MW00613056

William Henry Harrison and the
Conquest of the Ohio Country

JOHNS HOPKINS BOOKS ON THE WAR OF 1812

Donald R. Hickey, Series Editor

Also in the series:

Carl Benn, *Native Memoirs from the War of 1812: Black Hawk and William Apess*

Ralph E. Eshelman, *The War of 1812 in the Chesapeake: A Reference Guide to Historic Sites in Maryland, Virginia, and the District of Columbia*

Ralph E. Eshelman, *A Travel Guide to the War of 1812 in the Chesapeake: Eighteen Tours in Maryland, Virginia, and the District of Columbia*

Donald R. Hickey and Connie D. Clark, *The Rockets' Red Glare: An Illustrated History of the War of 1812*

Donald G. Shomette, Foreword by Fred W. Hopkins, Jr., *Flotilla: The Patuxent Naval Campaign in the War of 1812*

William Henry Harrison and the Conquest of the Ohio Country

Frontier Fighting in the War of 1812

David Curtis Skaggs

Johns Hopkins University Press
Baltimore

© 2014 Johns Hopkins University Press
Printed in the United States of America

Johns Hopkins University Press
2715 North Charles Street
Baltimore, Maryland 21218-4363

ISBN-13: 978-1-4214-0546-9

Frontispiece: William Henry Harrison, painted by Rembrandt Peale, National Portrait Gallery, Smithsonian Institution; gift of Mrs. Hebert Lee Pratt Jr.

A Book Club Edition

With Love and Hope for Our Grandchildren

Justin David Skaggs

Ryan Joseph Skaggs

Caroline Grace Skaggs

Elaine Wells Skaggs

Julia Katherine Skaggs

Contents

Contents

Preface

About William Henry Harrison many Americans know only two facts: he campaigned for the presidency under the slogan "Tippecanoe and Tyler too," and he was in office the shortest time of any president. While some will tell you that "Tippecanoe" refers to a battle with the Indians (or was it the British?) fought somewhere in the Midwest, few can list any other episodes in his life, and fewer still recognize his military contributions to the early republic. Many others confuse him with his grandson, Benjamin Harrison, and assume he fought in the Civil War and was one of those hard-to-distinguish-between bearded men ascending to the presidency in its aftermath.

William Henry Harrison deserves better than this. He is the subject of two biographies that describe his military career but do not analyze it. They also lack the perspective of nearly three-quarters of a century of scholarship and the microfilm publication of the Harrison papers. Recent studies by Robert M. Owens and Adam Jortner on his dealings with the Indians and Hendrik Booraem's psychological study of his youth and young manhood add significantly to our understanding of an emerging political figure in the Old Northwest. Yet his military career remains little studied.

My interest in Harrison began over a quarter of a century ago. But my scholarly direction was diverted by a sideshow tangential to Harrison. The 175th anniversary of the battle of Lake Erie brought to my attention the collaboration between General Harrison and a young naval officer named Oliver Hazard Perry. That led to several articles and two books relating to the battle in particular and Perry's career in total. Some now thought I was a naval historian and pulled me into a biography of another naval leader of the War of 1812, Thomas Macdonough. By the time these studies were finished, I had retired from Bowling Green State University, and Margo and I were peacefully relaxing on the shores of northern Michigan's Burt Lake or wintering in coastal North Carolina.

The bicentennial of the War of 1812 brought me back to William Henry Harrison's long-forgotten, little-studied military contributions to the new nation. It is the story of a young man who received an apprenticeship in military leadership from one who proved a master at the art, Anthony Wayne. Few men in their late teens and early twenties received such an opportunity to closely watch a commanding general coping with personal rivalries, raising an army, disciplining and training raw troops, providing logistical support in a frontier environment, coordinating regulars with volunteer troops, and planning campaign and tactical operations against fierce native warriors supported by a foreign government. In the first dozen years of the nineteenth century, Harrison served as territorial governor of Indiana and expanded his administrative skills, sought solutions to political issues, became embroiled in political disputes, conducted treaty negotiations with Indian leaders, and eventually directed a campaign against an emerging pan-tribal coalition headquartered near the junction of the Tippecanoe and Wabash Rivers.

The Tippecanoe campaign could well have terminated Harrison's military leadership had not the United States declared war on Britain the next year. His hope for senior command was initially disappointed, but his own machinations combined with his rivals' military ineptitude brought him command of the Old Northwest theater. His successful defense of the Ohio frontier, his raising and supporting an army far from its logistical base, and his collaborating with Oliver Hazard Perry's naval squadron on Lake Erie eventually led to his triumph over the British and their Indian allies at the battle of the Thames in what is now southwestern Ontario. It was a significant triumph for the arms of the United States, but not a decisive one in the War of 1812. Its critical importance was in maintaining our national borders along the Great Lakes and in terminating British assistance to Native Americans within our national boundaries.

But this investigation is not just a description of Harrison's military career; it also involves a reinterpretation of the employment of the often maligned volunteer soldiers of the early national era in a series of engagements from Fallen Timbers to Tippecanoe, Frenchtown, Fort Meigs, and the Thames. In this he was no different in the leadership of volunteers than such successful citizen-soldier commanders as Jacob Brown at Sackets Harbor, Samuel Smith at Baltimore, and Andrew Jackson at New Orleans. By his support of volunteers, Harrison remained an unreconstructed Jeffersonian in defiance of Secretary of War John Armstrong's emphasis on regular army troops. An unusual aspect of his military leadership was the use of mounted troops as dragoons, mounted riflemen, and mobile infantry. Nowhere else in the War of 1812 were mounted forces more successfully employed than in the Old Northwest. He also learned to use former white captives and friendly Indians as scouts and as gatherers of military intelligence data, providing him with a solid understanding of his opponents' capabilities. Nothing personified his unique leadership capabilities more than the successful conduct of an amphibious invasion into southwestern Upper Canada.

This study also entails an analysis of the politics of military leadership in the early republic. Along with many others, William Henry Harrison used political connections to achieve high command, and in the process he created numerous enemies. That same political process combined with what he thought were affronts to his personal honor resulted in his resignation. By the spring of 1814, what once appeared to be an even more promising military career was at an end.

Acknowledgments

No scholar can completely express his appreciation and gratitude to those who directly or indirectly contributed to such a study. At the center of this study is the fine work done by Douglas E. Clanin of the Indiana Historical Society, and his staff, on the ten microfilm reels of the William Henry Harrison Papers, 1800–1815, which provide the most recent and most thorough compilation of the surviving correspondence to and from the future president. For those wishing to know more of this effort, see Clanin's "The William Henry Harrison Papers Project," in Darrel E. Bigham, ed., *The Indiana Territory, 1800–2000: A Bicentennial Perspective* (Indianapolis: Indiana Historical Society, 2001), 149–66.

Mary Beth Zachary and Coleen Parmer of the Jerome Library staff, Bowling Green State University, allowed an emeritus professor library privileges that permitted me to check out dozens of books for four years and to haul them back and forth between northern Michigan and eastern North Carolina. I'm sure they are relieved that all have been returned. Mary Keil of the Inter-Library Loan Department complied with numerous requests from a long-departed and far-away former professor for scholarly articles through its ILLiad program. Again I'm indebted to Stephen Charter and Lee McLaird of Bowling Green's Center for Archival Collections and the center's excellent collection of Great Lakes–related materials—most particularly, on this project, the microfilm edition of the Draper manuscripts.

Hendrik Booraem and the Kent State University Press kindly allowed me to read and cite page proofs of his *A Child of the Revolution: William Henry Harrison and His World, 1773–1798* (2012). Carl Benn and the Johns Hopkins University Press gave me permission to read Carl's manuscript proposal for Black Hawk's and John Norton's memoirs. Both of these expanded my understanding of Harrison's career.

The staff of Cheboygan Area Public Library in Michigan allowed the use of their microfilm reader-printer by this part-time resident—also known as a "fudgie"—in the inland lakes region. Similar accolades go to Mary Smith of the Indian River Public Library and Nicky Haller of the Alanson Area Public Library, who secured interlibrary loan books for a wandering scholar. Brian Jaeschke of the Mackinac State Parks library allowed me access to its extensive collection of regional historic volumes.

Former student Nan Card of the Rutherford B. Hayes Library in Fremont, Ohio, patiently allowed her old professor to use its fine library of nineteenth-century materials relating to Harrison's career. Another former student, Larry Nelson, until recently the site manager at the Fort Meigs State Memorial, continued to add his insights regarding Harrison's military career, especially relating to the Fallen Timbers campaign and the defense of Fort Meigs. He even published some of my preliminary findings in *Northwest Ohio History*, as did Christopher Phillips and Glenn Crothers in *Ohio Valley History* and Mary Graham in the *Michigan Historical Review*.

Archival specialists at the Manuscripts Division of the Library of Congress, the Filson Historical Society in Louisville, the Indiana Historical Society in Indianapolis, the Cincinnati Historical Society, the William L. Clements Library of the University of Michigan, the Swem Library at the College of William and Mary, and the Alderman Library of the University of Virginia very professionally assisted this visitor in the use of their fine collections. I am indebted to the Welsh Regimental Museum, Cardiff Castle, South Wales, United Kingdom, for permission to quote from James Cochrane, "The War in Canada, 1812–1814" (MS ca. 1840). Jon Parmenter of Cornell University promptly responded to my queries regarding Native American affairs.

Over the years Margo and I have been privileged to visit numerous sites related to Harrison's career. These include Berkeley Plantation in Charles City County, Virginia; North Bend, outside Cincinnati; Grouseland, in Vincennes; and the Tippecanoe Battlefield. Of course, anyone who has spent thirty-six years in Bowling Green, Ohio, has toured Fallen Timbers, Fort Meigs, and Put-in-Bay many times. Bill Nelson (billnelsonmaps@verizon.net) made a few modest alterations on two Benson Lossing battle maps that erased mid-nineteenth-century roads, railroads, bridges, and buildings that did not exist in 1813. He also slightly altered the Lossing diagram of the battle of the Thames to more closely reflect the actions of Col. Richard M. Johnson's mounted riflemen that my research indicated were the case.

Bob Brugger, Melissa Solarz, Linda Strange, and the staff of Johns Hopkins University Press have been very forgiving of one who slowly produced this study. They have corrected numerous literary infelicities, but any surviving mistakes are mine. Both the University of Oklahoma Press and the Michigan State University Press kindly allowed the use of maps from their earlier publications.

Accompanying me on all these trips and bearing with my seemingly endless hours at the computer has been my patient and long-suffering wife of over fifty years, Margo. For her understanding, tolerance, and dedication to this and previous scholarly efforts, she merits special commendation. My CINCFAM has made this task far easier than it would otherwise have been.

Overleaf:
Great Lakes region, 1775–1795, and Great Lakes region, 1795–1814. Reproduced with permission from David Curtis Skaggs and Larry L. Nelson, eds., *The Sixty Years' War for the Great Lakes, 1754–1814* (East Lansing: Michigan State University Press, 2001), xii–xiii.

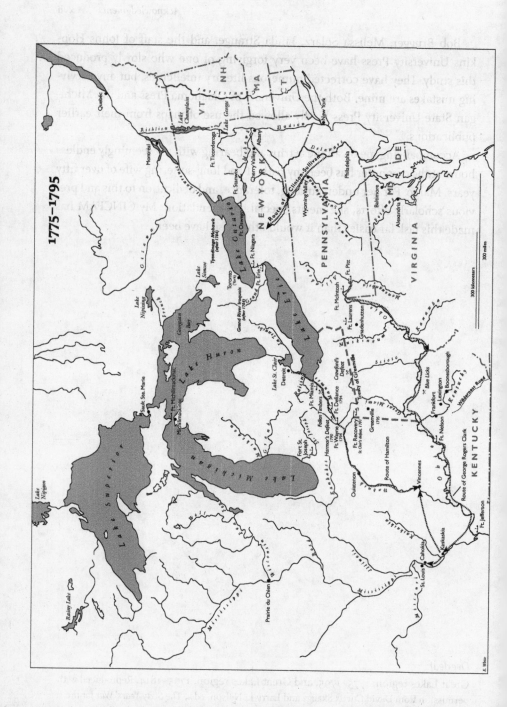

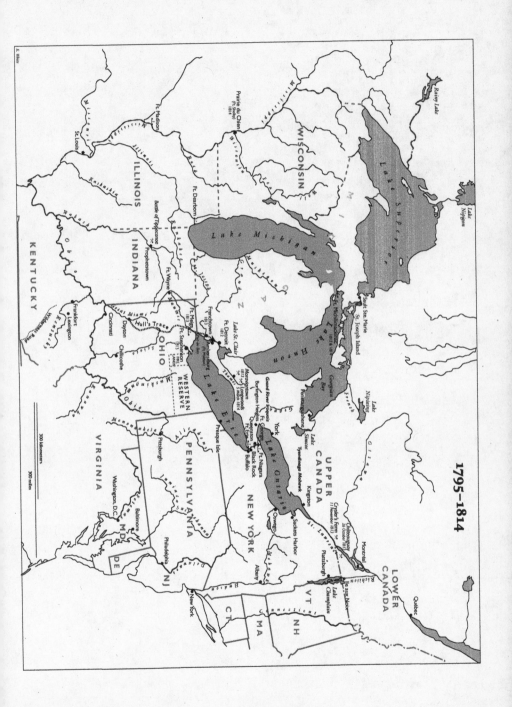

1795–1814

William Henry Harrison and the
Conquest of the Ohio Country

Chapter One

Apprenticeship in Frontier Warfare

About a mile and a half from Prophetstown (east of modern Lafayette, Indiana), the army paused in its approach to the native village. William Henry Harrison, Indiana territorial governor and militia brigadier general, sent Capt. Toussaint Dubois, commander of his scouts and guides, to request a truce and conference with Tenskwatawa (the "Shawnee Prophet"). Hostile natives derided his overtures with insulting gestures. Harrison ordered his soldiers to halt and load their packs into wagons. They dressed their lines, assuming attack formation, and those who had bayonets fixed them. This show of aggression seemed to surprise the Indians, who sent out three representatives to speak to the army's advance guards. Through interpreters, Harrison informed them that he wished to talk, not fight. The chiefs told him that Tenskwatawa was unavailable because he thought Harrison was approaching on the opposite bank of the river. Harrison probably doubted this story, for his army had been on the right bank for several days. Understanding that the Indians would meet with him the following morning, he then asked one chief where he might encamp for the night. The chief pointed to nearby high ground. Harrison sent two staff officers to assess it, and they found it acceptable. Although Harrison later described the site as "not altogether such as I could wish it," he ordered the troops to take up positions.[1]

They found themselves in an oak wood on a small triangular ridge rising above the marshy Wabash floodplain, about two miles from Prophetstown on nearby Tippecanoe Creek. On one side of the American camp were the waters of Bennett's (or Burnet's) Creek; thus the location provided high ground, wood, and water. Harrison posted his men in a camp with the shape of an elongated trapezoid, with the 4th U.S. Infantry and militia infantry holding the long sides (about 150 yards) and facing the Wabash lowland and Bennett's Creek. Kentucky and Indiana mounted riflemen and dragoons held the two ends of the formation (50 to 75 yards wide). The commander held three companies of militia infantry and two of mounted troops in the center in reserve. He also placed baggage and horses inside the perimeter; cattle and draft horses he corralled below Capt. Spier Spencer's mounted Indiana riflemen, known as the Yellow Jackets. Reinforced by a detachment of Indiana mounted rifles, they commanded the far left. As he had done several times during their march north from Vincennes, Harrison ordered his men to sleep in their uniforms, weapons loaded.

He did not issue directives to fortify the encampment. In all probability, the reason for this mistake was their arrival at the site late in the afternoon of a fall day. There was little time to make such preparations before nightfall, and no doubt in the cold fall weather many of the men preferred to build fires rather than log barriers, but why a disciple of the ever-cautious Gen. Anthony Wayne and a student of ancient military history would fail to fortify his position remains an unanswered question. Caution in the vicinity of an armed, aggressive foe should have outweighed acceptance of the Indians' promise of negotiations the following day. Harrison's deference to Secretary of War William Eustis's preference for negotiation over combat and his willingness to delay talks (which he clearly felt would be unsuccessful) while his expeditionary force was poised to take Prophetstown called his tactical judgment into question. Harrison violated a basic military principle: never assume that a foe will act agreeably.

What discussions took place among the warriors assembled at Prophetstown that afternoon and evening remain unknown. Before leaving on a diplomatic mission to add southern and western natives to his coalition, Tecumseh had implored his brother Tenskwatawa not to engage the Americans. Yet the Prophet now found himself facing some hotheaded young warriors, especially among the Potawatomi and Kickapoo. These war hawks wanted to attack the Americans. They were joined by many Winnebago, Delaware, and Shawnee. Earlier, Harrison had made it clear that their intertribal village had to be disbanded. If he accomplished this object, Tenskwatawa's and Tecumseh's dream of a union of native peoples with a common pan-Indian background would be seriously disrupted, perhaps destroyed. Reversing his brother's instructions, the Prophet now consulted with the spirits and informed his followers that his spells would drive the Americans blind and crazy and make the native warriors invisible and invulnerable to American bullets.

The natives devised a two-part attack. First, a substantial number would attempt to infiltrate the American lines and assassinate leaders early in the

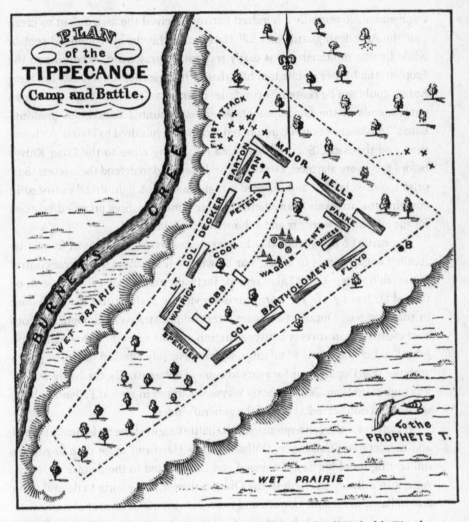

Battle of Tippecanoe. Reprinted from Benson J. Lossing, *Pictorial Field-Book of the War of 1812* (New York: Harper Brothers, 1869).

engagement. Reportedly a hundred natives received the assignment to creep past the American guards and kill Harrison, either in his command tent or while he was mounted on his easily recognized gray mare. According to the Prophet, the Master of Life told him that if the governor did not die, the Long Knives could not be beaten. Second, the main assaults would begin at the two narrow ends of the encampment, where dismounted militiamen predominated. Tenskwatawa's force numbered around six hundred to Harrison's fewer than one thousand. Success depended on getting close to the Long Knives before they were alarmed, awakened, and prepared to defend themselves. Surprise required stealth and dictated a night assault. A light drizzle assisted in covering the attackers' movement. Blazing American fires provided beacons for the advancing warriors and silhouetted their targets.

The battle of Tippecanoe that followed remains one of the most frequently recalled engagements in a long war between whites and natives over control of the Ohio Valley–Great Lakes region. Tactically and strategically, Tippecanoe proved far less significant than Harrison's victory at the battle of the Thames in southwestern Ontario two years later. Administratively, though, his conduct created a controversy between himself and his second-in-command, Col. John Boyd of the 4th U.S. Infantry, which adversely affected his relationship with the War Department for years to come. Diplomatically, the battle was far less important than Gen. Anthony Wayne's triumph in 1794 at Fallen Timbers, where Harrison served as one of the general's aides.

Yet whatever the consequences of the battle fought at the melodically named and memorable Tippecanoe, William Henry Harrison, more than any other military figure of his day, witnessed and contributed to the demise of Native American military strength in the Old Northwest. His efforts to defend Ohio and Indiana, to reclaim Detroit, and to secure American control of southwestern Upper Canada contributed significantly to the maintenance of the United States' boundary with Canada negotiated at the Peace of Paris thirty years earlier. And he did this with a combination of regulars and volunteers that personified the military aspirations of the new nation that he and many others saw as a reincarnation of the Roman republic.

Harrison represents the last generation of senior military leadership going to what might be called the American Cincinnati. The War of 1812 constitutes the last time in our national history when senior military leadership went to men coming from civilian life—Harrison along with such men as Jacob Brown, Andrew Jackson, and Samuel Smith, all following in the footsteps of the revolutionary generation. Except for Brown, all these men would return to their homes after the war's end and continue their careers without wearing a uniform, although taking advantage of the memory of their military achievements for political success.

William Henry Harrison Goes West

The April 1815 issue of *Port Folio*, one of the young republic's leading literary journals, published a twenty-page biographical sketch of one of the heroes of the War of 1812—Maj. Gen. William Henry Harrison. It began with a significant query: should greater credit go to one "who, by the mere force of his own natural talents and personal exertions has emerged from obscurity and humble birth to honors, wealth, and distinction," or to "he who, born to all the advantages or opulence and splendid descent, performs actions which tend rather to augment, than to impair his family stock"? Biographers, the author continued, alternately adopt and reject "either side, as it appears to be more or less favorable to the particular subject upon which they are at the time employed." One of those in the second category, who distinguished himself "by an early victory over sloth, sensuality and ease, and by a magnanimous oblation of life and personal services at the shrine [of] patriotism and military glory," was "the conqueror of Tippecanoe and the hero of the Thames."[2] Because Harrison was born into the gentry, we must begin a study of his career with his upbringing on a James River plantation in the midst of the upheaval of the American Revolution.

To her husband, Benjamin Harrison V, and a rapidly changing world, on 9 February 1773, Elizabeth Basset Harrison presented an eighth child and third son. The Harrison family's Berkeley Plantation—with its two-and-a-half-story brick Georgian manor house and adjoining buildings, several dozen slaves, many cattle, hogs, and chickens, fields of tobacco and corn, and gardens and orchards—proved a comfortable place in which to grow up. The Harrisons had committed themselves to American independence and willingly risked their lives and fortunes for that object. The child's father served in the Continental Congress, was a signer of the Declaration of Independence, and became governor of the Commonwealth of Virginia as the "dogs of war" were unleashed in the Tidewater. When, in January 1781, now-British Maj. Gen. Benedict Arnold raided eastern Virginia towns and plantations—up the James River to Richmond and then downstream—he did his best to destroy the governor's home and household goods, burning clothing, portraits, and furniture, killing cattle, and making off with slaves and horses. It was a devastating loss from which Governor Harrison never financially recovered. This vengeful act helps explain the hatred of all people and all things British that permeated the son's life (just as it did that of a notable contemporary, Andrew Jackson).

The Harrison scion emerged as a young man expecting deference from those in subordinate positions, even though they might be senior to him in age and worldly experience. "Massa Billy" the family slaves called him from infancy. We know he dined frequently with relatives and family friends and that at least from his teen years, he participated in conversations concerning government and politics. Not only was he Governor Harrison's son, but he was also future Congressman Carter Harrison's brother. While the Harrisons might economically be classed as living in genteel poverty, they were still one of the first families of the Old Dominion. They expected deference from whites of less gentlemanly trained families, a factor that provides insights into Harrison's favoritism toward Kentuckians (most of whose leaders came from Virginia) and his strained relations with Midwestern political leaders who lacked familial credentials. His family's connections provided him with another important benefit: access to influential individuals who opened up for him appointments outside the norm for one so young and inexperienced.

Benjamin Harrison the Signer presciently directed his sons' futures. He understood that long-term financial prospects for tobacco plantations in the Chesapeake were quite dim. His eldest son, Benjamin VI, became a paymaster general in the Virginia militia and associated himself with a Philadelphia mercantile house before establishing his own firm in Richmond. The second son, Carter, became a planter-lawyer and a member of the Virginia House of Delegates and eventually the United States Congress. Both studied at the College of William and Mary. For the youngest son, the father sought a medical career.[3]

William Henry Harrison was reasonably well educated for his time—there were private tutors at home and a brief attendance at the fledgling log college known as Hampden-Sydney Academy, where the institution's faculty contained a well-known trainer of physicians. He also spent a few months as an apprentice in the office of Dr. Andrew Leiper in Richmond. Then he transferred to the Medical College of Pennsylvania in Philadelphia, the country's first medical school. While the young William was en route to Philadelphia, his father died, freeing "Billy" from the dominance of an overbearing, hard-drinking parent and allowing him to make his own career choices.

Somewhere in all his traditionally oriented education he read and reread Charles Rollin's multivolume classics *Histoire Ancienne* (1730–38) and *Histoire de Rome* (1738–48) (translated from the French). Rollin's histories were popular among eighteenth-century Chesapeake planters, and throughout his life Harrison frequently made reference to ancient military examples. Rollin saw history as a means of criticizing the immorality of his present-day world and as a vehicle for preaching the virtue of intellectual honesty in an age of hypocrisy. For Rollin and for Harrison, history had a purpose: it allowed one to discover and promulgate moral laws and constant truths that could affect contemporary conduct. Rollin also emphasized military campaigns and the role of honor in the conduct of personal relations. Coupled with Julius Caesar's *Commentaries*, these studies significantly affected Harrison's outlook toward military affairs and personal values.[4]

Military valor was a prime prerequisite of ancient honor, and this attitude prevailed in young Harrison. Certainly it was a value Rollin expressed, and the writings of Caesar endorsed it. It was also a creed espoused by his father's generation, the men who fought and led the American War for Independence. Contemporaries considered military rank prestigious. For example, Governor Harrison favored being addressed by his militia rank—colonel—rather than by his political title. Military affairs dominated the world of the younger Harrison's youth; it is no wonder Billy Harrison sought to secure honor and fame through a military career.[5]

On reaching Philadelphia, young Harrison learned that although he inherited three thousand acres of undeveloped land, there was no money to continue his medical studies. While under the guardianship of the famous revolutionary war financier Robert Morris, a former colleague of his father in the Continental Congress, William Henry Harrison sought employment in the new federal government. According to his recollections, it was a visit with another family friend, former Continental Army general and Virginia governor Henry "Light Horse Harry" Lee, that led to his new career. Lee promised to secure a commission for him in the new United States Army. Lee's visit to President George Washington resulted in young Harrison's appointment as ensign (the lowest commissioned rank) in the 1st U.S. Infantry, effective 15 August 1791.

This was done without the permission or knowledge of Robert Morris. The financier subsequently warned the young man that someone raised in genteel surroundings on the James River might not find the rough and tumble, primordial life on the Ohio frontier to his liking. Morris warned that the officers were middle-aged veterans of the Continental Army unable to fit into civilian life; the enlisted ranks were filled with the most "worthless and depraved," dragged from the streets of seaport cities. There would, Morris argued, be no glory fighting Indians in the wilderness. Even if Harrison survived the primitive conditions and constant skirmishes, there were few chances of promotion in such a small military establishment. There can be no doubt that Harrison was about to undertake something for which his training and experience counted little and might work against him. Short in stature, spare in physique, bookish in interests, he nonetheless accepted the commission, received orders to take three hundred recruits west, and (carrying a copy of Cicero and a book on rhetoric) began the long march from Philadelphia to Pittsburgh. There he and his motley force proceeded by flatboat down the Ohio River to Fort Washington in Cincinnati.[6]

The army he entered was not an effective military force; it was an insignificant and impotent instrument of national power. Under the leadership of Brig. Gen. Josiah Harmar, it suffered defeat at the headwaters of the Maumee River in what are known as the battles of Kekionga in September 1790. Although it contained some capable leaders such as Maj. John F. Hamtramck, the officer corps was filled with incompetent, intoxicated, illiterate, and ineffective men. Brig. Gen. James Wilkinson called them "Beasts & Blockheads" who lacked "science, pride, principle, & polite education." He claimed there were captains who could barely read and majors "who can scarcely write their names."[7]

Morris had correctly observed the hazards of Harrison's becoming an army officer. He did not seem to recognize, though, that the young ensign brought with him certain characteristics that might assist him in a military career. Harrison spoke articulately, wrote with a legible hand, drank with moderation, and exhibited the self-confidence of one well educated, well read, and well connected. Given the right circumstances and the right superiors, he might blossom in the West. The rebellious behavior he demonstrated in taking the commission is not uncommon in later-born siblings, who are more likely than first-born children to engage in risk-oriented activities, to be more extraverted, and to be more receptive to and active in political, economic, and intellectual change.[8] He also represented what Professor Joyce Appleby calls the "first generation of Americans"—those born during the revolutionary era who had never known British rule and who slowly but surely gained control of the national and state political and military systems during and after the War of 1812.[9] Few men took greater advantage of the opportunities offered by the evolution of the new republic than would the youngest son of Benjamin Harrison V.

While Ensign Harrison and his accompanying recruits made the trip down the Ohio River, there occurred in what is now western Ohio the most disastrous defeat of the United States Army by Native Americans in the nation's history: the battle of the Wabash, or what is usually called "St. Clair's Defeat," on 4 November 1791. In the Ohio Valley, Harrison entered a military environment that had evolved on the North American frontier over several centuries. It was far different from the one he observed as a youth, where British, French, and American professional soldiers fought and conducted themselves according to well-understood rules.

Frontier Warfare

Warfare in the Eastern North American Woodlands consisted of both small-scale operations and larger, more violent conflicts and revolved around a shifting system of alliances between and among various Indian tribes, government figures, white settlers, and business interests. Given the characteristics of Indian societies and the nature of disputes that often had to be decided outside what European society deemed the rule of law, most native-versus-native military operations consisted of limited objectives and actions.[10] There were restraints to the intensity of warfare that the tribes of the Eastern Woodlands could wage. Foremost was an individualization of military prowess that focused on the desire of young Indians to achieve status through personal valorous conduct in combat. This characteristic required the warrior to bring home enemy scalps or prisoners as individual possessions, not as group trophies. This emphasis on individual achievement rather than unit reputation diminished the combat effectiveness of native warfare. Coupled with this was the lack of efficient control of warriors by their supposed commanders.

There were several levels of Native American violent confrontation. Most warfare by Indians was based on blood revenge. The mandate was that relatives and tribal allies must take revenge for the killing of one of their own. Whether a family member died due to accidental death, murder, or combat, it became a moral imperative to avenge the loss, not necessarily on the perpetrator of the loss but on any member of the killer's people. Such a system perpetuated an endless cycle of violence that produced endemic states of conflict. The blood feud limited the intensity of combat because it did not require the annihilation of a whole people.[11]

Limited warfare could also be employed to teach political lessons to one's rivals. A tribe conducted raids at the fringes of a territory to limit the activities of those whose expansion into territorial or hunting grounds might be threatening. These raids generally consisted of limited campaigns that posed little or no threat to the central residency of the opponent. Indian raids of the 1780s and 1790s against farmsteads north and south of the Ohio River exemplify such efforts and became a constant problem for both the settlers' defenders and the natives' leaders.

This concept of "petite war" contrasted sharply with "grand war" waged by hundreds of warriors seeking to achieve political dominance of a people or control of an enlarged geographic region. Considerable debate continues on whether the introduction of Europeans into North America increased the intensity of violence and modified the tactics of Native Americans. One recent summary of the current state of scholarship in this regard contends that before 1492, natives had not "scaled down warfare into some kind of ritualized, not lethal nonentity," but rather, given "the opportunity and the right motive, Indians were prepared to wage intensely lethal violence on another people."[12]

Archaeology provides considerable evidence that major conflict prevailed among the Eastern Woodlands tribes in the pre-Columbian era. Cross-cultural studies of preindustrial societies conclude that primitive wars over territorial change were very common.[13] An eighteenth-century French officer commented, "They [Native Americans] believe that the master of life caused them to be born in the territory they inhabit and that no one has the right to interfere with what they possess . . . This instinctive feeling makes them very touchy over the matter and it is always a cause for war when one nation comes to hunt on the territories of another."[14] Thus territorial disputes were a common cause of large-scale intertribal wars. They also formed the core of disputes between whites and Indians from the dawn of European settlement.

Among the limitations on the intensity of intertribal warfare, and the most critical, was logistics.[15] Without pack animals and carts to transport baggage, Native Americans were unable to sustain distant and prolonged combat far from their main base without allies in the combat region. Even though women provided their men with agricultural supplies, the native warriors lacked logistical support units. While logistical impedimenta hindered rapid advancement by European-styled forces, they allowed the conduct of warfare far from one's home bases without the necessity of local support.

Without horses, oxen, and wagons, the most effective transportation mode for men and equipment in the woodlands involved canoes on the extensive lakes and rivers. In regions accessible by canoe, they carried warriors from the upper Great Lakes as far east as Lake Champlain. French Captain Pierre Pouchot wrote in amazement of these artistically decorated birch bark craft, which carried from three to nine people with gear. With oars that were four to five feet long and a freeboard of a few inches, the largest could carry a cargo of up to three thousand pounds. "One only has to make sure that they do not run aground," the Frenchman observed. "When they approach land, they are very careful not to let the canoe run aground, because it would break up. They carry it ashore & place it in the water again to relaunch it. They used the vessels especially for their war parties." If the canoes sustained damage, native warriors used the spare pieces of bark and tar they carried to make repairs.[16]

For the Native Americans, their logistical disadvantage compelled them to rely on the British Indian Department and on fur traders for critical support. While warfare demands required the Indians to depend on the British for guns, bullets, and gunpowder, most scholars ignore the natives' requirement for European goods for clothing, hunting and fishing equipment, and cooking utensils, which accounted for over 85 percent of all trade goods between the two groups. Captain Pouchot observed, "To the misfortune of the Indians, we arrived in their land & taught them to use our materials for their garments. They could not now dispense with gunpowder & brandy without the majority of them perishing."[17] Naturally, in those areas where combat situations deprived natives of their traditional agricultural produce, the Indians found themselves additionally dependent on their European allies for food. And if warfare deprived the Native Americans of the crops produced by the tribes' females, it also deprived the males of acquiring the furs and skins used to exchange for necessities provided by the fur traders, thereby placing them in an even more dependent status.

A combination of disease and combat losses dramatically reduced the number of warriors the tribes could bring into combat. Consequently, various Indian war chiefs sought to overcome traditional intertribal rivalries and combine forces against the constantly increasing number of American settlers moving into the Ohio Valley. Despite extraordinary efforts for pan-Indian resis-

tance by such leaders as Little Turtle, Blue Jacket, and Tecumseh, demograph-
ics doomed them to failure. By 1812 whites in the trans-Appalachian West outnumbered Indians by a margin of seven to one.

A realistic appraisal of the outcome of a military solution to their problems
caused some native leaders to seek accommodation with the advancing American settlement. By the early nineteenth century, former warrior chiefs such
as the Miami Little Turtle near Fort Wayne, the Delaware Buckongahelas near
modern Muncie, and the Shawnee Black Hoof near Wapakoneta, Ohio, abandoned their combative ways for accords with the "Long Knives."[18] The Indians
of the Old Northwest reached their maximum combat effectiveness in the early
1790s, and their relative military power declined appreciably after the battle
of Fallen Timbers in 1794. American diplomatic policy sought to keep as many
natives as possible either supportive of or neutral toward any United States military effort.

Even though the Indians' combat effectiveness declined, this does not mean
natives could not inflict considerable losses upon their American opponents.
Two traditional native tactics were particularly effective: the raid and the
ambush. The first of these became especially obnoxious to settlers who found
themselves under attack without any declaration of war. There is no doubt that
natives inflicted hundreds of casualties—dead, wounded, and captured—by
using this tactic. Ohio Valley settlers (Marietta, Ohio, being an exception) preferred individual farmsteads rather than fortified hamlets and thereby made
themselves vulnerable to such raids.

Native Americans utilized the ambush time and time again. A famous
ambush came in the aftermath of a failed Indian siege of Bryan's Station in Kentucky. Pursuing the natives was a party of 182 Kentuckians who soon engaged
in their usual practice "to impetuously assume the offensive" and "to inflict
punishment and take revenge." While Lt. Col. Daniel Boone cautioned his colleagues they were walking into a trap, a rival accused him of cowardice and led
the forces to disaster at the battle of Blue Licks, on 24 August 1782.[19]

By the late eighteenth century a third native tactic had emerged—the attack
on enemy encampments. Such an operation required more warriors than an
individual tribe could muster and necessitated intertribal alliances and cooperation that emerged as Euroamerican expansion became ever more threatening. The object was to encircle a foe and pick off enough of the troops to cause
panic and flight, which destroyed unit discipline and made the Euroamericans
vulnerable to individual combat. The battle of the Wabash was the most suc-

cessful example of such an effort. The battle of Tippecanoe represented a failure of an encampment assault.

By the eighteenth century, Euroamericans had devised four principal means of combating Native Americans. First was the raid. Usually employed against Indian villages, it normally included the destruction of homes, fields, and storage facilities. The objective was to force native dependence on the colonists, who normally possessed a surplus of agricultural products that were used to solicit concessions from their foes. These attrition campaigns lacked long-term impact but normally achieved the short-term goals of temporarily eliminating opposition and achieving territorial concessions that would eventually lead to more conflict. One of the best examples of this was the Kentucky raid into the Wabash Valley in 1791 led by Charles Scott.[20]

The second form of warfare involved the employment of conventional European campaigns into natives' homeland and the construction of fortifications that demonstrated a permanent occupation of a strategic site and dominance over a region. Forbes's expedition into western Pennsylvania and the erection of Fort Pitt at the headwaters of the Ohio River was an extraordinarily effective example of this military style. Such a policy required regular forces to permanently garrison such outposts.[21] Europeans and Americans established fortifications at critical geographic constraining points and portages—for instance, Niagara, Detroit, Michilimackinac, and Fort Wayne. Major problems at these forts included maintaining a garrison for what was normally a very boring duty and keeping the wooden structure of these forts in repair. Typical of these fortifications and the surrounding community was Detroit: the central stockade, the palisaded town, and the surrounding farms and Indian villages. The fort constituted a military base, depot, and place of refuge. The town became a commercial center, with fur traders conducting business throughout the upper Great Lakes and Midwest. Local farms provided produce for the soldiers and the community, and the nearby Indian villages provided produce from their fields and furs and skins from the forest. The native warriors were potential recruits for expeditions against the British and, later, the Americans to the south.[22]

Repeated attempts by native warriors to take European and American fortifications failed because they lacked artillery. But sometimes they succeeded with ruses like the one that allowed them to take Fort Michilimackinac in 1763.[23] Throughout the years of William Henry Harrison's life in the Ohio Valley, various forts of the Old Northwest were critical components of frontier strategic policy.

Natives began settling near European fortifications, especially those of the French at such places as Niagara, Detroit, Michilimackinac, St. Joseph (Michigan), and Vincennes. These native communities became socially interactive with French soldiers and traders. The resulting *métis* population provided kinship networks that rewarded these settlements economically and diplomatically. On the other hand, as historian Francis Jennings wryly notes, "when the Indians asked for forts, they wanted places of refuge for their women and children, but the British wanted them to control the Indians. Obviously there were different sorts of constructions subsumed under the same word."[24]

A third Euroamerican strategy involved the use of short-term volunteers, many of whom had extensive military experience. Veteran "rangers" operated deep into the wilderness—often with Indian allies or former white captives—and provided scouting, screening, and raiding services that disrupted enemy offensive and defensive operations. Despite the many problems in dealing with volunteers, especially in the area of discipline, they often proved valuable assets when combined with effective leadership.[25] As early as 1677 colonial militiamen adapted the "skulking way of war" used by Native Americans. One authority concludes, "Frontier militias, composed of men who had learned the 'skulking way of war' by direct and prolonged experience, were thus usually more effective at fighting tribesmen than were European regulars."[26] It was to counter the failure of Gov. Arthur St. Clair's expedition to thwart his opponents' "skulking" tactics that Ensign Harrison began his apprenticeship in the employment of armed force in the Old Northwest. He learned to appreciate the contribution of such tactics to the military effort during Gen. Anthony Wayne's campaign.

Traditionally, Euroamericans called up local common militiamen to counter Indian raids. These untrained, ill-armed, and often ill-led troops proved to be of little value, and frontier families demanded more effective forces. Various colonies created volunteer militia units with officers appointed by the colonial governors and with enlisted men serving for the duration of the campaign or conflict. As one might expect, there were insufficient numbers of volunteers, and during the French and Indian War, the Virginia Assembly instituted a draft of militiamen to fill the vacancies. This proved exceedingly unpopular and unenforceable. Finally, Virginia resorted to a bounty of £10, which lured sufficient troops into the Virginia Regiment. The bounty and increased monthly pay proved successful in recruiting for both Virginia and Pennsylvania.[27] The wartime volunteer units proved much more effective than common militia units and constituted the core of most military units that fought on the frontier. The use of such men would become the source of many issues between Harrison and more traditionally oriented military leaders in the nation's capital.

A fourth element of Euroamerican strategy involved the employment of native allies as scouts and informants. French, British, and American military campaigns used Indian allies to assist their efforts against their European foes. Utilizing intertribal animosities to their advantage, Euroamerican commanders sought the protection and information only provided by friendly natives.

The 1758 march of Brig. Gen. James Forbes from Philadelphia to Pittsburgh was a model of military organization and efficiency, combining all of these strategic factors. With British and American regiments Forbes painstakingly built a series of forts and supply depots at places that come to mind every time one drives the Pennsylvania Turnpike—Carlisle, Loudon, Bedford, and Ligonier. He and his superior, Maj. Gen. James Abercromby, pushed for negotiations with the Ohio Indians, which alleviated some of the opposition to Forbes's advance into the upper Ohio Valley.

Both the Braddock and Forbes campaigns provide examples of a serious weakness in Native American tactics. In both instances, the Indian warriors took scalps, hostages, and booty and returned to their tribal areas, thereby reducing the military effectiveness of the remaining French troops at Fort Duquesne. This tendency to withdraw after achieving short-term objectives constituted a significant flaw in native military operations and opened them to defeat in detail by westernized forces with sufficient logistical support and a willingness to construct fortifications far from their home bases. Similarly, the divide-and-conquer diplomatic policy of western-oriented communities traded on traditional intertribal and intratribal enmities to their advantage.

The French and Indian War brought about a policy of integrating European regular troops with colonial volunteers. While Braddock's defeat represented a failure of this course of action, Forbes's success demonstrated its usefulness. Natives proved useful not only to the French but also to the British in the latter years of the conflict. However, the promises made to Indians to secure their assistance, or at least their neutrality, demanded that the British maintain regular forces on the frontier to protect both natives and colonists and to honor agreements made to both sides. In the long run, the British Army would be unable to thwart expansion of the frontiersmen.[28] The same demands and the same failure bedeviled American efforts to control violence on the frontier once the United States gained control of the region.

Among the frontiersmen of Pennsylvania and Virginia, the crises of the French and Indian War and Pontiac's Rebellion of 1754-1765 created social and political turmoil that would eventually have long-term consequences for the military situation west of the Appalachian Mountains. In the Pennsylvania and Virginia backcountry, the war threatened the backcountry elite's influence, aggravated anti–regular army sentiment, especially over the quartering of troops and impressments of supplies and wagons, intensified deep ethnic and religious divisions in western communities, exacerbated anti-Indian racial attitudes, and opened economic opportunities for aggressive, daring entrepreneurs.[29]

Forbes and subsequent British leaders recognized that peace treaty conferences were often as critical to success as victories on the field. Reluctantly, the Ohio Valley Indians came to see the 1768 Treaty of Fort Stanwix (Rome, New York) as their guarantee of sovereignty in what the United States would later call the Old Northwest. One of the factors in this agreement was the English promise not to allow permanent settlement in the Ohio Valley. After Lord Dunmore's War in 1774, the Shawnee gave up title to Kentucky and laid their claims to the lands north of the Ohio to the Fort Stanwix line. But that treaty was with the British, and when in 1783 the northern boundary of the United States became the Great Lakes, the Americans saw the Fort Stanwix agreement as passé.[30]

If British officials saw the outcome of this Great War for Empire as confirmation of the desire to protect the Indian homelands from colonial settlement, the colonists drew different conclusions. They saw the vast acreage of the Ohio Valley and Great Lakes as potential farms, towns, and cities. They had not suffered the havoc and misery of war so as to restrain their quest for some of the richest soils in the world. With control of the interior by France and its native allies eliminated, the colonists expected His Majesty's government to open the region to settlement. Instead they faced a decade of attempts to restrain their westward movement, as exemplified by the Proclamation of 1763, the Treaty of Fort Stanwix of 1768, and the Quebec Act of 1774. Moreover, from Philadelphia to Williamsburg to London, land speculators sought royal approval for new colonies and land companies with names like Vandalia, Transylvania, Ohio, Wabash, and Illinois. These groups found their ambitions frustrated, however, because countering their pressures were the fur traders from Montreal and Quebec who sought to keep settlement from disrupting their profitable commerce in furs, hides, and skins from Hudson's Bay to the Ohio River.

Frontiersmen took advantage of the British inability to enforce their rules by settling in Kentucky and moving west of Fort Pitt. Imperial discipline, social restraint, and provincial control broke down just as the First British Empire began to break up. For many, the Quebec Act was the last straw in a long list of grievances. The royal restrictions aroused hot anger among westerners who dreamed of a trans-Appalachian empire, and that anger rose to a fury when the crown attempted to enforce restrictions by imposing such policies as incorporation of the whole of the region north of the Ohio River into the province of Quebec.[31]

There can be little doubt that the postwar frontier became ruled by individualistic, self-willed men who knew little government and resented political interference with their desires and ambitions. The lack of formal government institutions in the vast spaces of the frontier and the conflict over boundaries (such as, "Is Pittsburgh in Virginia or Pennsylvania?") and land titles induced frontiersmen to resort to the *lex talionis* (law of retaliation) and retributive violence in which the keeping of order was accomplished by self-appointed groups of men.[32] There is no better example of this than the events of December 1763, when the so-called Paxton Boys of Lancaster County, Pennsylvania, marched on the Christian Conestoga Indian settlement, killed and scalped six Indians, and burned houses and personal effects. Frustrated by the colony's inability to protect settlers from the raids during Pontiac's Rebellion and erroneously believing that the Conestoga cooperated with the raiders, western Pennsylvanians exhibited this retributive violence in a cruel but logical way. Moreover, the inability of the provincial administration to prosecute the participants reflects the growing tensions between the backcountry settlers and Pennsylvania's traditional leadership.[33] The same sort of antagonisms confronted Harrison during his career,

Limited as it had always been, Native American cohesion eventually broke down. For years the Iroquois Confederacy claimed suzerainty over the Algonquin tribes to the west, a level of dominance such tribes as the Shawnee, Miami, Delaware, and others resented. While the Fort Stanwix Treaty of 1768 protected Iroquois interests, its relinquishing of claims to lands south of the Ohio River that the Shawnee considered their hunting grounds brought great bitterness.[34] Resentful of Iroquois righteous arrogance and presumed dominance, in 1770 representatives of various Algonquin-speaking tribes met at Chillicothe (in modern Ohio) to coordinate future diplomatic relations with the British government separate from Iroquois interference.

The Great War for Empire of 1754–63 and Pontiac's Rebellion that followed it forced many among the provincial elite to compromise principle for power. Those who could do so were among the most successful of the political leaders of the new republic in North America. But such compromise did not apply only to politics; military leadership required a subtle understanding of available resources, of frontiersmen's willingness to serve, of compromises with strict discipline that were necessary to retain an adequate number of soldiers, of integration of regular and volunteer troops into an effective fighting team, and of compensation through enlistment bounties, higher-than-usual enlisted pay, and offers of land grants. William Henry Harrison would spend twenty years learning these leadership skills in preparation for his command of westerners during the War of 1812.

The guarantee of no colonial British settlement in the Ohio country as negotiated in 1758 at Easton, Pennsylvania, and ratified in the Proclamation of 1763 seemed to assure the Delaware, Shawnee, and Miami of their lands in what would become the Old Northwest. But reliance on this guarantee demanded a British ability and desire to enforce the provisions and failed to forecast the changing political situation in colonial British America. In the long run, His Majesty's government became unwilling to protect Indian claims when political necessity dictated other choices. The Ohio Valley natives also found that Spanish control of Louisiana did not provide them with a countervailing ally that could and would assist their interests.

But such necessary lessons were not followed during the American War for Independence. The Continental Congress and its representatives in the West could not control the frontiersmen and natives, because they lacked the financial abilities to compensate their soldiers and to provide tribute to those Indians who sought to remain neutral.[35] All this came in the midst of a series of incidents that eventually ended Indian neutrality. Many leaders joined the British-Indian anti-American forces operating out of Detroit. The final straw was the brutal murder of about ninety Christian Indians in the Moravian mission community of Gnadenhutten in March 1782. There is no better example of the *lex talionis* and retributive violence than what happened in what is now eastern Ohio. Frontier leaders acquiesced in these events by their silence or vain attempts to justify them.[36] The consequence was a growing animosity between natives and settlers and an unwillingness by many on both sides to recognize nuances in positions around which they might make accommodations.

For the natives, future military success demanded they have a European ally. The only one left was Great Britain. Despite the Indians' support of Britain in the Revolutionary War, British negotiators at the Peace of Paris in 1783 gave the United States sovereignty over the region between the Great Lakes and the Ohio River, even though this area was controlled by Native Americans. The treaty marked the first betrayal of Indian interests by His Majesty's government. It would not be the last. Success for the Indians also required them to forego traditional rivalries and to unify against the advancing Americans who poured by the thousands into Kentucky and the Ohio Valley. This proved very difficult if not impossible.

Before Harrison arrived in the trans-Appalachian West, a new military ingredient emerged in the region: the introduction of mounted warriors. While water transport was the most critical element in western movement of supplies and soldiers, the horse proved a critical innovation in military activity. In 1791, Kentucky Brig. Gen. Charles Scott led mounted volunteers into the Wabash Valley, where they conducted devastating raids on native villages. The horse gave the Kentuckians a speed that infantrymen could not duplicate. Despite bogs made "almost impervious by brush and briars" and heavy rains that impeded progress and wore out the animals, Scott's troopers covered 135 miles in eight days. Indian communities had little warning as the mounted men approached. For instance, at one native village the inhabitants tried to flee across the Wabash as the American riflemen fired into their crowded canoes and sent many to their death.[37]

The horse provided speed, shock action, and maneuverability unknown in the days before its introduction into frontier military units. By 1800 Kentucky had the highest per capita horse population in the United States. Most of them were draft animals, but they proved useful in transporting troops and forwarding supplies on long expeditions north of the Ohio River.[38] Scott's expedition became an example for frontier warfare tactics that would be replicated many times in the ensuing years. Mounted units came in two types: cavalry and mounted riflemen. Mounted rifle units could fight dismounted or mounted when engaging an enemy. Few Ohio Valley settlers had swords, but most fired their rifles while on horseback with extraordinary accuracy, and they wielded tomahawks with deadly force as they rode through Indian villages. For young Harrison, Scott proved a tactical mentor whose example he would employ repeatedly in the first decade and a half of the nineteenth century.

A large proportion of the Virginians emigrating to what became Kentucky traveled via the Cumberland Gap. This overland route allowed them to bring their horses with them, and soon the mounted soldier became a mainstay of Kentucky-based operations into the Old Northwest. While the federal government found the maintenance of horses too costly following the demise of Anthony Wayne's Legion of the United States, most western militiamen and volunteers had their own horses and came to their musters mounted. Throughout the frontier wars of the 1790s, Kentucky sent numerous mounted units north of the Ohio River. Among them, Charles Scott attained considerable reputation as a frontier militia leader with his Kentucky horsemen and others, like Richard Mentor Johnson, learned the rudiments of mounted operations under these conditions.

Mounted units came in three types: rangers, cavalry, and mounted riflemen or dragoons. Rangers primarily served as scouts for larger units and as patrols designed to warn communities and settlers of threatening native forces. They were not members of the regular army but rather volunteers who furnished their mounts, harness, and arms, with the exception of sabers and pistols. Cavalrymen armed with sabers and pistols were scarce on the frontier; instead there emerged "mounted riflemen." When the British commander at Fort Malden noted that "the Indian Nations have a Fear of Cavalry," he appeared to be referring to a western variant of the term.[39] Using rifles rather than pistols and tomahawks rather than sabers, mounted riflemen became a Kentucky favorite. They began operations during the 1790s and reached their acme at the battle of the Thames in 1813. Dragoons, on the other hand, largely fought as dismounted riflemen and used the rapidity of advance that the horse afforded them to surprise a foe and to scout for infantry.

Both sides had horses, but the Americans used them more effectively, as rangers, dragoons, or mounted riflemen. The Indians adopted ranger-like tactics, and in at least one incident in the fall of 1812, mounted native forces encountered similarly armed and mounted Americans along the shores of the Maumee River. In the second battle of Frenchtown (or the River Raisin) in January 1813, mounted Wyandot wielding tomahawks killed fleeing members of the 17th U.S. Infantry with abandon. Such combat was rare, and usually the Indians lacked unit discipline to effectively employ mounted warriors during a battle. They also lacked the systematic procurement of forage and the stables, corrals, blacksmith shops, and harness and saddle factories that support an equestrian-oriented community.

Indeed, the largest problem that horses presented was the logistical support required—the need for shelter, fencing, pasture, forage, blacksmith shops, saddles, and harness dramatically raised the cost of equipping and maintaining any mounted force. For the financial reason, the U.S. government did not maintain cavalry or mounted rifle regiments in the early years of the republic. Before Anthony Wayne created the Legion of the United States, mounted units consisted of short-term volunteers who furnished their own animals and equipment. It was these logistical requirements that limited the Indians' ability to utilize the horse for anything beyond scouting.

The Geographic Environment

The new region Harrison entered in 1791 was far different from the Chesapeake Bay and its tributaries, where he was raised. The dominant geographic features were the Great Lakes to the north and the Ohio Valley to the south. These waterways provided the transportation net that bound the region's economy internally and externally. The St. Lawrence–Great Lakes system provided the British and their Indian allies with commercial connections that stretched across the Atlantic. By the early nineteenth century, a limited number of sailing vessels plied the lakes engaging in trade. A few carried light artillery. Much of the commercial and military transportation was by birch bark canoe on the region's many rivers. Many of the larger river systems such as the Ottawa, Cataraqui, Grand (Ontario), Thames, and French Rivers drained deep into the Canadian Shield. Those draining from the south were normally much shorter— Oswego, Genesee, Cuyahoga, Sandusky, Maumee, Raisin, Grand (Michigan), St. Joseph, Fox, and Chicago—and therefore inhibited penetration into the interior of the United States and required portages to other rivers running to the Ohio watershed.

As noted earlier, at portage sites at the mouths of many of these rivers and at critical chokepoints, the French, British, and Americans erected fortifications—Forts Oswego, Kingston, George, Erie, Niagara, Malden, Detroit, Wayne, Michilimackinac, St. Joseph (on St. Marys River, Ontario), St. Joseph (Niles, Michigan), La Baye (Green Bay, Wisconsin), and Dearborn (Chicago). For the British and their native allies, one of the most critical of these chokepoints was the Niagara Falls. The portage was long and difficult, and one had to control both ends at Forts George and Erie. The most common way around this obstacle was to follow the long and tortuous route up the Ottawa and then west on the Mattawa River to the La Vase portage, which allowed access to Lake Nipissing; from there one could navigate down the French River into Lake

Huron's Georgian Bay. This involved twenty-two or more portages and over a dozen discharges of cargo. Only canoes could make this journey. By the early nineteenth century, a new route was established from Toronto (then called York) via a thirty-mile portage to Lake Simcoe, after a nine-mile portage from that lake's Kempenfeldt Bay to the Nottawasaga River, from where bateaux transported goods and men to the river mouth on Georgian Bay. Another route from Lake Simcoe used the Severn River to Georgian Bay. Control of the Niagara portage and travel via the upper lakes was preferred to the other routes, since larger cargo could be transported faster at less cost.[40]

There was another barrier to American logistical efforts: the Appalachian Mountains. For the United States, the Mohawk Valley between the Hudson Valley and Lake Ontario was the only natural water route into the interior. It proved difficult to navigate. Cohoes Falls at the mouth of the Mohawk made water navigation impossible. In the seventeenth century, a sixteen-mile "King's Highway" from Albany to Schenectady allowed access to the Mohawk River. The completion in the 1790s of Little Falls Canal and the Rome Canal between Rome and Wood Creek allowed bateaux to navigate via Lake Oneida and the Oswego River to Lake Ontario. Numerous oxbows on Wood Creek were circumvented by thirteen short canals cut across the necks. This route became the most efficient way to forward men and materiel to the Great Lakes interior during the War of 1812. However, its operational success depended on U.S. naval dominance of Lake Ontario and control of the Niagara portage. It eventually became part of the Erie Canal route westward, but that happened after the War of 1812.[41]

Another American route west involved an overland road to Pittsburgh and thence down the Ohio River. Forbes Road, built across Pennsylvania during the French and Indian War, was the most important portion of this route. Once in Pittsburgh, soldiers, munitions, and supplies were transported by barges to Wheeling, Marietta, Cincinnati, Louisville, and St. Louis for distribution to military units. Pittsburgh also constituted the starting point for a route northward to Erie, Pennsylvania, and hence to Lake Erie. By the early nineteenth century, Pittsburgh was already the largest manufacturing community west of the Appalachians. It provided cannon balls, wrought iron hardware, cordage, clothing, and other equipment—all of which did not have to be transported over the mountains. In this context it had no rival in the North American interior.

The third route west lay through the Cumberland Gap in what is now southwest Virginia. It became the most important pass through the Appalachian Mountains between the Mohawk Valley and the terminus of the chain in northern Georgia. Through the Cumberland Gap, starting in the 1750s, came the long hunters in search of deer skins, buffalo hides, and bear furs, which they carried by packhorses to tidewater and piedmont exchange points. It would not be until 1774 that Harrodsburg, the first English-speaking settlement west of the Appalachians, was established. Although temporarily abandoned during Lord Dunmore's War, it became the harbinger of rapidly advancing settlements in the Kentucky River Valley over the next decade.

Lord Dunmore's War of 1774 marked the beginning of twenty years of frontier conflict in the trans-Appalachian West that ended only with the battle of Fallen Timbers. For Kentucky pioneers it was a time of alarms, mobilizations, and encounters with Native Americans. During the War for Independence they conducted mostly a defensive strategy. But under the leadership of George Rogers Clark there were offensive forays across the Ohio River into southern Indiana, Illinois, and Ohio. The Americans scored numerous victories in this struggle, most significantly at Vincennes, but also tragic defeats at the hands of natives and Loyalist allies, most importantly the battle of Blue Licks in August 1782. There were no regular army forces in the region, and with the continued mobilization efforts, most of the adult male citizens became familiar with military organization, campaigns, and fighting. The expansion of settlement in the Bluegrass Region grew amazingly during the Revolutionary War. Bardstown in 1778 and Louisville and Lexington in 1779 are only a few of the new settlements begun while warfare raged throughout the region. After the war, settlement intensified, and Kentucky would be admitted as a full-fledged member of the Union in 1794.[42]

Robert McAfee, a Kentucky cavalry captain in the War of 1812, wrote that "the old method of sending regulars, under a general unskilled in savage warfare, was . . . employed in the case of [General Arthur] St. Clair's campaign [of 1791], with disastrous consequences of a total defeat."[43] Most commentaries on the regular army campaigns of the 1790s place the blame for failure on the ill-equipped, ill-led, and ill-disciplined militia. Most scholars concentrate on the campaigns of Generals Josiah Harmar and Arthur St. Clair and ignore the volunteer militia campaigns from Kentucky into Indiana during the same period. As noted earlier, the Kentuckians brought a new tactic and new weapons into Midwestern combat: the cavalryman with his rifle, tomahawk, and audacity and the mounted infantryman with his rifle, hunting knife, and boldness. Mounted raids into the Wabash Valley forced many hostile Indian groups to settle farther up the valley for greater security. The same raids trained the Kentuckians in the intricacies of mounted warfare, a military style that suited them and provided relief from Indian attacks south of the Ohio River. Throughout Harrison's career, the effective utilization of mounted troopers would be an important component in his operations.

The Junior Officer

While Harrison and his accompanying recruits made the trip down the Ohio River, the United States Army experienced, in what is now western Ohio, its most disastrous defeat by Native Americans in our national history: the battle of the Wabash, or what is usually called "St. Clair's Defeat," on 4 November 1791. In three centuries of warfare between Euroamericans and Native Americans, never before and never again was there such a calamitous defeat for British or American armies—the better known Indian triumphs on the banks of the Monongahela (1755) and the Little Bighorn (1876) notwithstanding. Little Turtle's triumph at the Wabash constitutes the apogee of native victories in what became the United States.[44]

This triumph for the great coalition of tribes in the Old Northwest represented the total collapse of an American expedition. The butcher's bill was exceptionally high; nearly one thousand of the fourteen hundred men commanded by Maj. Gen. Arthur St. Clair were killed, wounded, or missing. Indian losses stood at approximately twenty-one killed and forty wounded. The shattered remnants of St. Clair's army filtered into Fort Washington as Harrison and his recruits arrived. All was chaos in Cincinnati. For Harrison's career, though, it represented an opportunity—Generals Harmar and St. Clair were eliminated from direction of the western military campaign. Who would the new commander be? And would he be favorably inclined toward an untried ensign?

Among the men returning from the Wabash, one whom Harrison met was a Virginian who had been a guest at Berkeley and was surprised to find Ensign Harrison in uniform. He may have been Capt. Joseph Brock, who commanded one of the four Virginia volunteer militia levies in the battle. Whoever it was, he tried to discourage Harrison and to entice him into resigning his commission rather than committing his fortunes to a war with few opportunities for glory and with fellow officers who were more inclined toward alcohol and

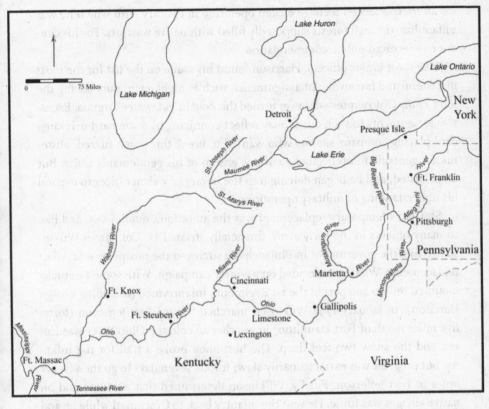

Theater of military operations, 1972–94. Reproduced with permission from Alan D. Gaff, *Bayonets in the Wilderness: Anthony Wayne's Legion in the Old Northwest* (Norman: University of Oklahoma Press, 2004).

cards than gentlemanly pursuits. Such an environment might lead the young ensign into similar excesses.[45]

But Harrison disregarded this advice, as he had that of Robert Morris. He had entered the army without telling his family or Morris. He was not now going to back down from a decision made on his own, a decision that went against the advice of those more experienced than he, and a decision made with the apparent self-confidence of a young man who considered himself capable of overcoming the biggest of obstacles on a road to valor, honor, and advancement. Just a few days after his arrival at Fort Washington, he commanded a twenty-man guard escorting supplies bound for Fort Hamilton, the post twenty-five miles to the north. This was a pretty significant responsibility for an inexperienced teenage ensign operating in country with which he was unfamiliar, through forests supposedly filled with native warriors. For his conduct he received public commendation.

Like most junior officers, Harrison found his name on the list for the most distasteful and inconvenient assignments, such as night guard duty during the long, chilly Ohio winter—it never turned this cold in Tidewater Virginia. Excessive assignments to such duties may reflect conniving by some hard-drinking, card-playing company seniors who wanted to break this peach-fuzzed, abstemious, gentrified, intellectually curious ensign of his gentlemanly traits. But he persisted, and he began delving into the library of a slain officer to expand his understanding of military operations.

St. Clair's temporary replacement was the ambitious, duplicitous, and like so many officers in the early army, financially striated Lt. Col. James Wilkinson. While the government in Philadelphia surveyed the prospective St. Clair replacements, Wilkinson decided on a winter campaign. With some Kentucky mounted militia and part of the 1st Regiment's infantrymen (including Ensign Harrison), in January 1792 Wilkinson marched toward Fort Jefferson (forty-five miles north of Fort Hamilton) in weather so cold the Ohio River was frozen and the snow two feet deep. The horsemen broke a trail for the infantry, but progress was extraordinarily slow; it took seven days to go the seventy miles to Fort Jefferson. Finally, Wilkinson determined that a winter raid on native villages was futile. He sent the infantry back to Cincinnati while he and a mounted party went the additional twenty-nine miles to the Wabash battlefield site. They observed the aftermath of the disaster—human remains, some in skeletal condition with others preserved by the cold weather, with all the carnage that animals and Indians had inflicted. After burying all the bodies they could find, the horsemen returned to Fort Washington. It was not a successful expedition—Wilkinson did not recover the cannons at the battle site, nor did he attack any Indian villages. This did not impress those in Philadelphia and, consequently, Wilkinson did not receive the coveted command of the North West Army.[46] Tales of the battle scene, of course, became common fare in the officers' and enlisted messes. The experience undoubtedly increased Harrison's respect for the role of mounted troops on the frontier and began his acquaintance with some of the leaders of these Kentucky volunteers, many of whom were native Virginians.

Wilkinson determined that the gap between Forts Hamilton and Jefferson was too extended for expeditions to the former, so in March he directed two hundred regulars and militia to build a small fortification, to be known as Fort St. Clair, near modern Eaton, Ohio. Ensign Harrison found himself commanding the guard every other night for three weeks. He remained in good health and apparently became more acceptable to the company-grade officers that accompanied this enterprise. Some of his regimental adversaries also left the scene. Maj. David Zeigler resigned in a huff and was surprised to see the resignation accepted. (There is a lesson here that Harrison should have learned.) Capt. David Strong became commander of Fort Jefferson, thereby removing another Harrison nemesis from the Cincinnati environment. By late spring Ensign Harrison was in good graces with most of his fellow officers.[47]

Harrison's social experiences went far beyond the regimental mess. Slowly but surely his sophisticated manners and family reputation gave him access to individuals outside the norm for young ensigns. Significant among these was Winthrop Sargent, the territorial secretary. This classically educated Harvard graduate had an office inside Fort Washington. Even though he reputedly was somewhat aloof, his scientific, natural history, and anthropological interests coincided with some of Harrison's and the two got along well. It was Sargent who introduced the ensign to a five-foot-high, six-hundred-foot-diameter circular mound in the village and a fifty-foot-high conical mound nearby. Who were the people who constructed these edifices? How long ago were they built? What happened to the builders? Questions like these percolated through the minds of Sargent, Harrison, and a few other scientifically oriented individuals in the community.[48] However romantic might be Harrison's answers to such questions, his association with this activity demonstrated a growing intellectual curiosity and expanded friendships in a wider community. He acquired the social skills and acquaintanceships necessary for future advancement. Most critical was the growing favoritism of Colonel Wilkinson toward the ensign.[49]

In Philadelphia, President Washington and Secretary of War Henry Knox made critical staffing decisions regarding the western armed forces. Politically, the issue was divisive—although the emerging Republican faction leader James Madison, with his western Pennsylvania allies William Finley and Albert Gallatin, normally favored the use of militia over regulars, they agreed to support an enlarged United States Army. For the most part, Federalists wanted the creation of a strong national armed force. As delay followed delay in deploying the new federal troops, the Republican opposition became less enamored with the regulars and counseled using more numerous and less expensive militiamen. An elaborate congressional investigation of the defeat at the Wabash exonerated St. Clair and placed the blame on the War Department, especially on its logistical inadequacies that had delayed the general's departure until late in the season. Thus the Republicans attacked the administration to salve their wounded consciences for supporting an enlarged regular force. At the same time, the Republicans caved in to western pressure for a stronger national military presence.[50]

The administration created the Legion of the United States with four legions of twelve hundred men, each with three-year enlistments and increased pay. These combined arms teams of infantry, cavalry, and artillery constituted an innovative organizational development that would not survive. Washington kept St. Clair as the territorial governor and, after considerable debate, selected Continental Army Maj. Gen. Anthony Wayne as the Legion's commander and promoted Wilkinson to brigadier general. Although many found Wayne's appointment controversial, Washington and Knox viewed Wayne as the best of a series of bad choices. In the final analysis, Wayne proved an effective commander for the new military instrument that the administration was hoping would destroy the natives' confederation in the Old Northwest.

The new "Act for making further and more effectual provision for the protection of the Frontiers" combined with the new senior officer appointments were part of the Federalists' efforts to develop a grand strategy that would let them recover from the recent defeats on the frontier. Washington, Knox, and Secretary of State Thomas Jefferson knew there had to be more than military might to achieve their objectives. Besides the Indians there was the continued British occupation of military installations inside the 1783 boundaries of the new republic—especially Detroit and Michilimackinac. The aftermath of defeat necessitated the integration of military and diplomatic aspects of national power to meet common goals. The recovery of the next three years required the successful implementation of a grand strategy on all levels.[51] All this allowed Ensign Harrison an opportunity to be in the midst of national policymaking at the highest operational echelon.

Before this happened, the young man exhibited a rashness often attributed to teenagers. It all began when Wilkinson allowed soldiers to visit the village of Cincinnati, with permission of their commanding officers. As one might expect, all too many over-imbibed in local alehouses and annoyed many of the townspeople. Moreover, the post guardhouse was filled with men adjudged guilty of being drunk on duty. To stop this behavior Wilkinson issued an order that any private observed drunk and disorderly in the village would receive fifty lashes on the spot—without a court martial. As one might expect, enforcement duty fell on the junior officers, and this included Ensign Harrison. Acting as a military police officer, Harrison and his squad of enforcers found one of the fort's men inebriated in town. Despite the protests of his companion that the man was not a soldier, the officer in charge had the drunken man stripped and lashed. When the other man continued protesting, the ensign ordered him to be given ten lashes. Later Harrison discovered that the men were civilian artificers at Fort Washington, not privates. They were subject neither to Wilkinson's order nor to Harrison's discipline. The two victims eventually went into town and swore out a warrant for Harrison's arrest on grounds of assault. The resulting confrontation between the town and the army grew more heated when General Wilkinson closed the post gates to the deputy sheriff as he was trying to serve the warrant on someone the general thought to be "one of the best disposed and most promising young Gentlemen in the Army." Eventually, Acting Governor Sargent concluded that the two men had "voluntarily subjected themselves" to military discipline by becoming civilian employees and thereby ordered that Harrison could not be prosecuted in a civilian court.[52]

Both Wilkinson and Harrison needed a way out of the mess. Because an escort was needed for Mrs. Wilkinson and the children on a trip to Philadelphia that spring, the general ordered Ensign Harrison to accompany them—at least as far as Pittsburgh. This took the young man out of the contentious environment and allowed tempers to cool. The keelboat trip upstream took almost three weeks, and the ensign reported to General Wayne, the new commander of the Legion. The general procured horses for Mrs. Wilkinson and her three boys, and the ensign received instructions from Wayne to take "particular care to inquire for the best and *safest* roads" during the trip to Philadelphia.[53] The escort duty finished, Harrison returned to Pittsburgh. Although Wilkinson expected him back in Cincinnati, the new commanding general kept him. Harrison's reputation as an effective drill instructor made him just the man to help train the large numbers of new recruits.

Wayne intensified drill instruction and included a new method of musket fire. The normal tactic was for the men to fire in volleys with their weapons pointed in the general direction of the opponent. Since musketry was erratic and marksmanship allegedly ineffective, eighteenth-century armies relied on close order formations and volley fire. Wayne thought such a tactic unwise and directed aimed-fire practice. He began rewarding the best marksmen with an extra liquor ration, a practice designed to increase competition. Given that they were fighting Indians who also used aimed fire and did not employ close order formations, American soldiers had to be marksmen. In addition the men learned to use a "buck and ball" load, which, when aimed at dispersed opponents, was more likely to inflict wounds rather than kill as when using a single ball. Skilled musket fire became a characteristic of the Legion. Its effectiveness impressed the young Virginian, and he emphasized it throughout his military career. The Legion also trained with bayonets; Wayne knew that effective bayonet charges would break any native formation, because Indians lacked similar weapons in an age of slow-loading muskets. Both aimed-fire and bayonet skills would be useful in the close combat expected in the forests of the Old Northwest. Wayne summed up his training objectives in a letter to Knox: "I am also endeavouring to make the riflemen believe in that arm, the Infantry in heavy buck shot & the bayonet, and the Dragoons in the sword, & the Legion in their United Prowess."[54]

Wayne took the nomenclature of the Legion and formed four sub-legions, each supposedly commanded by a brigadier general. Each sub-legion he divided into battalions and companies. Each twelve-hundred-man legion contained eight companies of infantry (one company consisted of riflemen), with a troop of dragoons and a battery of light artillery as part of its organization. The 1st Sub-Legion (filled mostly by men from the 1st U.S. Infantry Regiment) wore white binding and white plumes on their caps. The 2nd Sub-Legion had red binding and plumes, and so forth. The legionary organization was primarily of Knox's design (he was formerly Washington's chief of artillery) and did not long outlast his tenure as secretary of war. Its principal liabilities were the difficulty of moving artillery in a wilderness containing no roads and the enormous expense of mounted troops compared with foot soldiers. But it gave junior officers an opportunity to see the interaction of foot, mounted, and artillery units in a way unknown to most of them.

The reorganization found Harrison assigned to a company commanded by Capt. Ballard Smith, a fellow Virginian with personality traits directly opposed to those the ensign expected of a military officer. Few officers in the new sub-legion had a reputation as bad as Smith's—he quarreled with superiors, drank excessively, and maintained an equally hard-drinking mistress who was the common-law wife of one of his sergeants. On one occasion, he and the mistress became so intoxicated that she threatened to shoot a noncommissioned officer with the captain's pistols and then began waving his sword in a threatening manner, before both were subdued by a squad of soldiers. A subsequent court martial suspended the captain from command, and this allowed the nineteen-year-old Lieutenant Harrison to become temporary company commander. Captain Smith exemplified a style of military leadership in sharp contrast to that followed by the prim and proper son of Benjamin Harrison V.

While his company command time was relatively short, Harrison left the impression of a commander concerned with the welfare of his troops. Just prior to Smith's court martial on 10 September, Harrison had received promotion to lieutenant, with a date of rank retroactive to 2 June 1792. Nothing indicates the growing reputation of the young man more than his receiving this promotion less than a year from his commissioning.

Fort Fayette proved too close to Pittsburgh for Wayne to control his troops' behavior, so in November he moved to a new encampment twenty-two miles below the town, on a high bluff to be called Legionville. Lieutenant Harrison still commanded Smith's company when it moved to the site later that month. For weeks the soldiers cleared brush, felled trees, shaped the trunks into logs, and fitted them into huts. Wayne reversed what is too often the order of comfort by having the troops' quarters finished first, the officers' second, and his own last. By the end of the first week of December, the troops had finished the primitive quarters so that all personnel were out of the linen tents and into some sort of housing. Soon the men were back to the routine of morning parade, musket practice outside the camp, and bayonet and marching drill. It was a rigorous and demanding schedule, designed as much to keep the men busy as to increase their proficiency in the profession of arms. But there can be no doubt that Wayne's troops were better trained than any the young republic had fielded since the end of the War for Independence. This attention to drill, marksmanship, and the men's protection from both the elements and the enemy would characterize Harrison's command procedures in both the Tippecanoe and Canadian campaigns.

The lieutenant learned more about the harsh realities of frontier military life. Not only was the second winter spent in sparse and crude conditions, but it opened to him all the problems of closely confined young men seeking a way out of their frustrations. Drunken behavior resulted in a major being dismissed from the service; a captain committed suicide by slitting his throat; an inefficient logistical system meant inadequate rations, uniforms, and equipment; paymasters only infrequently visited the post. Duels arose between officers supposedly dishonored by some comment or conduct by another. According to Harrison, "There were more duels in the Northwestern Army between

1791 and 1795 than ever took place in the same length of time and amongst so small a body of men." Another officer recalled fifteen duels and three deaths in the year ending in February 1793.[55]

Brutal treatment of those involved in criminal activities typified Wayne's Legion—executions, floggings of up to a hundred lashes, branding on the forehead, and other forms of corporal punishment supposedly curtailed desertion, drunkenness, and theft. Nearly forty years after the incident, Harrison vividly recalled delivering the reprieve of a young corporal about to be executed for a minor infraction. Such incidents clearly affected Harrison's choice of more lenient forms of punishment when he commanded an army.[56]

Still the Legion did not campaign. Instead, the Washington administration tried negotiating with the natives rather than fighting them.[57] Emboldened by their victory on the Wabash, the Indians presented American negotiators with a nonnegotiable boundary—the Ohio River: north of it would be Indian territory. Throughout 1792 and 1793 negotiations went on, frustrated by Indian intransigence, British connivance, and American expansionism. But in 1793 Wayne moved his corps from Fort Hamilton to an encampment he appropriately named Hobson's Choice—take it or leave it.

Fallen Timbers Campaign

In June 1793, Harrison received appointment as General Wayne's aide-de-camp, along with Capt. Henry DeButts. This distinct honor for a very junior lieutenant came with a major's pay of $64 per month, plus $12 per month in forage pay for the two horses he had to purchase. Undoubtedly Harrison's neat handwriting, his classical education, and his social graces contributed to this appointment, which brought him in as a background observer to staff meetings and Indian negotiations and made him a secretary, receiving, keeping, and preparing the general's correspondence. Only twenty years old, Lieutenant Harrison found himself at the center of the largest military campaign undertaken by the young republic since the adoption of the Constitution. The stakes were high—the future history of North America lay in the balance. If the natives and their British allies could stop American settlement at the Ohio River line, this would jeopardize the northern boundary of the United States along the line of the lakes. Equally important was the future of the national military establishment. Many in Congress wanted reliance on the militia and volunteers rather than on regular troops. Wayne and his Legion carried a difficult burden as they began what is known as the Fallen Timbers campaign.

The appointment as Wayne's aide says much about Harrison's personality. He was considered a Wilkinson favorite, he had the special privilege of escorting Mrs. Wilkinson, and it would appear that Wilkinson wanted the young lieutenant on his own staff, as part of his official "family." Instead, Wayne appointed him into his "family," even as the tensions between Wilkinson and the commanding general were becoming obvious. That Harrison could negotiate between the two contentious generals provides an interesting commentary on his affability and adaptability. Wilkinson sought to undermine Wayne by corresponding directly with Knox in Philadelphia, by attempting to separate the western command from Wayne's supervision, and by fomenting opposition to the commanding general within the officer corps. Harrison kept out of the increasingly tense situation between the two generals. For example, during the winter of 1793–94, Harrison frequently carried letters between the two generals, one at Fort Jefferson, the other at Fort Greenville. It seems he respected both men and refused to be drawn into their increasingly bitter recriminations.[58]

Although an interpreter provided a summary of the failed peace conference negotiations shortly after they concluded, official news of the failure did not reach Cincinnati until 11 September 1793; Wayne ordered a march northward to begin. Anticipating the news, he had issued "Order of March" and "Order of Battle" on 25 August, but still the movement could not begin until 7 October. For Harrison and the other aides this was indeed a busy time. In effect, they—along with the adjutant general, quartermaster, and surgeon—were the operational staff of the army. Their pens wrote the general's orders and their eyes observed the orders being successfully implemented.

Joining the army were five hundred Kentucky mounted riflemen, one fourth of what Wayne hoped would come. Commanded by Brig. Gen. Charles Scott, these volunteers constituted the main mounted arm of the army. The Kentuckians did not remain long and were sent back when Wayne decided to halt the campaign due to insufficient supplies and the lateness of the season. Harrison's acquaintanceship with the Kentucky general would last for twenty years and eventually resulted in Governor Scott appointing Harrison a major general in the Kentucky militia near the start of the War of 1812. Friendships are important factors in successful military careers, and Harrison made and kept friends

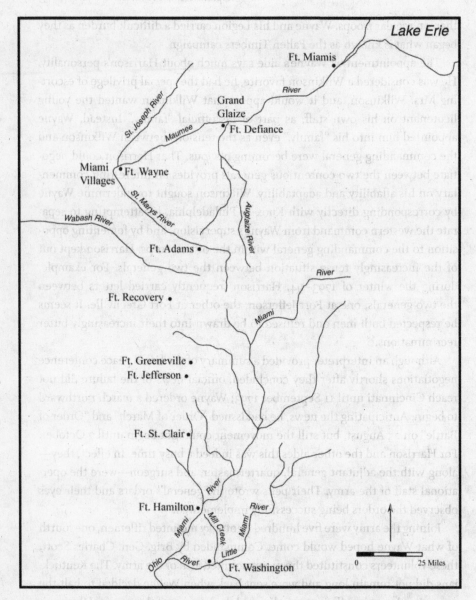

Northwestern forts. Reproduced with permission from Alan D. Gaff, *Bayonets in the Wilderness: Anthony Wayne's Legion in the Old Northwest* (Norman: University of Oklahoma Press, 2004).

throughout his military service. Another lesson learned involved Scott's desire to conduct mounted raids against Indian villages in the valleys of the St. Marys and Auglaize Rivers, tributaries of the Maumee. Wayne denied this maneuver, but given Scott's previous success in similar endeavors in the Wabash Valley, the idea may have been the genesis for Harrison's use of mounted raids during the War of 1812.[59]

Harrison also witnessed Wayne's continued alertness and discipline as the army moved northward. As he advanced, the commanding general had his dragoons patrolling in advance and on the flanks of his infantrymen. Every night the army encamped and set up breastworks and abatis around the camp—there would be no open encampment like that contributing to the disaster on the Wabash. Wayne seemed to want an attack, but it never came. Instead he became furious when some of the dragoons encountered an Indian party and withdrew in confusion. He ordered a court martial for the whole group and had a grave dug for its commanding officer. Convicted of cowardice, the officer was sentenced to be executed. It was a hard lesson and a sobering one for the entire corps as it assembled in front of the young man, blindfolded and standing in front of his grave, before Wayne issued a last-minute reprieve. The commanding general took the opportunity to harangue the force on the consequences of cowardice.[60]

General Wayne was particularly conscious of the possibility of an encounter in which the natives might attack the flanks and rear of a deployed force. He trained the Legion to react promptly and correctly to such circumstances. As Harrison recalled years later, Wayne's tactics were "devised with a reference to all the subtilties, which those of the Indians were well known to possess. It united with apparently opposite qualities of compactness and flexibility, and facility of expansion under any circumstances, and in any situation, which rendered utterly abortive the peculiar tact[ic] of the Indians in assailing the flanks of their adversaries."[61] It was this type of preparation that proved useful to Harrison nearly two decades later.

At the time it seemed insignificant, but in 1792 a young Kentuckian who had been captured eight years earlier by the Miami and brought up in their ways came to Cincinnati. While a captive he had married, and he came to Fort Washington to secure the release of his wife and son who had been captured earlier. (The Americans often held warriors' families hostage as guarantees for peaceful behavior.) General Wilkinson soon recognized the importance of this young man as a cross-cultural mediator between the two worlds. William Wells was his name, and he became highly useful to the United States as a scout, liaison, and negotiator in the years that followed. During the advance toward Fallen Timbers, he and another former captive, Henry Miller, served as "spies" or scouts in Capt. Ephraim Kibby's company, which blazed the trail for Wayne's army. Such men became critical intelligence assets in Wayne's campaign. For Lieutenant Harrison these men provided a good example of how to use the talents of former white captives and friendly natives in frontier warfare.[62] Wells would remain a factor in Harrison's life for the next twenty years.

Harrison became familiar with one of the commanding general's most pressing problems—logistical support. Supplying the western army was the bane of operations throughout the early national era. Most manufacturing was done on the east coast, and in this time before canals, steamboats, roads, and railroads, difficulties abounded for contractors trying to meet the demands of armies operating in the trans-Appalachian region. Contractors seemed more interested in profits than performance, and accusations of ineptitude and malfeasance dominate the letters written by the aides for Wayne's signature. For instance, in 1793 the contracting firm of Elliott & Williams failed to deliver 250,000 rations to Fort Jefferson and instead provided 70,000, with another 12,000 supposedly en route. This forced the commanding general to stop operations just six miles north of Fort Jefferson at a post he named Fort Greenville.[63]

The demands that Wayne placed on Elliott & Williams were extraordinary given the inadequacy of the road network and the dangers of unescorted supply trains and cattle droves being ambushed by the Indians. Some of the blame for the problems might be placed on Quartermaster General James O'Hara, a Wayne confidant, who operated out of Cincinnati and catered to the general's whims without much regard to contractors' problems.[64] Wayne found that the lack of supplies forced him to send Scott's horsemen and his own dragoons to Kentucky for the winter. His hopes for an early spring campaign northward seemed frustrated by logistics as much as by the enemy. Supply issues in the same region would frustrate Harrison in the winter of 1812–13. However, Harrison appreciated the efforts of one of the firm's partners, Robert Elliott, who was killed by Indians while trying to forward supplies. For this reason, he refused to openly condemn Elliott's son, Capt. Jesse Duncan Elliott, USN, whose altercations with Capt. Oliver Hazard Perry in the aftermath of the battle of Lake Erie generated considerable controversy.[65]

And so the Legion of the United States spent another winter in hastily constructed quarters built of green logs cut down in late fall. Even with all the perquisites of an aide-de-camp, for Harrison this was not pleasant duty. Certainly, managing social affairs, escorting visiting dignitaries, conveying the general's orders to subordinate commanders, attending senior officer conferences, coordinating with other staff officers, letter writing, record keeping, and inspecting troops kept the young aide busier than many of his fellow officers. During three long winters Lieutenant Harrison observed activities at the highest level of command. Such an understanding would stand him in good stead years later.

Despite his reputed mercurial temperament, Wayne could be both prescient and prudent. For instance, at the outset of the 1794 campaign he made detailed preparations for the outfitting of units and individual soldiers. He had all "heavy and Useless Baggage" left at a rear post, each company received ten axes for the construction of nightly encampments and more permanent fortifications, and soldiers were issued summer uniforms and told to fold their blankets and knapsacks in tight bundles to allow ease of marching along narrow trails and underbrush.[66] This anticipation of the tough duty facing the Legion and how to ameliorate it left a lasting impression on Lieutenant Harrison.

The young aide also observed the commanding general's operational caution. In contrast to Generals Harmar and St. Clair, and despite his reputation for impetuosity, as implied in his nickname "Mad," the commanding general of this campaign was a paragon of prudence. A recent biographer summarized it thus: "shrewd caution was to be the hallmark of Anthony Wayne's methodical assault on America's enemies north of the Ohio River."[67] "Shrewd caution" became a notable characteristic of William Henry Harrison throughout his military career; it was a technique he witnessed successfully implemented in the march to the Maumee River in 1794.

In January 1794 General Wayne continued his counteroffensive by moving north from Fort Greenville to the site of St. Clair's defeat. There Harrison witnessed the burial of the skeletal remains of the fallen and the construction of a new post named Fort Recovery. Wayne hoped to overawe the natives, and he observed a truce with the Delaware that he recognized might give the Indians time to move their nearby villages before attacking the Americans. His suspicions were justified; three major tribal war leaders met—Buckongahelas of the Delaware, Little Turtle of the Miami, and Blue Jacket of the Shawnee—and rejected the peace offer. Instead they drafted plans for an attack on their foe and expected British assistance. The governor general of Canada, Sir Guy Carleton, recently elevated to the peerage as Lord Dorchester, promised such aid because he expected the United States and Great Britain to be at war shortly and, if so, they could expect direct assistance from His Majesty's government. To implement this, Carleton ordered John Graves Simcoe, the lieutenant governor of Upper Canada (modern Ontario), to construct a fort near the rapids of the Maumee River. (Named Fort Miamis, though often designated Fort Miami on early maps, was located in what is now the eastern edge of Maumee, Ohio, on the river's north bank.) All this was an aspect of a British desire to create an Indian barrier state between the lakes and the Ohio River that protected Britain's Canadian territorial and fur trading interests. To the Americans this was an invasion of their territory under the provisions of the Peace of Paris of 1783; to the British and Native Americans it was a defense of native rights to the lands north of the Ohio River from unauthorized American settlement. How this was handled short of war constituted a delicate diplomatic problem to be handled by frontier commanders on both sides. Lord Dorchester's aggressiveness (which was without London approval) turned an Indian campaign into a potential for international war, at the outset of the wars with revolutionary France in Europe.[68] Harrison watched closely how this interaction unraveled.

Before the Legion marched northward, a group of Indians attacked the garrison at Fort Recovery, to which Maj. William McMahon had brought a convoy containing supplies from Elliott & Williams. Friendly native scouts warned Wayne, and he alerted Fort Recovery of the native confederacy sending braves into its vicinity. Had the native confederacy, which now included Ottawa and Chippewa tribesmen from the upper Great Lakes, concentrated its forces a day earlier they might well have destroyed the supply train. When the first indications of an attack appeared, an impulsive charge by McMahon and his dragoons was a disaster and cost the lives of the major and many of his officers and men. Such a brazen native assault on the fortification, even one so far north of the Ohio River, reminded the army's leadership of the logistical vulnerability of campaigns so far from their supply base. Capt. Alexander Gibson and the garrison, including several Choctaw Indians allied with the Americans, stoutly resisted the attackers, and eventually the natives withdrew with significant losses. For Harrison, the memory of this attack against the army's supply system served as a constant remembrance of the need to protect the links necessary to keep an army in the field. It also pointed out the importance of friendly Indians to success in wilderness warfare.

For the Indian confederacy, the defeat at Fort Recovery may be more important than that at Fallen Timbers. Little Turtle of the Miami lost confidence in the British, who refused to support a second Fort Recovery attack with a small artillery battery. He would not participate in the Fallen Timbers battle. The Potawatomi, Ottawa, and Chippewa warriors took their scalps and other trophies and returned to their Great Lakes villages. The confederacy slowly disintegrated. Equally important, British policy changed as the possibility of an American victory became increasingly probable. Caution rather than direct support became the word of the day. Recent commentators conclude that the war was really over after the Fort Recovery defeat.[69] Of course, none of this was obvious to Anthony Wayne or William Henry Harrison.

Wayne understood that warfare against the Native Americans was concluded successfully if one destroyed their villages and the nearby fields of corn and vegetables. Far more important than achieving a tactical military victory, Wayne needed to make the natives dependent on American annuities for their subsistence. This meant that the concentration of natives in seven communities near the junction of the Auglaize and Maumee Rivers became the primary objective of the 1794 campaign. Instead of advancing up the St. Marys River to the headwaters of the Maumee as General Harmar had done in 1790, Wayne chose the direct route to the midst of the new native communities along the center of the Maumee,[70] at present-day Defiance, Ohio.

Wayne moved cautiously, erecting a post at the headwaters of the St. Marys River and then marching directly to the mouth of the Auglaize River, where he erected Fort Defiance at its confluence with the Maumee. Now at the center of the native settlements, he moved down the Maumee toward Fort Miamis (Maumee, Ohio), where he finally encountered the somewhat depleted Indian confederation in a mass of tornado-downed trees.

At Fallen Timbers, Wayne's forces included the Legion of the United States plus approximately fifteen hundred mounted Kentucky riflemen commanded by Maj. Gen. Charles Scott. In contrast to the Legion troops, these men were veterans of years of frontier warfare. Their mobility and the shock action of their mounts allowed a flanking movement toward the Indians' right wing and into their rear. Meanwhile, the Legion attacked the center with rifles, muskets, and bayonets. Archaeological evidence indicates that the Americans fired mostly "buck and ball" rounds; as noted earlier, these were less likely to kill, but wounding created more problems for the warriors than did deaths. In the midst of flying bullets, a conspicuously mounted Harrison displayed considerable courage carrying Wayne's orders to various subordinates. The young aide feared the commanding general might become so engaged in the fighting that he neglected to inform him of the latest field orders; Wayne abruptly told Harrison the standing order of the day was "Charge the damned rascals with the bayonet." Lt. Bartholomew Schaumburgh recalled that "Harrison was in the foremost front of the hottest battle . . . Wherever duty called, he hastened, regardless of danger, and by his efforts an example contributed as much to secure the fortune of the day, as any other officer subordinate to the commander-in-chief."[71] Harrison claimed that the "great strength, activity & fleetness" of his mount allowed him to escape from being hit while delivering one of General Wayne's orders.[72] These examples of personal courage undoubtedly enhanced his reputation among both regulars and volunteers. Harrison's baptism to combat brought home the drama, trauma, and consequences of men killing one another. Only twenty-one, he, like the other aides, demonstrated

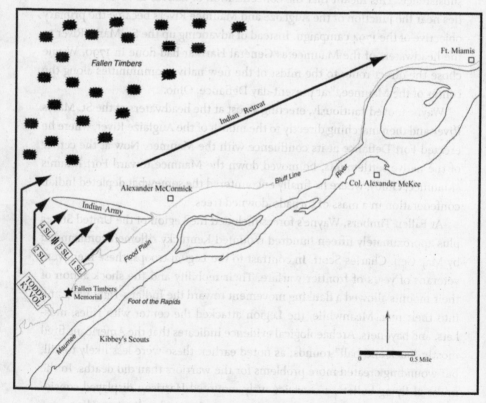

Battle of Fallen Timbers. Reproduced with permission from Alan D. Gaff, *Bayonets in the Wilderness: Anthony Wayne's Legion in the Old Northwest* (Norman: University of Oklahoma Press, 2004).

bravery, fortitude, and composure that merited mention in Wayne's report to Secretary Knox.

For Harrison the lessons were clear. Well-trained infantry utilizing firepower and bayonets combined with mounted troops and overwhelming manpower superiority could overcome their opponents' positional advantage in the downed timber. Critical to all this was the lieutenant's appreciation of the role of the mounted volunteer riflemen. For all his years in the regular army, Harrison never lost his understanding of the important role that volunteer units could play in western military operations. Charles Scott, both as a general and as governor, became a military mentor to Harrison nearly as important as Anthony Wayne. Harrison would repeat Scott's formula nearly twenty years later at the battle of the Thames.

For the British and the Indians, the defeat at Fallen Timbers was a disaster of enormous proportions. The fleeing natives found the doors of Fort Miamis closed to them, and they limped northward toward Detroit, knowing they had been betrayed by British promises of assistance. Wayne refused to attack the British outpost but paraded his troops in a taunting fashion outside its walls. The redcoats did not accept the challenge, as they knew defeat was their only option; war with the Americans was not what they wanted while they were engaged in more serious combat on the European continent. They eventually vacated the post and withdrew northward, and they finally retired from their posts on American soil as a consequence of Jay's Treaty. For Harrison, Wayne's demonstration of military force without provoking international war was a lesson in military discretion.

Equally important was Wayne's return march up the Maumee Valley. He had native fields and villages destroyed, reinforced Fort Defiance, and established a new post at the head of the Maumee River, which is known as Fort Wayne to this day. Humbled by their defeat, betrayed by their supposed allies, and desperate for provisions, the Indian chiefs accepted a treaty at Fort Greenville in 1795 that formally opened up lands north of the Ohio River for American settlement.

The conduct of this negotiation provided Harrison with a lesson in how to treat with the Indians. It was a tutorial he would put into practice time and time again in his subsequent career.[73] The lieutenant and Wayne's two captain aides signed a final Greenville document—singular honors for men so young and junior in rank. For the next twenty years, negotiations with the Northwestern tribes revolved around the Treaty of Greenville. Native chiefs made constant reference to it; they knew Harrison had been there, and his understanding of the treaty's contents and meaning was understood on both sides. After Fallen Timbers, most native leaders recognized the repudiation of the Treaty of Fort Stanwix. Hereafter, Greenville became the basis for negotiations. Harrison watched closely as General Wayne used threats, spies, bribes, and presents while treating with the natives. For the general's aide, these lessons learned just a few miles from the site of the most disastrous defeat of the U.S. Army by Native Americans would be used over and over again in the following years.[74]

Although finally promoted to captain, Harrison continued in military service only until 1798, when his friendship with Winthrop Sargent opened a new opportunity. Sargent received an appointment as governor of Mississippi Territory and suggested to the Adams administration that Harrison replace him as secretary of the Northwest Territory. Just twenty-five years old, Harrison took up this appointment with what was then considered a lucrative salary of $1,200 per annum, terminating his military apprenticeship.

But it did not terminate Harrison's interest in national defense. His experiences in the Legion of the United States provided him with an understanding of military affairs. His career in the Eastern Woodlands impressed upon him essentials of military operations: of the need for military drill and combat training, of organizing and conducting a major campaign, of the necessity for incorporating regular and volunteer units during operations deep into the wilderness, of the critical importance of logistical support to operational success, of the interaction between military and diplomatic policy, and of the relations of a theater commander to both higher headquarters and subordinate officers. Few had been better apprenticed for senior command responsibility than the Virginian who, in 1811, would find himself a leader of an expedition facing the rise of a new Indian coalition led by two brothers—Tenskwatawa and Tecumseh.

Chapter Two

To Tippecanoe

The years between Harrison's becoming secretary for the Northwest Territory and 1812 forced the young Virginian to acquire both personal and administrative skills. In those years he demonstrated ability as a territorial administrator, exhibited a talent for negotiations with Native Americans that opened thousands of square miles of western lands for white settlement, and eventually fought a campaign against hostile Indians in the Wabash Valley. Besides political adroitness, he acquired a wife and children. With the possible exception of Andrew Jackson, no one of his generation achieved so much so quickly.

These formative years revolved around two critical issues: developing a functional militia system and conducting relations with Native Americans, all while allowing for the expansion of white settlement. In neither of these efforts did he fully succeed, but both help explain his later conduct.

Territorial Secretary and Congressional Delegate

The post to which William Henry Harrison received an appointment in 1798 originated in the Northwest Ordinance, which the Confederation Congress passed in 1787. That seminal document established an office of secretary, whose incumbent served a four-year term and bore responsibilities "to keep and preserve the acts and laws passed by the legislature and the public records of the district and the proceedings of the governor in his executive department and to transmit authentic copies of such acts and proceedings every six months to the Secretary of Congress."[1] Far from holding a minor administrative post, the secretary stood second only to the territorial governor, Arthur St. Clair, and served in his place during any absence. (Given St. Clair's repeated absences, Harrison's predecessor in the office, Winthrop Sargent, had frequently occupied the governor's chair.)

That the Federalist Adams administration would appoint this Virginia Republican as territorial secretary makes sense only if one understands Harrison's marital good fortune and the regional politics in the territory. Four regional/partisan factions had begun to emerge: New England Federalists, centered in Marietta; the heavily Virginia-born Scioto Valley Republicans; the pro-statehood citizens of Cincinnati; and the Francophone communities around the old French trading settlements of Vincennes, Cahokia, and Detroit. Harrison lived in Cincinnati, the leverage point in the political struggle, and in 1795 he married Anna Symmes, daughter of John Cleves Symmes. An outspoken rival of Governor St. Clair and one of three territorial judges constituting both the supreme court and the territorial council, Judge Symmes consistently opposed the policies of the governor, whose administration he considered dictatorial.[2] Again, Harrison exploited his connections—Sargent recommended him to the administration, declaring that he had "sustained a fair, indeed unblemished reputation as a Military Officer . . . [and] I think him a very deserving young man." Harrison himself wrote congressional Federalist and family friend Robert Goodloe Harper in May 1798, soliciting support. In petitioning Harper, Harrison mentioned his various connections to Federalist leaders, from President Adams and Alexander Hamilton to former Gen. Daniel Morgan. Six weeks after writing this epistle, Harrison received his commission as secretary.[3] Thus at the age of twenty-five he became the second-ranking political officer in the Northwest Territory. When St. Clair returned to Cincinnati a few days later, he found the son-in-law of a political rival in the secretary's office. How much of the background to this appointment the governor knew about one cannot say, but he cannot have been delighted.

Harrison as secretary did not incur the hostility from St. Clair he might have expected. Perhaps he managed to trim between the governor and his father-in-law as he had negotiated between Anthony Wayne and James Wilkinson. Thus Secretary Harrison seems to have worked well with the governor and with the latter's rivals. But he became increasingly identified with the Scioto faction in the new territorial legislature that sat in 1799. As the Northwest Territory emerged into the second stage of development under its governing ordinance, the legislature had a new task: choosing a territorial delegate to Congress. The governor sought to have his son and namesake elected to the post. He seems not to have known that three leading Scioto Valley Republicans— Thomas Worthington, Edward Tiffin, and Nathaniel Massie—had visited the secretary and proposed supporting Harrison's candidacy if he would agree to support "an amelioration of the laws for the sale of Public Land." One can easily imagine the surprise of the governor and Arthur St. Clair Jr. (whom St. Clair Sr. had appointed territorial attorney general) when Harrison won the election in the territorial assembly, with an 11 to 10 vote.[4]

Despite what should have been his gratitude to the Adams administration and to Congressman Harper for the appointment as territorial secretary, Delegate Harrison now returned to form as a Virginian and worked mostly with Republicans during his term in Congress. While he was a nonvoting member of the House of Representatives he became a chair of the Committee on Public Lands. It was here that he proposed and secured passage of what is known as the Land Act of 1800, which reduced the minimum size of a purchase from a section of land (one mile square, or 640 acres) to a half section. The act also established a system of installment payments beginning with a one-fourth-price down payment and subsequent remittances over four years. While the minimum price remained $2 per acre (still higher than the amount for which speculators were selling public lands acquired at bargain rates in previous years), the bill satisfied Harrison's Scioto Valley backers and made him popular in the territory. He pushed for the settlement of land title claims in the Vincennes Cession that had long frustrated Congress. This issue would take years to resolve during his Indiana governorship. He also thwarted Governor St. Clair's attempt to forestall statehood. Delegate Harrison backed a proposed State of Ohio that kept Cincinnati in the new state and moved the capital to the Scioto Valley town of Chillicothe.[5]

Only once during his brief tenure in Congress did Harrison concern himself with national defense policies, which would dominate his tenure there two decades later. In his first congressional speech, the young congressman spoke against the drastic reduction of the regular army being considered by the House. In opposition to the anti-regular speech of another newcomer, John Randolph of Roanoke, Harrison warned that the "disbanding of so large a proportion of the military force would be attended with disastrous consequences." The advocates of the reduction placed "too much reliance" on the militia, which was not well disciplined and was incapable of engaging professional forces of a possible enemy. Militiamen did not want for courage, valor, or alertness, but in his experience with them in the 1790s, "after a very short service they wanted to go home, they were anxious to see their families, and therefore numbers deserted, and left the army in a state which was almost the cause of its destruction." When utilized with regulars, militiamen did well, but Harrison "never could think of trusting the country entirely to their protection."[6] This appears to be a very Federalist position, in opposition to that of the militia-favoring Jeffersonian Republicans. The search for a well-organized, well-trained, and well-armed militia would be a hallmark of Harrison's career for the remainder of his life. He knew a militia had to be coordinated with an effective regular army.

Like any congressman then or now, Harrison also looked after the interests of veterans and war widows. He sponsored a bill allowing veterans an extension on the time they could register and locate their land claims.[7] He also sought to amend the Committee on Claims' unfavorable report on a petition of Mrs. Ann Elliot, widow of Robert Elliot, who lost his life to Indians as he sought to supply General Wayne's army in 1794. This motion failed, and it would not be until 1805 that an "act for the relief of the widow and orphan children of Robert Elliot" passed Congress.[8]

The law that greatly reduced the Northwest Territory to what would eventually become Ohio also established a new territory of Indiana that included all the Old Northwest not in Ohio. This new territory needed a governor, and the Adams administration searched for someone to appoint. By law, the citizens of the new territory were to enjoy "all the singular, rights, privileges, granted and secured" them by the Northwest Ordinance.[9] As a former Northwest Territory secretary, Harrison presented the Adams administration with a candidate familiar with territorial affairs. Nothing better indicates Harrison's ability to traverse the path between Federalist and Republican partisans than his conduct in the gubernatorial negotiations.

When Congress adjourned, the future governor of Indiana and his pregnant wife headed to Richmond for an extended visit with his family. Although the appointment was made in mid-May, Harrison waited until July before accepting it. The delay in all probability was a consequence of his political maneuvering with the Republicans over the continuation of his governorship. He sought out some of Thomas Jefferson's allies. Before accepting Adams's appointment he wanted assurance that he would be reappointed by a possible Jeffersonian administration when his three-year term expired. After spending time in Richmond while Anna (called Nancy by her family) went through another of her frequent pregnancies, he thought he had such guarantees. Keeping his options open, he also indicated to Ohio friends that he would forego the Indiana position if a more suitable one were available for him in the soon-to-be-admitted State of Ohio. This opportunity did not pan out.

Finally he was assured that Jefferson, if he became president, would retain him in office; later he would become moderately apprehensive about his tenure when Sargent was dismissed from his post by Jefferson. The birth of a daughter at Richmond in August brought a delay until October before the family began journeying toward the Ohio Valley. Harrison left the family in Frankfort while he finally moved to Vincennes, where he assumed the governorship on 10 January 1801.[10]

Gubernatorial Activities

Arriving in Vincennes, Harrison found "the affairs of the whole territory were in greatest confusion; both among white people and Indians, discord and anarchy rule with undisputed sway."[11] The newly minted governor sought to remove this "discord and anarchy" by imposing the rule of law in the administration of the various counties of the territory. By modern standards the counties were huge—Knox County, for instance, encompassed the entire modern state of Indiana except for the southeastern corner, which was in Clark County. However, most of this land was still under native tribal control. Over the twelve years of Harrison's gubernatorial tenure, the number of counties increased and their territorial dimensions decreased.

For the first four years the governor and the territorial judges ran the government, until the population rose sufficiently to allow the move to phase two of territorial government and the introduction of an elected territorial assembly. During the early years Harrison and the judges governed without any political opposition. Even after initiation of an elected assembly, Harrison was able to keep tight control over its legislative actions. But slowly, opposition to his government and its policies arose. Harrison found himself increasingly facing opponents who found his rule arbitrary and cliquish; ironically, the charges echoed those Harrison and his allies used against Governor St. Clair of the Northwest Territory. Some of this rivalry can be traced to the typical ins and outs of political favoritism, but in 1802 Harrison and his associates made a serious political blunder that turned an increasing portion of the citizenry against him.

A major problem in the development of Indiana Territory was the lack of employable free labor and the provision in Article VI of the Northwest Ordinance prohibiting slavery. In reality there had been few slaves in the Vincennes area from before the beginning of the territory in 1787, but Governor St. Clair did not enforce the antislavery article. From the beginning of his governorship Harrison had a black manservant, and he and others sought a ten-year suspension of the prohibition. This desire for the use of slave labor immediately brought a reaction from those who opposed the institution, and brought with it the rise of political rivals—particularly Jonathan Jennings, a New Jersey native who grew up in Pennsylvania. This hot-tempered antislavery advocate initially worked in the Public Land Office, directed by its very anti-Harrison superintendent John Badollet.[12]

By his adroit use of patronage, Harrison created a "court" party. Over time his responsibilities covered vast expanses stretching from modern Arkansas to the northernmost boundaries of the Louisiana Purchase, plus the modern states of Indiana, Michigan, Illinois, and Wisconsin. By 1809 Indiana Territory had been reduced to the size of the present state.

When Indiana moved to the second stage of territorial governance that allowed an elected assembly, an alternative version of Indiana's future emerged. Harrison's opponents used the electoral opportunities to portray the governor and his allies as aristocrats (wasn't he the son of a James River plantation gentleman?), as seekers of a slaveholder oligarchy, and as antidemocratic. Much to Harrison's chagrin, Jennings secured election as the territorial delegate to Congress, where he continued his fulminations against the governor in the nation's capital.[13]

Slavery became the catalyst for opposition to the territorial governor's policies. Some opposed slavery on moral grounds, some opposed it because of its competition with white labor, and others saw it as the harbinger of aristocracy. Harrison's political future in the proposed State of Indiana seemed doomed. There was a faction in the western counties that wanted division from Indiana in what would become Illinois, and a substantial group throughout the territory wanted statehood with its self-governing features. All of these groups opposed the governor.[14] The length of Harrison's tenure, his administrative cronyism, and allegations of his using the office to speculate in public lands all worked against his political future in the proposed state. Consequently, the governor began looking for a future in another area of expertise—the military.

Territorial Militia

As governor, Harrison was commander-in-chief of the territorial militia, and he almost immediately began appointing military officers in the vast territory. For example, on 6 February 1801 he named John Small as the territorial adjutant general, with the rank of lieutenant colonel, Henry Hurst and William MacIntosh as majors in Knox County (Vincennes), and Nicholas Jarrot as major in St. Clair County (Cahokia). Throughout the next several months he expanded the list of militia officers.[15] The absence of generals and colonels at this early stage indicates that the population base was so small that organization above battalion level was impossible.

As commander of the territorial militia, Harrison despaired over the failure of his efforts to organize and train those required to perform military service. He found "no effectual exertions had been made to rescue the militia from that disgraceful apathy which has been suffered so long to prevail." While visiting Detroit in 1803, the governor issued a general order to the territorial militia requiring the officers "to train and instruct their men in the duties of a soldier, and to infuse into them the principles of order and subordination, and of love and veneration for their country and its government." From the enlisted men he expected "a prompt and cheerful obedience to all the legal orders of their officers." A few weeks later he ordered Wayne County (the lower peninsula of modern Michigan) to raise a regiment of ten companies.[16]

At the meeting of the first territorial assembly in 1805, the governor urged a militia law that was less complicated than usual and endorsed a "system which would embrace simplicity with energy" and "would leave us nothing to apprehend from a rupture with our Indian neighbours."[17] The territorial assembly in 1807 passed a law requiring all males eighteen to forty-five years of age to be enrolled in the militia. Each soldier was to provide himself with "a good musket, a sufficient bayonet and belt or fuse, two spare flints, a knapsack and a pouch, with a box therein to contain not less than twenty four cartridges." Territorial law organized the militia into divisions of two brigades, each with two to four regiments divided into two battalions with four companies of not less than sixty-four privates. The companies were to muster every two months except for January through March. The governor could call the militia to active duty, when it became subject to the rules, regulations, provisions, and pay of the regular army.[18]

The ideal emphasized in this law (which incorporated the provisions of the federal Militia Act of 1792) and the reality of militia organization in the territory were two different things. Above all, the requirement for each soldier to equip himself with a musket (a weapon that had little practical value in a frontier household, where either a rifle or a fowling piece was used in hunting) imposed a tax on citizens that they were unwilling to accept. The mustering requirement was almost impossible to enforce. The financial situation of the territory made it difficult to pay militiamen for their service, and the federal government made no contribution to the militia.

The frontiersmen of Indiana Territory did have good reason to keep themselves organized. They would respond eagerly to emergency calls upon their service, because they had a fearsome opponent in the natives who threatened their farmsteads and villages. Moreover, many of them brought military experience from frontier communities in Kentucky, Tennessee, and Pennsylvania that could be mobilized.[19] As noted above, when he served as the Old Northwest's territorial delegate to Congress, Harrison had opposed the Republicans' efforts to place too much reliance on the militia ideal to the detriment of maintaining an adequate regular army. But this did not mean he opposed a territorial militia that was organized, equipped, trained, disciplined, and paid in the face of domestic and foreign threats.

The territorial governor kept some rangers on active duty in the Vincennes vicinity, commanded by Capt. William Hargrove. Harrison cautioned that the natives were "the most treacherous, cunning rascals on the earth and the most brutal as well," and he had blockhouses erected in rural neighborhoods to which settlers could come during an emergency.[20]

Particularly pleasing to the governor was the action of Col. George Atchison of the St. Clair County regiment, who authorized the organization of a company of grenadiers or light infantry under the command of Capt. Samuel S. Kennedy. This unit consisted of "young men from the age of 18 to 28 years old whose activity & Domestic Circumstances" admitted to "a frequence in training" and a state of readiness for "all cases of Emergency."[21] Another encouraging sign was the parade of the Vincennes Light Infantry at the 1808 Independence Day ceremonies. Governor and Mrs. Harrison entertained the company at Grouseland afterward. That October the entire first regiment of Knox County conducted maneuvers under the supervision of the territory's commander-in-chief. All officers, Harrison instructed, "particularly those of the higher grades, will exert themselves on this occasion and endeavor to understand the evolutions herein directed."[22] That which he had learned under the tutelage of Anthony Wayne was now being put into practice. As we shall see, these were the types of units and training that Harrison thought exemplified what he wanted from the militia.

Unfortunately, as the crisis in Indian affairs increased, by 1810 the governor admitted that the militiamen of the region were entirely "without discipline and vastly inferior to what they were at the close of the late Indian War. In an encounter with the Indians they would inevitably be beaten unless *greatly* Superior in numbers."[23] Yet he was not above activating two militia companies for a short period to protect settlements in the Vincennes area until a company of regulars arrived to relieve them. He deactivated them not because he thought their services were no longer necessary but because their farming occupations dictated returning to their fields in harvest season.[24]

At this time the Indiana governor wrote two lengthy letters to his Kentucky counterpart and former comrade-in-arms Charles Scott, bemoaning the lack of military preparedness among westerners.[25] Basing his conclusions on his rereading of Charles Rollin's ancient histories and on modern history, Harrison argued, "We must become a nation of warriors, or a nation of Quakers." "We have indeed, no militia" because that is a term that can only be applied "to citizens who are disciplined or trained for war." "There is no political axiom more generally defused amon[g]st the people of the United States, than that which declares militia to be the only proper defence of a republic." Despite this, "Why is there so much indifference manifested upon this all-important subject?" His apprehension came when he feared warfare could break out again with the Native Americans, or the British, or a combination of the two. This erudite, more than 7,500-word treatise must have impressed the Kentucky governor, who two years later would make Harrison a major general in that commonwealth's militia. The need for an organized and disciplined militia arose out of the growing tensions with Native Americans that emerged in the first decade of the nineteenth century. Central to Harrison's thesis was that republics could not survive unless most of their young men experienced military training, service, and discipline. This former regular army officer deplored the possibility of consigning national defense to a greatly expanded federal force instead of the body of its young male citizens. Without a capable, broad-based citizen force, Harrison believed, we could become the subjects of a military dictator or dominated by a foreign invader. In other words, should we fail to maintain an effective militia, "the fate of Rome" with the fall of its republic to the emperors "will be [the] fate of America, and of every other republic, which does not take effectual means to inspire its citizens with a military spirit, and train them to the use of arms."

His solutions mark the culmination of two decades of military service, self-education on defense policies, in-depth reading in classical and modern military history, acquaintanceship with the problems of Indiana's territorial militia, and fear of an outbreak of conflict when so little had been done to prepare the nation for possible internal and external warfare. Governor Scott was someone with whom he could release his frustrations and expect a sympathetic hearing. His "Thoughts on the Subject of the Discipline of the Militia" constitute the summation of all these frustrations, readings, and apprehensions. Our "militia laws have been of no use" and militia muster days "are generally devoted to riot and intemperance." "How it could be supposed that the *science* of war could be learnt in this manner is most surprising," especially since those "on whom the task of instruction is devolved" are seldom "better informed than the men whom they attempt to teach." Harrison concluded that to bring the militia into "that state of perfection as entirely to supercede the necessity of a [large] standing army, the [militia] system . . . must be entirely changed."

His solutions were about three generations ahead of their time—which came toward the end of the nineteenth century with the development of a National Guard. But in many ways his suggestions involved military probabilities highly unlikely in the early part of the century—for example, an invasion of the southern states by a European army of fifty thousand. Harrison's proposed reorganization of the militia included the following ingredients:

- Maintaining a regular army of six thousand with a hundred-thousand-man active militia that would be paid, armed, and equipped by the federal government. (He recognized that this may require additional taxes but thought this was a national necessity.)
- Appointment of able officers. (He made no comment on the militia custom of enlisted men electing company-grade officers.)
- Stimuli "to engage our youth to enter [the militia] with ardor"—occasional military history orations, frequent military parades and other exhibitions of the "pomp of war," and "rewards and distinctions" for those who excel in military activities.
- Early instruction in military discipline, maneuvers, and organization that commences "as soon as their mental and bodily powers have acquired sufficient strength."
- Establishing professorships on tactics at all schools and colleges. (Throughout the treatise Harrison placed considerable emphasis on "the military knowledge of their leaders," with examples of good and bad generalship throughout history.)

At the same time he recommended several tactical and organizational approaches:

- Utilizing light infantry armed with rifles: "If our Western militia should ever encounter an European army, they would be astonished to find themselves opposed by a body of men using the same arms, with equal dexterity to themselves—making their attacks with the same unexpected velocity, and eluding their enemy with all the celerity and address which distinguishes our back woods riflemen." But the undisciplined American soldiers would find that "their own operations would be directed by no fixed plan, but such as might be formed on the moment by their leader; their attacks dissultory, uncombined, ill supported, and their retreats disorderly."
- Emphasizing light horse artillery to accompany the light infantry, in much the same way as in Anthony Wayne's Legion of the United States.
- Employing rifle corps in forests or behind fences and hedges, but in open country using the musket and bayonet, which are best adapted for military success. (However, Harrison argued that the rifle is a weapon with which westerners are so familiar that "at least two thirds of the [western] militia" should be allowed "their favorite arm.")
- Because some sections of the country may be better endowed with weapons and organization adapted to their situation, "the whole militia of the union should be considered as one great army, and in the distribution of the several corps particular regard should be had to the manners, the habits, and even the prejudices of the people"

Throughout this two-letter treatise, Harrison supports his arguments with examples ranging from ancient Sparta to his own experiences under Anthony Wayne. The references are prodigious and reflect his reading from Polybius (ca. 200–118 BC), Julius Caesar (ca. 100–44 BC), and Charles Rollin (1661–1741) to the present. For many modern readers, his list of ancient generals will require a Google search to find out just who they are: Epaminondas and Pelopidas of Thebes, Leonidas and Agesilaus of Sparta, plus a host of Romans and their opponents, to include Marcus Licinius Crassus, Mark Antony, Flavius Claudius Julianus, Lucius Papirius Cursor, Gaius Fabricius Luscinus, Fabius Maximus, Scipio Africanus, Pyrrhus, Hannibal, Flavius Aetius, Count Boniface, Flavius Belisarius, and Narses. His eighteenth-century list includes Frederick the Great, Kurt C. von Schwerin, Edward Braddock, Friedrich Wilhelm von Steuben, Arthur St. Clair, George Rogers Clark, James Wilkinson, William Crawford, and Archibald Lougherty. His list of battles stretches from Leuctra (371 BC) to Fallen Timbers (AD 1794).

It was an impressive display of learning, but his solutions were somewhat impractical. At one point he acknowledged a new military development that avoided the need for a universal common militia and the expense of arming, equipping, and training particular militia units. Emerging by the first decade of the new century were "voluntary military associations entirely independent of militia laws." But he did not see this as a solution to the problem of a universal white male obligation. He also avoided discussing temporary volunteer units like those commanded by General Scott during the Indian campaigns of the 1790s. Both types of units epitomized the wave of the future more than Harrison's proposals did.

That does not mean all of Harrison's militia ideas were impractical. He constantly reminded the territorial legislature of the necessity for reforming the territory's militia laws so "that the discipline of the Militia shall be such, as the General Government looks for, and our exposed situation requires." What he wanted was a militia institution formed "by discipline and frequent trainings" so that Indiana would have "a body of Citizen soldiers, which shall be equal to the defence of our country against every invader."[26] In particular he lamented the "want of coercion to produce the returns & reports" from militia officers, without which "no great progress can be made in any other part of the Military art."[27] While he never fully received what he wanted, he did try as much as his executive authority allowed to create a disciplined, trained, and responsive defense force.

Indian Policy

Living in Vincennes, Harrison learned how the French and Indians interacted as two separate but interconnected societies. Vincennes constituted a unique and, for Harrison, unknown culture that enabled the two communities to coexist while each retained its essential value systems and did not appear to threaten the other's survival. The *métis* served as cross-cultural mediators and connecting links that assisted in this development.[28]

But the leaders of the young republic wanted another outcome. Both the Federalist and Republican administrations sought to convert the Indians from a hunter-gatherer society to one involving male-dominated commercial agriculture. This flew in the face of native tradition and was based on two false premises. First, it assumed the Indians would give up a traditional tribal culture and become peaceable, individualistic American farmers. Second, it thought they would tolerate the encroachment of white Americans close to their territorial areas and acquiesce peacefully to the consequent loss of game and agricultural land. For the natives this required them to face within a single generation an economic and cultural transition that would destroy their communal hunter-gatherer village societies. In effect, there was a paradox in American policy toward the trans-Appalachian tribes: a quest for settlement expansion that conflicted with the desire of the first three presidential administrations to treat the natives honorably.

But this arrangement was not entirely confrontational. A complex set of relationships emerged in which individuals reacted to one another in a variety of ways. From the twenty-first-century perspective, the situation remained constantly at odds with one culture versus the other. But the nineteenth-century reality of cross-cultural communication and interactions included everything from dietary exchanges to political and religious interactions. Thus we must always keep in mind that there were social interactions that went far beyond the traditional view of cultural conflict and military confrontation.[29]

From rifles and steel traps to iron kettles and woven blankets, native culture underwent a material transformation and dependency in the years following white contact. Many Indians took considerable steps toward what whites described as "civilization." But, as historian Bernard Sheehan argues, "the tribal order remained intact." The philanthropic ideology of the first years of the new nation failed to recognize "the tendency of culture to persist or the inherent tentativeness in the acculturative process . . . [that] asked the Indian to abandon totally his ancient manner of life." With considerable naivety, Jeffersonian philanthropic idealism "utterly misconstrued the nature of tribal culture and the possibilities for its reform."[30] Moreover, while the early administrations wanted "American Indian policy to assume new standards of morality and justice," concludes Reginald Horsman, "they were thwarted by the complete ethnocentrism of the Enlightenment view of human progress, by the frontiersman's desire for land, by the phenomenal rate of population and economic growth in the young United States, and by the desire of most Indians to preserve their lands and their own way of life."[31]

Nonetheless, the governor of Indiana Territory found himself compelled to carry out the best intentions of President Thomas Jefferson toward both Native

Americans and American settlers. He found some accommodationist natives among those living in the territory. They included the famous Miami war chief Little Turtle (Mishikinakaw), who lived outside Fort Wayne, and Delaware (Lenni Lenape) chief William Anderson (Kikthawenud), who resided on the White River in modern Anderson, Indiana.[32] "The Indians," Harrison learned, "are remarkable for deliberation in all their Councils & they are Still More So When ever the Subject before them relates to their lands."[33]

During the 1780s, American negotiators recognized that their territorial boundaries in the Peace of Paris of 1783 did not allow a line-of-lakes border to the United States by right of conquest. The British had not ceded the natives' right to the land, and the Americans understood that they had to negotiate cessions for the expansion of white settlement.

One of Harrison's first problems when he became governor involved a double standard of justice for Indians who murdered whites and whites who murdered Indians. He recounted the story of two Indians who were convicted in Kaskaskia for murdering a white, and one was executed. On the other hand, the governor said, none of the white murderers had been given up despite the provisions of the Treaty of Greenville, and none had been punished. Repeated instances of this appear in Harrison's correspondence during his governorship.[34]

Another issue involved white trespass on Indian lands for hunting purposes. Harrison and Secretary of War Henry Dearborn noted with regret the complaints of visiting Indian chiefs about whites hunting game on what were clearly Indian lands. In his capacity as the superintendent for Indian affairs in the territory, Harrison agreed that this was a problem, but he had virtually no way of enforcing the rule. He bemoaned the fact that "one white Hunter will destroy more game than five of the common Indians." As early as 1801 Harrison asked for a garrison at Fort Knox: "I do not think that a military force is so necessary on any part of the fronteers as at this place." But it wasn't until the summer of 1810 that the governor received one company of regulars at his disposal. This was an inadequate organization to counter violations of the Treaty of Greenville by both sides in an area of thousands of square miles.[35]

From the outset of his governorship, Harrison found that despite the provisions of Jay's Treaty, the "British have been unremitted in their exertions to preserve their influence over the Indians resident within our Territory." This was not unexpected, since, as he admitted, British traders supplied a greater quantity of goods and a better market for the natives' furs, skins, and hides than could the Americans. But he exaggerated British hostile intentions in the first few years of his governorship.[36]

It was not the British but fellow Americans that presented one of the most dangerous and recurring problems with the Indians. The sale of alcoholic beverages brought continuing difficulties, which despite all Harrison's efforts seemed irresolvable. His complaint to Dearborn on this matter was followed by a July 1801 proclamation forbidding any trader from selling or giving "Spirituous Liquors to any Indian or Indians in the Town of Vincennes" and ordering traders to make such exchanges either a mile from town or across the Wabash River.[37] This effort paled to insignificance when compared with the distribution of alcohol throughout the territory. Harrison informed the president of the failure of his efforts in this regard: "It is my Opinion that More Whisky has been Consumed by the Indians & More fatal Consequences ensued from the use of it Since the traders have been prohibited from taking it into the Indian Country than there ever was before." He wanted legal authority to prohibit trading with the Indians without a license and to forbid those with a license from commerce in alcohol. In 1805 he despaired that the "humane and benevolent intentions of the government will be however forever defeated unless effectual means can be devised to prevent the sale of ardent spirits to these unhappy people." He described the current congressional legislation as "entirely ineffectual" in addressing this issue.[38]

Another constant problem facing the governor was the pressure to open more lands for white settlement while trying to make Native Americans adapt to agricultural policies that copied those of the Euroamericans. For more than a decade after the Treaty of Greenville, the Americans took advantage of intra- and intertribal infighting in their negotiations with various native chieftains. As one scholar recently described it, "The turmoil and division engendered by power struggles among and between the tribes only made the United States more powerful. As chiefs fought each other for the scraps their father threw them, they made it easier for him to divide and conquer."[39]

A good example of this process can be found in the notes from an Indian council held at Vincennes in the fall of 1802. Lapoussier of the Wea band of the Miami discussed the boundary of the supposed Vincennes Grant. "We only lent" the French "the land to live on," he argued, it was not sold to them. Fusee, another Wea, contended that "the treaty of Greenville was a good one—the annuity was for our friendship not for our Lands." Harrison countered with the argument that the Greenville Treaty mentioned the Vincennes Grant and that the only problem was its size and location. The subsequent Memorandum of Agreement defined the Vincennes Grant boundaries along the Wabash and White Rivers. Central to the agreement was the acquiescence of Little Turtle and Jean Baptiste Richardville of the Miami and Topenebee and Winamac of the Potawatomi. The final document contained the signatures of Potawatomi, Eel River, Wea, Piankeshaw, Kaskaskia, and Kickapoo chiefs.⁴⁰

Over the next several years Harrison negotiated treaties with various tribes that led to the opening for settlement of thousands of square miles from the Mississippi to the lower Wabash Valley. In so doing he carried out the cynical policies enunciated by President Jefferson in a private letter of early 1803. While the president proclaimed that the American system was "to live in perpetual peace with the Indians, [and] to cultivate an affectionate attachment from them," he wanted them to "withdraw themselves to the culture of a small piece of land" so that they would "perceive how useless to them are their extensive forests." This could best be accomplished by creating situations "to pare them off" from their excessive landholdings "in exchange for necessaries for their farms & families." One suggestion was to have their principal leaders run up so much debt with government traders that they would be forced to reduce their tribal holdings to pay off these obligations. While the president still clung to his prediction that many natives would "incorporate with us as citizens of the U.S.," those unwilling to do so would have to "remove beyond the Mississippi." And, if they became so foolish as "to take up the hatchet" against the Americans, the consequence would be "the seizing of the whole country of that tribe & driving them across the Mississippi."⁴¹

From an acreage standpoint, one of the largest cessions was that negotiated with Chief Jean Baptiste Ducoigne of the Kaskaskia. In 1803 this small, largely Roman Catholic tribe, which feared the Potawatomi and Kickapoo more than they did the Americans, gave up claims to eight million acres comprising the southern fourth of Illinois. There is a hint that Harrison plied the Kaskaskia with liquor to secure this generous settlement.⁴² If so, this was a tactic he would utilize again. When accused of using alcohol to secure concessions, he claimed its use was "strictly interdicted until the object for which they Were Convened was accomplished."⁴³

But inside what would become the State of Indiana, there were few concessions in its northern half. In southern Indiana Harrison completed a coup in negotiations with the Delaware, who in 1804 ceded territory between the

Wabash and Ohio Rivers, title to which lay with the Miami Confederacy, the land being occupied by the Delaware by their permission. Since the Delaware planned to migrate west of the Mississippi to join tribal members living there, their right of cession was disputed by Miami Indians.[44]

The Delaware's cession without the approval of the Miami Confederacy opened a breach between Harrison and William Wells, the Indian Agent at Fort Wayne. Wells, who was Little Turtle's son-in-law, claimed to speak for the entire confederacy. But Harrison argued that he spoke only for the Eel River portion of the tribe and that 90 percent of the confederacy was led by Richard-ville and his brother-in-law, the Miami civil chief Pacanne, who "utterly abhor both Wells & the [Little] Turtle." According to the governor, objections to the Delaware treaty by the Miami or Potawatomi were without foundation, since they had not hunted in this tract for some time. Little Turtle would use whatever "Artful & Mischevious reason" was at his disposal to frustrate any agreement to which he did not consent. "Conscious of the Superiority of his Talents over the rest of his race & Colour he [Little Turtle] Sighs for a More Conspicious theatre to display them." Wells, argued Harrison, had adopted "a Submissive defference" to the opinions of his father-in-law and had not devoted his limited talents to the best interests of the United States. Moreover, "Some rediculous spice of jealousy towards myself may have Mingled itself with his motives." In a letter to Secretary Dearborn, Harrison urged the federal government to admonish Wells for his failure to support the official policy initiatives that the governor thought he was carrying out. Six weeks after composing this letter, he denounced Wells as one who would "not rest until he has persuaded the Indians that their very existence depends upon the rescinding [of] the Treaties with the Delawares & Piankeshaws . . . Much Mischief may ensue from his knowledge of the Indians [and] his Cunning & his perseverance." There would be a subsequent reconciliation between Harrison and Little Turtle and Wells, but at this time the governor's animosity toward the two was embittered and may have adversely affected relations with the Miami Confederacy, which Little Turtle was trying to keep from being coopted by the growing influence of Tenskwatawa (the Prophet) and Tecumseh.[45]

To mollify the several parties, President Jefferson directed Harrison to "cause a meeting of the Delaware Chiefs and some of the principal Chiefs of the Miamies and Puttawattamies, for the purpose of such an explanation of the doings, so much complained of, as well satisfy the Chiefs generally." He authorized Harrison to distribute a few hundred dollars among the chiefs as a "way of quieting their minds in relation to the sale of the lands." In the subsequent 1805 Treaty of Grouseland, the governor secured the Miami, Eel River, and Wea tribes' consent to the Delaware's cession in exchange for payments.[46] He regarded the Potawatomi, Ottawa, and Chippewa residing in the Detroit vicinity as "the Most perfidious of their race. They have been so long used to play a double game between our Agents & those of the British that they are perfect in the Arts of deception."[47]

Harrison proudly reported to President Jefferson that one of the native "orators at the breaking up of the [Grouseland] Council assured me in the name of the rest that they would in future look upon the United States in the same light that they had formerly done their fathers the French—An unexpected Compliment and one which I never Supposed I should hear from an Indian."[48] Such optimism or naivety flies in the face of what was happening among many Midwestern natives following the revelations of the Master of Life to a previously dissolute Shawnee shaman who now called himself Tenskwatawa—the open door.

The story of William Henry Harrison's military career became intimately tied to the tale of Tenskwatawa, the Shawnee Prophet (1775–1834), and his older brother Tecumseh (c. 1768–1813). Originally known as Lalawethika, the younger brother was an outcast, disliked by many in his tribe. Blind in one eye because of an accident, a poor hunter, and a well-known braggart, he eventually turned to alcohol as a solution to his problems. He became a little-respected shaman until he experienced a series of visions in which the Master of Life told a story of heaven's opportunities for the Native Americans if they reformed and threw off the White Man's ways. He took the new name Tenskwatawa, the "open door," to symbolize his representing a new avenue through which they might revitalize traditional Indian culture and values. Now a reformed alcoholic, he told of the horrors of the afterlife that awaited those who left their earthly life unreformed. While he could tolerate the French, Spanish, and British that lived in North America, Tenskwatawa had nothing but contempt for the Americans, whom he called children of an evil spirit.

He urged the abandonment of Christianity and the adoption of a new set of values involving prayer to the Spirit of Life, restoring some traditional native ceremonies and accepting several new ones. After successfully predicting an eclipse of the sun in 1806, his reputation grew, and two years later he established a new multi-tribal village known as Prophetstown on the Tippecanoe River, in the upper Wabash Valley of modern Indiana. Among the Shawnee his appeal was somewhat limited (they knew of his previous activities, and their response may well typify the old adage that "a prophet in his own country is without honor"), but other tribes received his message well. Miami, Delaware, Wyandot, Kickapoo, Sauk and Fox, Potawatomi, Ottawa, Menominee, Winnebago, and even very distant Ojibwa all journeyed to the Prophet's community to hear his message and carry his words to their home villages. One of the most fearsome recruits was Main Poc of the Illinois Potawatomi, whose influence brought in a number of leaders whose loyalty to the Shawnee brothers would last until the end on the Thames River.

A few years later Shawnee Chief Yelabahcan, one of Tenskwatawa's disciples, summarized this desire to avoid the White Man's ways:

> Brothers listen! . . . if the Great Spirit above should kill all the game then we should suffer, then we should be oblig'd to change our mode of living, but he has not done so! He will not do it! He made the women to raise corn, he made *us men* to hunt, we can live no other way . . . We cannot live as *you* do, while game lives, we wish to live on it, we wish to live by hunting, we wish to live as our Fathers liv'd before us.[49]

Yelabahcan's declaration epitomizes the traditionalism and appeal of Tenskwatawa for those wishing to restore traditional values and a way of life under severe stress. To the Prophet's adherents, male farming involved emasculation.

Historian Colin Calloway sees the Prophet as one in a long line of revitalization leaders who sought to halt the shift from traditional values and a return to traditional ways. "Tenskwatawa's message," he concludes, "drew on longstanding beliefs that associating with white men and their ways contaminated and diminished Native sources of sacred power; disassociating themselves was necessary to restore that power."[50]

As the political leader of the movement, Tecumseh went beyond time-honored methods; he advocated intertribal unity, with himself as leader; he championed collective Indian ownership of lands; and he threatened assassination of tribal chiefs who negotiated land sales. Tecumseh advocated destroying those chiefs who ceded lands without the consent of all the tribes. Harrison witnessed the impact of this intimidation when Winamac of the Potawatomi was physically threatened by Tecumseh, and he expected Winamac to "be assassinated by the Prophets party for the active part he has taken against them." According to the governor, Chief Lapoussier of the Wea band of Miami declined, out of fear, to speak against those advocating a united resistance to land sales. At the same time, Tecumseh advanced a displacement of traditional civil chiefs by tribal warriors.[51]

In 1809 Tenskwatawa sent his brother Tecumseh to Amherstburg to talk with the deputy superintendent-general of Indian Affairs William Claus and Upper Canada's lieutenant governor Francis Gore. From the latter Tecumseh received a beautiful wampum belt that symbolized the King's continued friendship with the Indians. Since all this followed the 1807 *Chesapeake-Leopard* Affair that nearly brought the United States and Britain to war, the major purpose of this meeting was to bolster the covenant of friendship between the British and the Native Americans in a time of international stress. While Claus supplied the assembled natives with provisions, rifles, and gunpowder, he made sure it was understood that so long as the two nations were at peace, the British would do nothing that implied direct military support of those Indians living within the United States. At the same time, Tecumseh secured status among the leaders of the several assembled tribes and established a rapport with the representatives of His Majesty's government.[52] Tecumseh became minister of foreign affairs for Tenskwatawa, and he journeyed from modern Alabama to Wisconsin in his efforts to bind various tribes to a common religious and political purpose.

Particularly disturbing to Harrison were Tenskwatawa and followers' policies of issuing threats of intimidation and assassination to those chiefs who cooperated with the Americans. Despite provocations from Indians who stole horses and other property, Harrison remained somewhat optimistic about future American-Indian relations. As long "as no blood is spilt I shall have the hopes of bring[ing] the prophet to reason."[53] One way to do this was to invite Tenskwatawa to visit the nation's capital, which he proposed because he thought "it is probable that the knowledge which he will acquire of the strength and resources of the United States will prevent him in the future from attempting hostilities against us."[54] But the Prophet refused the invitation and, concluded the governor, became "as actively employed in poisoning the minds of the Indians as ever."[55]

Placing much of the blame for the natives' hostility on the "implacable enmity" of British Indian Agent Matthew Elliott, who was known to be furnishing arms, munitions, supplies, and advice to friendly Indians, Harrison acknowledged broader causes of the antagonism between the races: "Instability & fickleness are the characteristics of Indians, & the inattention which the great bulk of them pay to remote consequences, is truly surprising; The convenience & safety of the passing moment is all they regard."[56] This habit of blaming others for the problems he faced characterized much of the governor's outlook on the complexities of the situation.

While Tenskwatawa's prophesies probably did more to create Native American unity during the years following his trances of 1805 than did the political visions of his brother, there is no doubt that Tecumseh was "the most ambitious of a small number of leaders who dreamed of a brotherhood of tribes capable of resisting white expansion, and who tried to replace intertribal indifference and conflict with unity and common purpose."[57] For Tecumseh and Tenskwatawa, preservation of a female-agriculture, male-hunting society and traditional religious values justified an alliance with the perfidious British.

Harrison, meanwhile, was beginning to doubt aspects of the Jeffersonian solution of "civilizing" the natives. The former president was "Seduced . . . to commit political error when he caused his agents to effect a peace and enjoined them to preserve concord and friendship between the various Tribes of Indians which inhabit our frontier." The native "hunts in the winter [and] he must go to war in the Summer." The consequence of Jefferson's policy of "the establishment of tranquility between the neighbouring Tribes will always be a Sure indication of war against us."[58] The short-term consequences of Jefferson's policies were a unification of native warriors against whites that Harrison's frontier experience found detrimental to the expansion of settlement. From the governor's viewpoint, it was better that the various Indian tribes fought one another than joined in a common bond against the Americans

The Strategic and Tactical Situation

The Native Americans faced several serious disadvantages when opposing the Americans. First, their proportion of the region's population had been reduced by epidemics and by the rising tide of Euroamerican emigrants in the trans-Appalachian West. The leading authority on pan-Indian unity efforts writes, "By 1812 American citizens outnumbered Indians in the region between the Appalachian and the Mississippi by a margin of seven-to-one . . . This weighty American presence . . . meant that the pan-Indian effort associated with Tecumseh would be more a severe aftershock than a seismic rift, a mere reminder of the greater deeds done long ago."[59]

Second, traditional intra- and intertribal rivalries made it difficult for pan-Indian leaders like Tecumseh to fully mobilize the available manpower. The natives were divided on their political, economic, and military strategy. Some, the so-called accommodationists, wanted to live with the Americans, adapting Native American culture to Euroamerican agricultural practices and some social customs. Perhaps the most notable of these were the groups surrounding Moravian and Quaker missionary outposts; others were natives and their *métis* relatives who lived in Roman Catholic communities from Vincennes to Mackinac Island. Of particular note were the Shawnee of Wapakoneta, Ohio, led by Chief Black Hoof, a rival to Tecumseh and Tenskwatawa. There is no more telling commentary on the internal divisions among the Indians than the observation that more Shawnee were with Harrison at the battle of the Thames than fought with Tecumseh.[60]

Third, the nativist faction wanted to maintain Indians' hunter-gatherer society and territorial control. But because the natives lacked a sense of common ethnic identity or nationalism, there was no government or leadership providing coordination, capital, and resources to engage in extended and extensive warfare. The Shawnee brothers Tenskwatawa and Tecumseh hoped to create a combination of native tribes to oppose the intrusion of Americans into the Old Southwest and the Old Northwest and to preserve Indian customs and lands. We now know the quest was doomed. There was a sense of fatalism among those who led the Indian warriors. Potawatomi orator White Pigeon spread the angst from the Auglaize River in Ohio to Lake Peoria in Illinois. He spoke with resignation about the natives' options: "to remain still they must die, and should the Americans overcome them they can only die and it is better to die as men at once than die a lingering death."[61] His fatalistic message, combined with the religious nativism of Tenskwatawa and the pan-Indian political appeal of Tecumseh, unified some but not all of the Indians of the area between modern Peoria, Mackinac, and Detroit.

Finally, the Indians were dependent on Euroamericans for weapons, bullets, and gunpowder. Even though they were accomplished horticulturalists and hunters, their food supplies were vulnerable to declining wild animal stocks, to raids by their opponents, and to the vagaries of weather. The destruction of their fields and storage facilities raised the specter of dependence on the British for food. Because there was little surplus of agricultural supplies produced by the few Americans and Canadians living on the Detroit frontier, and because there was no industrial support west of Montreal, food supplies and weaponry for both the aborigines and the British troops relied on a vulnerable logistical trail that stretched across Lake Erie, over the Niagara escarpment, across

Lake Ontario, and down the St. Lawrence River. This dependency became even more critical during Britain's twenty-year war with revolutionary France and the Napoleonic Empire. While the nativists' reliance on the British increased, the United Kingdom's capacity to supply them and defend them decreased.[62] The British loss of naval control of either Lake Erie or Lake Ontario imperiled the supply line necessary to support their army and allies in Upper Canada and the Old Northwest.

The Native Americans had some advantages. Geographically, the Americans had to conduct operations at a considerable distance from their main population centers in the Ohio Valley. Even then there were sparse settlements in the region, especially in Indiana and Illinois. Consequently the Indians had forewarning of American advances toward their villages and could avoid combat by not defending them. The Indians' raiding tactics required the Americans to divert limited military resources to protect a large geographic area. Moreover, the American industrial base was mostly east of the Appalachians. Military expeditions imposed logistical burdens on attacking forces that limited their ability to wage warfare at great distances from their base. The Americans' logistical train was particularly vulnerable to surprise attack by native warriors, as were regular and militia expeditions, whether on the march or encamped.

The agricultural cycle tied most American settlers to a schedule that required them to be at home during planting and harvesting seasons. Since the late summer and fall were the most meteorologically favorable time for both ground campaigns and grain harvests, the Americans faced a manpower problem during the best combat season. A defense-in-depth by the Indian tribes might result in destruction of their fields and storage bins, but so long as they could be resupplied by His Majesty's government or their British-favoring fur trader allies, these losses were not devastating.

Because the natives traveled via the Great Lakes and connecting rivers, they could mobilize and concentrate their forces more rapidly than was possible with the overland marches required of the Americans. Over half of the world's freshwater surface is in Canada and the adjacent United States Great Lakes, and the natives employed this vast system of inland waterways as woodland highways.[63] So long as the British kept naval superiority on the upper lakes, the journey by water from Green Bay to Detroit was much faster and more secure for the Native Americans than was the shorter overland route from Cincinnati to Detroit for the United States Army. With Anglo-Indian control of the waterways and such critical outposts as Green Bay, Chicago, Michilimackinac, and Detroit, native mobility and waterborne logistical support for their operations allowed much greater flexibility than was possible for the ground-bound Americans.

Despite their dependence on the British, experience taught the Indians not to trust them. They found their interests betrayed at the peace treaty ending the American Revolution, which awarded the United States nominal control over the lands between the Ohio River and the Great Lakes. And again the British betrayed them at the negotiating table that resulted in Jay's Treaty, which forced the natives to surrender territory north of the Ohio River at the Treaty of Greenville. These First Nations (as Canadians call them) had to be very cautious when dealing with His Majesty's representatives. Still, they had no one else to turn to. Their only hope was that this time they would not be deceived. While the United States and the United Kingdom remained at peace, no formal assistance to the Indians could be given by His Majesty's representatives living in the region. Following the *Chesapeake-Leopard* Affair of June 1807, the likelihood of Anglo-American war increased, but negotiations postponed conflict for five years. Nonetheless, British Indian Agents, fur merchants and traders, and others encouraged the natives to expect material and military support should conflict between the two nations begin.[64]

The 1809 Treaty of Fort Wayne may be seen as a critical dividing point in the history of American-Indian relations in the Old Northwest. Governor Harrison made use of the differences among the Potawatomi, Delaware, Miami, and Eel River tribes to secure a concession of 2.9 million acres. This involved tall grass prairie acreage in the Wabash Valley that would become luxuriant agricultural land between the Vincennes Grant and modern Terre Haute.[65] Conspicuously absent from the negotiations were representatives from the Shawnee, who were considered not to control any lands affected by this document. Despite tribal leader Black Hoof's efforts to control discontent, many among the Shawnee resented the surrendering of any Native American homelands to American pioneers. Tenskwatawa and Tecumseh used the 1809 treaty to bolster their standing among the outraged of all tribes in the Wabash, Maumee, and Illinois Valleys.

Profiting from his gubernatorial experience, a cautious Major General Harrison sent two long letters to Secretary of War John Armstrong concerning the relationships between the United States and the various Indian nations of the territories of Indiana and Illinois. He advised against trying to extinguish tribes' land titles until after the war (the War of 1812). At that time he expected "that a cession of all the lands we want or may want for a considerable number of years, might be obtained." Trying to exact such concessions during the war would excite the wrath of those tribes with whom he had recently secured armistices. He reminded the secretary that the Fort Wayne Treaty of 1809 became the "rock upon which the popularity of Tecumseh was founded and that upon which the influence of *Little Turtle* was wrecked." Seldom does one find such an astute appraisal of the various tribes and their geographic entitlements as in this summary. Harrison clearly recognized that land title claims "founded upon reason and justice" should be acknowledged and that tribes living on lands traditionally the property of another tribe should be compensated, as well as the traditional owners. "Upon this principle" he compensated such migratory tribes as the Shawnee, Delaware, Potawatomi, and Kickapoo, as well as the more ancient inhabitants of the area.[66]

The Decision to March

"The aspect of Indian affairs at this moment is a little gloomy." So wrote Harrison in a classic understatement of the situation in the summer of 1811.[67] The Indiana governor attempted to ascertain Tenskwatawa's military strength and intentions. A French-American, Michael Brouillette, went to Prophetstown as a trader and spy. He provided the governor with intelligence until the Prophet discovered his activities and drove him from the village. Harrison then sent Toussaint Dubois as a messenger to the Prophet to warn him that Indiana and Kentucky militiamen and regulars were coming to Vincennes. They were not intending to attack the native village but would do so if the Shawnee's "disposition to commit hostilities could no longer be doubted." Both men provided intelligence information that Governor Harrison forwarded in weekly reports to Secretary of War William Eustis. Eustis authorized the governor to establish a post inside the 1809 treaty area. In July 1810 the governor sent Joseph Barron, an interpreter, to Prophetstown with an unusual proposition: an invitation to the Prophet to visit Washington, DC. Listening to the proposal, the Prophet declared, "For what purpose do you come here? Brouillette was here; he was a spy. Dubois was here; he was a spy. Now you have come. You too are a spy." Only Tecumseh's intervention saved Barron from execution.[68] One of those contingencies of history revolves around what would have happened if either

Tenskwatawa or Tecumseh had gone to Washington. Would it have changed their attitudes regarding the possibility of a military solution to the Midwestern confrontation between the races?

For Tecumseh, the central ingredient in any successful effort to thwart American advancement into Native American homelands was political unity among Indians. This was a remote possibility, but one he sought. In July 1811 he began a half-year journey to seek such coordination by visiting tribes in the Old Southwest, where he would visit the Chickasaw, Choctaw, and Creek and to Missouri to consult with Osage leaders. Before leaving Indiana he paid a visit to Harrison at Vincennes.

Accompanied by over two hundred warriors in fifty-three canoes, Tecumseh paddled down the Wabash to Vincennes for a conference. It was a stand-off—Tecumseh feared Harrison might capture or kill him; Harrison feared this large a native force would overwhelm the small Fort Knox garrison and the local militiamen protecting him. After a series of armament reduction talks, a reduced number of less-well armed soldiers, militiamen, and warriors confronted each other at an arbor not far from Harrison's imposing Grouseland mansion. For two days they exchanged speeches.

In the course of these talks, Tecumseh made several critical disclosures. First he indicated that he wanted a union of native tribes similar to the "seventeen fires"—states—of the American republic. Harrison knew that the crux of this Indian confederacy would be a refusal to negotiate subsequent territorial concessions. Implicit in this discussion was the obvious desire of the natives to control thousands of square miles of potential farmland so that they might maintain their hunter-gatherer way of life for an increasingly small population base. Tecumseh exaggerated the size of those allied with him, while Harrison realized that the Shawnee brothers' confederacy was far smaller than the one that existed in the 1790s.

Second were Tecumseh's repeated threats of assassination of any chief who negotiated land concessions to the United States. What in the eyes of Tecumseh and Tenskwatawa was a punishment for native treason was to Harrison a terrorist tactic against Indian leaders who recognized the realities of the situation.

Third, Tecumseh refused to acknowledge the legitimacy of the Fort Wayne Treaty of 1809 and said that the brothers would establish settlements within the ceded lands. Even though Tecumseh acknowledged that no new villages in the disputed lands would be built before the following spring, to Harrison the statement was a direct and immediate threat to his opening lands in the rich soils of the Wabash and White River Valleys to white settlement. This was a tactical error by Tecumseh. The information merely reinforced Harrison's desire to make "short work with the Prophet & his adherents" so that surveys could be conducted in the 1809 treaty lands. A territorial surveyor informed the surveyor general that one should not "go to the woods . . . [judging] from the surly Disposition of the Indians."[69] But the advance of white settlement required the safe conduct of surveyors, and Harrison meant to ensure that this would be the case.

Finally, Tecumseh divulged one more piece of information that the governor decided to act upon. Tecumseh would be gone for several months on his visit to the south, and Harrison decided to make use of his absence to break up the multi-tribal village. Before leaving Prophetstown, Tecumseh cautioned his brother not to provoke the Americans during his trip, but his release of this information to Harrison was a blunder of the first magnitude.[70]

The governor made an astute appraisal of Tecumseh's abilities in a letter to Secretary of War William Eustis in which he described the Shawnee as one "of those uncommon geniuses, which spring up occasionally to produce revolutions and overturn the established order of things . . . His activity and industry supply the want of letters . . . wherever he goes he makes an impression favorable to his purposes."[71] For the Prophetstown residents, the consequences of the Harrison-Tecumseh confrontation were disastrous. The governor resolved to chasten Tenskwatawa before Tecumseh returned.

Just after the Shawnee warrior chief left the Indiana capital, Harrison requested authorization from Secretary Eustis to move against Prophetstown. The governor wanted to destroy the multi-tribal community, which, in his mind, engaged in terrorism by threatening the lives of friendly Indian leaders and by allowing small native war parties to prey on frontier settlers. This appeal was consistent with warnings the War Department had received from other frontier government officials. Governor Ninian Edwards of Illinois Territory warned that the Prophet and his party "have taken a hostile attitude against us and so long as we permit them to continue it, their confidence will increase, the seeds of discontent will be sown far and wide and they will be continually adding to their strength." The secretary of war agreed with Governors Harrison and Edwards and told President Madison that he would send Col. John Boyd's 4th U.S. Infantry from Newport, Kentucky, to Vincennes to accompany the militia that Harrison would mobilize. Madison agreed with the secretary's decisions and with his desire to use caution and intimidation to achieve the desired results. Reluctantly the secretary conceded that some militia might be required, so he allowed Harrison to raise a force that, in the governor's estimation, would be sufficient. Eustis wanted the governor to be as frugal with expenditures as possible.[72]

The secretary assumed the expedition would intimidate Tenskwatawa and his followers; he hoped to avoid combat. He authorized Harrison to disperse the natives at Prophetstown and to force from Tenskwatawa a pledge not to assemble a hostile gathering there or elsewhere. If he refused, Harrison could attack Prophetstown and capture the Prophet. To ensure compliance, the secretary authorized the governor to take some tribal leaders as hostages. Harrison was to inform the assembled natives that should they not return to their homes, the United States would send an armed force against them that would drive hostile tribes "beyond the great waters, and [that they would] never again be permitted to live within the Jurisdictional limits of the United States." Presumably this was a threat to force them across the Great Lakes into Upper Canada. Eustis authorized Harrison to build a fort along the Wabash within the limits of the 1809 land cession. The War Department presumed that no direct evidence would be found of British direction of the Indians other than supplying provisions and weaponry at Amherstburg. Given the delicate nature of diplomatic relations with Britain, the governor was not to act in a manner that might be considered aggressive toward His Majesty's officials and subjects.[73] In this respect Governor Harrison faced a diplomatically delicate issue similar to that confronting General Wayne at Fort Miamis.

By the time the 4th Infantry Regiment arrived at Jeffersonville, opposite Louisville, its strength had been reduced by desertion and disease from six hundred to four hundred men. To awe the Prophet and his allies, Harrison found it necessary to augment Eustis's original allocation of four militia companies to twelve or fourteen. Joseph Hamilton Daviess, Kentucky's attorney general, volunteered to bring mounted riflemen on the expedition. Like so many of the field-grade militia officers, Daviess was a veteran of the Fallen Timbers campaign. Harrison mobilized the Indiana militia, and approximately eight hundred officers and men left Vincennes and headed up the Wabash Valley. With Harrison commanding as brigadier general of the Indiana militia and Colonel Boyd as second-in-command, the other main subordinates were Col. Joseph Bartholomew, leading the Indiana militiamen, and Major Daviess, commander of the two hundred mounted men. Harrison's aides and staff included chief of staff Abraham Owen plus Henry Hurst, Waller Taylor, Marston G. Clark, and Thomas Randolph. Capt. William Piatt of the 2nd U.S. Infantry served as the quartermaster. Never one for military formality, the commanding general wore a calico hunting shirt trimmed with fringe and a beaver fur hat with a large ostrich feather.

Before they departed Vincennes, Harrison directed his officers to drill the men and conduct battlefield maneuvers. Neither the regulars nor the militiamen performed effectively; these men were without the discipline he had seen General Wayne insist upon before marching toward Fallen Timbers seventeen years earlier.[74] Throughout the march northward, Harrison directed his troops to conduct drills to increase their competence in battle formations. Still unsatisfied with the results, on 2 November at the daily parade, Harrison threatened to break the officers if they did not comport themselves in a more military manner and maintain better discipline.[75]

By this time the governor's army amounted to about a thousand men, including 400 Indiana militiamen, 120 mounted Kentucky volunteers, 80 Indiana mounted riflemen, and 300 regulars from the 4th U.S. Infantry.[76] Nothing better indicates the enthusiasm for this operation than the participation of Samuel Wells, a Kentucky militia major general, who took a demotion so he could command a battalion of the state's militia in the Tippecanoe campaign, with the rank of major. Wells was the older brother of William Wells, former Indian Agent at Fort Wayne.[77] Among the Indiana mounted riflemen were Capt. Spier Spencer's Yellow Jackets from Harrison County, Indiana Territory, northwest of Louisville. They became the general's favorite scouts and hunters and would play a critical role in the battle at Tippecanoe. With the operational intelligence gathered by his emissaries to Prophetstown, the advice of friendly natives, and his evaluation of Tecumseh in his visit to Vincennes, Harrison accumulated considerable information regarding his foe's numbers, capabilities, and vulnerabilities.

On 3 October they reached an old Indian village a couple of miles north of modern Terre Haute, where they began construction of a fort. This post was within the land ceded in the 1809 Fort Wayne Treaty and would be named Fort Harrison. Delaware chiefs he had sent to Prophetstown reported back to him that they had been ill-received and insulted by Tenskwatawa, and the general and his officers determined that nothing remained but to chastise the Prophet and his allies.[78] After leaving a small garrison at Fort Harrison, the troops advanced northward to the mouth of the Vermilion River in modern Vermilion County, Indiana. Because they knew Prophetstown was nearby, they built a small stockade, which was named Fort Boyd, and left the supply barges that had accompanied them from Vincennes. At the same time Harrison became concerned that Indians might attack settlements like Vincennes, so he sent a detachment of mounted riflemen southward and urged the senior militia officer at the territorial capital to remain on the alert for hostile natives. After reveille on 3 November, they began a march into Tenskwatawa's locale.[79]

Like most of his contemporaries, Ensign John Tipton of Captain Spencer's troop eagerly examined the countryside for its agricultural potential. His diary is filled with often misspelled, grammatically inconsistent notations like "we moved through good land. Passt three springs. Some Beautiful prairie some timber."[80] Entry into Tenskwatawa's homeland enticed Americans into an area where they found soil, water, and timber most suitable for white settlement. The spread of such information was not in the best interests of those natives hoping to retain possession of the fertile Wabash Valley.

In the governor's mind, the efforts of his emissaries and the Delaware chiefs "to induce the Prophet to lay aside his Hostile designs" had failed, and no option remained but to "chastise" Tenskwatawa. Harrison demanded that Prophetstown be denuded of its Potawatomi, Winnebago, and Kickapoo residents and become a Shawnee village, that Tenskwatawa return all stolen horses, and that he surrender all warriors guilty of depredations on frontier settlements. If he complied with these demands the Prophet would lose face, so combat seemed inevitable.

Tippecanoe

With his army encumbered by wagons loaded with supplies and driving forty cattle at the rear, Harrison followed an example learned from Anthony Wayne: the infantry marching in columns of two files, with the cavalry and mounted rifle troops covering the front and rear. From the mouth of the Vermilion River the army moved slowly along the right bank of the Wabash a few miles northeast of modern Lafayette. Near Prophetstown, they encamped on a low ridge overlooking the Wabash Valley.

Harrison awoke in his tent at 0430 hours on 7 November 1811 when he heard a shot from a sentry followed by yells from natives attacking under Tenskwatawa's spell. Alerting the sleeping garrison of the attack, the sentinels served well. Soon the 4th U.S. Infantry's drummer boy was calling men to their stations. As the general dashed from his tent he found that his horse had bolted from its picket, so he took another, darker one. That change in mounts may have saved his life. One of the general's aides, Col. Abraham Owens, mounted his own white charger, rode near the general, and was killed by an infiltrating Indian. This was the first of the deaths on Harrison's staff, which would also include his secretary, Thomas Randolph. Even though an officer on a white horse was dead, the natives found that the Americans did not, as Tenskwatawa had predicted, "run and hide in the grass like young quails."

Only a small number of attackers reached the center of Harrison's encampment, but for a few minutes fighting went on inside and outside the American lines. On the right flank, militia companies commanded by Captains James Biggers and David Robb collapsed during the initial assault. The two companies withdrew, and some soldiers ran and hid among the wagons, especially the soldiers in Captain Robb's company. Col. John P. Boyd, commanding the 4th U.S. Infantry, pulled two unengaged companies from the Bennett's Creek line to plug the vacated position. Realizing the campfires were illuminating the defenders, the sergeants doused the flames.

The natives used a tactic unfamiliar to Harrison: "They rushed up to our lines in large bodies and by signals from their chiefs, fired, and then retreated to load again."[81] Such a procedure maximized individual marksmanship and allowed its participants to retreat for concealment while reloading. Aimed fire brought significant losses among American officers. The commanding general rode from one end of the line to the other, encouraging his men with a strong voice and moving reserves into holes in the line. His presence and calm in the midst of chaos brought confidence to those in his command.

In the midst of the combat on the right flank, Lt. Col. Joseph H. "Jo" Daviess of Kentucky repeatedly solicited Harrison's permission to lead a mounted charge against the attackers; the commanding general urged patience. Finally, in exasperation the general said that the colonel could attack when he thought it opportune. Daviess took about twenty cavalrymen toward an endangered segment of the battlefield, but only nine followed him through the American lines. Daviess's white jacket attracted native marksmen, and he soon fell to the ground with a mortal wound. Thus ended one man's quest for the military fame he expected would enhance his political career; Harrison would be accused by a few Kentuckians of deliberately sending Daviess on a forlorn mission.[82] The impetuosity of officers like Daviess frustrated Harrison's command and control efforts throughout his frontier campaigns.

While shots came on all sides of the encampment, a second major assault came on the left flank against Captain Spencer's Yellow Jackets. The Indians drove off the cattle and draft horses as they moved against the Hoosiers. Two lieutenants fell early in the encounter, and the company commander received three wounds. "Close Up, men! Steady! Hold the line!" shouted the veteran Spencer as he attempted to mount his horse, when a fourth shot to the head killed him. When Harrison reached the endangered position he asked, "Where's your captain?" "Dead, sir," Ens. John Tipton replied. "Where's your first lieutenant?" "Dead, sir." "Where's your second lieutenant?" "Dead, sir." "Your ensign?" "Here, sir." Tipton took command, and the company held the line until reinforced by Captain Robb's re-formed Indiana mounted rifles and Capt. Joel Cooke's regulars. This type of bravery and determination affected most of those engaged. Their stance reflects an adage from Anthony Wayne's 1794 order book that admonished his men to stand their ground, as the natives were more formidable when confronting a retreating foe than one standing its ground.

During the night, Harrison rode his horse throughout the encampment and attracted native marksmen, whose shots penetrated his uniform several times; he received a slight wound to the scalp and lost one horse to gunfire. Meanwhile he ordered men to stand and others to reinforce. Colonel Boyd effectively deployed his regulars from one threatened area to another, and the two long flanks of the American line repelled the limited offensives against them.

As dawn approached, the Indians' fire decreased and Harrison called off a charge by the 4th Infantry. Both sides withdrew from combat and paused to bury their dead, tend to their wounded, and plan their next step. That day, 7 November, saw the Americans fortify their position and the natives withdraw from Prophetstown. The next day, Harrison's men entered the village and destroyed the grain caches they found and the homes (except for that of an elderly woman with whom they left a seriously wounded Indian).[83]

Harrison had skillfully distributed his forces around the campsite during the engagement, and in all, his conduct during the battle was exemplary. The significant criticism revolves around his failure to entrench or barricade his encampment. The experience retaught Indiana's governor two tactical lessons he should have remembered from Wayne's campaign: fortify your position daily and bring artillery. He would not make those mistakes again, although his subordinates would.

The principal controversy would be over whether the Tippecanoe expedition "won" anything. The two sides seem to have suffered similar losses. American casualties included 62 dead and 122 wounded; native losses cannot be accurately determined, but 36 bodies were left on the field and several graves found in the village. There must have been at least 50 Indians killed and an unknown number wounded. Proportionally, the native losses were higher than those of the Americans, and the latter held the ground at the end of the day. That the Indians scalped only three Americans indicates that except for the few that penetrated to the American center, the warriors failed to close with their foes. Harrison concluded that for the most part his volunteers fought effectively and determinedly. There was no question that his regulars performed well.

Casualty comparisons do not determine the long-term meaning of a battle; strategic consequences do. The immediate result was just what Governor Harrison and Secretary of War Eustis had aimed to achieve. Less than two weeks after the encounter, Capt. Josiah Snelling reported from Fort Harrison that most Indians had abandoned their faith in Tenskwatawa and were "very much exasperated at their loss & reproaching the Prophet in bitter Terms for the defeat he had brought upon him."[84] Although limited raids into the territories of Indiana and especially Illinois continued during the winter and spring, major encounters ceased. Tecumseh cautioned moderation and probably would have restrained his more militant adherents had not the United States and Britain gone to war the following June. Suddenly the natives could expect more British assistance and direct military support at Fort Malden. After suffering a winter of food deprivation due to the razing of their upper Wabash community, Tecumseh and his allies defiantly rebuilt Prophetstown.

The battle of Tippecanoe was more catastrophic for the Native Americans than it first appeared. Tenskwatawa lost his reputation as a prophet and miracle worker. Tecumseh understood that such a loss before finalizing the native alliance constituted a major setback in his efforts to forge a united opposition to the American advance. He knew that his only hope was support from the British.[85] The mantle of Indian leadership passed from the Prophet to his brother. For the following two years, the struggle in the Ohio Country revolved around Harrison and Tecumseh.

Chapter Three

The Politics of Command

B y early 1812, Governor William Henry Harrison recognized that, as his political rivals gained control of the territorial legislature, his political career in Indiana was about to end and that, with the territory soon to be admitted into the Union, he was too unpopular to win major elective office. Always looking for public employment to supplement his income, Harrison sought a general's commission in the expanding regular army.

Military Policy for the Old Northwest

Even before the collapse of his political fortunes in Indiana, Harrison had proposed major changes in military policy in the Old Northwest. In a letter to Secretary of War William Eustis in July 1809, he replied to the secretary's request for comments on positioning of troops in the region. In a geography lesson, Harrison noted that there were no critical mountain passes in the region and so a novel fortification system was required. Instead of creating posts to protect each settled area (which, he said, Arthur St. Clair and Anthony Wayne had tried), he advocated the construction of several posts on the straits uniting the Great Lakes and the Mississippi. He also argued for fortifications at critical portage junctions that would inhibit movement from one water course to the other. His list of sites was extensive: Detroit, Michilimackinac, Sault Ste. Marie, and Prairie du Chien. At critical junctions like Chicago, Fort Wayne, and Wabash Valley points such as the mouth of the Tippecanoe and Terre Haute, he would establish or continue the existing outposts. He saw no reason to retain Fort Massac (southern Illinois Territory), although he did support the retention of Fort Madison (on the Mississippi in modern Iowa) as a support base for Prairie du Chien and a defensive outpost for St. Louis.

That he did not suggest Green Bay is interesting since it was a hotbed of pro-British sentiment and traders who operated in defiance of American trading regulations. The Prairie du Chien fortification was critical to blocking trade between Montreal and the western tribes, he noted, given that the Fox-Wisconsin River waterway was "the most used & the most interesting & important" British trade route to the upper Mississippi and regions west. He understood that Green Bay was more difficult to support logistically than the Mississippi River post.

Harrison's attitude toward the defense of Detroit was most interesting. Instead of the current fort, he suggested building a post on one of the Detroit River islands, at a site that commanded the shipping channel. He hoped to entrap armed British vessels in Lake Erie by constructing a formidable fort capable of resisting attack and interdicting trade from Lake Erie. In a bit of irony, given what he would have to campaign to retake a few years later, he predicted the British "could never think of defending upper Canada, & no valuable purpose to them could be answer'd by a temporary possession of Detroit & the neighbouring settlements." On the other hand, he recognized the need for naval superiority on the upper lakes, where it would be necessary "to build a number of Vessels equal to theirs," or to rely on holding a Detroit River fortification that would interrupt British trade with the fur traders and natives on Lakes Huron, Michigan, and Superior. He did acknowledge that the British had a canoe route up the Ottawa River and through the Lake Nipissing portage to the French River and Lake Huron that circumvented Detroit. Although acknowledging that "the post of Michilimacinac is of considerable importance," he advocated neither its reinforcement nor naval vessels on Lake Huron for its defense.[1]

This letter was of considerable importance for Harrison's military career. It marked him in the eyes of the War Department as an authority on northwestern defense policies; it demonstrated a capacity to perceive regional military policies; and, for the first time in his career, it pointed to an awareness of the interaction of military and naval operations. All this came before the Tippecanoe campaign, when he renewed his military career.

Learning of the Army Act of 11 January 1812, which authorized the appointment of two major generals and five additional brigadier generals, Harrison promptly wrote Secretary Eustis of his desire "to resume the La guerre if the Government should think me worthy of a commission in the New Military establishment." He then recounted his seven years of service in the 1790s, when he had been "not an inattentive observer nor neglectful of those studies which appertain to the military art." His status on Anthony Wayne's general staff had allowed him "to apply to the test of experiment those Rules for the Construction [and] the Substance [and] the Marching & Manoevreing of Armies which I had acquired from Books." Even after leaving military service, he had maintained his study of military subjects, and his recent campaign emphasized his ability to maneuver soldiers better than anyone available. Julius Caesar's famous *Commentaries* were a choice reading in the Harrison household. For all these reasons, combined with his "Ardent zeal for the Service of my Country," he offered himself "to the Government as a Candidate for a Military Appointment in the Army that is contemplated."[2]

But criticism of Harrison's conduct at Tippecanoe reverberated in Washington. Particularly important was the censure of Col. John P. Boyd of the 4th U.S. Infantry, his second-in-command in the campaign, which attacked the conduct of many militiamen in the battle, and that of Jonathan Jennings, his Indiana political rival and the territory's delegate to Congress.[3] Several of Boyd's subordinates wrote certificates on Harrison's behalf, arguing that "throughout the campaign and in the hour of battle," Harrison "proved himself the soldier and the general . . . Indeed one sentiment of confidence, respect and affection, towards the commander in chief, pervaded the whole line of the army." Signed by Captains Joel Cook, Josiah Snelling, and R. C. Barton, plus five lieutenants, two surgeons, and an ensign, these certificates appeared in the *National Intelligencer* in early February.[4] Disappointing from Harrison's point of view was the absence from the signatories of any of the field-grade officers of the 4th Infantry Regiment. (It is appropriate to note here that as a brigadier general during the War of 1812, Boyd proved inept, undistinguished, and unsuccessful.)

Secretary of War Eustis and President Madison had other candidates for the new brigadier generalships. One was quite obvious. William Hull (1753–1825) rose from captain of a militia company to lieutenant colonel in the Continental Army. After the war he practiced law in Newton, Massachusetts, and eventually became a major general commanding the 3rd Division of the Massachusetts militia. In 1805 Thomas Jefferson appointed him governor of the newly created Michigan Territory. Of all of James Madison's appointments to high command in 1812, Hull probably brought the most military experience as a field-grade veteran of the Revolutionary War with both command and staff duties, along with the administrative familiarity of a militia general and territorial governor. Yet there were those in the administration who had reservations about Hull's abilities for such responsibility. The fifty-nine-year-old, corpulent Hull eagerly sought the appointment as commander of ground forces in the Old Northwest and even went to Washington to secure it. After receiving a brigadier general's commission in the regular army, Hull journeyed to Cincinnati, where he secured one regular regiment, commanded by Lt. Col. James Miller, and three Ohio militia regiments commanded by querulous, ambitious Colonels Lewis Cass, James Findlay and Duncan McArthur.

As General Hull assembled his North West Army in Ohio, apprehension about his talents grew. Lewis Cass wrote U.S. Senator Thomas Worthington that he feared Hull "was not our man . . . I am now told by men capable of appreciating his talents and who have had opportunities of observing him, that he is indecisive and irresolute, leaning for support on persons around him." Colonel McArthur, on the other hand, claimed Hull appeared "to give entire satisfaction; he is both friendly and attentive."[5]

Hull's appointment was not unexpected and certainly would not affront Harrison. The Detroit region was far more vulnerable to British attack than any place in Indiana or Illinois. Hull was familiar with the region, and he knew political leaders in the new State of Ohio. But the Madison administration's appointment to the second western generalship certainly did offend Indiana's governor. The Tennessee congressional delegation pushed for James Winchester (1752–1826), a Tennessee businessman and militia officer, for a regular brigadier general's commission, which he received in March 1812. While both Hull and Winchester brought maturity (they were twenty years older than Harrison, who was only thirty-nine in 1812) and Revolutionary War experience to their positions, Winchester lacked familiarity with the Ohio Valley–Great Lakes region to which he was now sent and had no acquaintanceship with local leaders. According to a conversation between Senator Thomas Worthington of Ohio and Madison several months later, the reason Harrison's name was not put forward for the brigadier rank was that there was little probability of such an offer being ratified in the Senate without Harrison's resigning the governor's post. The president, said the Ohio senator, did not want to put Harrison "on such uncertainty otherwise he should not hesitate to nominate" him. Soon after Winchester set up a recruiting headquarters in Lexington, his arrogant personality aroused the enmity of Kentucky politicians and potential soldiers. A pro-Harrison Kentuckian described Winchester as a man "advanced in years" who lived "in a degree of elegant luxury and ease, which was not calculated to season him for a northern campaign in the forest."[6]

The notice of Winchester's appointment disappointed the Indiana governor, whose critics now seemed to have the upper hand. Most conspicuous was intelligence that the victory at Tippecanoe had an opposite effect from what

Harrison expected. Tecumseh returned to northern Indiana to find his brother's village in shambles but the natives willing to carry on. Through the winter and early spring, on the outskirts of Fort Madison, Iowa, and Fort Dearborn, Illinois, Indian raids killed frontier families, but little could be done to counter such small-scale attacks. These forts, along with Michilimackinac and Harrison, were considered relatively easy prey for native warriors. With British assistance, Forts Detroit and Wayne might fall. In May an intertribal council met on the Mississinewa, a Wabash tributary, with representatives of the Delaware, Kickapoo, Miami, Ojibwa, Ottawa, Piankeshaw, Potawatomi, Shawnee, Wea, Winnebago, and Wyandot tribes. Although the conference counseled peace not war, it represented a decided effort at unity among most of the native peoples of the Old Northwest.

John Badollet, a long-time Harrison critic and registrar of the land office at Vincennes, capital of Indiana Territory, wrote his old friend Secretary of the Treasury Albert Gallatin about the failure of the Tippecanoe expedition: "The bloody tomahawk is now in fact raised, the work of murder has begun . . . [I]t is now ascertained that large collections of Indians are forming on the Wabash above us, with a view . . . of retaliating upon this place [for] the inhuman burning of the Prophet's town."[7]

The British were assisting this effort to reinforce the Indians' military capabilities. According to a report from Detroit in February, "Since the battle of Tippecanoe, large numbers of savages who have visited the British fort at Amherstburg [Fort Malden] . . . have been there liberally supplied with arms and munitions of war."[8] As it became increasingly clear that war between Britain and the United States might ensue, from the British perspective it was to their advantage to use native allies to assist in the defense of Canada and in revising the Great Lakes boundary with the United States.

Tecumseh faced the problems of revitalizing the resistance to American encroachment on Indian lands, of cowing the accommodationist chiefs, of playing the Americans off against the British, and of counseling caution among his younger warriors who sought revenge for Tippecanoe. He saw an opening during a conference with the Americans at Fort Wayne in June 1812. There he learned that General Hull was advancing with an American army toward Detroit and that an Anglo-American war loomed—in fact, it would be declared while he sat with the Americans. He immediately left Fort Wayne and journeyed to Fort Malden, where he would talk with British representatives. For Tecumseh, the opportunity long sought was at hand. The long hoped for Anglo-

American war had begun; he expected British weaponry and soldiers to assist his expanded pan-Indian alliance. His confederacy, though never as large as that of Blue Jacket, Little Turtle, and Buckongahelas in the 1790s, was a formidable one, and he expected at least the Creek to engage in warfare with the Americans in the Old Southwest.[9]

The Detroit Campaign of 1812

The signs looked ominous to Harrison, who received notes about the advancement of one company of regulars to Fort Harrison and a company of rangers to be raised in the territory. As the situation became graver, Secretary Eustis ordered Col. William Russell to command all the regular army troops in Indiana Territory and the five companies of rangers raised in Kentucky, Ohio, Indiana, and Illinois. More serious for Indiana was the withdrawal of the 4th U.S. Infantry Regiment from Indiana to Cincinnati and eventually to Detroit, with General Hull. From Fort Wayne came information that Indians were passing over to Malden in large numbers. One junior officer reported that parties as large as three hundred received weapons and munitions from British Indian agents at the fort.[10] There remained just a thin blue line for the defense of such a large frontier, and both Harrison and Tecumseh knew it. American hopes for a peaceful summer depended on Hull's capture of Fort Malden at Amherstburg, Upper Canada (modern Ontario), downriver from Detroit.

On 19 April, Hull received his orders from Secretary Eustis: (1) march with "little delay" to Detroit with the 4th Infantry Regiment and Ohio militia, (2) take command of all troops within Michigan, Chicago, and Fort Wayne, and (3) "adopt such measures with the chiefs and the several Tribes of Indians [that] in your judgment may appear to be best calculated to secure the peace of the country."[11]

On 11 June 1812, the North West Army marched out of Urbana, Ohio, for Detroit. Instead of taking the route chosen by Generals St. Clair and Wayne, which circumvented the Black Swamp of Northwest Ohio by heading northwest to Fort Wayne and down the Maumee River, Hull decided to blaze a more direct route heading through the heavily forested uplands and the Black Swamp for the Maumee Rapids (modern Perrysburg, Ohio). It took nearly three weeks to reach the rapids, where Hull made his first major mistake of the campaign. He engaged a schooner to carry much of the heavy baggage to Detroit. He did not know that war had been formally declared and that the British at Fort Malden knew of the congressional declaration, and as the vessel sailed by Malden it fell to the British. Besides the loss of critical supplies, especially medicines, the commanding general's personal papers containing confidential information of immense value to his opponents were on the ship.[12]

Hull's army arrived in Detroit on 5 July. It consisted of slightly more than 2,000 officers and men of whom 450 were regulars and 1,450 Ohio militiamen. At Fort Malden there were 325 British regulars, 850 militiamen, and 400 native warriors. Hull's unwillingness to attack Fort Malden in the ensuing weeks drew sharp criticism from the Ohio militia colonels. At the same time, the Indians, fur traders, and a few British regulars made a coordinated attack on Fort Michilimackinac and captured it on 17 July. This triumph at the critical intersection of Lakes Huron and Michigan caused many natives who had wavered in their support of the British to abandon their neutral status and combine with the redcoats. It also unnerved Hull, who withdrew his troops from Canada to Detroit. He feared a combination of Indians from the north would destroy his forces, now divided on the two sides of the river. Part of Hull's concern was the increasing insecurity of his supply lines between Detroit and the Maumee Rapids. He wrote Col. Samuel Wells of a newly recruited regular regiment that the North West Army was "in a most perilous condition—his [Hull's] communications cut off almost entirely by the enemy—in danger of want of provisions, and instead of carrying on offensive operations" he found himself "reduced to act on the defensive."[13]

Gen. Isaac Brock of Upper Canada exploited British control of Lake Erie to transfer troops from the Niagara Frontier to Fort Malden. Hull allowed Brock's troops to land on the Michigan shore of the Detroit River without opposition and then surrendered, without firing a shot, to Brock's troops and their native allies on 16 August.[14]

The surrender of Detroit changed everything on the northwestern frontier. Panic set in from St. Louis to Pittsburgh. Kentucky's Robert McAfee recalled that "it created an excitement and indignation as great as the catastrophe was unexpected." According to the Chillicothe, Ohio, *Scioto Gazette*, General Hull "has let loose thousands of merciless savages on our defenceless frontiers—the blood of many hundred helpless women and children must rest on his head. God grant, that their cries may reach his ear, and pierce his heart, with anguish and with agony." A Dayton, Ohio, correspondent to the *National Intelligencer* reported that news of Hull's surrender "created considerable alarm," which he suspected would result in "Savages, whose roving, active & restless disposition, instigated by the British officers, would soon transport them to our neighborhood and excite them to a barbarous warfare upon the defenceless frontier."[15] The surrender sent shock waves through the Madison administration. Former U.S. Senator Jonathan Dayton (1760–1824) wrote the president that "Your political enemies are taking every possible advantage of our unaccountable disasters at Detroit, to render your Presidency unpopular, & your cabinet Council odious & contemptible."[16] For William Henry Harrison, the crisis presented an opportunity to demonstrate his military leadership capabilities before a much larger audience than in earlier years.

As news of the Detroit debacle reached political leaders in Ohio and Kentucky, many saw Harrison as the best possibility for command of a rebuilt North West Army. Robert Johnson of Kentucky (1745–1815) wrote the president: "The Idea with us is, that Hull is a traitor or nearly an Ediot or part of both. To take a View of the whole of his Conduct, it would seem as if he has played the Grandest Yanke[e] Trick [Hull was a native of Connecticut] that has been played on the U.S." Johnson, whose sons Richard M., John T. and James would serve with distinction in the War of 1812 and in postwar Kentucky and national politics, had been raised in Orange County, Virginia, with Madison, and he wrote his old acquaintance of the political maneuvering going on in the Ohio Valley on Harrison's behalf. Harrison, as territorial governor, was ex officio commander of Indiana's militia and a territorial brigadier general. However, this made him inferior in seniority to regular army Brig. Gen. James Winchester of Tennessee, who was heartily disliked by the volunteers of Kentucky, Ohio, and Indiana who composed most of the troops raised, or that would be raised, in the Ohio Valley. General Winchester in command of the North West Army, wrote Johnson, would create "a great deal of uneasiness in the Army" where the men have "great Confidence in Harrison but with Winchestor they have very little."[17] But Harrison's status with the Indiana legislature was such that he could not expect support from that quarter.

The land office registrar in Vincennes kept up his barrage of mocking criticism of Harrison, who was putting a palisade around his home. The Hero of Tippecanoe, Badollet wrote sarcastically to Secretary Gallatin, "that brilliant meteor in the galaxy of military heroes, who has sung & caused so many sycophantic pens & venal presses to sing his unparalleled military talents, is at last eclipsed behind a wooden fence, and the New Washington has sunk into a pitifull and selfish Sir John Falstaf not daring to defend those he has exposed, nor to face the enemy he has ostentatiously and wantonly provoked."[18] If Harrison was going to receive support for a regular army generalship, it was going to have to come from outside the territory of which he was the chief executive.

Before receiving news of the Detroit defeat or of his new commissions, Harrison sent Secretary Eustis his proposals for the conduct of war in the Midwest. Nowhere else did Harrison so explicitly describe his conception of frontier warfare. Against the Indians there were two tactical maneuvers. The first was the "rapid and desultory expeditions by mounted men having for their object the surprise and distruction of Particular Villages"—in other words, a raiding strategy. The second was "the more tardy but more effectual operations of an Army Composed principally of Infantry penetrating the Country of the Enemy and securing the possession by a chain of Posts"—in other words, a persisting strategy. Gen. Charles Scott's raids with the Kentucky militia in the Wabash Valley in the 1790s best exemplified the former; Anthony Wayne's campaign to the Maumee Valley in 1794 provided a successful illustration of the latter. With the exception of the construction of Fort Harrison (north of modern Terre Haute), the Tippecanoe campaign became much more a combined arms version of the raiding strategy than the persisting strategy that Harrison had learned from General Wayne.[19] To implement the latter and to secure the more northern frontiers, Harrison advocated construction of a chain of posts on the Illinois River from the Mississippi to Chicago plus the reinforcement of Fort Wayne.

Most everyone from Secretary Eustis to Governor Harrison recognized that the small garrisons at Forts Michilimackinac, Dearborn (Chicago), Wayne, and Detroit had to be either reinforced or evacuated. Permanent garrisons required regular army soldiers in sufficient numbers to sustain them in case of attack. The modest size of the detachments at these most forward outposts of the United States Army—50 men at Fort Harrison, 54 at Fort Dearborn, 57 at Fort Michilimackinac, 70 at Fort Wayne—made them particularly vulnerable to attack. With the news of Michilimackinac's capture, Harrison immediately concluded that Hull was in grave danger.[20] In a prescient commentary, he wrote Eustis: "It is possible Sir, that every-thing may yet go on well, that no considerable Number of Indians may be collected at Malden and that our Detachments and Convoys may reach their destination in safety, the reverse however appears to me to be the most probable." To secure his territory's outposts, they should raise two thousand Kentucky and Indiana volunteers, not militia, to relieve Fort Wayne. But he warned the secretary of war that the fall of Michilimackinac "will give such *éclat* to the British and Indian Arms that the Northern Tribes will pour down in swarms upon Detroit, [and thus] oblige Genl. Hull to act entirely upon the defensive, & meet and perhaps overpower the Convoys and reinforcements which may be sent him."[21] How much these strategic analyses of the situation in the Old Northwest affected Eustis's decision to award Harrison a brigadier generalship is unknown.

Kentucky Major General

Harrison wrote this strategic commentary from Lexington, Kentucky, after conferring with that state's political leaders in Frankfort at the time of Isaac Shelby's inauguration. It was there that Governor Shelby and retiring Governor Scott, both experienced military figures, along with U.S. House of Representatives Speaker Henry Clay and other local dignitaries, conferred and decided to take their own course of action in the absence of the regional military leadership they thought necessary for the situation. For some time Governor Scott had feared for Hull and his army in distant Detroit. He and others sought a novel solution to the choice of regional commander. Scott defied the commonwealth's constitution and state law and named Harrison a brevet major general of Kentucky's militia on 20 August 1812.[22] This placed the commonwealth's militia and volunteers under Harrison's, not Winchester's, immediate command. Two days later the federal government commissioned Harrison as a brigadier general in the U.S. Army by recess appointment. This commission made Harrison junior in rank to Winchester, something neither Scott nor Harrison wanted; consequently, Harrison refused the federal commission and continued to operate under the Kentucky appointment.

Speaker Henry Clay wrote effusive letters on Harrison's behalf to those in power in the nation's capital. He informed Secretary of State James Monroe "that throughout all parts of the W. Country there has been the strongest demonstrations of confidence in him given." To Secretary of War Eustis he expressed the hope that the president would "see fit to approve substantially what was done . . . with the respect to the appointment of Govr. Harrison." Col. John Allen, commander of a Kentucky volunteer rifle regiment, wrote the president that notwithstanding the attempts by a few to denigrate Harrison's abilities, he "did not Know one who would be dissatisfied with serving under him but believe all would be pleased with it and a large proportion highly Gratified."[23]

All this occurred before news of Detroit's capitulation arrived in either Frankfort or Washington. If Harrison had gotten to Detroit before the surrender, would Brigadier General Hull have recognized the Kentucky brevet major general rank as superior to his regular army commission at a lower grade? We do not know whether this was a consideration at the Frankfort conference where Harrison received his Kentucky rank. Secretary Eustis had said in a letter to the Indiana governor in mid-July that if he could raise fifteen hundred volunteers in Kentucky or elsewhere, the president would authorize a regular army brigadier generalship. The conferences in Frankfort between Harrison and the political leadership of the Bluegrass State in early August brought forth pledges of at least this number of volunteers. On receiving this information, Eustis informed Harrison of his federal brigadier generalship, before learning of the Detroit disaster. He initially placed him in command of the Indiana and Illinois frontiers and urged his cooperation with both General Hull and Governor Benjamin Howard of Missouri Territory. When news of Hull's surrender reached Washington, Eustis modified these instructions: "You will extend your eye over all the circumstances, & communicate with General Winchester . . . It is left to your discretion to join him with any part of the force under your Command, and to afford such other aid and cooperation as may be in your power."[24] Nothing in this directive indicates that Harrison was either superior to or subordinate to Winchester.

Harrison's support was not solely from Kentucky. In a letter to Harrison, Ohio's William Findlay wrote, "That gloom of indignation, which manifested itself at the news of the surrender of Detroit and of our brave men, is dissipated, and every body, possessed of patriotic zeal and ardour, is ready to enrol themselves under your conduct, to defend their Country and fight her battles."[25] Findlay apparently assumed that Harrison commanded the troops destined to regain Detroit, something Eustis's directive did not specify.

Not only was Harrison's Kentucky commission legally suspect (he was not a resident of Kentucky, as law required), but as a federal brigadier he would be junior to Winchester, who held seniority with the regular army commission and therefore became the senior officer in the Midwest. Did a Kentucky major general outrank a federal brigadier? Maybe yes, maybe no. But, and this was the rub as far as Winchester was concerned, most of the available troops were assigned to Harrison. Kentucky could raise far more infantrymen and cavalrymen than Ohio and the rest of the Old Northwest. Governors Scott and Shelby placed these volunteers under Harrison's direction.[26] Soon doubts arose regarding Winchester's status. On 1 September, Secretary Eustis sent a letter to Winchester "or officer commanding the N. Western Army," and four days later he told Maj. Gen. Elijah Wadsworth (1747–1817), who was commanding a division of Ohio militia, that "The Governor of Ohio will furnish Reinforcements on the requisition of General Winchester or Officer Commanding the North Western Army."[27] Those "ors" indicated unease in Washington regarding Winchester's status.

New rumors circulated in the West that Isaac Shelby would be named to the command of the North West Army. Informed of this possibility, two Ohio brigadier generals, Edward W. Tupper and Simon Perkins, wrote Governor Meigs a highly laudatory letter favoring Harrison, who "has the unshaken confidence of ourselves & of the whole army under his Command." Writing less than a month after the disaster at the River Raisin (second battle of Frenchtown in January 1813), they continued, "He has ever conducted himself like an officer of foresight—skill & prudence . . . If in his operations, he has been retarded beyond his own expectations and the expectations of an impatient people, his momentary or partial failure, cannot, with any justice, be ascribed to him." The calamity at Frenchtown "cannot claim him as its author," they concluded.[28]

The Madison administration considered an option other than Harrison as commander in the Midwest—Secretary of State James Monroe. Madison proposed that Monroe be given a volunteer rank of brevet major general and sent westward. The president saw "no evil" in sending the secretary of state to the Midwest with such a commission. In fact, he felt "the critical good to be expected from the presence, the influence, & counsels of Mr. Monroe." "If Winchester is to retain the command," he continued in a letter to Eustis, "such an expedient is the more necessary. Any new calamity, or even failure of success, under him, following the oppressive disaster of Hull, would shut every ear agst. arguments for not appointing a Commander, preferred by the public voice." Obviously the "public voice" preferred Harrison.[29]

In a carefully crafted, private letter to Monroe on 6 September, the president analyzed the situation:

> Hull has shewn himself utterly unqualified for such a trust. Is Winchester
> equal to it? His want of that enthusiastic confidence on the part of those who
> are to support & co-operate with him so peculiarly essential to his success,
> alone answers, this question. Is Harrison, if substituted, every thing that the
> public would ask? Without disparaging his qualifications, and allowing their
> great superiority to W.s, his military knowledge must be limited, and a more
> extensive weight of character, would be of material importance. Should a

junction of the two take place what then? No small degree of danger, that jealousies & jars might weaken, more than the union of their talents, would strengthen their measures. I am thus led to the idea . . . of availing the Crisis, if possible of your services. You would carry with you the confidence of all, would be the most unexceptionable depository of the necessary powers, and be most able to give impulse & direction to the only force now applicable to the object.[30]

While the president remained at Montpelier in Orange County, Virginia, Eustis and Monroe conferred about Madison's suggestion in Washington. They agreed that Monroe's appointment would have a positive "moral effect . . . on the public mind, being one emanating immediately from the govt. itself." But they thought there might be "doubtful" consequences with "the advantages quite precarious." Madison continued to push for the secretary of state in a letter to Eustis: "Nothing is wanting in the Western Country, to cure the evil proceeding from Hull but supplies of the necessary sorts, and a head to combine & apply the volunteer force every where springing into service. Without such a head, in which all wd. Confide, there is danger of much waste of military patriotism & money also; I am more desirous that Mr. Monroe should patronize & guide the efforts on foot." At the same time, he wrote Monroe that he wanted "a head that will inspire confidence, concentrate their force, and direct the application of it. I am not without hopes that in some way or other this critical service may proceed from you." The Monroe gambit depended on Madison bringing Thomas Jefferson into the cabinet as secretary of state, but it became apparent that the former president would not leave Monticello— thereby dooming the appointment of Monroe as commander of the northwestern army.[31]

Harrison realized he had exceeded his instructions in actively reorienting his orders to assist Hull in the defense of Detroit to the relief of the Indian siege of Fort Wayne. "It appeared to me necessary that some one should undertake the general direction of affairs here," he wrote Eustis, "and I have done it . . . [S]hould it be considered by the Government to have been improper, I shall, I hope, be pardoned for the purity of my motives." To his letter he added a personally written, deferential postscript: "I shall cheerfully acquiesce in any arrangement which the president may make & shall not think that I have the least right to complain at being removed from it."[32]

To Winchester, Secretary Eustis wrote that the "immediate object appears to be the protection of the Frontier," with Fort Wayne's relief receiving the highest priority. "You will also keep in view such further operations relative to the Michigan Territory & Upper Canada as may become expedient."[33] All this left the command relationship between Winchester and Harrison vague; who was to be in charge of a campaign to retake Detroit? Harrison received a letter from Eustis noting the president's desire to "regain the ground which has been lost by the Surrender of Detroit." Once the frontier was protected, Harrison was to join Winchester in the campaign against Detroit. Meanwhile, Eustis ordered artillery to be sent from Pittsburgh and volunteers from Pennsylvania and Virginia to join Winchester in Ohio. But the confusion on command relationships continued, for at the same time Eustis wrote Governor Return J. Meigs of Ohio that the Virginia troops would "cooperate" with Harrison's force.[34]

Eustis's instructions placed Harrison in command of troops in the Indiana and Illinois Territories. Harrison quickly undertook command of the newly raised Kentucky regiments and set his sights on the relief of Fort Wayne, then under siege by British-allied natives. He acknowledged receipt of the brigadier's commission but decided not to accept it until the command relationship between himself and Winchester was settled. He demanded of Secretary Eustis a determination of just "how far I am to be subordinate to" Winchester. There is, he pointed out, "a necessity of having one head in the Western Country to direct all the military Movements." Obviously, Harrison thought himself the better qualified. Winchester's "extreme solemnness," his lack of regional friends, and his ignorance of the local geography made him less qualified for senior command. "Woodsmen are a singular people," Harrison continued solicitously, "they are susceptible of the most heroic atcheivements but they must be taken in their own way. From the affection and attachment every thing may be expected, but I will venture to say that they never did nor never will perform anything brilliant under a stranger."[35]

Concurrently, Winchester wrote Eustis a letter implying he would subordinate himself to Harrison. But when Harrison and Winchester met at Fort Wayne on 19 September, Harrison issued a general order: "The President of the United States having designated Brigadier General James Winchester to the Command of the army originally destined to relieve General Hull and that officer having arrived at this place, the command is accordingly relinquished to him." But a few days later at St. Marys, Ohio, he told army officers that the latest message from Eustis did not resolve the question one way or the other.

He asked the officers to draft and sign a statement that their troops would rather be under his command than Winchester's.[36] They refused to follow this recommendation.

News of this incident was soon received by Winchester, who viewed it as a double cross and an indication of the governor's duplicity. One of Winchester's subordinates claimed that Harrison, from the time he connived to be named a Kentucky brevet major general until he was nominated for a similar regular army rank, "conceived and incessantly labored to execute a plan for the destruction of" Winchester's "military character, then the only barrier between him and the idol of his ceaseless exertions—the command in chief of the northwestern army." The venom spewed from Capt. S. G. Hopkins's pen indicates the level of contempt for Harrison that characterized his enemies. Such men saw the general as a "wily and unprincipled intriguer" and an "insidious though specious reptile."[37] But Hopkins had an ax to grind over Harrison's appointment, which had given Kentucky troops to the Indiana governor rather than to his father, who held a major generalship in the commonwealth's militia and should have commanded these troops.

Tensions between the two senior officers in the Old Northwest continued. When Harrison proposed they "divide the force and act in support of each other," Winchester disagreed, believing that he should direct a coordinated and maybe combined force. Nonetheless, Harrison began making plans for an expedition against the Indians along the southern shore of Lake Michigan, which was clearly within his operational area. Harrison continued to refuse the federal brigadier appointment because "it was the almost unanimous wish of the people of the Western Country that I should not accept of an appointment which would place me in a subordinate situation in this Army." Nor did the devolution of senior command on Winchester sit well with many who had participated in the relief of Fort Wayne. Richard M. Johnson, congressman and Kentucky militia colonel, wrote President Madison that the "united exertions of us all" could not reconcile the volunteers to the transfer of command. He continued the Kentuckians' extravagant championing of General Harrison: "He has capacity without equal. He has the confidence of the forces without parrellel in our History except in the case of Genl. Washington in the revolution." Johnson's father, Robert, hoped the president would not take the command of the North West Army from Winchester and give it to another. Appalled at the apparent replacement of Harrison in command of the North West Army,

Governor Meigs of Ohio urged he be retained in command or else "the Objects of the Campaign may be lost."[38]

Harrison left the Tennessean in command at Fort Wayne while he returned to Ohio. When he received an order from Eustis to join Winchester with newly arrived troops, Harrison would not subordinate his Kentucky major general-ship to Winchester. He forwarded the new troops to Winchester while remaining in the Buckeye state.[39]

Letters crossed back and forth between Harrison and Eustis and between Winchester and Eustis and between Kentucky political leaders and members of the administration, with no definitive resolution. When the president returned to the capital, he, Monroe, and Eustis finally reached a decision regarding the western command.[40]

In a letter to Clay, Monroe expressed a "willingness to obey the [Madison's] summons, altho. it was sudden, and unexpected, as indeed the event which suggested the idea was. On mature reflection however he [Madison] concluded that it would not be proper for me to leave my present station." Monroe then wrote the president that Major James V. Ball of the dragoons (who had served with Harrison during the Fallen Timbers campaign) "thinks that Harrison is much better qualified for the trust" of command than Win-chester. Finally, in mid-September, the administration decided that command in the West devolved to Harrison, "who it is believed will justify the favorable expectation entertaind of him, by those who are best acquainted with his merit." Monroe told Clay that he and his Kentucky allies "will find that the utmost attention has been paid to your opinions & wishes, on all these subjects."[41] Secretary Eustis sent notices to Harrison and Governors Meigs and Shelby, but apparently not to General Winchester, that the president assigned command of the North West Army to Harrison. When news of this decision reached Fort Wayne, the leadership of the North West Army passed to Harrison. But, by virtue of what commission was his superiority recognized? Harrison still declined to accept the federal brigadier generalship. He inquired of the secretary whether his seniority claim was the consequence of a dubiously legal Kentucky major general appointment or a presidential directive to a man without a federal officership.[42]

Thus it took a month after Hull's surrender to resolve the command situation. How much that delay affected the fall-winter campaign to retake Detroit is incalculable. The solution left Winchester deeply humiliated and desirous of proving his military leadership capabilities. It may well have affected Winchester's decision to march to Frenchtown, Michigan Territory, in January 1813, a move that led to the defeat of his force and the resulting "River Raisin massacre." That incident terminated the Harrison-Winchester rivalry; Winchester became a disgraced prisoner of war. There was now no competition for the senior post in the North West Army.

Federal Major General

Yet Harrison's brigadier general appointment had not been confirmed by the U.S. Senate. The key seems to have been Harrison's desire to keep his governorship at the same time. Senator Thomas Worthington of Ohio wrote General Harrison in November that senators were worried about the general's holding both the governorship and the generalship. They wanted him to resign the former to hold the latter. Worthington mistakenly noted that Hull had been required to resign his governorship when accepting the command of the North West Army. The senator expected that more major generals would be created and that Harrison would be a prime candidate for one of these posts. Worthington concluded his letter with an astute summary of Harrison's character:

> I presume you will not suspect me of flattery when I tell you you are ambitious and pray do not be surprised when I tell you too that you are not more so than I would have you be only I fear you are a little impatient and now let me add and with a sincerity of heart which I will ever manifest to my friends and with that pleasure which I shall always feel even in the anticipation of the gratification of their wishes. If your ambition is not most fully gratified it will be your own fault.[43]

As Mark Antony described Julius Caesar in one of Shakespeare's most famous orations, so Worthington correctly analyzed William Henry Harrison—he was an ambitious man. The Senate confirmed his brigadier rank on 2 December 1812. Senator Worthington admitted "that the western people are more partial than perhaps your services heretofore might strictly justify" such high rank, yet he "was fully satisfied they could not more properly have directed their choice or partialities in reference to future services."[44]

Even though the Senate approved his federal brigadier general rank in early December, Harrison refused to accept it. As late as mid-January 1813, he signed orders under the rank of "Major Genl. Kenty Quota."[45] It is obvious that he did not want any question regarding his rank to affect his position as commander of the North West Army. Meanwhile, alarm arose in Ohio that Harrison might resign his command unless he received a major generalship. Citizens in Hamilton County, Ohio, petitioned him not to leave his post. Arguing that his presence was "indispensably necessary for a continuance of that discipline and harmony, and implicit confidence, which we feel confident no other commander which government may please to appoint will ensure," the assembled supporters expressed their "ardent wishes" for the continuance of Harrison as the North West Army commander. This group resolved to petition the president to appoint Harrison a major general in the U.S. Army. A similar petition was sent by residents of Franklin County, Indiana Territory.[46]

Congressman Richard M. Johnson of Kentucky conveyed Harrison's resignation of the governorship to Secretary of State Monroe in early January 1813 and subsequently wrote President Monroe regarding Harrison's interpretation of the situation. The Indiana governor wanted a major general's commission should the opportunity arise. Before he accepted the brigadier general's commission, Harrison wanted a date of rank that placed him third or fourth on the list of brigadiers. Otherwise he would continue to exercise his command as a Kentucky brevet major general. He did not want any federal appointment that would make him junior to Winchester. Congressman Johnson strongly recommended Harrison for a two-star appointment.[47]

In a long letter to the new secretary of war, John Armstrong, written at Fort Meigs (modern Perrysburg, Ohio) on 16 February 1813, Harrison explained his problems of command and summarized the situation as it stood at that date:

> The date of my appointment as Brigadier, made me the youngest of that grade in the whole army (one only excepted) altho' the sphere of my command embraced two Militia Major Generals and a Brigadier of the Regular Army, who by the articles of war was entitled to command me. To the rank of Brigadier, I could certainly make no other objection than that it could not give me that authority which was necessary to effect the object of my command; I was obliged, therefore, to resort to my Kentucky commission, by which along, I was enabled to command gen. Winchester.—It was not, however, sufficient to warrant either gen. [Samuel] Hopkins [of Kentucky] or gen. [Elijah] Wadsworth [of Ohio] to receive orders from me, both of their commissions being of older date than mine . . . It appeared to me that from the difficulties which had occurred as well as from the importance of the Western Depart-

ment—that the appointment of Major Gen. was necessary to the officer who was intrusted with it. That there might be no obstacle to my obtaining it if the government should think me worthy of that rank, I determined to give up my civil appointment, which situated as I am with a large family and a very unproductive property was a great convenience to me, but I did not positively decline the appointment of Brigadier . . . I have never been so tenacious of rank as to suffer it to influence me for a moment in opposition to the public interest. My only aim has been to obtain that which appeared to me necessary to perform the duties assigned to me.

[Consequently] I resigned the government of Indiana, and intimated an intention to decline the appointment of Brigadier. The latter step was called for by the circumstances under which I received the command, which might give room for the suggestion that I was rather forced upon the government by the partiality and importunity of the Western people in my favour. As the affair now stands, it remains with the President to determine whether I shall continue in the command of the Northwestern Army . . . All that remains for me to say is, that I will continue in the command in any grade which he may assign me.[48]

Despite the final sentence, Harrison had thrown down the gauntlet: either promote me to a federal major generalship or I'll resign. With Hull and Winchester in disgrace, with the decision not to send Monroe, and with the major generals of the western militia willing to subordinate themselves to Harrison, the administration caved in. On 27 February 1813, President Madison sent two nominations to the Senate: Harrison to be a major general and Thomas Posey to be governor of Indiana Territory. The major general promotion received Senate approval on 1 March, and Posey's appointment came two days later. With this position Harrison also became commander of the newly created Eighth Military District, which included the states of Kentucky and Ohio and the territories of Indiana, Illinois, Michigan, and Missouri. As an additional responsibility he was to direct an invasion of western Upper Canada.[49]

His new superior, Secretary of War Armstrong, thought Harrison was "an artificial General—but the West and South, were only to be satisfied by his appointment, and our's is, you know, a Government of opinion."[50] Armstrong despised the use of militia troops when, so he thought, a much smaller contingent of regulars could do the job, and he was determined to restrain Harrison's use of militiamen and short-term volunteers in the future. Moreover, Harrison was not his kind of leader. Instead of wearing an elaborately decorated general's uniform in the field, Harrison wore a hunting shirt, not unlike most of his volunteer soldiers.[51] This endeared him to his subordinates but flew in the face of the conventions of a straight-laced former regular like Armstrong. The relationship between Armstrong and Harrison began strained and it never warmed.

His ambition gratified, Maj. Gen. William Henry Harrison now had to demonstrate a competence as military commander that, thus far, most of President Madison's appointments had failed to do.

Chapter Four

The Failed Counteroffensive

B oth the British and American leadership recognized that the critical North American strategic objective was the St. Lawrence lifeline to the lakes. British leadership saw the Midwestern natives as allies that might divert American military efforts away from this vital point. Thus the Indians found a willing ally in the British, but the lifeline between the St. Lawrence Valley and the Great Lakes was long and tenuous, and its disruption made military assistance difficult to obtain. Moreover, Canadian officials correctly concentrated their military assets in preserving the St. Lawrence line rather than focusing on the Great Lakes, particularly the upper lakes. So natives fought their war for cultural survival with only modest British military assistance and with promises of continued support that were subject to the whims of His Majesty's government's imperial interests.

Besides British naval dominance on the lakes, two key locations were vital to the maintenance or disruption of British military support and commercial intercourse between the Midwest and Montreal: Detroit and Michilimackinac. Detroit controlled the sailing vessel route between Lake Huron and Lake Erie, the most convenient and rapid way for the exchange of goods and military materiel between the Niagara portage and the upper lakes. Michilimackinac was the center of trade and communication between Lakes Huron, Michigan, and Superior and the vast interior of lakes, rivers, and forests that stretched beyond the Mississippi.

Three agents of British imperialism became essential ingredients in renewing British-Indian ties in the early nineteenth century: Isaac Brock (1769–1812), commanding general of British troops in Upper Canada and president of the Executive Council of the province; Robert Dickson (1765?–1823), a fur trader headquartered at Green Bay; and Matthew Elliott (1739?–1814), a British Indian agent operating out of Amherstburg.[1]

Major General Brock wanted to conduct offensive operations should there be an outbreak of warfare. This was particularly necessary because he relied on Native Americans, not only of his province but also of the Old Northwest, to stop any American invasion. In December 1811 he wrote Governor General Sir George Prevost that "before we can expect an active cooperation on the part of the Indians" we must capture Michilimackinac and Detroit. He believed such an achievement would encourage the natives to join with the British and encourage Canadian settlers to reconsider the possible success of their cause. Brock recognized that to protect their frontier from Indian depredations, the Americans would have to deploy troops across the Great Lakes region—troops that could not be used against critical Canadian targets. Unless this western diversion were instigated, he expected "an overwhelming force" to be sent against the Lake Ontario littoral and the St. Lawrence Valley. The Americans, he observed, were "an enterprising hardy race, and uncommonly expert on horseback with the rifle."[2] That capability might eventually spell the doom of the British military in the Midwest, but initial success in the western theater refocused American military effort in the secondary theater of the Upper Lakes rather than in the more critical Lake Ontario–St. Lawrence theater. Brock astutely evaluated the strategic consequences of undertaking offensive operations in the West. Subsequent events proved him eminently correct.

Brock also recognized the criticality of naval dominance on the Great Lakes: since no overland transportation net existed to support ground operations, naval superiority was essential to the protection of the Canadian shore from American invasion. Lake Erie was particularly vulnerable; "From Amherstburgh to Fort Erie," he noted, "my chief dependence must rest on a naval force for the protection of that extensive coast." He instituted cooperation between the provincial marine forces and the North West Company and its lightly armed vessels to combat the Americans' ground mobility and numerical superiority. But the provincial marine and fur traders were a slender reed on which to base a naval strategy.[3]

By aggressively attacking the weak upper Great Lakes frontier before the Americans were ready to focus on the decisive strategic targets, Brock envisioned an economy-of-force measure designed to use Native Americans, fur traders and their employees, and small contingents of British regulars and Canadian militiamen to divert the Americans from concentrating on the strategic lifeline of Upper Canada. Few generals have done so much with so few while at the same time placing at risk so many who stood to lose all should the Americans retain the line-of-lakes boundary negotiated in 1783.

Today Robert Dickson is virtually forgotten, but in 1812 he was a most critical partner in the British domination of the upper Great Lakes. Born in Scotland, he emigrated to Canada as a young man and became a fur trader in the firm Robert Dickson & Co., operating out of Mackinac Island. This firm eventually became part of the Michilimackinac Company. His anti-American business policies strained relations with the American authorities at Mackinac Island, and he was known as one who supported British interests in the region. He also had close personal and business ties with a number of embittered Canadian Loyalists. Because he was married to a Sioux woman, he maintained close kinship ties to that tribe and others operating between Lake Michigan and the upper Mississippi Valley.[4]

Writing for Brock, Capt. John B. Glegg sent a highly confidential letter to Dickson in February 1812. If war broke out between the United States and His Majesty's government, the Upper Canada leader wanted to know "the degree of cooperation" that Dickson and his friends "might be able to furnish" to a possible war effort. By return message Dickson promised that at least 250 voyageurs plus Indian allies would rendezvous by 30 June at Fort St. Joseph in the St. Marys River, not far from Mackinac Island.[5] Dickson secured Sioux, Menomonie, and Winnebago support for the war effort before news of the official opening of hostilities reached the shores of Lake Michigan. More than Tecumseh and his allies, these Native Americans risked their futures on British promises, even though they had not been affected by the Tippecanoe campaign or threatened by Hull's march to Detroit. While many Shawnee and Miami warriors waited to see the outcome of Gen. William Hull's Detroit campaign, these natives of the upper Great Lakes won two surprise victories over garrisons at Michilimackinac and Chicago that changed the military situation in the western Great Lakes and upper Mississippi Valley.

In January 1813 Dickson received an appointment as agent and superintendent "for the Indians of the Nations to the Westward of Lake Huron." At the same time, Maj. Gen. Francis de Rottenburg authorized him to tell the Indians that, this time, His Majesty's government would not forsake them: "My Children, listen not to the Songs of the wild birds who may tell you that the English will make Peace with the Enemy when it suits their own convenience without consulting your Interest. My words are pledged to you that this will never happen." And de Rottenburg warned that American land grabbing was unabated by temporary treaties: "The policy of the Big Knives . . . which they will never lose sight of and of which you have had so many proofs, is to possess themselves of all the Indian lands and to destroy one Nation after an other until they get the

Whole Country within the Rocky Mountains."[6] Unfortunately for the Native Americans, "the songs of the wild birds" were as truthful as the general's prophecy of American land-grabbing desires.

The final partner in this leadership triad was Matthew Elliott, superintendent of Indian affairs in the Detroit area. For many years he had lived with a Shawnee woman who bore him two sons. This provided him with a fictive relationship with that faction of the Shawnee opposed to collaboration with the United States. Although numerous Indian tribal leaders were apprehensive about close associations with the British after their betrayals in 1783 and 1794, Tecumseh and Tenskwatawa hoped to bring most of them to the British side should conflict break out between the United Kingdom and the United States. As it was, the largest share of Native Americans joining Tecumseh were the Potawatomi led by Main Poc.[7]

Harrison's Operational Plans, 1812

At the time of the declaration of war, the United States Army found its regular army regiments scattered in detachments of seventy or fewer men. For instance, the 1st Infantry Regiment was scattered from Fort Detroit to Fort Osage, Missouri Territory, east of modern Kansas City. The Detroit garrison had 50 enlisted men, Fort Dearborn (Chicago) 54, Fort Madison 40, Fort Wayne 70, Fort Osage 54, and Fort Bellefontaine (outside St. Louis) 68, and at Fort Knox, Indiana, the paymaster had a sergeant's guard of 6 men.[8] As was generally agreed, the small garrisons at Forts Michilimackinac, Dearborn, Wayne, and Detroit should be reinforced or evacuated; permanent garrisons required larger numbers of regular army soldiers.

While awaiting his possible federal generalship, Harrison faced the requirement to defend the Wabash Valley. In January 1812 Congress authorized the creation of six ranger companies, one of which was allocated to Indiana Territory. Secretary Eustis sent the governor blank commissions, which Harrison filled with a captain, two lieutenants, and one ensign. The enlisted complement consisted of four sergeants, four corporals, and sixty privates who were to serve for a year and furnish their own rifles or muskets, horses, and forage. As governor, Harrison received permission to mobilize the company and to "direct them to march to such places, and perform such duties, as in your judgement may be necessary for the protection of the frontier." When native hostilities increased in the spring, Eustis ordered Col. William Russell of the 7th Infantry,

in early May, to command the regulars in Indiana and the five ranger companies then serving there. Harrison received authorization to raise militia companies if the need for more troops arose. At the same time, the 4th Infantry
Regiment was sent to Cincinnati to support General Hull's march to Detroit,
although Harrison did have permission to delay the 4th Infantry's march until
he was "satisfied that the rangers & regular troops under Colonel Russell . . .
are equal to the protection" of the Indiana frontier. In the late spring, the territory's defense fell to these rangers plus one undermanned company at Fort
Harrison, commanded by Capt. Zachary Taylor, and another at Fort Wayne,
commanded by Capt. James Rhea. Eustis believed that Hull's pending march
to Detroit would deter Indian attacks on the Indiana-Illinois frontier.[9]

Colonel Russell, on the other hand, found himself confused about how
to deploy his troops along a five-hundred-mile frontier. He tried using his
mounted rangers as scouts, but soon dropped this course. Instead he planned
to construct "strong points" at Peoria and Prophetstown. He did not call these
"forts," but he planned to construct blockhouses to protect his men at these
locations. One of his biggest problems was keeping his rangers from attacking
friendly Indian villages. A member of the "force-'em-out-of-the-area" school
of soldiers, Russell argued for a policy of burning natives' villages and driving
them onto ever-smaller reservations. He saw the need to mount frontier regiments because their alacrity, mobility, and shock action could be decisive in
combating Tecumseh's warriors.[10]

An understrength company of infantry at Fort Harrison, another at Fort
Wayne, and a few companies of rangers seemed insufficient to defend the
northern Indiana and Illinois frontiers. But without British allies, Tecumseh and the Native Americans restrained themselves from all-out war. They
observed the concentration of American forces in Ohio as General Hull prepared to march to Detroit and presumably on Fort Malden and Amherstburg,
and they recognized the possible deprivation of the Indians' logistical lifeline.

By mid-May, Euroamerican settlers from Terre Haute to Vincennes withdrew from their villages and farmsteads to various fortifications. The Indiana
governor found his territory being depopulated, and this included his own family, which he sent to Cincinnati. The five hundred muskets Harrison received
from the federal government were quickly distributed to eager militiamen, but
the need was for hundreds more and there were none to be purchased in the
region.[11]

Governor Ninian Edwards of Illinois reported in May that he did not consider a major Indian attack probable. The losses in crops and munitions sustained during the Tippecanoe campaign had so depleted native resources that the chances of their attacking Illinois towns were low. In mid-June Capt. William Perry, commander of a ranger company at Piqua, Ohio, noted that although "the Indians appear peaceble," the settlers were "very much alarmed—and a great deal of uneasiness prevails amongst them for feare we [the rangers] will be called away to the Wabash." At Fort Wayne the new Indian Agent, Benjamin F. Stickney, wrote Hull that he had "lengthy conversations" with Tecumseh, who was going to Amherstburg to assess the situation with British authorities.[12] There can be no doubt that the mobilization of Hull's army and its threat to the natives' supply base at Amherstburg forced caution among most Indians from the Maumee to the Illinois Valley. As long as the British connection was tenuous, Tecumseh and his allies exercised restraint toward the American men and women of the frontier. There were certainly a few Potawatomi renegades who conducted scattered attacks on isolated farmsteads, but these did not constitute a significant threat to the American settlements in the Ohio Valley. Thus, unbeknownst to the American authorities, the most immediate native threat came not from Tecumseh's shaky confederation but rather from those Indians being gathered by Robert Dickson at Green Bay.

The Fall of Forts Michilimackinac, Detroit, and Dearborn

Hopes for a peaceable summer disappeared when information about a series of events reached both white and Indian ears. First was the news of Little Turtle's death on 14 July 1812. The warrior chief of the Miami, who was known for his leadership in the anti-American wars of the 1790s and subsequently resolved to live peaceably with the United States, had been a critical factor in restraining his fellow tribesmen from falling into the Tenskwatawa-Tecumseh orbit. Now his son-in-law, William Wells, found this influence lessening as more young Miami men drifted away from the old warrior's accommodationist path.[13]

The second dramatic event involved the fate of Fort Michilimackinac. As noted earlier, General Brock planned for the capture of the key American outposts at Detroit and Michilimackinac during the winter of 1811-12. His message to Robert Dickson at Green Bay was not received until early May, however, because the trader was operating in the upper Mississippi Valley. He met the couriers with Brock's letter at the portage of the Wisconsin and Fox Rivers and immediately gathered all the warriors he could to proceed with Brock to St. Joseph Island in the St. Marys River, just forty-five miles from Mackinac Island. Meanwhile, messages to the North West Company's operators at Fort William at Thunder Bay on the western edge of Lake Superior brought skilled Canadian boatmen to the same rendezvous point. British Capt. Alexander Gray, Army Deputy Quartermaster General, noted that the North West Company would exert "all the influence they possess over the Canadians and Indians to induce them to follow their Example" of supporting His Majesty's government should war break out. The Michilimackinac Company agent Toussaint Pothier reported that the company would exert all its energies to bring both Indians and Canadians to St. Joseph Island. Brock's adjutant wrote Capt. Charles Roberts at Fort St. Joseph with news of the American declaration of war and authorized him to "observe the greatest vigilance and Caution for the Protection" of his post and to cooperate with the North West Company representatives in the area, especially William McKay, one of the company's proprietors.[14] Dickson and Pothier combined warfare with economic advancement as their business ventures were being undercut by introduction of an American government factory system that traded for furs with Indians at a rate designed to undercut private fur traders. Thus the factories (as they were called) at Mackinac Island and Chicago threatened the fur trading enterprises of men like Dickson.[15]

Thirty-nine-year-old Captain Roberts was a sickly veteran of numerous Caribbean island campaigns who had received command of Fort St. Joseph the previous fall. He brought with him three officers, two sergeants, and forty-two rank and file of the 10th Royal Veteran Battalion plus three enlisted men from the Royal Artillery. Veteran battalions contained "meritorious Soldiers, who by Wounds, Infirmity or Age, are become unequal to the more active Duties" of regular infantry forces. One of Roberts's subalterns was a fifty-nine-year-old ensign. Obviously these officers did not come from families that could purchase their commissions, and for all of them this was an end-of-career assignment. The officers and men of this unit seemed more inclined to alcohol-drinking contests than military valor, and with its licentious reputation, Mackinac Island seemed an ideal place for them to garrison. The detachment constituted more a symbolic representation of the Crown's authority than a real military threat.[16] The major inducement for soldiers to come to this cold, remote, westernmost outpost of the British Empire was the offer of two hundred acres of land for doing so. Brock expected that his plan to place younger, energetic Canadian voyageurs and Indian warriors under Roberts's command would create a combination of vigor and military experience that could capture the weakly held American post.

Robert Dickson brought more than 100 Sioux, Menominee, and Winnebago warriors, and North West Company agent John Askin Jr. added about 280 Ottawa and Chippewa men. There seem to have been about 200 Canadians, some of whom were without arms. They also brought with them two six-pound cannons. This approximately 630-man British force greatly outnumbered the Fort Michilimackinac garrison of less than 60. Moreover, Dickson brought a familiarity with the island's topography that greatly assisted the endeavor.

Although Brock's letter of June 25 did not expressly authorize the Fort St. Joseph commander to conduct offensive operations, Captain Roberts understood that the window of opportunity was narrow. He assumed that Lt. Porter Hanks on Mackinac Island did not yet know of the declaration of war and would not be prepared for an attack. He also feared that General Hull's troops would reinforce the Michilimackinac garrison shortly after the Americans' arrival at Detroit. Besides, the natives were eager for combat and would abandon the endeavor if he did not act promptly. So on the morning of 16 July, just a day after he received Brock's somewhat ambiguous instructions, Roberts's small armada left St. Joseph Island, went down the St. Marys River, through Detour Passage, and around Les Cheneaux Islands, arriving at a rendezvous point off Mackinac Island at 0300 hours of the next day.

Shortly before the British-Indian departure, Lieutenant Hanks received information that something was afoot on St. Joseph Island and sent Michael Dousman to investigate. Dousman paddled to the Les Cheneaux island area, where he met the British flotilla "of 50 canoes 10 warriors in each, 12 Barges with 200 Canadians two Iron six pounders & 40 men of the 10th R.V. Battalion." (There may well be an exaggeration of the number of Indians or canoes in this statement by Askin.) The British captured Dousman and came ashore on Mackinac Island at 0600 hours. The strong Canadians hauled one of the six pounders to a position above the fort's landward side, and Roberts demanded Hanks surrender the garrison or he could not vouch for the Indians' behavior should the post be taken by assault. This threat of an Indian massacre of resisting Americans would be a common British tactic in the next several months. Finding the situation hopeless, Hanks surrendered the garrison.[17]

This victory rearranged the military situation in the upper lakes. "The Indians are flocking in from all Quarters," wrote Captain Roberts.[18] This happened not only in the Mackinac Straits area but also all over the Lake Huron and Lake Michigan littorals. Many who had been cautious but resentful neutrals now became defiant, committed opponents of the United States. British-favoring fur traders now had unimpeded access to Lakes Michigan and Superior and the natives who lived there. And with Mackinac Island under its control, the United Kingdom had a depository for military supplies and an ideal location for launching military expeditions to the west and south.

The news of the fall of Fort Michilimackinac impacted Gen. William Hull in Detroit, leading to the denouement of his expedition. Fearing that a combination of Indians from the north with the forces at Fort Malden would destroy his troops, now divided across the river, he withdrew his troops from Canada to Detroit. Part of Hull's concern was the increasing insecurity of his supply lines between Detroit and the Maumee Rapids. Finding his supply line to Ohio interdicted by British-Indian forces and fearing a wave of native warriors coming from the north, Hull found himself reduced to the defensive rather than the expected alternative.[19]

Making use of British control of Lake Erie, Gen. Isaac Brock transferred troops from the Niagara Frontier to Fort Malden. Hull did not oppose Brock's landing on the Michigan shore of the Detroit River. Given the wide number of landing options, this was probably a wise move. Using the threat of an Indian massacre if the Americans resisted, Brock demanded capitulation of the territorial capital, and on 16 August Hull surrendered.[20] For the second time the threat of a massacre was made but went unexecuted. Native restraint, however, reached its limits in Chicago.

Another consequence of the Michilimackinac surrender was Hull's decision to withdraw the garrison from Fort Dearborn. Capt. Nathaniel Heald commanded a depleted company of men trying to defend this remote outpost at the mouth of the Chicago River; to Hull this seemed a wasteful and perilous exposure of limited resources. Hull ordered withdrawal to Fort Wayne. He undoubtedly knew what Antoine LeClair reported in mid-July: the Indians from Milwaukee southward "were only waiting (and that with impatience) for the word from the British, and the first place they meant to attack was the Garrison at Chicago."[21]

Capt. William Wells, son-in-law of the late Little Turtle, carried Hull's order and commanded an escort of approximately twenty-five Miami from Fort Wayne. They arrived to find the Fort Dearborn garrison surrounded by over four hundred warriors of various tribes. Wells apparently told the Indians they would receive all the goods in the store at the post, including arms and ammunition, if they allowed the garrison to withdraw. But a consultation with Captain Heald concluded that the arms and gunpowder should be destroyed, which was done. The local Indian agent distributed the other store goods. Meanwhile, Potawatomi chief Main Poc sent a belt of red wampum (a symbol for war) and a message from Fort Malden, including notice of the fall of Michilimackinac and of Brock's successful crossing of the Detroit River. He also said that the British would provide the natives with the food, arms, ammunition, and clothing they needed.

Heald evacuated the post on 15 August, accompanied by two hundred military and civilians. As they walked along the sand dunes south of the Chicago River, they were ambushed by Potawatomi led by Black Bird. The Miami refused to assist the Americans, and when Heald surrendered, many of the prisoners were executed—including Wells, whose heart was removed and eaten by the triumphant natives. Heald and his wife were among the few who were taken captive and were eventually paroled.[22]

Young Indian warriors were facing starvation because of the loss of their crops and stores in raids like those by Harrison the previous fall and because of a drought that deprived them of even more provisions. They lacked ammunition for their weapons and were irritated by American unwillingness to provide it. They were deprived of normal commerce with the Mackinac traders because of the war and were motivated by revenge because of the dispossession of their lands. They were eager to take up the tomahawk against the United States.

The loss of Michilimackinac, Detroit, and Chicago completely unhinged the American defense in the Old Northwest. Britain and its native allies controlled the upper lakes, the key straits necessary for the transportation of goods and people, and the loyalty of most Indian tribes. Tecumseh and Dickson coordinated Indian attacks on posts from modern western Missouri to the Maumee Valley. Fort Osage in Missouri, Fort Madison in modern Iowa, Forts Wayne and Harrison in Indiana all came under attack. Some threats went as far as Vincennes and northeastern Ohio. General Brock's economy-of-force measure reaped rewards far in excess of what he probably expected.

But the "Chicago massacre" had a downside that Brock knew would adversely affect his objectives. The treatment of prisoners of war at Michilimackinac and Detroit was in keeping with the laws of war observed in the western world. But Captain Roberts's and General Brock's threats of massacre if there was resistance became reality on the sandy shore of Lake Michigan. There were no British at the engagement outside Fort Dearborn; however, agents of His Majesty's government endorsed an attack on Fort Dearborn and its garrison. The slaughter of the prisoners infuriated Midwestern settlers. Thousands flocked to join the various regular, volunteer, and militia units being organized in the region. Revenge combined with fear brought to the American flag many who might not have supported an invasion of Canada. Now the United States was the invaded country, and the panic over Indian terrorism became a recruiting tool exploited by General Harrison and the governors of the Ohio Valley states and territories.

The fall of these three fortifications underscores that there were two major native coalitions against the Americans. The first was that under the leadership of Tenskwatawa and Tecumseh, which saw their native lands and traditions facing a last-ditch stand. They operated mostly between Detroit and Chicago. The second was that coordinated mostly by the British-aligned fur traders operating from the upper Mississippi Valley and from Lakes Superior and Michigan to Mackinac Island. These Native Americans had experienced less of the British betrayal familiar to Tecumseh's group and were not immediately threatened by American encroachment, but they appreciated the traders' loyalty to them and saw alliance with the Crown as a means by which they could maintain their way of life.

Harrison was not alone in his apprehensions about native activities in 1812. In January, Governor Benjamin Howard of Missouri Territory reported that "our difficulties with the Indians are not at an end, and my own opinion is that so soon as the winter is over we have much danger to apprehend from them. I feel no hesitation in recommending a Campaign to be carried on in the Spring against the hostile Indians on the Illinois [River] for untill some of those tribes are punished we shall not have a durable peace with them." From Prairie du Chien, Nicholas Boilvin wrote that the "news of Govr. Harrisons Victory [at Tippecanoe] does not appear to please the Indians here." And writing from what is now northern Illinois, Maurice Blandau noted that the Fox Indians "determined to parish or revenge themselves on the Americans for what Governor Harrison had done [to] their nation." In the aftermath of Tippecanoe, Harrison was optimistic about the consequences of his victory. He thought "there will be no further hostilities."[23] But Midwesterners soon learned this was not the case. After the snow and ice melted, Indian attacks on isolated farmsteads began in earnest. An early April attack just four miles from Fort

Dearborn on the Chicago River resulted in the deaths of two men. Soon such depredations occurred as far distant as southwestern Ohio.[24] The militia officers of St. Clair County, Illinois, concluded in early February that the Indians were "in an actual state of warfare with the U. States, and that the said frontier inhabitants is as much exposed to the hostile violence of these savages as any other part of the Union."[25]

Thomas Forsyth, American Indian agent at Peoria, warned Governor Benjamin Howard of Missouri Territory "to acquaint Governor Harrison to be guarded in every quarter, otherwise they will make great havoc. You may rely that an Indian War is inevitable." He advised "the Governors of the different territories to set, immediately, all in motion against the Indians & to make use of every advantage against such barbarians which 'God & nature have put into their hands' for your Excellency may be assured that no conciliatory measures will do—the time is past for that & a War of extermination must do the business."[26] "A war of extermination" was just what many frontier settlers envisioned. Distinctions between friendly, unfriendly, and neutral natives were lost to many. Most settlers saw the British as collaborators in the bloody terror they witnessed taking place from the Missouri Valley to the Sandusky Plain. General Hull warned that the "first stroke with the Tomahawk the first attempt with the Scalping Knife will be the Signal for one indiscriminate scene of desolation. *No white man found fighting by the Side of an Indian will be taken prisoner.*"[27] This somewhat pretentious take-no-prisoners doctrine portended "a mutual and bitter exchange of atrocities in which no quarter was asked nor given."[28]

If concern with larger issues was not enough for political leaders, officials like Governor Howard found it necessary to give precise tactical orders to one of the captains of a ranger company. For instance, the company commander was to keep scouts out thirty miles in advance of his main formation and other scouts three hundred yards to the front, rear, and flanks of his column. With such inexperienced young men in command of independent units, the need for such ordinary orders to such junior officers by someone of the governor's position indicates the degree of amateurism in the newly raised units.[29]

General Harrison Takes Command

The three American disasters in the summer of 1812—the surrender of Fort Michilimackinac, the destruction of the Fort Dearborn garrison as it sought to evacuate, and the surrender of Detroit—dramatically changed the military situation in the Midwest. What Harrison intuitively recognized but never articulated was that the war against British regulars and Canadian militia required different tactics than those necessary to defeat the Indians. The first requirement was to preserve the surviving frontier outposts—Forts Wayne, Harrison, and Madison. The second was to retake the lost fortifications—Forts Detroit, Dearborn, and Michilimackinac. Finally, he presumed that fighting the British forces in formal combat required soldiers willing to stand and face British regulars and Canadian militiamen. He thereby assumed the dual obligation of destroying the Indian coalition and defeating the British Army and its Canadian allies. He knew the necessity of occupying what is now southwestern Ontario in the vicinity of the Detroit River to protect Detroit from future counterattack. Subsequent operations obligated him to retake Fort Michilimackinac and to regain control of the upper Mississippi Valley. To accomplish this he required both newly recruited regular army regiments and volunteer militia units from the Ohio Valley states and territories. Besides Kentucky and Ohio, this included western Pennsylvania and that part of Virginia now known as West Virginia.

In his earliest 1812 planning, Harrison never sought naval assets in the quest for military dominance of the Old Northwest. From the time Ensign Harrison reported for duty in Cincinnati and throughout his career in Ohio and Indiana, the transportation node of his world was the Ohio Valley and its river's greatest tributaries—the Kanawha, Muskingum, Scioto, Miami, Kentucky, Wabash, Cumberland, and Tennessee. Certainly he knew the importance of the great portage rivers—the Cuyahoga, Sandusky, Maumee, St. Joseph (of Michigan), Chicago, and Fox—that drained into the Great Lakes, but naval control of the lakes was something alien to his military understanding. In the summer and fall of 1812 he concentrated on the retaking of Detroit without naval assistance; this was predicated on the conclusion that there was no way an American naval force could be constructed, armed, and manned before the end of the shipping season. Only gradually did Harrison envision naval superiority on Lake Erie as a requirement for the reconquest of Detroit. His first intimation of any Navy Department effort on the Great Lakes came in a letter from Eustis dated 1 September.[30] Harrison had no reason to believe the navy would achieve dominance before he expected to control the Detroit River Valley that fall or winter.

Given the manpower at his disposal and the personnel weaknesses of his opponents, Harrison adopted a strategy of annihilation against the Native Americans—the overthrow of their military power. It fit neatly into his own and his regional contemporaries' war aims, which were expansive and involved total destruction of the Indians' war-making potential. As the Fallen Timbers and Tippecanoe campaigns demonstrated, it was not the tactical superiority of the Americans over native warriors that adversely affected the Indians' fighting capacity but rather the attrition strategy of destroying their fields and storage facilities, combined with killing the wildlife on which their hunting depended. All had to be conflated with severing their logistical connections with the British and thus forcing them to curtail warfare and sue for peace.[31] He also knew that the Americans must destroy the military capabilities of the British Army in the region. This required gaining control of Fort Malden and Amherstburg in Upper Canada, retaking Fort Michilimackinac, and, as he soon learned about it, gaining naval superiority on Lakes Erie and Huron.

The great weakness in Harrison's strategy of annihilation was that it required financial resources and logistical abilities in excess of what the young republic could provide and support. Throughout 1812–13 the Madison administration sought to constrain Harrison's desire for what those in Washington thought were excessive numbers of troops and the extravagant logistical expenses supporting them, which exceeded the economic resources of a nation fighting a war on several fronts outside the Old Northwest.

With his Kentucky brevet major generalship in hand, Harrison began to take charge of the defense of the Old Northwest, even though command relationships with James Winchester were still unclear.[32] His priorities for action included the following:

First, he would muster, train, equip, support, and project a new North West Army composed of regular, volunteer, and militia units.

Second, his first priority for action would be the relief of the Indian siege of Fort Wayne.

Third, he would retake Detroit and gain control of the Fort Malden–Sandwich area of Upper Canada.

Fourth, he contemplated destroying the hostile Indian forces in northern Indiana and the Illinois River region of Illinois Territory.

Fifth, he would retake Fort Michilimackinac. Once taken, this objective closed the route of British supplies to the natives west of Lake Michigan and hindered the Lake Superior supply line.

This was a complicated, diverse, overly ambitious set of objectives. The Eighth Military District was a huge operational area. Harrison immediately recognized the need for concentrating on the more threatened and strategically more important eastern areas of his district—Ohio, Indiana, and Michigan. He needed a subordinate to command operations in the western territories—Illinois (which included modern Wisconsin) and Missouri (including modern Iowa and Minnesota).

The Detroit defeat and the failures on Lakes Champlain and Ontario forced the Madison administration to reconsider its unwillingness in early 1812 to secure naval superiority on the North American Lakes. The strategic situation had changed; the conquest of Upper Canada involved more than just marching soldiers into the British province. Canadian Capt. William Merritt aptly summarized the reason for the British victories: "By means of the lake of which we had the entire command, we were enabled to transport from the different posts with little expense and greatest facility." Concurring with this summary of the tactical situation, Kentucky Capt. Robert McAfee diagnosed the "great want of foresight" of sending General Hull into Canada "without having taken the necessary measures to obtain command of Lake Erie."[33]

At the end of August, Secretary of the Navy Paul Hamilton ordered a redirection of departmental interest to the lakes. The president, he wrote Capt. Isaac Chauncey, USN, in New York, "has determined to obtain command of Lakes Ontario & Erie, with the least possible delay—and the execution of this highly important object is committed to you." He authorized Chauncey to purchase, hire, or build as many vessels as he thought necessary to gain control of the lakes. In addition to sailors and officers from New York, the secretary authorized Chauncey to bring ship carpenters, caulkers, riggers, sail makers, and other personnel to the lakes, as well as to requisition the naval agent in New York for clothing, ammunition, cannon, powder, small arms, and other munitions of war. Chauncey was to establish a headquarters at Sackets Harbor, New York, on Lake Ontario, and a subordinate headquarters at Buffalo, New York, on Lake Erie.

"You will cooperate with the American army" in your area, said Hamilton in the first directive to a service commander for joint operations. No such order went to Harrison from the War Department, but sending naval forces to Lake Erie was still in the future. In a second letter, Hamilton made an extraordinary prediction that he expected naval operations on Lake Erie to commence before those on Lake Ontario.[34]

Commodore Chauncey sent one of his young subordinates, Lt. Jesse Duncan Elliott, to investigate the situation in the Buffalo area for the construction of the Lake Erie squadron. While this was going on, an upper lakes merchant mariner came to Washington with his recommendations for where to build naval vessels on the lake. Daniel Dobbins of Presque Isle (now Erie), Pennsylvania, influenced the decision makers in Washington before Lieutenant Elliott's commentaries reached the national capital via Sackets Harbor.

Completely unknown to the Washington establishment, Dobbins secured an introduction to Secretary of State James Monroe, who sent him to the secretary of the navy. Nothing so demonstrates the urgency in late summer as the rapidity with which Secretary Hamilton digested Dobbins's advice, sent his intelligence information on Lake Erie's naval and commercial vessels to Chauncey, appointed Dobbins a U.S. Navy sailing master, and sent him back to the lake with a contract to build a forty-ton gunboat in Erie. All this was done over just five days in mid-September.[35]

At the same time, Lieutenant Elliott forwarded his commentaries after his visit to Buffalo. He could not find a safe, defensible anchorage on Lake Erie and therefore sought to build a construction base at Black Rock, a short distance downstream from the headwaters of the Niagara River. Even this site had its liabilities: the four-knot current of the river posed difficulty in bringing vessels upstream into the lake, the deeper water was on the north (Canadian) side of the river, there was a British battery that could fire on Black Rock (but American Gen. Stephen Van Rensselaer promised to eliminate it—which he did not), and the British had several armed ships in the vicinity. On the other hand, a good logistical support system and a road system were in place, construction personnel were en route, and several merchant vessels had taken refuge at Black Rock where they could soon be conveniently armed. General Van Rensselaer suggested that the emphasis on Lake Erie be curtailed and that the navy concentrate its efforts on the more critical Lake Ontario situation. Commodore Chauncey agreed, although Elliott started arming the merchant vessels at Black Rock. Before the winter season closed in, the enterprising Chauncey had temporarily secured naval dominance of the lower lake.[36]

More important for Harrison's campaign was a cutting-out expedition at the head of the Niagara River, led by Lieutenant Elliott. Anchored near Fort Erie on the Canadian side of the river were two brigs: the former North West Company armed brig *Caledonia* and the former U.S. Army brig *Adams*, renamed the *Detroit*. If these two ships could be captured and joined with the vessels being armed at Black Rock, Elliott believed he could change the balance of naval power on Lake Erie. He organized approximately one hundred sailors and soldiers into two boats that drifted downstream in the early morning hours of 8 October. They surprised crews of not-very-alert Provincial Marine, who surrendered the vessels—which Elliott then attempted to bring to the American shore. The *Detroit* ran aground on Squaw Island, and the Americans burned it to the waterline to make sure it would not be recaptured. The *Caledonia* was successfully brought to the American shore and added to the small American force being assembled at Black Rock. The *Caledonia* along with the merchant vessels *Amelia*, *Catherine*, *Ohio*, and *Zephyr* and the sloops *New Contractor* and *Commencement* were enough to give General Brock second thoughts about the status of British superiority on Lake Erie. With typical self-aggrandizement, J. D. Elliott addressed his after-action report directly to Secretary Hamilton instead of to his immediate superior, Commodore Chauncey. This little exchange on the Niagara River reduced the British Lake Erie squadron by two and increased the American squadron by one. Brock cautioned Sir George Prevost that the Americans were "making every exertion to gain a naval Superiority on both Lakes which if they accomplish I do not see how we can retain the Country."[37]

The balance of naval power on the lakes began slipping toward the Americans' favor that fall and winter. All-too-optimistic assumptions foresaw the United States Navy gaining control of Lake Erie's waters the following spring. Instead, it would take eleven months to achieve Secretary Hamilton's objective. General Harrison expected to achieve his goals long before the new fleet had been constructed.

While the navy discerned the importance of gaining naval dominance of the lakes, the army needed to set its organizational, personnel, and logistical house in order. The organization of the United States Army was rudimentary at best and in 1811 consisted of a secretary of war and a few clerks in Washington. There was no commanding general to advise the secretary, usually a politically connected individual with little military and administrative experience. As the leading authority on public administration during the years of the early republic concluded, "It must be recorded at the outset that the administration of army affairs before 1812 was wretched, and that while more adequate means of management were provided by Congress in 1812 and 1813, much too late, the record remained wretched throughout the conflict with Great Britain." The handicaps on military administration "stemmed from popular distrust of a standing army, which was part of the Republican ideology, and from the determination of the Republicans to economize on current expenditures until the debt was discharged."[38] At the start of the conflict there was no general staff to plan strategy, project the numbers of troops needed, or purchase and transport supplies to the desired locations—in other words, it was as though there was no preparation at all. The secretary of war had eight clerks, none of whom had more than a year's experience. He and this modest staff faced the enormous task of performing the duties of quartermaster general, commissary general, and master of ordnance while at the same time directing strategic policy, appointing senior officers, raising new regular army regiments, looking after Indian affairs, and paying pensions.[39]

Secretary of War William Eustis was an army surgeon in the War for Independence and had served in Congress for five years. Since his appointment to the post in 1809, he had become absorbed in the petty details of administration to the neglect of wide-ranging strategy. In the eyes of his contemporaries, he had a second-rate mind heading a third-rate organization. Senator William H. Crawford of Georgia (himself a future secretary of war) described him derisively in a letter to Monroe: "A Secretary of War who, instead of forming general and comprehensive arrangements for the organization of his troops and for the successful prosecution of the campaign, consumes his time in reading advertisements of petty retailing merchants to find where he may purchase one hundred shoes or two hundred hats . . . cannot fail to bring disgrace upon himself, his immediate employers, and the nation."[40]

As it moved toward open warfare with the British, Congress revised the supply and administrative departments. It reestablished the quartermaster department, reorganized the ordnance department under the commissary general for ordnance, augmented the Corps of Engineers, and removed military purchasing oversight from the Department of the Treasury to a commissary general of purchases. In Washington there was an adjutant general in poor health, a braggart as inspector general, an over-age, incompetent quartermaster, and a paymaster general so overwhelmed by the burden of his expanded role that troops mutinied for lack of pay. In June 1812 the inspector general admitted he did not know the actual strength of the army and its readiness for combat.[41]

Given the disorganization in Washington, one of the critical aspects of Harrison's command was to assemble a competent group of staff officers. At a crossroads in a career that would see him become a U.S. Army general, Lt. Col. Edmund P. Gaines became the North West Army's adjutant general. He was the chief administrative officer of the district, principally concerned with personnel and their assignment. Assisting him were Captains Nathaniel F. Adams and Robert Butler and Assistant Deputy Adjutant General Lt. Levi Hukill. Col. James Morrison of Kentucky received orders to be Harrison's deputy quarter-master general concerned principally with supply. John S. Wills became the judge advocate, with Ens. Charles S. Todd assigned as assistant judge advocate. Todd became a critical staff officer in varying capacities throughout Harrison's command of the North West Army. Col. Thomas Buford of Kentucky became deputy commissary for subsistence, and Col. John C. Bartlett served as the army's field commissary general. Critical in forwarding supplies from Cincinnati was Lt. James W. Bryson, who served as assistant deputy quartermaster there.[42]

Maj. Amos Stoddard became Harrison's chief of artillery, a post he held until his death during the first siege of Fort Meigs. The War Department sent Capt. Henry Brevoort as chief engineer and, as his assistant, Capt. Eleazer Wood. Brevoort was a hard drinker often unable to attend to his duties and hence not much appreciated by General Harrison. On the other hand, Wood, the seventeenth graduate of the new U.S. Military Academy, became one of Harrison's most trusted staff officers. He eventually served as the equivalent of the North West Army's operations officer. He designed and supervised the construction of Fort Meigs and directed the upgrading of the defenses of Fort Stephenson in Ohio. A versatile young officer, he would serve in combat roles in the artillery, cavalry, and infantry and held a brevet lieutenant colonelship before dying in a sortie from Fort Erie on 15 August 1814. Maj. James V. Ball of the 2nd Regiment of Dragoons served as Harrison's cavalry chief. Harrison also appointed additional staff officers, including some from among the volunteers, even though staff officers normally had to come from regular army units. For instance, Harrison named as deputy inspector general Henry Clay's brother-in-law, Capt. Nathaniel G. S. Hart of the 5th Kentucky Volunteer Regiment. Eustis eventually ratified this appointment.[43] Harrison augmented his staff with three Kentucky aides—Congressman Richard M. Johnson, William S. Hunter, and John Logan. Johnson championed the efficiency and effectiveness of mounted riflemen and became an ardent advocate of their employment.[44] He would become an important figure in the 1813 campaign as a mounted riflemen commander. The aides changed from time to time throughout the campaigns of 1812 and 1813. For instance, Colonels Duncan McArthur and Lewis Cass, captured at Detroit, served as Harrison's aides following their exchange. Both would become brigadier generals and governors, of Ohio and Michigan, respectively.

Logistical Issues

Victory on land or sea depends on three components: logistics, logistics, logistics. A tried-and-true army adage holds that "amateurs talk tactics, professionals talk logistics." Technically, logistics involves the planning and supporting of military forces through the acquisition, distribution, maintenance, and storage of materiel; the training, movement, and hospitalization of personnel; and the construction and maintenance of military facilities.

Mustering troops was not a problem in the fall of 1812. There was an overwhelming enthusiasm to officer and enlist volunteer regiments from Ohio, Kentucky, Virginia, and Pennsylvania and from the Ohio and Mississippi Valley territories. In fact, Eustis authorized and Harrison allowed an over-enrollment of troops far beyond military necessity and logistical capabilities. Given the limited size of his opponents in the Detroit River region, Harrison needed fewer troops than came to his aid and a much more sophisticated and efficient supply system than he could develop in the few months before winter set in.

From the beginning, General Harrison and Secretary of War Eustis—and his successor in 1813, John Armstrong—disagreed on how many and what type of units should be enrolled, trained, equipped, and marched. The national treasury became increasingly hard-pressed to meet the financial obligations of the war, and those in Washington wanted to keep expenses to a minimum. The western penchant for cavalry over infantry units greatly increased expenses because horses, tackle, and forage were far more costly than infantrymen. Since most cavalrymen furnished their own mounts, who was going to pay for losses due to illness, injury, combat, theft, and so forth? These may seem trifling problems, but they are the type that consumed time at the War Department and at the moving headquarters of the North West Army.

No greater problem confronted the war on the northwestern front than that of logistics. Shortly after naming Harrison as the region's commanding general, Secretary Eustis wrote the general, "As the difficulty of obtaining Supplies particularly of provisions, through the wilderness, appears to be one of the greatest obstacles with which you have to contend, which difficulty is well known [to] increase as the season advances, your own judgment, the information you possess & will acquire on this subject, will enable you to determine how far it may be practicable to advance & what posts or stations it may be expedient to maintain during the winter."[45] Eustis's letter book for September and October is filled with directives to governors, quartermasters, ordnance personnel, contractors, and others concerned with food, forage, uniforms, tents, weapons, gunpowder, cannon shot, and other items necessary to support an army in the field.

For instance, on 30 September, Eustis named Capt. William Piatt at Pittsburgh as deputy quartermaster general for the army on the Ohio frontier. A letter in early October gave his directions: "You will consider it among your first and most important duties to forward all the mounted Ordnance . . . while the Roads are good, without waiting for the Carriages, which must follow as soon as Major [Amos] Stoddard can prepare them. To facilitate your movements, you are hereby authorized to require any Commanding Officer [of] such Detachments of Regular Troops or Militia as you may find necessary . . . to furnish him [General Harrison] with Artillery; and until you receive his instructions, you will continue to forward the Ordnance to the Frontier."[46]

On 6 October, Eustis wrote Col. Duncan McArthur that the "public Agents & Stores in every Quarter are in requisition to meet the wants & conveniences of the Troops on the Frontier."[47] Yet all this effort could not rectify differences between Eustis and Harrison over personnel and policy and the logistical bottlenecks caused by competing agents and agencies for vessels, wagons, horses, oxen, teamsters, and other workers necessary to support a growing army.

As one example, Eustis named Maj. Ebenezer Denny at Pittsburgh as contractor for the commissary of subsistence for the army and directed Denny to establish deposit posts at Urbana and Piqua, Ohio. He also directed Capt. William Piatt to serve as deputy quartermaster general from Cincinnati. Harrison, to the contrary, named James White and John Piatt as special commissaries and James Morrison as his quartermaster general. Because Colonel Morrison and Captain Piatt held coequal authority, Harrison faced problems regarding who was responsible for what he wanted resolved at the War Department level.[48] The conflicting lines of authority and nature of duties contributed to the support confusion of the fall campaign. These disputes only helped to confound the supply situation in a region stretching from the Missouri Valley to the Cuyahoga Valley, where logistical support was inherently difficult, where Eustis was unfamiliar with both the geography and the personalities involved, and where the command relationship was confused.

One fairly astute transportation decision Harrison made was to employ as many ox teams as he could get to bring supplies forward, because oxen could "live on the food which the forests will furnish . . . whilst our horse teams

require a constant supply of grain." He authorized Colonel Morrison to purchase a hundred teams of oxen and wagons for the route to Sandusky, "being
convinced that purchasing will in the end prove more oeconomical than hir-
ing."[49] A frustrated assistant deputy quartermaster wrote directly to the president complaining that his counterpart in Pittsburgh forwarded inferior wheels,
axletrees, wagon tongues, and wagon bodies that contributed to the loss of
horses, many of whom were also sick and lame. In addition, the axes necessary
to clear roads "made by his [the Pittsburgh officer's] Brother in Law, are after
the enormous expence of transporting them to this place [Mansfield, Ohio] not
worth their weight in Iron." This same officer commended a Pennsylvania militia lieutenant who supervised twenty-five pioneers in building a road across
northern Ohio and exhibited "that order & regularity which Might be expected
from men better acquainted with Service."[50]

Mississippi Valley Command

Meanwhile, controversy emerged over control of the western portion of
the Eighth Military District. The two concerned territorial governors, Ninian Edwards in Illinois and Benjamin Howard in Missouri, felt that Harrison
neglected the Mississippi Valley.

Eustis had to instruct Edwards to suspend purchases of supplies unless on
Harrison's requisition. On 22 August, Eustis wrote to both Edwards and Howard reminding them that Harrison commanded all troops in their territories.
Later, the secretary reiterated to Howard that "General Harrison . . . is charged
with the defence of the Frontiers."[51] To these governors the general's focus on
Detroit meant that the Mississippi Valley settlers were endangered by exposure to the not-too-tender mercies of the natives supplied by fur traders. To
some extent the governors exaggerated Harrison's inattention to the western
portions of the district. He did order Col. John Miller's 19th Infantry Regiment
to Vincennes and Col. Philip Barbour's Kentuckians to Kaskaskia, Illinois. But
Harrison had to admit that both of these regiments were poorly armed and
equipped.[52]

Both of these governors seemingly recognized that natives and traders
hoped the upper portions of these territories would be returned to the British Empire at the war's conclusion. In fact, when he received Hull's surrender,
General Brock assumed that Hull surrendered both his soldiers and Michigan
Territory to the United Kingdom. This revanchist approach to the situation in

the West altered the balance of forces in the regions affected.[53] While Harrison attended to the Detroit River campaign, the whole West from Saginaw Bay to Green Bay, from St. Marys rapids (Sault Ste. Marie) to St. Anthony's Falls (modern Minneapolis–St. Paul), from the shores of Lake Superior to the banks of the Illinois River, lay in the hands of the natives and their allies. If the United States could not militarily reassert its presence in the region, the region could be lost at a peace treaty table.

A series of letters from Governor Howard and William Clark, the federal Indian agent in the trans-Mississippi West, delineated the problems along the Mississippi and its tributaries throughout 1812. In February, Clark noted that prospects of peace with the Indian bands in the Lake Michigan vicinity were "more gloomy than I could wish," and he proposed devising means to cut off their ability to communicate with British traders. He thought mounted rangers above the Illinois River were a necessity, and a post at Green Bay would deny British traders such as Robert Dickson commercial and military support of Winnebago, Kickapoo, and Potawatomie to the west and south of that point.[54] Just how the United States would support such a remote installation was never stated, but one must remember that this letter was written before the declaration of war.

Writing to Lt. Col. Daniel Bissell, commander of the U.S. Army garrison at Fort Bellefontaine near the mouth of the Missouri River, Governor Howard requested he move troops to protect a settlement a few miles upstream, as he assumed that "the object of the Govt in sending Troops here must be to afford protection to the People." Colonel Bissell also found himself beseeched by Governor Edwards to send troops to Illinois at the same time. Neither governor controlled federal troops in his territory. Were this not enough, Capt. Horatio Stark of the 1st Infantry, who commanded Fort Madison, pleaded that, given the increasing Indian threat, he did not have an adequate force.[55] Deficiencies in troop numbers, training, and equipment, a huge territorial obligation, and a numerous, wily, and feared opponent all made the defense of these territories difficult and frustrating.

Howard feared the Indians were concentrating their strength in the vicinity of modern Peoria where "the extensive navigable rivers, emptying into the Mississippi . . . hold out inducements, to an extensive enterprise against" Illinois and Missouri. So in May, Missouri's governor personally led a company of rangers commanded by Capt. Nathan Boone and a small detachment of 1st Infantry regulars to a site on the Mississippi (about ten miles south of modern

Hannibal) to establish a small outpost named Fort Mason. He claimed the site was more defensible than Fort Madison in modern Iowa. That a territorial governor paid such close attention to tactical fortifications says much about General Hull's lack of concern for the western portion of his theatre of operations.[56]

By September, Howard found the situation even more desperate: "The entire failure of our arms on the upper Lakes has placed this Country in a most dangerous situation, not one liable merely, to much injury, but to total overthrow." He feared not only the Indians but also that the French and British traders in the vicinity might combine against his government. There were, he believed, British scouts in the St. Louis vicinity. He sought a regiment of regulars to come to St. Louis as soon as possible. But he noted that the regular officers, "however, long they may have been in service, and whose views of military operation have been confined, to the ordinary routine of Garrison duty are . . . of little consequence."[57] This may well be a not too subtle attack on Colonel Bissell's leadership. Thus Howard estimated the situation shortly after Harrison took command of the Eighth Military District.

Shortly thereafter, the two territorial delegates to the U.S. House of Representatives told the secretary of war that more companies of mounted rangers and two regiments of six-month volunteer mounted riflemen (following the example of those raised by Kentucky Congressman Richard M. Johnson) were critical to the protection of frontier settlements. They asked that a regular brigadier general and his staff be appointed to coordinate operations in the Mississippi Valley region. These troops would not only provide frontier defense but also allow the construction of forts at Peoria and Prairie du Chien and offensive operations to retake Chicago and Michilimackinac. (They did not describe just how the latter was to be achieved from the Mississippi Valley.) They also advocated building three "bullet proof" gunboats to cruise the major waterways to prevent Indians from utilizing these routes for their attacks.

Both congressmen recognized that the long-term obligations of regular army duty were incompatible with the economic situation on the frontier. They noted that volunteers could be raised after the planting season and for a duty of three months or longer, but only "when it was known that at the completion of their time other patriotic men would take their places and that they might then return to their usual occupation."[58] This requirement for limited tours of duty did not sit well with those in Washington, especially with John Armstrong, the incoming secretary of war.

As noted above, Eustis constantly had to remind the two governors and congressmen that Harrison commanded the troops in the Eighth Military District and that they should communicate their desires through him and his staff.[59] At the same time, Governor Edwards discovered he could not compel regular army lieutenants to obey his orders unless Colonel Russell directed them to do so, and his requests for assistance from the governor of Kentucky went unanswered. The governors claimed they did not demean all activities by the regulars in the Mississippi Valley—for instance, Colonel Russell and his 7th Infantry Rangers raided a large Indian village at the head of Lake Peoria in October.[60] However, for several months the problems of military command and operations in the Mississippi Valley would become a major issue among authorities in that region, General Harrison, and the War Department.[61]

Defending the Midwest

The campaign to defend Illinois, Indiana, and Ohio continued. The results did not redound to General Harrison's reputation as a military commander. The Indiana governor faced increasing small-party raids against farmsteads as close as five miles from Vincennes. These raids, he wrote Secretary Eustis, are designed to distract and divide the settlers and thereby prevent the militia from turning out for duty away from their home communities—"and certainly no plan could be More Successful than that which they have fallen upon." Militiamen refused calls to serve because they felt compelled to defend their homes, families, and farms. But Harrison did have a limited number of short-term rangers that he deployed beyond the settlements who were to reconnoiter 150 miles of frontier. Their presence made it "impossible for any large number of Indians to pass them unobserved and very difficult for a Small party" to elude their observation.[62]

Still, Lt. Col. James Noble of the 7th Indiana Militia Regiment wrote that the "minds of the people are much agitated, upon the reports of the different murders, committed on the frontiers of our Territory by the Indians." To keep more residents from fleeing Franklin County, he sent a rifle company to the west branch of the White River where they would construct two blockhouses and act as rangers in that area. Harrison understood the problem of evacuating the territory, which was fast depopulating "and will no doubt continue to do so until effectual measures are taken for its protection."[63]

The governor sought to employ the friendly Delaware as a screen against water-bound and overland-marching hostiles. They were, he reminded the secretary, a people of "Uncommon faithfulness" to the United States, but "the bravery of their Warriors and their intimate acquaintance with our Settlements" made them a possible foe of greater potential than any other tribe. For this reason, he sent Maj. Davis Floyd as a special messenger to the Delaware with the hope of keeping them in the American camp. Floyd's efforts proved most fruitful, and Harrison assured Secretary Eustis that the Delaware were "entirely to be depended on" and "have determined to follow the Wishes & directions of the President."[64] In this manner he used a time-tested Euroamerican tactic of utilizing friendly Indians against hostile ones.

With mobilization of the Indiana militia, Harrison faced another recurring problem: how to pay for the volunteer troops, uniforms, weapons, munitions, equipment, food, and forage. He asked Eustis whether the federal government would assume these obligations.[65] They would be compensated eventually, but it took a long time.

Concurrently, Capt. Zachary Taylor at Fort Harrison notified the governor that a large number of hostile Indians were in his vicinity. After reading Harrison's dispatches, Eustis authorized the governor to halt the movement of the 4th U.S. Infantry to Ohio until the replacement troops under Colonel Russell and the territorial militia were "equal to the protection" of the Indiana frontier. Harrison feared that Vincennes was endangered, and he began fortifying his large brick home, Grouseland, and other prominent edifices in the town.[66]

A council with Indians at the Miami village of Mississenwa in modern Miami County, Indiana, in mid-May seemed to relieve the situation for a while. Isadore Chaine, a mixed-blood Wyandot who served as a British emissary, cautioned peace as long as the Americans had not gone to war against His Majesty George III. Tecumseh blamed the Potawatomi for both the attack at Tippecanoe and the spring raids into Illinois, Indiana, and Ohio. More importantly, he scorned the accommodationist chiefs who sold Indian lands that belonged collectively to all Indians, not to individual tribes. Writing to Christopher Greenup of Kentucky, Harrison said he had "no faith in the sincerity" of the Mississenwa council declaration of peaceful intentions toward the United States. Moreover, Tecumseh and Tenskwatawa reestablished the Tippecanoe village (Prophetstown) and there augmented their warriors to a force equal to that of the previous November. Harrison concluded "that their intentions were entirely hostile."[67]

Because the United States had not declared war against the British, Chaine cautioned the natives not to expect significant support out of Malden. Thus the combat in the spring and early summer consisted of depredations by small raiding parties that frightened settlers but did not endanger major communities and fortifications. Chaine moved to Tippecanoe, where he displayed two sets of wampum—one white, indicating peace; the other red, indicating war. The latter he shared only with those most hostile to the Americans.[68]

With the declaration of war in June and the fall of Forts Michilimackinac, Dearborn, and Detroit in July and August, the situation underwent a dramatic change. The Indians found themselves released from any British restraints. In the period between the declaration of war and the fall of Detroit, Harrison undertook to assist General Winchester in Cincinnati in organizing an expedition to provide the necessary supplies to Hull. This was made difficult by a series of circumstances. The first was geographic: the Black Swamp (between the Auglaize River and the mouth of the Maumee) either had to be crossed with difficulty or circumvented via the St. Marys River in western Ohio to Fort Wayne and then down the Maumee. From there one had to follow a swampy road along Lake Erie's western shore to Detroit. The second problem was the British command of Lake Erie, which allowed them to intercept supply trains by crossing the Detroit River at a time and place of their choosing. To overcome these difficulties, Harrison proposed a "covering Army" large enough to protect the large logistical convoy necessary to relieve Hull's force. But he realized that the chances of acquiring the necessary troops and supplies in time to assist Hull in his dilemma were limited.[69]

In the midst of this concern for Detroit, natives began full-scale attacks against Forts Harrison, Madison, and Wayne. While Governor Harrison feared Fort Harrison at Terre Haute and Fort Knox at Vincennes would come under attack, Fort Wayne became his first objective. There is little indication that he paid much attention to the defense of the Mississippi Valley as represented by Fort Madison. After the fall of Detroit, Indians began a siege of Fort Wayne, and British artillerymen were expected to reinforce them. The artillery did not arrive before Harrison relieved the siege on 12 September. Utilizing his Kentucky major generalship, Harrison ordered Kentucky Gen. John Payne to march from Cincinnati toward the Indiana outpost. Supply shortages delayed Payne's advance. He sent one company of mounted infantry in advance of the Fort Wayne expedition, hoping it could relieve that fort before the main body arrived.

Logistical support became an increasing problem. Even regular regiments were without arms and supplies. For instance, regular army Col. James Miller's 4th Infantry recruits were without arms and received orders to await them in Cincinnati while those with weapons went to Vincennes. Kentucky Lt. Col. Phil Barbour's regiment went to Kaskaskia without being fully armed, under the expectation that the weapons would be forwarded to them before they engaged in combat.[70]

Considerable concern existed regarding Harrison's authority over regular army Colonel Russell's troops in Illinois and that officer's desire to engage in offensive warfare. Harrison feared that the termination of hostilities after the Mississenwa council would be endangered if Russell went on the offensive. In fact, in early June, Harrison anticipated a low probability of offensive operations and sent several volunteer units home.[71] Hull's army en route from Cincinnati to Detroit temporarily raised a level of caution among the Indians of the Old Northwest.

In mid-August the situation changed. War had been declared, Forts Michilimackinac, Dearborn, and Detroit had fallen to the Indians and British, and native warriors rallied in opposition to the Americans. By then Winchester and Harrison commanded approximately twenty-one hundred men at Cincinnati, with various degrees of materiel, training, experience, and enlistment times. Winchester left Harrison in charge as he went to Kentucky for more recruits and supplies. When word came of the Chicago massacre, Harrison relayed this information to Eustis. Shortly thereafter he learned that several hundred Indians had besieged Fort Wayne since 5 September. As a forlorn hope, he sent a message to the garrison that a relief force was on the way. The messenger made it through, and the news encouraged the defenders to continue their resistance in defiance of the post's usually intoxicated commander, Captain Rhea. The defenders beat off two serious assaults from several hundred natives, who maintained the siege and awaited the arrival of a British force coming up the Maumee with light artillery.[72] A race ensued between the Americans and British over which contingent would arrive first.

General Harrison organized a campaign to relieve Fort Wayne from the Indian siege—his "first object" after receiving the news of Detroit's capitulation. He spent the last days of August in Cincinnati, dictating general orders to his troops, ordering Kentucky regiments to proceed across the Ohio River as soon as possible, and sending messages to Secretary Eustis, Acting Governor of Indiana John Gibson, Kentucky Governor Isaac Shelby, Brig. Gen. James Winchester, Ohio Senator and Gen. Thomas Worthington, Speaker Henry Clay, Assistant Deputy Quartermaster James W. Bryson, and others.[73] The letters to

Eustis and Clay concerned matters of regional strategic and logistical policy, those to the various governors and generals concerned their state and territorial troop deployments, and those to Lieutenant Bryson provided detailed directions on what quartermaster supplies should be forwarded and to what destinations.

Typically citing examples from ancient history, Harrison acknowledged Fort Wayne was in imminent danger, and he wrote Clay that he had "an army competent in numbers & in spirit equal to any that greece or Rome have boasted of but destitute of Artillery, of many necessary equipments & absolutely ignorant of every military evolution, nor have I but a Single individual [Capt. Nathaniel F. Adams] capable of assisting me in training them."[74] Harrison became dismayed about the military competence of the Ohio volunteers assembled in Cincinnati and the logistical inadequacies confronting a movement northward. Unlike Anthony Wayne, he could not spend two years training his army. He expected more reliable Kentuckians would arrive shortly, and they did.

Almost simultaneous with the Fort Wayne siege, the natives began one against Fort Harrison. Captain Taylor commanded only fifty men, most of whom, including the commandant, were convalescing from a virulent fever. Only twelve were healthy when the garrison learned on 4 September that two settlers had been killed just outside the fort. When natives informed Taylor that their chief would parlay with them the next morning, Taylor, conscious of the same ruse used at Tippecanoe to lull the Americans into a false sense of security, did not take the bait and alerted his guards to maintain constant vigilance. Before midnight, sentinels discovered Indians advancing on the outpost, and Taylor brought his entire garrison to the defense. Even though the Indians were able to set one of the post's two blockhouses on fire, Taylor's men contained the fire and repulsed the attack.[75]

A third native attack occurred at Fort Madison, on the Mississippi some twenty-five miles above the mouth of the Des Moines River in Missouri Territory (modern Iowa). On 5 September some two hundred Winnebago attacked the small garrison commanded by Lieutenants Thomas Hamilton and Barony Vasques of the 1st U.S. Infantry. The Winnebago warriors laid siege for three days, but the stalwart defense of the outpost by the regular army infantrymen discouraged their assailants.

The successful defense and relief of these three frontier outposts by late summer saved the whole region from Lake Erie to the Mississippi from Indian depredations.[76] Fortunately for the Americans, none of the Indian attacks involved British artillery, otherwise the outcomes would probably have been different.

After the relief of Fort Wayne, Harrison began organizing raids on the villages participating in the siege. Col. Samuel Wells commanded a detachment of Kentucky and Ohio mounted riflemen and four companies of the 17th U.S. Infantry Regiment against a Potawatomi village at Elkhart. Brig. Gen. John Payne commanded two regiments of Kentucky militiamen that raided recently abandoned villages on the upper Wabash, where they destroyed the Indians' homes and fifteen hundred bushels of corn. Even Little Turtle's town had to be destroyed because the Miami chiefs were unable to control "the licentious part of their tribe."[77]

For some Indians, these raids and the successful defense of Forts Harrison, Madison, and Wayne tempered their military optimism. In early October some Miami leaders came to Fort Wayne with the hope of securing peace. Harrison described them as "prepared to palliate or deny the hostility of their tribe," but when confronted with Harrison's evidence establishing their aggressions in previous months, they "threw themselves upon the mercy of the President." Harrison thought them duplicitous and demanded they convey five of their more notorious chiefs for custody in Piqua before he would recognize their solicitations as genuine.[78] It is clear that Harrison wanted more guarantees than mere words before he would terminate his raiding strategy. Nonetheless, these initial peace probes constituted a break in the solid wall of hostile native warriors against the United States. Harrison, however, needed more obvious demonstrations of his military dominance before he was going to see significant fractures in Indian determination to wage war against the "Long Knives."

Harrison proposed gathering between eleven hundred and eighteen hundred cavalrymen and making a surprise attack on Detroit by heading north from Fort Wayne and then riding down the River Raisin to a point south of Detroit. This maneuver would circumvent the traditional route via the Maumee Rapids crossing at modern Perrysburg, Ohio. At the same time, Harrison recognized that such an expedition would outrun its ability to resupply itself and leave it vulnerable to being cut off by British and Indian forces from Fort Malden.[79] In other words, this cavalry expedition might find itself in the same isolated dilemma that Hull had faced the previous summer. Moreover, such a campaign required a coordination between Harrison and Winchester that the strained command situation precluded. It never came to fruition.

As it became increasingly probable that Harrison would become commander of the North West Army, he began directing the campaigns against Detroit and the Native Americans allied to the British. Secretary William Eustis and he coordinated a huge mobilization of personnel, equipment, munitions, horses, and artillery toward the southeastern portion of Michigan Territory and across the Detroit River where Fort Malden lay. Other operations conducted against Indian villages between Chicago and St. Joseph, Michigan, attempted to prevent the natives from harassing American settlements in Indiana and Illinois Territories. Their disappointing outcomes were largely the consequence of leadership failures, logistical complications, short-term enlistments, effective British and Indian opposition, geographic impediments, weather difficulties, and misfortune.

There can be little doubt that Harrison's presence invigorated many of those disillusioned by the fall of Detroit. One correspondent to the Zanesville *Messenger* noted that the general's "presence appears to inspire every person with courage, and make even cowards brave." In a dramatic attack on Hull's leadership, the writer concluded "that the American army will no longer be commanded by an old woman." At the same time the general talked to the friendly Shawnee of Piqua and promised them protection.[80]

General Harrison waged two different campaigns against his foes. Against the natives he employed the centuries-old tactic of raiding their villages, depriving them of homes, fields, and storage facilities, and consequently forcing them to sue for peace or to flee to British-held areas for sustenance. The latter consequence, of course, placed increased stress on the British supply system as it expanded to support Indian warriors and their families. So long as they controlled the Great Lakes lifeline this would work, but if they lost it, the difficulties of supplying the soldiers, settlers, warriors, and families would jeopardize their entire effort in Michigan and the Western District of Upper Canada.

The second campaign involved a persisting strategy directed toward the recapture of Detroit and taking of Fort Malden, elimination of the British Army in the region, and restoration of American government in Michigan Territory. This objective required the mobilization of a large, conventional military force directed against His Majesty's soldiers and their native allies in the Detroit River region. It also necessitated a huge logistical effort over wilderness terrain with few roads, a densely forested countryside, and impassable swamps where a wily foe impeded American efforts.

At St. Marys, Ohio, Harrison paraded his army, assembled the troops in a hollow square, and mounted a wagon to address them. The affable general wore his customary hunting shirt as he described the absolute necessity of subordination in the military (something he may have violated in his pursuit of rank) and confidently predicted retaking Detroit and reducing Fort Malden before Christmas. With his permission, the thirty-day volunteers went home, and he stationed the six-month men in local garrisons.[81]

At the same time, Harrison directed Kentucky Maj. Gen. Samuel Hopkins to command the troops operating along the Wabash and Illinois Rivers.[82] This allowed Harrison to concentrate his efforts toward northwest Ohio and the Detroit River region. Hopkins, however, proved a weak commander on whom to rely for the western Indiana and Illinois frontiers.

There is no better example than that in October when the elderly Kentucky militia general, commanding U.S. troops in Indiana and Illinois, failed as a senior officer. Hopkins's two thousand Kentuckians crossed the Wabash at Fort Harrison on 14 October with ten days' rations and headed into Illinois. His troops became lost and mutinied, and he finally led them back to Fort Harrison in disgrace. Like so many Revolutionary War veterans who assumed major commands in this war, Hopkins was not up to the task. Kentucky Governor Isaac Shelby reacted with frustration: "This event has terminated most dishonourably to the Volunteers." Harrison responded by bringing charges of incompetence against Governor Edwards. However, the Illinois territorial legislature complimented Edwards's conduct and was highly critical of the failures to pay troops, contributing to a decline in patriotism and enlistments in the area until rectified.[83] Of course, the antagonisms between Harrison and the Mississippi Valley governors and generals increased as a result of this episode.

Maj. Gen. Sir Isaac Brock was mortally wounded at the Battle of Queenston Heights (13 October 1812), but his strategic concept of offensive operations in the American Midwest—diverting extensive American military assets to the Mississippi Valley and the upper Great Lakes frontier through a massive economy-of-force effort—was successful throughout 1812. It continued to affect American military policy for the remainder of the war. Every month of occupation at Detroit and Michilimackinac kept American troops and materiel focused away from Upper Canada's more vulnerable and strategically decisive points on Lake Ontario and in the St. Lawrence Valley. It remained to be seen whether control of these two locations could be maintained by the British and Indians and whether the politicians in London would again sacrifice the interests of Indians and fur merchants for the perceived larger well-being of His Majesty's dominions. Those natives allied to the British risked everything they had in one last desperate gamble to salvage their lands and culture.

Before winter set in, the British and their fur trading allies forwarded large quantities of goods to the frontier and deposited them at Mackinac and St. Joseph, Michigan, and at Prairie du Chien. Governor Edwards recognized that these supplies kept the Indians allied with the British, who would "not cease to employ the Savages against the U.S." Moreover, until General Harrison succeeded in cutting off all British transportation routes via Mackinac, Edwards recognized that the British could keep up the hopes of the natives between the Mississippi and Lake Michigan "from whom we have most to apprehend and they already have got their supplies." The governors understood that American control of the Detroit River area was not enough to stop the British from maintaining supply routes to their territories. Both Howard and Edwards saw the necessity of employing mounted troops and gunboats on major rivers to defend their settlements. Echoing these sentiments were Shadrach Bond and Edward Hempstead, the two territories' delegates to the House of Representatives.[84]

In April 1813, Secretary Armstrong issued an order promoting Governor Howard to brigadier general and authorizing him to have a "special command" in the western part of the Eighth Military District, commanding both regular and militia troops in the territories of Illinois and Missouri.[85] In effect, this order allowed Howard to operate independently of Harrison, who concentrated his efforts in the Detroit campaign. Harrison remained uninformed of this modification to the district's command structure.

Logistics Again

The district commander began his fall 1812 campaign by directing Winchester to advance down the Maumee from Fort Wayne and establish a post at the Maumee Rapids. With the leaves starting to turn, Harrison found himself facing chronic problems of logistics. At St. Marys there was neither the expected number of cavalrymen nor the required number of mounts for those that had arrived. Instead of two thousand mounted men he found only eleven hundred, enough to conduct raids on Indian villages along the upper Wabash and upper Maumee Valleys but not enough to stage a *coup de main* on Detroit.[86] As we shall see, his raiding strategy began in earnest in September.

As indicated by the volume of letters and orders Harrison issued in late

September, he was in thorough command of the situation and cognizant of the difficulties he faced. Adequately arming and provisioning his troops was a constant problem. In one instance he kept Kentucky cavalrymen because they were the only such troops with sabers and pistols. He lamented that many of his dragoons were armed with muskets rather than rifles. He directed Winchester to advance with two thousand regulars, Kentucky volunteers, and dragoons to the confluence of the Maumee and Auglaize Rivers where old Fort Defiance lay in ruins. Because that site was denuded of timber, he suggested Winchester establish a new post across the river. However, the Tennessean had the fort built a few yards from the old site. The new post would be named in Winchester's honor.[87] All this was in preparation for the attack on Fort Malden and Detroit.

Meanwhile, Eustis began to recognize the logistical problems and their impact on operations in the Old Northwest. He wrote Harrison, "As the difficulty of obtaining Supplies, particularly of provisions through the wilderness, appears to be one of the greatest obstacles with which you will have to contend, which difficulty is well known [and] increases as the season advances, your own judgement . . . will enable you to determine how far it may be practicable to advance & what posts or Stations it may be expedient to ma[i]ntain during the winter." Concurrently, Harrison asked Maj. Ebenezer Denny in Pittsburgh to restrain his purchase of rations in Pennsylvania and establish a depot at Cincinnati where they might be acquired more cheaply. He recalled his experience on Gen. Anthony Wayne's staff regarding difficulties in procuring supplies from Pittsburgh when they might be more conveniently secured in Ohio. Thus he limited Denny to four hundred thousand rations from Pittsburgh until he received directions from Eustis. Attempting to shorten the supply route to support Winchester's advance, Harrison ordered Col. William Jennings of the 2nd Kentucky Militia Regiment to follow the Auglaize River toward what is now Defiance, Ohio. Jennings's men were to escort packhorses to Defiance and establish a road along the river, as well as two blockhouses. The size of this operation boggles the imagination—it involved at least 145 packhorses (carrying flour) and 240 beef cattle. Colonel Jennings deemed it "impracticable to take care of the cattle upon a march" while at the same time he was to open a road and construct blockhouses.[88]

But logistical problems hampered every effort. Maj. Richard M. Johnson's mounted riflemen had to be withdrawn from Fort Wayne to St. Marys because of the lack of grain for their horses. Harrison requisitioned 550,000 rations for

Urbana and St. Marys and expected to have 300,000 of these at the latter point and at a more forward station before the end of September. Additional requests for packhorses and quartermaster supplies amounted to $10,000, a huge sum for that day.[89]

Forwarding supplies down the St. Marys and Auglaize Rivers proved difficult. Eventually the army established a boatbuilding site at St. Marys, which provided the means to use that waterway to Fort Wayne and then down the Maumee. Winchester left Fort Wayne with six days' rations, and he desperately needed to meet with Colonel Jennings's pack animals to continue. Low water levels due to the drought on the Auglaize hampered its being used. Winchester also needed his troops' baggage forwarded since it contained their winter clothes. Like Harrison, he expected these difficulties to be overcome and to move on to Detroit in a short time.[90]

Harrison gradually understood that the recovery of Detroit was going to take months, not weeks. If rations and forage were short, so were blankets and winter clothing. When the quartermaster corps could not meet the requirements, the general made a unique appeal. On 25 September he issued a proclamation to the people of Kentucky, asking for assistance. Acknowledging that he was leading the brave men of the Bluegrass State "into a rigorous northern climate," he found that many were without blankets and most were "totally destitute of every article of winter Clothing." He appealed to his "fair countrywomen" to provide "Blankets, overalls, roundabout jackets, shoes, socks and mittens" for their home state's "brave defenders." He also ordered 150 watch coats for those on sentry duty.[91]

On 24 September, Harrison received Eustis's directive giving him command of the North West Army. The secretary of war gave him three missions: (1) protect the frontier, (2) retake Detroit, and (3) undertake a "conquest of Upper Canada" by penetrating "that Country as far as the force under you[r] Command, will in your judgement justify." In addition to the regulars already assigned to the North West Army and the Kentucky and Ohio volunteers that already accompanied Harrison, regular cavalry commanded by Maj. James V. Ball and three thousand volunteer militiamen from Virginia and Pennsylvania would arrive shortly. This made his whole force about ten thousand strong.[92]

In the fall campaign Harrison suffered from an embarrassment of riches—he had more soldiers than his logistical system could accommodate. Troop strength of half that size might have accomplished the mission, and the supply system might have been adequate for such a force. Neither Harrison nor the Washington authorities fully comprehended the impact of so many soldiers, horses, wagons, and supplies on a frontier environment where the enemy controlled the most convenient transportation route—Lake Erie—and overland transportation used either primitive roads or newly established trails and involved construction of barges and pirogues to navigate the Maumee River waterway. Harrison developed four supply routes to support the three wings of the army he expected to consolidate at the Maumee Rapids. The first ran from Cincinnati and followed Anthony Wayne's 1794 route up the Great Miami River and Mad River Valleys to Urbana, Ohio, then overland to St. Marys, Ohio, and along the St. Marys River to Fort Wayne. A variant of this route went to Fort Amanda, Ohio, and down the Auglaize River to its junction with the Maumee at Fort Winchester. At both St. Marys and Fort Amanda, boat builders constructed bateaux and pirogues for the transport of men and supplies. Beside each river were trails along which infantry, cavalry, packhorses, wagons, cattle, and hogs moved forward. Packhorses were not a good substitute for bateaux since they consumed in forage almost all the weight they could carry. On the second route, the central wing commanded by Ohio Maj. Gen. William Tupper followed Hull's Road. Although the most direct route to the Maumee Rapids, it involved long overland transportation and crossed the Black Swamp at its widest point, between modern Van Buren and Perrysburg, Ohio.

Supplies for Harrison's right column followed two routes. One went via the Scioto River from Portsmouth through Columbus (then called Franklinton), Ohio, and overland to Upper Sandusky, where Harrison eventually established a major supply post. Harrison increasingly favored this route as he could use water transportation as far north as Franklinton. However, the road north of modern Delaware was inadequate between Franklinton and Upper Sandusky. The other route involved an overland march from western Pennsylvania to Wooster and Mansfield, Ohio, roughly following modern U.S. Highway 30. From Mansfield he anticipated going to either Upper or Lower Sandusky before crossing the Black Swamp. Although this required a longer overland journey than the other routes and involved several major river crossings, it ran through the Seven Ranges and just south of the more settled Western Reserve of northeastern Ohio and therefore could supply provisions, forage, teams of oxen, teamsters, packhorses, wagons, and oxcarts from local farmers, merchants, and mechanics.[93]

Much to his surprise, Harrison discovered that despite Royal Navy control of the lake, a few ambitious, risk-taking entrepreneurs in Cleveland and Erie endeavored to transport small amounts of supplies by bateaux to the mouth of the Huron River on the Lake Erie shore (east of Sandusky Bay). When he visited the Huron River mouth in early November, Harrison rejected the location and instead requested that bateaux and their cargos be sent up the Sandusky River to Lower Sandusky (modern Fremont). Harrison directed the Augustus Porter Co. to forward at least five hundred thousand rations to Lower Sandusky to support the advance of an expected forty-five hundred troops, first to the Maumee Rapids and then to Detroit.[94]

But the Augustus Porter firm refused to comply with Harrison's request. The contractor allegedly met its obligations to supply merchandise to Lower Sandusky, Maumee Rapids, River Raisin, and Detroit, which had been lost with Hull's surrender. With Lake Erie navigation closed due to Royal Navy control and these designated points of deposit in enemy hands, the company's agent, Samuel Tupper, refused "to supply the army at [Lower] Sanduskey or any place beyond." He did agree to supply 950 barrels of whiskey and flour if the government would pay transportation expenses beyond Cleveland. Contractors' inabilities to supply his troops drove Harrison to distraction. At the end of November he wrote John Piatt that the "circumstances in which the army is placed will no longer permit me to suffer the contractors to trifle with us in the manner they have done." In fact, his employment of John Piatt as a deputy commissary general would be a source of difficulties for Harrison for years to come.[95]

Despite the problems with the Augustus Porter firm, the Cleveland to Lower Sandusky logistical route increasingly beckoned. In mid-November, Harrison urged Deputy Quartermaster General Capt. William Piatt to drop his work on the overland road from Mansfield to Upper Sandusky and go to Cleveland to purchase boats and transport grain and flour to Lower Sandusky. He concluded, "the facility of conveyance from Cleaveland by Water on the Lake now, and on the Ice when it shall be frozen, points out that as the proper route for any article of supply." Given the supply post at Lower Sandusky, Harrison expected Gen. Simon Perkins to begin constructing a road from there to the Maumee Rapids. This involved crossing the Black Swamp in the midst of a rainy fall, but such a causeway was thought to be within the capabilities of General Perkins's men. Another plan was to move supplies from Sandusky Bay across the narrow neck of the Marblehead Peninsula and, after crossing the Portage River near modern Port Clinton, to haul supplies by wagons along the shore of Lake Erie to Maumee Bay and thence upstream to the rapids. All this was necessary because General Winchester was expected to arrive at the rapids in a few days. But logistics was the bane of Harrison's operational plans. Finally, in exasperation he told the secretary of war that he had not made "sufficient allowance for the imbecility and incompetence of the public Agents and the Villainy of the Contractors."[96]

Another recurring logistical problem involved personnel. Most volunteers enlisted for a short period—three to six months. Often these obligations began to expire just as Harrison hoped to mount a counterattack. Time and again he had to replace those who departed.

Nothing could have hampered the already difficult situation in northern Ohio had all the natives living in the region turned against the Americans. They could have sent their families to join the other hostile tribes gathering in the Detroit region while hundreds of warriors familiar with the terrain harassed the Americans' logistical lifeline. Throughout the 1812 campaign, Harrison reinforced his relations with those Indians loyal to the United States. Forgotten in the legends of Tecumseh are the loyal natives who assisted the United States during this war. At the center of the pro-American tribes were the Shawnee living in the Wapakoneta area of western Ohio. These accommodationist or "civilized" Indians settled near the headwaters of the St. Marys and Auglaize Rivers, which were launching points for the effort to support the left wing of Harrison's army as it moved from Fort Wayne to the Maumee Rapids. Led by Black Hoof, who denounced the British for making false promises before and who thought they would do the same again if it was in their best interests, the Wapakoneta Shawnee remained loyal to the United States.

No story is more telling of the divisions within the Shawnee nation than that of Spemicalawba, who had been captured by the Kentuckians in 1786 and took the name of Captain Logan to honor his favorable treatment by Gen. James Logan of Kentucky. Reputedly a nephew of Tenskwatawa and Tecumseh, Captain Logan remained at Wapakoneta with Chief Black Hoof rather than join his uncles at Prophetstown. In 1812 Captain Logan, Captain Johnny, Bright Horn, and others became scouts for General Winchester and the left wing of Harrison's forces. In November, Logan and his companions were detained by a Potawatomi and Ottawa scouting party led by Capt. Alexander Elliott, the son of British Indian agent Matthew Elliott and a Shawnee woman. Logan and his companions killed Captain Elliott and hostile Potawatomi Chief Winamac (not to be confused with another Potawatomi of the same name), but Logan died of wounds received in a successful escape. According to one contemporary writer, Logan "was a brave and enterprising warrior, sincerely attached to the Americans, and possessed a powerful influence over the Indians."[97] Logan of the Shawnee, Tarhe ("The Crane") of the Wyandot, and Black Hoof and their followers were critical military intelligence gatherers and defenders of the supply line for Harrison's North West Army.[98]

Advance to the Maumee

By late September, Harrison's forces began moving toward a variety of objectives. Winchester, with two thousand men, began a march from Fort Wayne toward the confluence of the Maumee and Auglaize Rivers. Maj. Richard M. Johnson's Kentucky mounted riflemen completed a raid on Little Turtle's former village on the Eel River in Indiana, destroying the village except for Little Turtle's house. Another party raided the Miami village of Mississinewa in northern Indiana. Other troops erected fortifications at St. Marys, Fort Amanda, and Fort Jennings. And Ohio Col. Samuel Findlay led a regiment of mounted men against an Ottawa village on the Auglaize.[99]

Of all these, perhaps the most successful was the Mississinewa raid by troops under the command of Lt. Col. John B. Campbell, 19th U.S. Infantry. This mostly light cavalry command marched from Franklinton with twelve-month U.S. volunteers from Pennsylvania and Virginia who would be mainstays in Harrison's army for the next several months. The order was to attack and destroy several Miami villages on the Mississinewa River, and Harrison provided Campbell with very detailed instructions concerning the order of march, constant readiness for possible attack either day or night, fortifying encampments, and engaging in surprise attacks. Harrison's directions allowed Colonel Campbell to advance on White Pigeon's town if the opportunity allowed and the risk was not too great. As far as the destruction of the Miami villages was concerned the raid was profitable, but it did not engage any sustained combat. The destruction of their villages and storage facilities forced the natives to be even more dependent on the British and their limited resources. The Americans lost eight killed in action, but they had a 50 percent casualty rate when they finally arrived at Fort Greenville, Ohio, after a month in the field. Most of those listed as unfit for duty were suffering from complaints caused by the inclement weather, especially frostbite.[100]

When forwarding Colonel Campbell's report to Acting Secretary of War Monroe, Harrison used the opportunity to recommend Campbell, Lt. Col.

James Simrall, and subordinates for War Department consideration in future promotions and assignments.[101] This consideration for his regular officers' career development reflects the maturation of General Harrison's leadership abilities. Harrison knew that service in the Eighth Military District was not considered as career rewarding as that in the Ninth Military District to the northeast, where most regulars thought the most career-enhancing assignments lay.

Harrison directed Ohio Brig. Gen. Edward W. Tupper to conduct a mounted raid toward the Maumee Rapids to ascertain the situation there. He placed General Winchester in charge of the "whole arrangement for the supply and march of the left wing" with the objective of occupying the rapids of the Maumee and securing any unharvested corn.[102] While Harrison directed his orders to each commander and implied that each commander was to operate under his command, Winchester presumed that while Tupper was in his area of operations, he was under the regular army general's command. This presumption produced fireworks later on.

Meanwhile, Winchester's advance stalled at Defiance, just down the Maumee River from Fort Wayne. Winchester knew why Harrison wanted a post at the Maumee Rapids, but he offered numerous excuses as to why he could not arrive there. At the intersection of three routes—via the Maumee, via Hull's Road, and from Eastern Ohio—the rapids would become the rendezvous point for the three columns of Harrison's army and the storage place for supplies for the campaign against Fort Malden and Detroit. Winchester and Tupper alerted Harrison that the British had destroyed homes and taken grain and livestock in the area from the lower Maumee River to Malden. In other words, most supplies would now have to be carried to the Maumee, not acquired from local sources. Winchester thought he needed more supplies, especially cold-weather clothing and ammunition.[103] This logistical excuse kept him at the newly constructed Fort Winchester at Defiance.

Personnel problems and differences continuously confronted the commanding general. The dispute between Winchester and Tupper grew intense as the former ordered the latter to conduct operations Tupper thought were contrary to directives he received from Harrison. Finally, Winchester preferred charges against General Tupper for slandering him and allowing reports injurious to his reputation to be circulated in Ohio. In February 1813 (after Winchester's defeat at the River Raisin), a court of inquiry exonerated Tupper of the charges against him. Ohio Col. Allen Trimble reported that his guides fostered mutiny among his troops that caused desertions by approximately one-third of the officers and enlisted men. Because of this he was able to conduct only the raid on Little Turtle's town and did not attack his intended target, White Pigeon's Potawatomi village at the headwaters of Michigan's St. Joseph River. Colonel Trimble concluded his commentary with the cry of many militia officers: "It is Lamentable Sir that Such troops as I commanded cannot on Short Tours be reduced to that Subordination & Discipline which is necessary, and are generally better calculated to ensure their commanders mortification & Disappointment that Success." The short enlistment times of volunteers caused Henry Clay to ask Acting Secretary of War James Monroe to reinforce Harrison's troops with new volunteers, since it was impossible to procure regulars in time to contribute effectively to the winter campaign. The conduct of many Kentucky and Ohio rangers frustrated Harrison. On top of all this, Ohio Maj. Gen. Elijah Wadsworth demanded a court martial of Brig. Gen. Reasin Beall. Harrison expressly forbade such a trial for those whose immediate responsibilities were to move their troops expeditiously to the Maumee. Compounding the issue was a directive from Wadsworth to Perkins that countermanded orders from Harrison. Finally, Governor Meigs directed General Perkins to be subject only to Harrison's orders, not those of Wadsworth. The latter went home in a huff.[104]

Were these problems not enough, Harrison took umbrage at the tone of a letter from Lt. Hezekiah Johnson, the assistant deputy quartermaster at Pittsburgh, which the general considered rude and lacking in due deference to a senior officer. He forwarded a copy of the lieutenant's letter of 3 November to Secretary Eustis to determine how far the letter was consonant with "the respect which is due from a Subaltern to his General." Another issue emerged when private citizens proposed a raid on friendly Delaware towns; Harrison had to write a letter to the Cincinnati *Liberty Hall* stating, "It certainly belongs to the government alone to determine upon offensive war."[105]

Each of these logistical, operational, and personnel problems interfered with Harrison's advance to the Maumee Rapids. General Winchester moved only five miles down the river from Defiance and waited there throughout November and December. All this time his troops consumed supplies. Most interesting was Winchester's comment that his "Kentucky Volunteers have improved greatly in disscipline and Subordination, and deserve the honorable distinction of Regular troops."[106]

While Winchester delayed moving downriver, General Tupper marched a column from McArthur's blockhouse (near modern Kenton, Ohio) to the Maumee. Under the direction of Capt. Matthew Elliott and with several boats lying near the rapids, the British and Indians were trying to seize all the grain available in the area. The British and their native allies were located near old Fort Miamis on the north side of the river, in modern Maumee, Ohio. Tupper attempted a nighttime crossing of the Maumee on 14 November, but the high waters swept soldiers downstream and Tupper had to cancel his surprise attack scheduled for the next morning. While the British left the scene in their boats, the natives attacked. Led by Splitlog, the Indians staged an unusual mounted attack. The warriors fired both mounted and dismounted; several of the Indians had pistols and fine horses. The Indians' marksmanship caused only one wounded casualty among the Americans, who claimed several natives killed. Tupper sent a message to Winchester to join him, but Winchester did not, and Tupper had to withdraw because of insufficient provisions. Harrison subsequently issued a general order commending this operation "as a worthy example of military spirit and enterprise" to the rest of the North West Army.[107]

This episode could not have enhanced Winchester's reputation with Harrison. And Tupper's success at marching from Fort McArthur to the Maumee Rapids had to embarrass Winchester and his colonels; they were nearly twenty miles closer to the rapids than Tupper had been at Fort McArthur. Could this embarrassment have influenced Winchester's decision to advance to the River Raisin in January? We will never know for sure.

In a letter to his father-in-law at the end of November, Harrison seemed overly optimistic concerning the prospects of being in Detroit before Christmas. The logistical efforts had to work, and Winchester had to advance quickly to the rapids. If this were done, the general expected the campaign's objectives would be accomplished.[108]

On 10 December, General Winchester justified his remaining in Defiance on the grounds of logistical inadequacies. On the St. Marys River, attempts to move supplies forward failed due to ice. General Perkins found himself "destitute of provisions" at Lower Sandusky. Were this not enough, Harrison's deputy quartermaster general reported that he was running out of cash and, if not immediately rectified, all Harrison's "efforts will be paralized when you may be on the Eve of accomplishing the object of the Campaign." Perkins noted that failure to pay the troops generated considerable distress among his soldiers. In a report to the secretary of war, Harrison acknowledged that the North West Army's expenses "greatly exceed the calculations of the Government." He complained bitterly of "the imbecility and incompetence of the public Agents and the Villainy of the Contractors," on which he blamed much of the delay.[109]

The question that emerges in all this is, was Harrison attempting to do too much given the seasonal and geographic difficulties? He had a direct order from Secretary Eustis to retake Detroit and take Fort Malden. Yet, more than anyone, he ought to have known the difficulties of advancing with three columns toward a junction at the Maumee Rapids in the middle of a wilderness during late fall and early winter. Two of those columns had to advance through the Black Swamp, and the third required river transportation along very crooked streams that often thwarted navigation because of low water or ice. One Harrison biographer speculated that had Harrison followed the prudent path and spent the fall and winter accumulating supplies and training troops (following the example of his mentor Anthony Wayne), "his popularity would have waned." Consequently, "Harrison opened a campaign which was to consume enormous amounts of money and supplies, and to dissipate large forces of men while it dragged slowly along to failure."[110]

In mid-December 1812, Harrison made plans for one last effort. He hoped to bring his forces to bear on Fort Malden after the ice formed on the Detroit River. Taking that post, he argued, was more essential to success than retaking Detroit. If it regained Detroit first, the North West Army would be subject to the interdiction of its supply route from Malden in the same way Hull had been. To achieve his objective, Harrison needed a supply post and rendezvous point at the Maumee Rapids from where he could attack Malden. A lesser option was to conduct a raid across the frozen Detroit River and burn the *Queen Charlotte* anchored there. The question that emerged was, could troops and supplies arrive at the rapids in time and in sufficient quantities to build a fort and concentrate provisions and equipment in the middle of a winter?

While in early November, Harrison had feared Winchester might advance to the rapids "too soon," by mid-December he found the lack of movement by both Winchester and Perkins frustrating. When no messenger from Winchester reached him at Upper Sandusky, he dispatched a letter with Assistant Adjutant General Charles S. Todd (Governor Isaac Shelby's son-in-law) instructing the commander of the left wing to advance to the Maumee Rapids and begin constructing huts there. This was a scheme for deception designed to induce the enemy to believe this was to be the winter quarters for the Americans. Winchester was to receive supplies from the other wings of the army in preparation for the advance to Fort Malden.[111] The need to send aide-de-camp Todd to Winchester's camp indicates the commanding general's impatience at his subordinate's inaction. On the right wing, General Perkins reported that no progress had been made on the road from Lower Sandusky to the Maumee Rapids, even though a possible route had been marked the previous summer.[112] The winter campaign was not going well.

Throughout December and early January, Winchester deliberately avoided keeping Harrison informed of his position and his intentions. Harrison received notice of Winchester's arrival at the Maumee Rapids in a message, not from the commander of the left wing himself, but rather via General Perkins in Lower Sandusky.[113] Some of this delay may have been caused by Winchester's sending letters to Harrison in Lower Sandusky rather than Upper Sandusky. In frustration, Harrison wrote Perkins at Lower Sandusky on 16 January indicating that he did not know whether Winchester was at the Maumee Rapids. One assumes Todd told Winchester where Harrison was located.[114]

Harrison began contemplating what would happen if he found his offensive stalled at the Maumee. In a letter to the secretary of war, he advised that it might require U.S. naval dominance of the lake to conduct a proper spring campaign. If, he proposed, we used a portion of those sums necessary for winter operations and devoted them to constructing a fleet that would command Lake Erie, "the wishes of the Government in their utmost extent could be accomplished without difficulty." The Eighth District commander indicated greater concern with the naval aspects of the war than he had previously shown. A secondary but important objective must be Michilimackinac and Fort St. Joseph. With these two in hand, the British logistical line to Lakes Michigan and Superior and beyond could be severed.[115]

He reviewed this option in a long letter to Acting Secretary of War Monroe in early January. He described his plans to occupy the Maumee Rapids and construct a fortification there (later Fort Meigs), which would become a fort of deposit as well as an assembly point for troops coming from his three avenues of advance. Still, he recognized the growing criticism over the lack of progress in regaining Detroit and the excessive costs of his fall campaign. Harrison justified the large number of troops as a product of his long experience in Indian warfare. While during the winter the British wisely encouraged most of their native allies to return to their home villages rather than remain a burden on the British commissary, the general noted that "but a Whistle will be almost Sufficient to collect them again." A seemingly too massive force was an important component in Harrison's strategy. The number of Indians opposing him "will be in an inverse ratio to the force which we employ," he wrote Monroe. The Americans must have excessively large garrisons at various outposts to overawe any ambitious British-Indian advance. Shortly after this epistle reached Washington on 19 January, the whole situation changed again as a consequence of the disaster at Frenchtown, Michigan.[116]

In both epistles Harrison articulated what eventually became the successful operational plan for reasserting American control of Lake Erie and southern Michigan. What he failed to comprehend was that instead of undertaking this task in late spring of 1813, it would be September before the necessary naval and military forces could be combined to achieve the first phase of this plan. That delay meant that the Lake Huron operations would be postponed until 1814, when Harrison would not be in command.

Meanwhile, President Madison searched for a new secretary of war, a post that eventually went to Maj. Gen. John Armstrong Jr. of New York. In another cabinet change, William Jones of Philadelphia became secretary of the navy. Whether either of these men read Harrison's proposal is unknown, but the Washington command center's operational directives for 1813 implemented Harrison's ideas. As a regional strategist, Harrison proved prescient and accurate; as an operational commander, he proved unable to execute the directives from Washington successfully during 1812. As he told his father-in-law, though some might criticize the emphasis on reclaiming what was lost in the Midwest rather than focusing on the truly critical and decisive attack on the St. Lawrence Valley, Harrison knew that the Madison administration emphasized his campaign and planned to persist with it.[117]

Battles at the River Raisin

Ensign Todd's mission to Fort Winchester bore some fruit. General Winchester finally began an advance on 31 December. His long-delayed movement from Fort Winchester (a short distance from Wayne's Fort Defiance) reached the Maumee Rapids eleven days later—a march of approximately forty-five miles. Harrison ordered Winchester to remain at the rapids while he directed the right wing toward the same objective. But Harrison's movement and that of General Tupper with the central wing were delayed because of limited supplies and transportation difficulties.

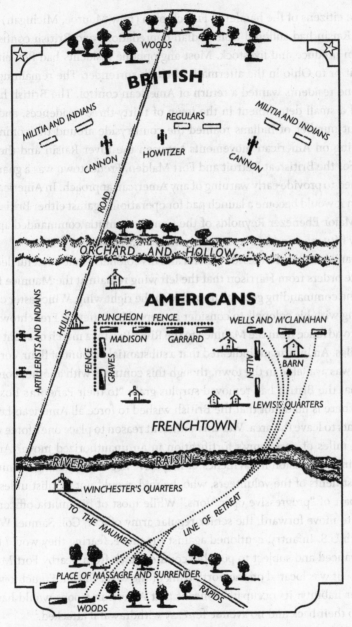

Labels within the image:

WOODS

BRITISH

MILITIA AND INDIANS REGULARS MILITIA AND INDIANS

CANNON HOWITZER CANNON

ROAD

ORCHARD AND HOLLOW

ARTILLERISTS AND INDIANS

HULLS

AMERICANS

PUNCHEON FENCE WELLS AND M'CLANAHAN

MADISON GARRARD

FENCE GRAVES ALLEN BARN

LEWIS'S QUARTERS

FRENCHTOWN

RIVER RAISIN

WINCHESTER'S QUARTERS

TO THE MAUMEE LINE OF RETREAT

PLACE OF MASSACRE AND SURRENDER RAPIDS

WOODS

Battle of the River Raisin. Reprinted from Benson J. Lossing, *Pictorial Field-Book of the War of 1812* (New York: Harper Brothers, 1869).

The citizens of the hamlet of Frenchtown (now Monroe, Michigan) on the River Raisin had suffered from Indian depredations and British confiscation of farm produce and livestock. Most anglophone residents had fled either to Detroit or to Ohio in the aftermath of Hull's surrender. The remaining, francophone residents wanted a return of American control. The British had stationed a small detachment in the town of thirty-three residences, and a significant number of Indians roamed the countryside around the community, reporting on American movements between the River Raisin and the Maumee. For the British at Detroit and Fort Malden, Frenchtown was a guard post designed to provide early warning of any American approach. In American possession it would become a launch pad for operations against either British position. Major Ebenezer Reynolds of the Canadian militia commanded approximately fifty men and had up to two hundred Indian allies.

Meanwhile, the Tennessee general and his colonels made a fateful decision. Despite orders from Harrison that the left wing remain at the Maumee Rapids until the commanding general arrived with the right wing, Winchester called a meeting with his colonels to consider an appeal by suffering Frenchtown residents to advance from the Maumee to the River Raisin, a march of about thirty-five miles. An informant indicated that a substantial amount of flour, corn, and wheat was available in the town, though this contrasts with another commentary that the British had removed surplus grain "to their Pandora's Box, Malden." There is no doubt that the British wished to force all American-favoring residents to leave the area. Was this sufficient reason to place one's force within fifteen miles of an enemy's fortification in an unauthorized move? Another factor in the decision for Winchester may have been the pending termination of enlistments of the volunteers, who, he said, would not reenlist unless they were part of "progressive operations." While most of his militia officers preferred to move forward, the senior regular army officer, Col. Samuel Wells of the 17th U.S. Infantry, cautioned against the move, fearing they would be too far advanced and subject to possible counterattack from nearby Fort Malden. Because it was located on the north bank of the River Raisin, Frenchtown had another liability: its occupation meant that American troops would have the river to their back and no avenue for easy withdrawal if attacked.[118]

Despite objections by Colonel Wells, Winchester decided to take Frenchtown. How much this reflected his chagrin that Harrison rather than he commanded the North West Army, how much he and his colonels resented the accolades the commanding general had heaped on General Tupper's troops after their raid to the Maumee in November, and how much this decision reflected Winchester's personal desire and the ambition of his colonels for military glory will remain unknown. Winchester claimed it was done for humanitarian reasons.[119] Whatever the reason or reasons, the decision proved costly. The advance to Frenchtown also violated Harrison's orders to await his arrival at the Maumee Rapids.

On the morning of 17 January 1813, Lt. Col. William Lewis left the rapids with 550 men, followed by Lt. Col. John Allen with 100 more. The two groups joined and encamped on the north side of Maumee Bay (in modern Toledo) for the evening. The next day they moved up the western shore of Lake Erie to the mouth of the River Raisin, marched up its southern shore, and began an attack over the frozen river in mid-afternoon. The Indian scouts warned Maj. Ebenezer Reynolds of the Americans' approach, but the British troops made little resistance before withdrawing; the natives, however, engaged vigorously and inflicted considerable casualties on their foe. The British successfully withdrew their small artillery piece. Had the Americans captured it, the subsequent engagement might have had a different outcome. Lewis's force suffered twelve killed and fifty-five wounded; Winchester reported at least twelve Indian dead. This was a substantial number of casualties considering the numbers engaged. Winchester informed Harrison of his sending troops into Michigan after the fact rather than requesting permission to do so. In a somewhat condescending note, Winchester said he intended to hold Frenchtown and that a cooperating force "from the right wing may be acceptable" to join his troops.[120]

Once he had learned of Winchester's arrival at the rapids, Harrison directed General Tupper to forward supplies up Hull's Road to support the newly arrived troops. He moved his headquarters from Upper Sandusky to Lower Sandusky, and General Perkins sent a battalion toward the rapids on 18 January. Harrison wrote Brig. Gen. Joel Leftwich of the Virginia volunteers at Upper Sandusky urging him to come forward "with nothing but Your tents" as the situation was precarious. He commended the "Kentucky Spirit" of the men at Frenchtown and predicted that if "the post at the River Raisin Can be Maintained for a few days all will be Well." But the satisfactory conclusion of this unauthorized expedition depended on a very big "if."[121]

"The Game has Commenced, rather earlier than I wished but there is now no alternative," Harrison wrote after receiving news of Colonel Lewis's victory of 18 January. Although he feared Lewis might be overpowered in such a forward position, he recognized that Winchester's decision obligated him to advance faster than he had anticipated. The commanding general told Elisha Whitlesey and Isaac Shelby of his anxiety about Lewis's holding onto French-town.[122] His apprehensions were part of a military caution that reflected his understanding of what happened to General St. Clair at the headwaters of the Wabash in 1791 and of his knowledge of military history that warned against rash actions. He stayed only one day at Lower Sandusky and began marching with Perkins's men toward the Maumee Rapids. He declared that Winchester made the correct decision to reinforce Lewis, but he still feared that Col. Henry Procter and his allies might overpower General Winchester before Harrison could reinforce him. On the day before disaster befell him, Winchester bragged that while he knew the enemy was preparing to retake Frenchtown, if they affected that purpose they would pay dearly for such a brazen attack. All this was said while he acknowledged that the ground he occupied was "not very favourable for defence and wood not Convenient but [it] is my only alternative unless I abandon the protection of the village."[123]

At Fort Malden on the night of 18 January, a gay party was going on commemorating the birthday of Queen Charlotte. Suddenly, at 0200 hours on the 19th, an exhausted messenger burst into the festivities. He told of the defeat at Frenchtown, and as one contemporary described it, the "scene was changed and mirth was transformed into melancholy." Rather than despairing, Colonel Procter decided to take advantage of the situation and counterattack before General Harrison brought the main body of his army forward. He quickly notified the British troops in Detroit and the Canadian militia and "whistled" to the Indians. He directed everyone to assemble at Brownstown (modern Trenton, Michigan).[124] The decision to counterattack constitutes an important example of how an effective commander can overcome adversity.

On the American side of the ledger, General Winchester brought forward Colonel Wells and the 17th U.S. Infantry, leaving only three hundred troops under Brig. Gen. John Payne at the Maumee Rapids. With Winchester now in command at the River Raisin, he had approximately one thousand officers and men. Colonel Lewis's Kentucky militia encamped behind a four- to five-foot picket fence that surrounded a block of homes in the village. Its purpose was not to serve as a fortification but rather to keep livestock and wild animals from the yards and gardens. Colonel Wells's Kentucky-recruited regulars pitched their tents in an open field about four hundred yards to their right. Although Wells protested that the position was indefensible, he did not require his men to build any barricades for their protection should the British counterattack. Both encampments had the frozen river to their rear. The Americans had no artillery for their protection. Ohio General Perkins attributed this lack of precautions to the troops being "too much impressed with the opinion that Kentucky bravery could not fall before so inconsiderable a force as indians and cannadians." As one veteran of this campaign recalled, the 17th Infantry thought it not worthwhile to fortify its position "though materials were at hand, to fortify the right wing, which therefore encamped in the open field." He sorrowfully observed, "This want of precaution was a great cause of our mournful defeat!"[125] Hubris is the curse of many armies; it made its appearance here again.

In all probability, in colder weather than most of the men had ever seen, the troops were more concerned about getting firewood than building protection from a seemingly improbable attack. General Winchester and Colonel Lewis stayed in the modest but comfortable home of François Navarre across the river from the town, about a quarter mile from the encampment. Colonel Wells went back to the rapids to urge Harrison to come forward quickly. Wells and Winchester were in disagreement. Thus the second-ranking officer left his unit without his leadership. When reveille sounded on 22 January, the three senior-most commanders were not with their troops.

Winchester later acknowledged that when the Navarre family and local residents alerted the Americans that the British and their allies were marching, Winchester and his senior officers dismissed the warnings as "conjecture." No scouts—or "spies" as they were called then—were sent out to verify the information. Officers posted a few sentries close to the encampment; however, no vedettes or mounted sentries were posted along the road from Detroit.

An entirely different appraisal came from Harrison's former aide, Capt. Nathaniel G. S. Hart, who sent a letter with Colonel Wells as he returned to the Maumee Rapids. Hart worried that Frenchtown might be lost and that "the people having taken an active part against the British, will be subjected to utter ruin—perhaps scalped." He and other officers urged Harrison to come as soon as possible because "[many] things ought to be done, which you only know how to do properly."[126] Hart was one of those company-grade officers and enlisted men who paid dearly for Winchester's neglect of normal military precautions.

While Winchester's men shivered in Frenchtown, the North West Army's commander began thinking ahead. Assuming Winchester could hold onto the River Raisin community, Harrison anticipated advancing on Fort Malden in two weeks. He ordered General Tupper to encourage his troops, whose terms of enlistment expired in February, to re-up for one month. If they would, he directed Tupper to bring them to the rapids where, as senior to General Perkins, he would have command of the entire Ohio quota. But many of Tupper's men were sick and others were obligated to return to their farms, and so few extended their obligation that his "brigade" was reduced to two hundred by the time it reached the rapids.[127]

At Brownstown, Procter assembled a conglomerate force of approximately 1,200, including 336 regulars, 212 militia troops from the 1st and 2nd Essex County Regiments, 28 provincial mariners, 19 Indian department men, and approximately 600 natives led by Wyandot chiefs Roundhead, Splitlog and Walk-in-the-Water, of which approximately 200 were mounted and armed with their very effective long-handled tomahawks. On 21 January they moved forward a dozen miles to Swan Creek.

The British, Canadians, and Indians made an early morning six-mile march from Swan Creek to the outskirts of Frenchtown. Without sentries to alert them, the Americans slept while Procter formed his troops and the natives encircled the town on both sides of the river. Just after American drummers beat reveille, the attack began. The initial artillery rounds passed over the heads of the Kentucky militiamen as the gunners had overestimated the range. The focus of the attack was down the road from Detroit at the Kentucky volunteers. The picketing provided excellent cover and concealment for the American defenders, and their rifles began to pick off the artillerymen as they manned their guns at close range. When the Royal Artillery gunners were eliminated, Provincial Marine gunners took their place, only to receive devastating fire. After half an hour, combat in the British center quieted down as both sides tried to determine what to do next.

On the American right the situation went from bad to worse. The exposed 17th Infantry troops faced crossfire from the Wyandot, forcing them to flee after less than half an hour of fighting. A few joined their comrades inside the pickets, but the majority ran across the river and, despite attempts by Winchester to rally them, dropped their weapons and tried to escape. They found themselves at the mercy of the mounted Wyandot, who were unwilling to take many prisoners. Swinging their tomahawks with abandon, they cut down the Americans, encumbered by two feet of snow, with grisly efficiency. As the horsemen went after more, the native foot warriors scalped the fallen. Among those killed was Lieutenant Colonel Allen who had encouraged the advance to Frenchtown. For all practical purposes, the 17th U.S. Infantry ceased to exist; this was not a distinguished day for the regulars. The disastrous panic-stricken retreat of the American right wing destroyed 40 percent of the American forces—220 killed, 150 captured by the Indians, and 33 escaped. The survivors included Maj. Elijah McClenahan (McClanahan) and his son and Capt. Michael Glaves, who fled on horseback along the Lake Erie shore rather than down Hull's Road as the infantrymen did. As the senior surviving officer of the 17th U.S. Infantry, Major McClenahan's unwillingness to remain with his troops reflected poorly on his professionalism.

Among the prisoners were Winchester, his sixteen-year-old son, and Lieutenant Colonel Lewis. This party was captured south of Frenchtown. Why the general was caught up in the panic that characterized the right wing of his army remains unexplained. The general was stripped of his uniform and had on only a white shirt and pantaloons when Roundhead presented him to Colonel Procter. The British commander eventually secured the American's uniform, and he decided to utilize Winchester's captivity to his advantage.

For the Kentucky volunteers and the British, the battle in the village turned into a stalemate. After a brief lull the fighting renewed; the British sought cover in nearby barns, which the Americans attempted to burn. Lt. Col. Thomas B. St. George of the 41st Foot suffered four wounds and remained *hors de combat* for the remainder of the war. Three direct assaults on the American position failed, and two British artillery pieces were silenced by Kentucky marksmen, who subsequently killed a British ammunition sleigh driver and horse. The long range of their rifles picked off the artillerymen attempting to man their short-range weapon. Almost all of Procter's artillerymen were casualties. After two and a half hours combat stopped while the Americans had their breakfast and Procter contemplated his next move. Meanwhile, Indians returning from the pursuit down Hull's Road were joining the battle from the Kentuckians rear and its unprotected flank along the riverbank. Without any picket fencing on this side, the natives could snipe away at the Americans on the river's north bank.[128]

In reality, both sides played a high-stakes poker game. Procter thought Harrison's troops were within a few miles and that such a relief force would force him to withdraw without a victory. Apparently, several Wyandot had seen hogs and cattle being herded on the Lake Erie ice to supply the Americans at Frenchtown. From a distance in the dim winter morning light, Procter's scouts mistakenly identified them as American infantry and cavalry and informed the British commander that Harrison was near at hand. Inside the American compound, Maj. George Madison, a future governor of Kentucky, discovered that his soldiers were running out of ammunition because the spare cartridges had been stored with Winchester at the Navarre home rather than with the front-line troops. Both men were bluffing, but Procter had an ace up his sleeve—General Winchester.

Procter demanded his prisoner surrender the Kentuckians or he would have to leave them to the not-so-tender mercies of the Wyandot. The British commander wanted a hasty decision and threatened to unleash the wrath of the natives on the survivors if Winchester did not immediately surrender the holdouts. Without demanding any terms, the American general sent a note to Major Madison informing him of his capture and directing the Kentuckians to surrender. Noting that such an order from a prisoner of war was probably invalid, Madison insisted on conditions, mainly a guarantee for the safety of all prisoners. Procter would insist that it was Winchester who surrendered without conditions and that there were no written terms between the British and Major Madison. Around 1100 hours, Madison agreed to surrender. In reality there were three groups of prisoners: those captured by the British, those captured by the Indians, and the severely wounded. How the latter two groups were handled has been a bone of contention between apologists for the Americans and for the British for two centuries.[129]

Generals Harrison and Perkins had arrived at the rapids on 20 January, and the next day Perkins led 660 men and one artillery battery toward French-town. Meanwhile, Harrison ordered Winchester to maintain his position at the River Raisin. He wrote the secretary of war that he feared "nothing but that the enemy may overpower Genl. Winchester before I can send him a Suffici[e]nt reinforcement." On the 22nd his troops were only a few miles below the rapids when word came that the British had counterattacked. This news confirmed the commanding general's worst fears. Harrison joined Perkins and began a forced march to relieve Winchester but soon learned that the American defeat at the River Raisin was total.[130] Rather than risk losing his whole army in a counterattack, Harrison withdrew to the Maumee Rapids.

Claiming to be a "cool, though not a disinterested observer of these events," Judge Augustus Woodward of Michigan Territory wrote that General Winchester's advance to Frenchtown was "a measure as erroneous and indiscreet, in substance; [as] it was weak, and defective, in execution."[131]

For all practical aspects, the campaign that had begun the previous fall was over three weeks into the new year. What had begun with optimism ended in frustration—frustration over logistical difficulties, frustration over financial inadequacies, frustration over short-term militia enlistments, frustration over leadership inadequacies and rivalries, frustration over tactical failures, and now frustration over an unauthorized advance to a precarious position that ended in the defeat of more than half of Harrison's army at a time he thought the North West Army was on the verge of success. Discouraged and unaware of his relative status vis-à-vis the British, Harrison withdrew a dozen miles from the rapids to the Portage River. He needed time to consider his next move.

Chapter Five

Defending Ohio

Both sides faced a quandary after the River Raisin battle. Harrison feared Procter and his Indian allies would push southward and attack his troops, who were without winter quarters or fortifications, along the Maumee. Colonel Procter, fearing an American counterattack, decided to withdraw from Frenchtown with his wounded and several hundred American prisoners. The two contending parties thus withdrew from the River Raisin, and for the next eight months the area between Frenchtown and the Maumee River became a no-man's-land. While the British went to Detroit and Fort Malden, and their Indian allies settled in around Brownstown and Amherstburg, Harrison retreated along the Lower Sandusky–Maumee Rapids trail over which he had come. The remnants of the North West Army stopped at the Portage River at what is now Woodville, Ohio, until they determined the British had not followed them. Thus both sides recoiled at what each expected would be an attack from the other.

The disaster at Frenchtown constituted another setback in a long series that plagued the American war effort. As Philadelphia publisher Matthew Carey wrote the president, "We are on the eve of a most tremendous explosion . . . [We] must put our shoulders to the wheel, or we may fast & pray forever in vain." To partially remedy the dire circumstances, an administrative change took place that would affect the remainder of Harrison's military career. President James Madison appointed Brig. Gen. John Armstrong of New York, former U.S. senator from that state, to be the new secretary of war, effective 18 January 1813. A Continental Army veteran of Maj. Gen. Horatio Gates's staff, Armstrong emerged from that conflict with a reputation as an intriguer, a characterization he never lost. He came to the post with numerous enemies in the cabinet (particularly Secretary of State James Monroe and Secretary of the Treasury Albert Gallatin) and in the Senate, which approved his nomination by a narrow 18 to 15 vote. From the beginning of his tenure, his relations with

Harrison were tension filled. Armstrong had presidential ambitions, and Harrison represented a threat as a potential presidential candidate rival. As a native Virginian (Armstrong's principal antagonist, Monroe, was another member of the Virginia dynasty) and as a westerner, Harrison possessed two characteristics Armstrong despised. The West was a region of the country that the sophisticated Armstrong—who had married into the prominent Livingston family of New York and was a former ambassador to France—treated with disdain.[1]

From the beginning Harrison followed Armstrong's directives to the letter, even when he thought them ill-advised. He knew long before Col. James Morrison wrote him about it in late April that Armstrong "is not over[ly] friendly to you." Nothing indicated this more than an article in the Philadelphia *Aurora*, edited by Armstrong's good friend William Duane, that blamed Harrison for Winchester's defeat at the River Raisin in January 1813.[2]

The River Raisin Massacre

When the British left Frenchtown, over five dozen seriously wounded American prisoners, unable to walk with the retreating redcoats and their colleagues who were now prisoners of war, were left behind in local houses. Procter resolved to use the limited number of sleds and sleighs at his disposal to transport his own wounded and left the Americans behind. He excused his failure to provide a guard over those left behind on the grounds that he expected Harrison to be in the village within a few hours. This supposition does not absolve him of responsibility for the security of his prisoners. Until Harrison arrived, Procter could have left a few British soldiers under a flag of truce to protect the wounded. Instead he left the Americans under the "guard" of Upper Canada militia Maj. Ebenezer Reynolds and a few British Indian Agency interpreters. Most of the Indians involved in the attack were already fully satisfied with the prisoners, booty, and scalps they had taken and withdrew with the British. Capt. William Elliott of Upper Canada's Essex County militia assured U.S. officers that sleighs would be sent to pick up the seriously wounded Americans by the following morning. This proved an empty promise.

Sometime during the night of 22–23 January, the British Indian Agency interpreters departed. They were replaced by at least fifty Indians who had been in a frolic at Stony Creek, just a few miles north of Frenchtown. Most of these were northern warriors allied to Robert Dickson, although there were some Potawatomi who had returned. The northern Indians had not been in

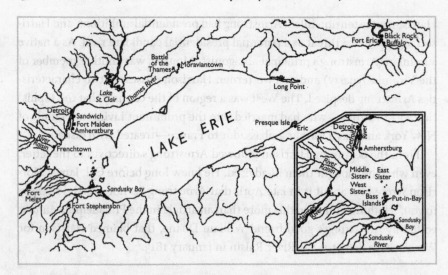

Lake Erie in the War of 1812. From William S. Dudley, ed., *The Naval War of 1812: A Documentary History*, vol. 2 (Washington, DC: Naval Historical Center, 1992), 408.

the battle and wanted trophies of the victory. Already intoxicated when they arrived in the town, they continued drinking and wasted no time in invading the houses where the American injured were staying, stripping them of their blankets and clothes; they then blockaded the exits and set the buildings on fire. Some of the wounded died in the flames; others tried to escape, and Indians tomahawked and scalped them. A few of the walking wounded and their caretakers were taken captive; these were later ransomed or executed and scalped. All the houses within the picketed area were left in ashes.[3]

This murder of the prisoners would be known as the River Raisin massacre, and its consequence was immediate. Most residents of Frenchtown and the surrounding area moved either to Detroit or behind American lines. In the following months, southeastern Michigan became the scene of the burnings of homes and outbuildings, stealing of livestock, looting of granaries, and theft of household items. The rationale for this was that the British did not want Frenchtown and other hamlets and farmsteads to become havens for advancing Americans. The Americans would use the same excuse when they occupied Moraviantown a few months later.

Although we do not know the exact number of Americans killed at the River Raisin on 23 January 1813, estimates range from thirty to sixty, with the probable loss closer to the higher number. Several times this number died in the panic-driven retreat down Hull's Road on the 22nd. The British forbade the interment of any remains, and feral hogs and wild animals consumed the bodies, leaving bones scattered throughout the vicinity. The disallowance of normal burial rites offended many, especially the Christian residents of Michigan. Months later, when Col. Richard M. Johnson's mounted riflemen came through the area, the sight of these remains incited them to revenge.

Far more than the larger losses among those fleeing the battle scene, the treatment of the wounded prisoners left behind disgusted most Americans. Blame focused on General Procter and Indian Agency Superintendent Matthew Elliott. In the eyes of the Kentuckians, these men refused to abide by the verbal commitments made to Maj. George Madison as part of the terms of surrender, and their "guards"—especially the Indian agents left behind—failed to provide security or transportation for the wounded prisoners. "Remember the Raisin" became a rallying cry for Midwesterners during the 1813 campaign. Especially in Kentucky, it became a recruiter's theme song motivating young men to volunteer for military service despite the defeats, sickness, and hardship that characterized the first year's operations north of the Ohio River. While defeat along the Detroit River may have been inevitable for the British, this incident at the River Raisin contributed significantly to motivating the Americans toward victory. Some argue that it sealed the doom for British control of the Detroit River Valley. Certainly it ended the prospects of those who had hoped there was a middle ground between American expansion and Indian claims to their traditional way of life. Many Canadians felt the failure to protect the prisoners constituted a stain upon His Majesty's officials. British Army Surgeon Dr. Robert Richardson described the Indians as having "murdered" the captives, and he considered General Procter personally "responsible for the lives of every one of them." Procter had promised protection for them, and Richardson warned that Canadians and Britons "have not heard the last of this shameful transaction."[4]

In the aftermath of the River Raisin debacle, Harrison received endorsement of his leadership abilities from a resolution by the Indiana Territorial Assembly and another from Generals Edward Tupper and Simon Perkins of Ohio on the occasion of the expiration of their troops' terms of service. According to one of his Indiana friends, the general's enemies were planting the rumor that he ordered Winchester to the River Raisin for the "special purpose of having him sacrificed because he was in your way as the future Command[er] of the North Western Army."[5] Both the tribute and the rumor in the aftermath of the River Raisin massacre indicate the diversity of Harrison's reputation among many Midwesterners.

For a while Harrison entertained the possibility of sending troops over the ice to Amherstburg to destroy the icebound vessels lying there. In his more optimistic moments, he contemplated that the frozen Detroit River might allow him to send enough troops across to seize Fort Malden. Finally, he sent Capt. Angus L. Langham and a party to undertake an expedition with the object of destroying the *Queen Charlotte*. The ice proved too thin for the success of this daring enterprise.[6]

The consequences of these failures for the 1813 campaign were daunting. Indian Agent John Johnston at Piqua, Ohio, noted that word of the River Raisin victory would "transport [the Indians] . . . beyond measure" and news of the event would "fly thro' their Country like lightening and will gather them in Swarms to Detroit in the Spring, expecting to reap a Similar harvest of plunder and glory. If Detroit Cannot now be regained this Winter I suspect you will have the largest Army of Indians to contend with in the Summer that has ever bee[n] embodied together in that quarter."[7]

An indication of the confusion existing in Ohio occurred at Upper Sandusky, where Pennsylvania Gen. Richard Crooks found himself without information regarding Harrison's intentions and thought he might be planning a retrograde movement toward the Sandusky Valley. Crooks sent scouting parties toward Lower Sandusky to ascertain whether the British were making any moves toward his position.[8] They would find that Harrison had begun a new fortification at the Maumee Rapids.

Building Fort Meigs

In the midst of this confusion, Harrison's scouts determined that Procter had not followed up his victory with an advance to the Maumee. So Harrison advanced his soldiers from their encampment on the Portage toward the rapids, where he began constructing a new fortification named in honor of Ohio's governor, Return Jonathan Meigs Jr. Just four days after construction began, Harrison reported to the governor that the foundations were laid and that "it will be [a] Strong work."[9] Supervising the construction was Capt. Eleazer D. Wood, Corps of Engineers. It became the largest log fort ever built in North America, covering ten acres with seven blockhouses and five gun emplacements. Wood required that between these structures, timber picketing should be placed, ten to twelve inches in diameter, fifteen feet long, and each set three feet into the ground. Each regiment tackled a particular section of the work, and it became a matter of pride as to whose section was the better built.[10]

Located on a bluff on the south side of the Maumee River, in modern Perrysburg, Ohio, Fort Meigs had three basic functions: resting at the critical north-south route between Michigan Territory and Ohio, it became a critical defensive outpost against any enemy incursion from the north; located at the junction of Harrison's three avenues of supply, it served as an advance depot for logistical support in the anticipated reconquest of Detroit; and finally, it served as a rendezvous point for American troops advancing northward. After the fort had withstood two British-Indian sieges, it received the moniker "Gibraltar of the Maumee."

Around the location of the fort was a large area of fields and meadow, which meant the men must travel some distance to secure the supply of timber necessary for the fort's construction. Throughout the period the fort was in use, Native American warriors lurked in the forested area, often picking off wood-cutting parties, deserters, fishermen, and duck hunters. In most instances the Indians were nimble enough to escape American attempts to capture them. A veteran quartermaster noted that the "idle curiosity of our young troops, the State of insubordination, & the impossibility to induce them to profit by advice" contributed to numerous deaths around the post.[11]

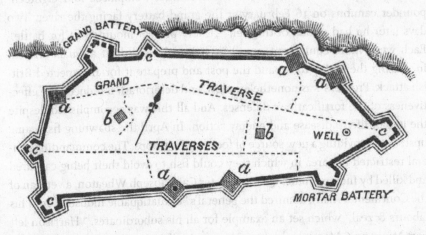

Fort Meigs. Reprinted from Benson J. Lossing, *Pictorial Field-Book of the War of 1812* (New York: Harper Brothers, 1869).

Not only the severe weather but also the lack of draft animals (there was not enough forage for the few they had) meant that bringing wood to the post required human labor. The forwarding of the eighteen- and six-pounder artillery was severely impaired by the rains, swollen rivers, and mud-clogged roads. Only gradually were these deficiencies overcome.[12]

According to Captain Wood, "It was not uncommon for the enemy to be about the camp at night, but probably his presence was more frequently imagined by the sentinels, than real, for scarcely a night passed without one, two or three alarms . . . The practice of turning the troops out because a frightened sentinel happens to hear a rustling in the bushes, or a bug fly over his head, is one of the most absurd practices that ever entered into the head of a general."[13]

In today's reconstructed Fort Meigs, the center area is covered with grass; this is very deceptive—not at all resembling the original conditions. During the first construction, the interior was a vast mud pot, with freezing and melting aggravating the living conditions. One officer recorded the scene: "Our camp is overwhelmed with mud and water; my eyes never saw such a place for mankind to live in—not a markee [marquee] tent in the whole encampment but what has more or less mud and water in it, and what makes it much worse is for the want of wood." There was "not a dry foot in camp" unless the soldiers stayed inside their tents. Sometimes the mud was so deep it came up to soldiers' calves. Spring rains increased the difficulties, and there was snow as late as 28 March.

Despite the Indian menace and the climatic conditions, work on the post went on. Capt. Daniel Cushing, 2nd U.S. Artillery, emplaced four eighteen-pounder cannons on 16 February at the grand battery facing the river. Two days later he had a total of thirteen artillery pieces "mounted fit for battle." Each week more equipment, supplies, livestock, and draft animals arrived, increasing the ability to expand the post and prepare it for an expected British attack. Progress was nonetheless slow, and deterioration reduced the effectiveness of the fortification's defenses. And all this was accomplished despite the loss of life to disease and enemy action. In April the spawning fish came upstream, providing a new source of food for the troops. The commanding general restricted the area in which they could fish to avoid their being captured and killed by Indian scouts. Quartermaster Capt. Joseph Wheaton, a veteran of the Continental Army, admired the general's "indifatiquable industry [and] his labours & zeal," which set an example for all his subordinates.[14] Harrison left Fort Meigs on 6 March and returned on 12 April.

Before he left, Harrison ordered Captain Wood to Lower Sandusky, where he spent about twelve days reinforcing Fort Stephenson before returning to Fort Meigs on 18 March.[15] Wood reinforced the outpost, which undoubtedly contributed to its successful defense from a British attack. Harrison then left for Cincinnati and put Virginia militia Gen. Joel Leftwich in command of Fort Meigs, with instructions to continue the post's construction.[16] On his return to the fort, Wood accused Leftwich, whom he called "a phlegmatic, stupid old granny," of stopping construction work and allowing his men to use timber brought in for picketing to be burned as firewood. In some instances troops tore down existing pickets for their fires. Despite the protests of regular army captains concerning this activity, it continued until Wood's return. About this time, news arrived that newly promoted Brig. Gen. Henry Procter was planning a British-Indian attack on Fort Meigs. With enlistment terms expiring, General Leftwich and his Virginia troops returned home. Fortunately, Gen. Richard Crooks and a few Pittsburgh volunteers remained until Harrison could bring more men to the outpost on the Maumee. The departure of some volunteers could be attributed less to a lack of patriotism and more to a lack of pay.[17]

Harrison began pushing men and supplies forward to the new outpost. By early April it became apparent that a British-Indian attack on Fort Meigs was imminent. Despite Secretary Armstrong's directives to curtail the use of militia, Harrison wrote Governors Shelby and Meigs asking for militiamen because of the "urgency of the occasion" and for which he took full responsibility. Moreover, he recognized that each of his small posts and the supplies he stored at them were vulnerable, as the enemy's command of Lake Erie allowed them to attack anywhere along his "extensive line of weak posts on the [Ohio] frontier," and he had insufficient troops to defend this vulnerable lines of communication.[18] He found the Ohio militiamen were "not to be depended upon" and insisted on having those raised in Kentucky, who were in his "opinion superior to any Militia that ever took the field in modern times."[19]

The military situation at Fort Meigs became more desperate as the temperatures warmed and the ice melted. Procter and his Indian allies planned to lay siege to the outpost. Because of their control of Lake Erie, they could bring to the Maumee much heavier artillery than that available to the Americans, who had to transport their cannons overland. Rumors in Ohio suggested that the British had offered the native chiefs "the whole Territory of Michigan—as a reward for their Services."[20] In addition to the natives on the Detroit frontier, Potawatomi Chief Main Poc brought warriors from northern Illinois with the expectation that General Harrison's army would be destroyed.[21]

Were these not enough worrisome items to bother him, Harrison faced continuing problems with his logisticians. Col. James Morrison wanted to leave his post as the army's deputy quartermaster general and return to his home in Kentucky. To replace him in this critical staff position, Harrison elevated Morrison's deputy, Lt. Col. John C. Bartlet. Before he departed, Morrison assured Harrison that he had procured a sufficiency of wagons and packhorses to transport the provisions and stores destined for Fort Meigs. Harrison grew increasingly outraged at the "fraud and peculation" involved in the logistical system, especially that of packhorse masters and wagon masters. He accumulated supplies along the Auglaize-Maumee route rather than trying to forward them by packhorses and wagons. The commanding general wanted to preserve these until the waters rose in the spring and he could make use of watercraft. His charges of embezzlement also included the assistant deputy quartermaster at Fort Meigs.[22]

The quality of militia officers also drove him to distraction. For a man known as an advocate of volunteer service units, Harrison complained freely of officers who could not read or write, and the "ignorance of many of those—even of Considerable Rank in the Western Country" infuriated him. One field-grade officer in the Ohio militia could not fill out a report form. It is not clear from this uncharacteristic display of outrage whether Harrison discriminated between common militia and volunteer leaders.[23] But he subsequently found similar issues with regular army officers.

On 12 April Harrison issued General Orders to the garrison praising the officers and men for "their past conduct as well as for the disposition which they at present manifest for the performance of their duty." Threatened as they were by a siege, Harrison determined that the "greatest exertion" by everyone in his command was necessary if they were to be successful in the post's defense. Therefore he "determined to exact from all the most punctual performance of every duty. Inattention & neglect will be immediately noticed and punished— Situated as we are even inactivity is a crime." He also began marksmanship training, ordering the officer of the day to take the guard being relieved of duty outside the post and instruct them to fire at a mark. "The best shot will receive a quart of whiskey and the second best a pint," a reward unlikely to have repeat winners the next time out. Daily drill of all units commenced on 23 April. "The General shall exact from every Officer the most punctual attention to this all important duty."[24]

Strategic Considerations

At about the same time, Harrison's close ally, Governor Shelby of Kentucky, concluded that to try to take Detroit without first taking Fort Malden was the wrong course. In a letter to Secretary of War Armstrong, Shelby advised, first, that "a decisive step" be employed to "secure the superior command of Lake Erie, which being effected would prevent the Enemy from reinforcing his troops in that quarter & the forwarding of supplies for their use." Second, the United States should exploit its newly won naval dominance by transporting troops, equipment, and supplies from Lake Erie's south shore to Canada. American use of waterborne transport would dramatically reduce transportation costs by reducing the need for wagons, wagon masters, packhorses, artillery horses, packhorse masters and their drivers, and the necessary forage and food to support them.[25] Few men spoke more eloquently for combined army-navy interaction in achieving the goal, and few could better satisfy the secretary's desires for economy than Governor Shelby.

Shelby's advice appealed to those in the War Department. It harmonized with Secretary Armstrong's habit of inserting his directives into Harrison's military district. While Harrison was building Fort Meigs as a supply post and rendezvous point for a land march toward Detroit, the secretary authorized Maj. Thomas Jesup to build, in Cleveland, flat-bottomed Schenectady bateaux for the purpose of transporting army troops across the lake after the navy secured control. Without consulting Harrison, Secretary Armstrong planned an amphibious operation from Ohio's north shore, escorted by the warships being built by Perry at Erie. Armstrong believed that Perry would be ready to sail by 1 June and that by then the Americans' regular regiments would be filled, negating the need to raise volunteer militia units. Jesup contracted with a Cleveland boat builder for sixty-five of these craft to be ready by mid-June.[26]

Finally, on 5 March the secretary of war issued a long directive to Harrison, listing several objectives. The first priority was obtaining command of the lakes, which he continued to insist would be achieved by early June. Land operations would be curtailed until naval superiority became a reality. Second, the approach to Malden should be achieved by a waterborne operation using the boats being built in Cleveland rather than by engaging in a "difficult, dangerous and enormously expensive" overland campaign out of Fort Meigs. The secretary clearly saw the interconnection between land and naval operations.

He and Harrison agreed that Malden had to be taken to curtail British-Indian interdiction of the logistical lifeline running roughly along what became U.S. Route 25 between Perrysburg and Detroit. The secretary envisioned an amphibious campaign starting from somewhere along the southern shore of Lake Erie that would be "easy, safe and economical." Third, since the Malden force reputedly contained no more than two thousand men, Harrison could raise no more than seven thousand for his campaign. (The secretary omitted any calculation of how many Native American warriors would support the British, which was eventually estimated to be over four thousand.) This limit was imposed for more than military reasons; the increasingly limited resources of the Treasury Department constrained troop and logistical expenditures. By the time the campaign began, Secretary Armstrong expected that the seven regular regiments raised in the West would constitute all the offensive forces Harrison would need. He did allow Harrison to call up militia to protect Fort Meigs and other outposts while the regulars were on the march. And the secretary gave the general another loophole in militia limitations: "should the recruiting Service go on less fortunately in the patriotic states of Kentucky and Ohio, than in other parts of the Union," Harrison received permission to call out militia units to make up the difference between the regular force authorization and its actual strength.[27]

After receiving Armstrong's directive, Harrison proposed an alternative operational plan: proceed by land from Fort Meigs toward Detroit, accompanied by the flatboats and pirogues being built on Maumee tributaries in Ohio, which would carry the army's baggage along the lake and Detroit River shore while the troops advanced and Perry's fleet (now dominating the lake) escorted them. Harrison did not see the need for the substantial number of Schenectady craft being built in Cleveland, and he expected that the watercraft coming down the Maumee, combined with the naval squadron's boats, could ferry the North West Army across the river to invade Canada. If the U.S. Navy attained naval superiority on the lake, the bateaux were not needed. Obviously Harrison and Armstrong were on different operational wavelengths regarding the best way to regain control of the Detroit River Valley.

Harrison again urged the necessity of volunteer soldiers; he knew full well that recruitment of the regular regiments envisioned by the secretary would not be successful. He also understood that the regular troops would be at least as raw as those volunteering and that the regular officers would be less experienced than many volunteer officers. The regular officers, he wrote, would with "scarcely an exception [have] to learn their duty before they could instruct their men." Such frank statements would not have been well received in Washington, even though the general sought to entreat the secretary's "pardon for the freedom with which these observations" were made and promised to execute "with promptitude and fidelity" any directives Armstrong sent him.[28]

Throughout the spring, tensions between the secretary and the general mounted. First, Armstrong imposed severe constraints on Harrison's expenditures.[29] Second, Harrison reported on "the dismay, and disinclination" of westerners for regular army service, thus denying the War Department the three new regiments expected to be recruited in Ohio and Kentucky. In fact, Harrison and his counterpart in Tennessee, Andrew Jackson, blamed "wicked machinations" by Armstrong to not pay volunteers for duty performed in 1812 and afterward as a device to induce them to join regular units. Third, Harrison questioned why Jesup's boats were being built when, if the navy secured control of the lake, the pirogues and boats used to transport supplies down the Auglaize and Maumee Rivers to Fort Meigs could coast along the western Lake Erie shore bringing supplies and assisting the movement of troops across the Detroit River against Fort Malden.[30]

Finally, the secretary authorized, but did not mandate, Harrison to evacuate Fort Meigs. This insulted the general. From Harrison's perspective the post was the linchpin in all operations directed toward Detroit. He had contemplated building it before Armstrong became secretary and had constructed it on a large scale to hold supplies and troops for the return northward without naval control of the lakes, an outcome Harrison knew was uncertain. Moreover, evacuation uncovered all the forts and depots below it on the Scioto-Sandusky and Great Miami–Auglaize–Maumee lines of communication and logistics. Harrison's problem was that the defense of the outpost required a large number of troops to repel attacks on its extended picket line. With the pending departure of the Virginia and Pennsylvania brigades that built the post, he needed soldiers immediately to operate it, and the slow regular army recruiting efforts meant that this could only be done with militiamen. "I must confess," he wrote the secretary, "that the Idea never occurred to me that the Government would be unwilling to keep in the field at least the Semblance of an army of Militia until the regular Troops could be raised."[31] At the end of March he implored the secretary to "call out the remaining part of the Militia that have been organised for service in Kentuck[y] & that they be Marched in the direction of Fort Wayne . . . [where] they will overawe the Indians tribes in that quarter & protect our deposits of provisions, as well as cover the Frontiers."[32] Their disagreement over the utility and necessity of employing volunteers would continue throughout the campaign.

Throughout March and April, Harrison pressed his subordinates to send as many soldiers as possible to Fort Meigs. Gen. John Wingate and Col. Mills Stephenson of the Ohio militia were specifically directed to forward troops to the Maumee outpost.[33] A small battalion from Gen. Richard Crooks's Pennsylvania brigade remained behind after the men's terms of enlistment expired.[34]

In April Harrison promised the secretary that his "Measures will therefore be entirely directed to the prosecution of the Campaign" as ordered. However, he advised that instead of departing from Cleveland, such a cross-lake expedition depart either from the mouth of the Portage River (modern Port Clinton, Ohio) or the mouth of the Maumee (modern Toledo).[35] Island hopping from either of these locations would be easier on the troops than the longer open-water voyage from Cleveland. Moreover, most of the supplies were stored at either Upper Sandusky or Fort Meigs, and the most convenient routes of advance for troops were over the left or central avenue of communications, not through Cleveland.

In mid-April Armstrong advised Harrison that General Procter's forces were not capable of mounting an expedition against the Eighth Military District. A week later he conceded that Procter might bring no more that two thousand effective troops against Fort Meigs and that he had only six- and eight-pounder guns. Regarding the caliber of available artillery, Armstrong was grossly mistaken; on the other hand, he overestimated the regular and militia strength available to the British.

At the same time, he indicated a desire to appoint a brigadier general to more effectively control operations in Illinois and Missouri Territories, a post that would eventually go to Governor Howard. On 24 April Harrison inquired of Adjutant General Thomas H. Cushing, "Is he [Howard] to be within my District & yet not report to Me?"[36] Although not a matter of controversy when it was announced, this appointment would become an important grievance between Armstrong and Harrison in succeeding months.

While the tensions between Armstrong and Harrison rose, the convivial relationship between the governor of Kentucky and the general continued; in fact, it improved after Shelby learned that Harrison was not responsible for Dudley's defeat. Governor Shelby provided sagacious advice, starting with the suggestion that Harrison employ "a Considerable force of Cavalry or mounted Infantry" during any land advance toward Detroit. He supported Secretary Armstrong's cross-lake invasion and implied that when information of Major Jesup's boatbuilding project reached Procter, this would compel the British general to divide his forces to protect against two invasions, by water and by land. Governor Shelby also promised to raise and organize Kentucky militiamen for an invasion of Canada. On the other hand, the governor thought Secretary Armstrong was "going in to[o] Small a Scale" with the North West Army troop allocations, and he argued that Harrison should "[call] out a force which you may deem Sufficient."[37] The collaboration between the veteran of the Revolution and the former aide to Anthony Wayne was just beginning.

Indian Policy

Throughout his campaigns of 1812 and 1813, Harrison used friendly Native Americans as scouts and informants. They proved immensely useful in providing military intelligence on enemy intentions, in protecting columns, and in serving as mail escorts. He employed thirty as scouts at fifty cents per day throughout the winter and spring of 1813, and they proved both extraordinarily useful and much cheaper than white scouts. Harrison had complete confidence in the natives' fidelity, and their employment kept them friendly to the United States. In mid-April he sent twenty of them to the vicinity of the River Raisin to take prisoners for the purpose of securing information about enemy intentions. Presumably from what they learned from fellow tribesmen living south of Detroit, the friendly Wyandot of the Sandusky River region provided him with information regarding General Procter's intentions and the state of his preparations. During the campaign up the Thames, they also provided useful military intelligence for the North West Army's advance.

Another issue revolved around professions of friendship from previously hostile native chieftains. Indian Agent John Johnston reported from Piqua, Ohio, that he had received overtures from Miami, Potawatomi, and Kickapoo representatives. Tenskwatawa "had become extremely unpopular" among many, but Johnston demanded hostages to ensure the good conduct of those supposedly coming over to the American side.[38] Operating out of Piqua, Brig. Gen. John Wingate of the Ohio militia constantly worried that visiting hostile Indians with their tales of scalps and loot taken during Dudley's massacre were influencing the friendly Indians to join the British.[39] Keeping the friendly natives allied with the United States in the aftermath of the first siege of Fort Meigs remained a problem for the Americans.

On the other hand, one of the general's worries was that "some Scoundrels in the Neighbourhood of Piqua would fall upon the friendly Delawares living in that area." This fear that white settlers would incite rebellion among the friendly tribes because of their universal hatred of all Indians was a constant theme in Harrison's correspondence. Nothing more justified the general's fear of Indian-hating whites turning against all natives, regardless of their affiliation with the American effort, than the attempted assassination of Shawnee Chief Black Hoof in January. Certainly there was a desire for revenge in the aftermath of the River Raisin massacre, but attempting to kill one of the native leaders most closely allied with the United States threatened everything Harrison thought necessary to successfully using Indians in his campaigns and reducing the numbers available to Tecumseh. The shot grazed the chief's left cheek near the eye, and he endured considerable pain before and after army surgeons extracted the bullet. Attempts to find the culprit with an offer of a huge $350 reward failed.[40]

Before heading north in June, Harrison called a council in Franklinton with approximately fifty chiefs of the Miami, Potawatomi, and Kickapoo plus the Ohio Seneca. Because of his suspicions about the fidelity of their warriors to the United States, he called upon those who had remained neutral thus far to take a stand for or against the Americans. Either the tribes should move their families near white settlements or they should have their warriors join his expedition northward. Led by Tarhe of the Wyandot, the "chiefs and warriors present unanimously agreed" to these terms and noted that "they had long been anxious for an opportunity to fight for the Americans." Harrison made a very specific charge to the Indians: those "who went with him must conform to *his* mode of warfare; not to kill or injure old men, women, and children, nor prisoners." This was done to belie the British canard that they were "not able to prevent Indians from such acts of horrid cruelty . . . for if the Indians under [Harrison] would obey his commands, & refrain from acts of barbarism, it would be very evident that the hostile Indians could be as easily restrained by *their* commanders." He concluded this instruction with the admonition that "none but a coward or a squaw would kill a prisoner."[41]

Two other problems with the militia and Indians emerged in mid-July. The first was the sale of liquor to Native Americans by soldiers at Upper Sandusky.

When Indian Agent Stickney protested to the commander about this, he was told "in a very angry manner" that he "meddled with that which was not [his] . . . business, & that he [the commander] would let me [Stickney] know that he Commanded the Fort." More pressing in many ways was the murder of an American scout by a Shawnee named Blackfeather. When the commander of Fort Amanda demanded the culprit be given over to the Americans, considerable opposition arose among the natives who felt this was a justifiable revenge killing for the murder of one of Blackfeather's friends earlier that year. Eventually the Shawnee gave up the young man but begged Harrison for mercy. This caused considerable unrest among Blackfeather's brothers, who threatened to commit atrocities if the confessed murderer were not freed.[42] For Harrison, the art of juggling relations between whites and Native Americans was a delicate matter demanding the wisdom of Solomon. It continuously confronted him while he sought to focus on defeating the British and their allies.

First Siege of Fort Meigs

By February the British had laid the keel of a new warship—to be named HMS *Detroit*—at Amherstburg. They hoped to have it completed by June, and it posed a distinct threat to the American vessels being built at Erie, Pennsylvania. It became the largest man-of-war built on the upper lakes during the war; fortunately for the Americans, the vessel's launching date would be late August.[43] But it is clear that Commodore James Yeo on Lake Ontario was trying to build a counterweight to the squadron that Perry was building at Erie. Whatever the time period between laying the keel and launching the completed vessel, the speed with which one side or the other could complete its squadron might well determine the outcome of the war in the Eighth Military District.

Before any naval decision could be reached, the defense of Fort Meigs became the main focus of American operations in Ohio in the spring and summer. Harrison's precautions for the expected British-Indian siege included a call to Brig. Gen. Green Clay of Kentucky to bring his volunteers to Fort Winchester (modern Defiance, Ohio). On March 26 Harrison ordered General Clay to march northward without losing a "moments time." From there he was to await further orders from the Eighth Military District commander. Harrison also ordered two companies from Fort Wayne to join him, along with Col. Richard M. Johnson's mounted riflemen supposedly being raised in Kentucky. Harrison recognized the strategic vulnerability not only of Fort Meigs but also of the several posts established along the three logistical routes toward the Maumee Rapids. Yet he promised Secretary Armstrong that the nearly completed fortification would "render all the efforts of the enemy unavailing." Governor Shelby advised Harrison that he would send Green Clay's brigade northward, but he had no authorization to raise the mounted riflemen that newspaper accounts said Johnson was to raise.[44] That authorization would soon arrive in Kentucky, but not in time to be useful in the first siege of Fort Meigs.[45]

Quartermaster James Morrison became apprehensive about the future prospects of Fort Meigs's survival as the Virginia and Pennsylvania troops left. "The enemy," he wrote Harrison, "*must know* how much, how greatly your force has *diminished* . . . and that weeks must pass once before reinforcements can be marched to the advanced posts—In a word, *I do not See what is to prevent disaster*." The alarms were such that Harrison set out from Cincinnati for Fort Meigs on 1 April.[46]

From his Washington vantage point, the secretary of war did not expect the British to assault the fort; instead he thought they would surround the post and intercept supplies and reinforcements that approached it. Given Harrison's force size (about which Armstrong seems to have had a complete misunderstanding), his available supplies, and his determination, Armstrong had "no fears with regard to Fort Meigs." On 28 April Harrison reported that enemy columns were in sight and that vessels bearing their artillery were moving up the Maumee River. Surrounding the post were "swarms" of Indians. To Governor Meigs he noted that his men were "in fine Spirits" and that "the enemy little dream of the bitter pill I have prepared for them." He directed his troops to take their posts and to "remember that the eyes of your Country are upon you."[47]

Harrison's "bitter pill" involved two ingredients. First, he expected the garrison to make a determined resistance, and second, he anticipated that the relief of the post by General Clay's troops coming down the river from Fort Winchester would discourage General Procter and his native allies.

The commanding general had an extraordinary confidence in the fortification built under Wood's direction. He did not send out a party to intercept the landing of British troops at the ruins of old Fort Miamis (modern Maumee, Ohio) on the river's north shore over a mile downriver from Fort Meigs, nor did he try to oppose the landing of the artillery brought from Detroit and Fort Malden. Instead he put the men to work constructing a series of traverses over twenty feet wide at the base and a dozen feet high, designed to provide cover and concealment for the troops. He hid this activity from the British and Indians by having tents raised on the river side of the fort. These were taken down just before the bombardment began on 1 May, exposing the traverses to the surprise of the British artillerymen. The troopers pitched the tents and corralled the two hundred horses behind the traverse, thereby protecting both men and animals from enemy fire.

Aboard the *Lady Prevost*, *General Hunter*, *Chippawa*, *Mary*, *Nancy*, and *Miamis* and his gunboats *Eliza* and *Myers*, Henry Procter, now a major general, brought 533 soldiers mostly from the 41st Regiment of Foot and the Royal Newfoundland Regiment. An additional 462 Canadian militia officers and men followed in bateaux. They landed first on Swan Creek near the Maumee's mouth (downtown Toledo, Ohio) and awaited the arrival of all the watercraft and the twelve hundred Indians led by Tecumseh and Roundhead that were coming overland. For several days they paused due to torrential rains, and then they advanced to the Fort Miamis ruins where two twenty-four-pounder artillery pieces weighing two tons each were unloaded on 29 April. These were moved overland to four gun emplacements completed by Royal Engineers in what is now downtown Maumee, Ohio, directly opposite Fort Meigs. The initial emplacements were constructed at night and confronted the American artillerymen in the morning. The two heavy artillery pieces provided the British with far greater firepower than any across the river, and they were joined by an 8-inch howitzer, a 5 1/2-inch mortar, and three twelve-pounder guns. The Native Americans encircled the post, and the North West Army was now without normal communication with the outside world. Sometimes the Indians climbed into trees and fired at the fort from the south side of the river, but few of their bullets could reach the fort itself. Nonetheless, they bothered American pickets and wounded a few. Captain Wood recalled that "we continued our operations, occasionally firing at the civilized savages across the river, as well as upon the wild ones in the woods, whenever the former exposed themselves, *or the latter became too troublesome*."[48]

On the night of 2–3 May, the Royal Artillerymen crossed the river and deployed three light howitzers to the east of the fort. They commenced fire the following morning. The inaccuracy of this fire caused Captain Wood to exclaim that the person who employed it "seemed to be a friend or possessed of very little skill in his profession, for notwithstanding he was about three or four hundred yards distant from the camp, yet not more than one out of four

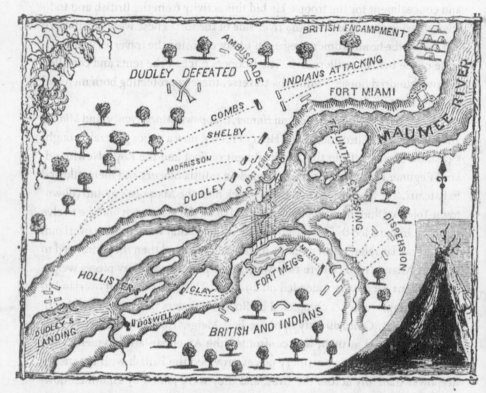

First siege of Fort Meigs. Reprinted from Benson J. Lossing, *Pictorial Field-Book of the War of 1812* (New York: Harper Brothers, 1869).

or five shells thrown every came inside the lines." On 4 May the fire from the British declined, and to the Americans it "appeared as if the enemy were convinced that their labor was entirely lost."[49]

With an extraordinary *sang froid*, Harrison allowed all this to happen without any serious challenge except for artillery fire across the river that had little effect on the British gun emplacements. The total enemy forces were double his own, but the second ingredient of his "bitter pill"—General Clay's Kentuckians—was on the move down the Maumee Valley; they arrived at Fort Winchester on 3 May. There Capt. William Oliver from Fort Meigs, certainly one of the bravest and most successful Americans to traverse native-infested woods, reported to General Clay and encouraged rapid movement down the river. The necessity to do so was reinforced by the rumble of cannonading that could be heard in the distance. Loading his men on eighteen flatboats, General Clay began his descent on the afternoon of 4 May. His hope to arrive in the evening was interrupted due to an exceptionally dark, moonless night that forced the Kentuckians to encamp. Meanwhile, an advance party headed by Maj. David Trimble and including Captain Oliver made its way to the fort and apprized General Harrison of Clay's approach.[50]

With this information Harrison made the most audacious tactical decisions of his military career. Normally risk averse, he decided to make three separate attacks the following day. First he sent Capt. John Hamilton back to General Clay with a new set of orders. The Kentucky general was to divide his command, with a regiment of eight hundred attacking the Royal Artillery batteries opposite the post and the other four hundred landing at Fort Meigs. The key portion of the order was that the element sent to attack the guns was, in the words of General Clay, to "spike them, cut down the Carriages and return to their boats." Second, a detachment of regulars, volunteers, and militia under Col. John Miller of the 19th Regiment, with two companies of the 17th and volunteers, were to attack the artillery position on the river's south bank. Third, Harrison ordered a detachment from the 19th Infantry and volunteers and militiamen from the fort to sally up the river to assist that portion of Green's men that came under attack as they attempted to land on the south shore. Such a complicated and multifaceted scheme of maneuver was uncommon for the usually cautious Harrison.

Colonel Miller's attack was eminently successful but resulted in numerous casualties for both sides. It captured the guns, two officers, and forty enlisted men at the south bank battery.[51] The sally to assist General Clay repelled the Indians and brought the general and his men to the fort. At one point in the latter operation, General Harrison loaned his own speedy mount to his quartermaster whom he sent as a messenger to his dragoon commander in charge of the relief.[52]

Col. William Dudley led Clay's Kentuckians against the main British batteries on the north bank and achieved a great success in capturing the guns and spiking them. They were aided by a spring morning fog that allowed them to land on the shore without being noticed, and they surprised the artillerymen before they could defend themselves. The British infantry encamped at Fort Miamis was unable to assist in the defense before the gun positions had been captured and the cannons there ineffectively spiked. Colonel Dudley apparently never told any of his subordinates that they were to withdraw to Fort

Meigs after spiking the enemy artillery. Moreover, the spikes to disable the cannon were in the boats allotted to General Clay rather than those of Colonel Dudley, so the British artillery was spiked with easily removed ramrods. With the artillery taken and the mission accomplished, success turned into disaster. As Harrison described it, "the intolerable perverse confidence" of too many Kentucky volunteers took hold, and they charged after the retreating enemy instead of withdrawing to the shore. That hubris induced Dudley and his men to disregard their instructions and to pursue retreating Indians and soldiers toward Fort Miamis, from which a relief force emerged. The natives drew their foes deeper into the woods and then surrounded them. Counterattacks led by Acting Majors Adam Muir and Peter L. Chambers of the 41st Foot sealed off the Kentuckians retreat. After a bloody battle the surviving Americans surrendered. As the prisoners entered Fort Miamis there ensued what Chambers called a "dreadful slaughter." In front of the British soldiers and General Procter, several of the prisoners were killed and scalped, and it was not until Tecumseh intervened that the murders stopped. This second mistreatment of Kentucky prisoners of war by Indians only increased the outrage of westerners toward both the natives and the British. Of the 800 men who landed with Dudley, only 150 escaped to Fort Meigs.

Even Ens. James Cochrane of the 41st Foot acknowledged that American "complaints of the supineness" of British General Procter during this incident were not "entirely without foundation." Combined with the River Raisin massacre of the previous January, the "Dudley massacre" provided ammunition for a vengeful attitude among westerners. After these two episodes one can imagine what sort of treatment British soldiers might expect from Americans in general and Kentuckians in particular if the situation ever were reversed.[53]

It had been a bloody day for the Americans: probably over 200 killed in action or while prisoners plus approximately 450 prisoners held in the holds of the British ships lying in Maumee Bay. British losses were relatively few, the most being those captured during Colonel Miller's sortie. The number of Indians killed and wounded is unknown. But there were enough scalps and other trophies of war to satiate most of the natives. They began returning to their homes with clothing and hostages the next day.[54] Harrison noted that he could now send messages to the secretary of war and Governor Meigs and expect them to get through. Despite his losses, the addition of General Clay's four hundred increased Harrison's strength as the British were losing their allies. Even the Upper Canada militiamen in Procter's command demanded to be released so they could plant their crops. Although his artillerymen regained their guns on the north shore and removed the ramrod spikes, they fired few shots at the American fortress. One suspects they were running low on cannon balls. Moreover, Procter learned that York (modern Toronto) had fallen to United States forces, and he feared an American attack from the east. While this fear proved groundless, military caution as well as military reality caused him to recognize that the siege was coming to an end.

Procter tried one last gambit with Harrison. After the encounters on 5 May, Acting Major Peter Chambers appeared with a truce flag and conveyed Procter's message demanding the surrender of Fort Meigs to "Save the effusion of Blood." Harrison feigned surprise that such a demand was being made after the attack rather than before the siege began, as was the custom. "Assure the general," said Harrison in closing the proceedings, "that he will never have this post surrendered to him upon any terms.—Should it fall into his hands, it will be in a manner calculated to do him more honour . . . than any capitulation could possibly do." Another report described a British soldier shouting across the river that the Americans "better hang out the white flag and surrender." To which a U.S. soldier replied, "Gen. Hull has not yet arrived; until he comes you may save yourselves the trouble of asking for surrender."[55] The young enlisted man was sarcastically contrasting Harrison's defiance with William Hull's capitulation at Detroit without firing a short.

His surrender demand rejected, Procter began withdrawing his artillery and men down the river. On 7 May Harrison and Procter began negotiations over a prisoner exchange. Harrison sent Maj. Levi Hukill of his staff and Maj. Thomas Fletcher of General Clay's staff to conduct the talks. The Kentucky prisoners in British hands were to be taken by the British gunboats to the Huron River of north central Ohio, where they would be released "upon the condition of not serving against Great Britain during the War." Capt. Samuel Price of the 1st U.S. Artillery and twenty army regulars and two British lieutenants were exchanged with the proviso that they would serve only on garrison duty until the end of May. What happened to the forty British soldiers captured in Colonel Miller's sortie is not mentioned in the surviving documents, but presumably they returned to His Majesty's service.[56]

Both sides sought to claim victory on the Maumee. Procter quite justifiably noted his modest losses and the infliction of significant casualties upon his foe. His losses included fourteen men killed, forty-two officers and men wounded among the regulars, and one officer and four enlisted men killed among the

Canadian militia. On behalf of the commander of His Majesty's forces in Canada, the British adjutant general proclaimed it a "complete defeat of the Enemy." What they did not focus on was the failure to capture Fort Meigs.[57] Harrison's butcher's bill was much higher, most of it due to the foolishness of Colonel Dudley. Nonetheless, Fort Meigs continued in American hands and remained a staging point for a possible expedition to retake Detroit. While Native Americans might circumvent it in their activities, they remembered the raids against Indian villages Harrison had authorized the previous fall and knew that leaving the fort in American hands while they attacked in Ohio or Indiana left their families vulnerable to a mounted sortie along the Detroit River. For similar reasons, as long as Fort Meigs remained under American control it constrained British land operations in Ohio and Indiana Territory. Therefore Harrison congratulated his troops for "having completely, foiled their foes and put a Stop, to that Career of Victory which has hitherto, attended their Arms." Tecumseh's biographer summarized the situation effectively: "Fort Meigs, with its network of earthen mounds, stood defiant—overcrowded, disease-ridden, and ill-provisioned, but utterly beyond immediate conquest. It seemed that neither side was able to stage a successful offensive."[58]

Governor Shelby was dismayed; again Kentucky had sent its men northward and again they had been slaughtered. This time he thought his son Maj. James Shelby was among the killed—it turned out he survived. Harrison's report, the governor averred, was "a mere plaister" covering up the general's errors. "This Mournfull event," he wrote Henry Clay, "has I assure you deadened the feelings of many of our best patriots, and abated their Confidence in the Commanding General. It will have an unhappy effect upon future calls on Kentucky for me." The governor had no objection to Clay showing the letter to Secretary Armstrong; but the speaker also brought it to the attention of the president. A year later Shelby admitted he based his first impressions on erroneous information.[59] Undoubtedly Shelby's epistle had an adverse effect on Harrison's reputation in Washington.

The Royal Navy still had superiority on Lake Erie and could transport army troops to points along its shore. For instance, James Morrison warned General Harrison that the British could utilize their naval dominance to threaten the logistical depot at Upper Sandusky.[60] But the American squadron being built at Erie, Pennsylvania, threatened that ascendancy. To keep Perry's ships in Presque Isle Bay, the British employed their naval force in blockade duties outside Erie. To employ the twenty-four-pounder guns used in the first siege in a possible second one, Procter needed the larger Royal Navy vessels to transport these large cannons back to the Maumee River. The Erie blockade denied him this support. It also limited naval usefulness in any attack up the Sandusky watershed.[61]

Planning for the Cross-Lake Campaign

Harrison left General Clay in charge of Fort Meigs and headed through Lower and Upper Sandusky to Franklinton and then on to Cincinnati. He conversed with Governor Return J. Meigs and newly appointed supply contractor Benjamin Orr. He also wrote a blistering condemnation of Assistant Deputy Quartermaster General Capt. Joseph Wheaton, whom Deputy Quartermaster General Capt. William Piatt accused of pilfering public funds. Governor Meigs found Wheaton "[so] entirely worthless and unfit for any kind of duty . . . that he was laughed at and Scorned" by all who knew him. Additionally, Harrison found Wheaton a man who "employs more of his thoughts and time in endeavours to conciliate and gain my confidence than he does in the discharge of the duties of his appointment." This was just one of several personnel problems that crossed Harrison's desk in the next several weeks. For instance, he allowed the dismissal of a 1st Artillery Regiment captain for repeated intoxication and absence without leave. He also approved the decisions of several courts martial within his district. Because there were unaccountable delays in the movement of some units, Harrison issued orders requiring every detachment commander to maintain a journal of his march from its inception to its completion.[62]

Logistical matters continued to concern him. He had supplies forwarded by several routes to the Lake Erie littoral. The first was the route via the St. Marys and Auglaize Rivers to the Maumee and downstream to Fort Meigs. Supplies also accumulated at Cleveland and Erie but could not be forwarded until Perry established naval dominance of the lake. Finally, logistical support supposedly under the supervision of the contracting firm of Orr & Greeley was sent up the Scioto River and down the Sandusky to Upper Sandusky, where Harrison had a supply depot. Before the United States achieved naval dominance of the lakes, Harrison focused on the Scioto-Sandusky route as the more useful one for both supplies and troops being sent northward. This avenue was less prone to be interdicted by hostile natives, and it brought troops and supplies close to a potential cross-lake departure point near the mouth of the Sandusky River.[63]

Col. Richard M. Johnson of the newly raised regiment of Kentucky mounted riflemen posed a particular problem for the Eighth District commander. Although the regiment had been raised for the relief of Fort Meigs and was no longer needed for that purpose, and although the secretary of war was not inclined to keep volunteer units on active duty longer than necessary, Harrison was particularly impressed with Johnson and his men and thought them necessary for deployment on the frontier. Hence he sent Johnson's regiment to Fort Wayne and sought the secretary's approval for keeping it in government service, because the deployment of such "a body of mounted men would be attended with very happy effects" in the Wabash, Illinois, and Mississippi Valleys. He would eventually receive Armstrong's approval for this enterprise. As he surveyed the situation, Harrison proposed a "Collateral expedition" to the cross-lake, one utilizing Johnson's regiment against Detroit combined with an amphibious attack on the Canadian side of the Detroit River. As we shall see, this corps would be most beneficial for United States military operations over the next several months. In another personnel matter, Harrison reduced the death sentence for three men charged with desertion but allowed the execution of one private who both deserted and threatened the life of his company commander.[64]

Nothing more graphically indicates Secretary Armstrong's micromanagement of Harrison's district than an order he wrote directing Johnson's regiment to report to General Howard at Kaskaskia, Illinois Territory. The order was sent to Cincinnati, and Harrison did not receive it until a month after its issuance; the general complained that the Indian menace in the Illinois and Missouri area was "groundless." Moreover, this directive would take Johnson's Kentuckians far from the main theater of operations in the Eighth Military District and involved a 450-mile trek from Fort Wayne. By early July Johnson's regiment had ridden seven hundred miles and it needed remounts. Johnson protested that his men did not enlist "to serve under cowards, drunkards, old grannies, nor traitors, but under one who had proved himself to be wise, prudent and brave"—that is, Harrison. The Kaskaskia order would eventually be rescinded by Armstrong. In fact, the secretary recognized that the mounted riflemen would protect "the frontier against small desultory attacks" and "be Useful in making demonstrations by land," while Harrison would advance by water against Fort Malden. Ironically, the same day Armstrong rescinded the order to Kaskaskia, Johnson wrote the president that he would be "satisfied & happy" to march to Illinois.[65] Obviously, the War Department ignored this letter.

Before receiving Armstrong's order, Harrison indicated a possible use of Johnson's men in a *coup de main* against British units or Indian settlements along the western bank of the Detroit River. The great danger of such an enterprise lay "in the inattention, (So Customary with Militia) of your Officers and Men to those measures which are necessary to guard against surprise, and the confidence and rashness which a first Success is So apt to inspire [in] our backwoodsmen." The district commander relied on Johnson's discretion and military expertise to restrain his men from a disaster similar to that befalling Colonel Dudley a few weeks earlier. Harrison clearly expected to make an advance on Detroit from Fort Meigs whether or not Perry secured naval control of Lake Erie and the cross-lake invasion took place. In fact, he proposed to Secretary Armstrong that if the rumor that General Procter had left Fort Malden for the Niagara Frontier was correct, Colonel Johnson should be sent to the Detroit Valley at once and not wait for naval dominance to be secured.[66] The rumor that Procter had gone to the Niagara Frontier proved false, but Harrison clearly intended to use Johnson's troops to advance toward Detroit while he moved by water against Malden.

Were these problems regarding Johnson's men and their deployment not enough, remounting his regiment caused troubles with the Native Americans. Indian Agent Benjamin F. Stickney accused Johnson's men of stealing horses from the Indians and of taking the fine horse belonging to an interpreter, who was laughed at by the mounted soldiers for wanting it returned. Stickney found himself without civil authority to assist in the case, finding that in northern Ohio it was a question not of legality but of might that governed individual and group actions.[67]

Another unit utilization issue emerged with the deployment of Col. William P. Anderson's 24th U.S. Infantry Regiment. This newly raised regiment was supposed to go to Cleveland to protect Major Jesup's boatbuilding project. Harrison, however, had sent Ohio militia forces there, and he assumed the boats would be used to move troops across the lake in short order. For that reason he stopped the regiment with its newly acquired enlistees at Franklinton. When it arrived on 7 June, the regiment consisted of only 314 enlisted men fit for duty, less than half its supposed enlisted strength and a third of its authorized manpower. By mid-June Harrison had the five viable companies of the regiment on their way to Lower Sandusky.[68]

But it was not just the want of regular army enlisted men that troubled the general. For instance, the 24th Infantry's officer corps lacked quantity, ability, and stability. Resignations and petty infighting characterized many of the few subalterns. Colonel Anderson urged Harrison to forward to Armstrong the resignations of three lieutenants because "they were worse than none." The 26th Infantry contained only three hundred men, a fourth of whom were former prisoners of war (Dudley's men) who were, by their parole, not allowed to engage in offensive operations. For its Canadian offensive, the North West Army needed far more men than the regular army units had enlisted.[69]

Because Harrison thought the British concentration of their Native American resources in the Detroit River area precluded there being significant Indian incursions in the Mississippi Valley region, he also sought Brig. Gen. Benjamin Howard's services with the North West Army. Even though Howard would remain in the Mississippi Valley portion of the district, the request indicates that in May, Harrison considered Howard his subordinate.[70]

Toward the end of June, Harrison learned from General Clay that escaped Kentucky prisoners reported that Indians from the upper Great Lakes had joined Tecumseh and Procter and a second siege of Fort Meigs was expected shortly. The men's informants grossly exaggerated Procter's strength to consist of four thousand Indians and fifteen thousand or more British and militia troops. The latter figure was at least ten times the real number of regulars and Canadian militia Procter could expect. The enemy was also expected to attack some of the small posts that supported the forwarding of supplies to Fort Meigs—for example, Forts Amanda, Winchester, and Stephenson—or maybe go down the lake and attack the boatbuilding facilities and supply depots at Cleveland and Erie. Harrison believed an attack on Fort Stephenson at Lower Sandusky might be made, because it was defended by "mutinous militia" and was not capable of withstanding the heavy artillery that Procter might bring by water. For that reason he deployed Maj. George Croghan (pronounced *Crawn*) and two companies of 17th U.S. Infantry to Fort Stephenson. He feared for this and other small posts because many contained large logistical supplies of which the British were alleged to be in dire need.[71]

About the same time, Harrison had his first disagreement with Benjamin Orr, the contractor recently sent to provide rations for the North West Army. One of the issues revolved around the large quantity of food in government hands before the contract with Orr & Greeley. Was the firm liable for an inventory of such supplies and for any losses sustained by them since the new contract went into existence? Who was to assume the costs of transporting the supplies to the troops in the field? Orr thought the firm was not liable for the inventory and that it could charge for transportation. Harrison rejected Orr's solution. Currently, the transportation to Lake Erie was being borne by teams and teamsters in government employ. Harrison did not see the need for Orr & Greeley to bill the United States for the transportation already being done at government expense. The real profit to the contractor lay in charging for rations, but Harrison knew sufficient rations were already available in Ohio and Kentucky, and he assumed that such supplies should last until 1 December without augmentation. Orr left Ohio for Washington, complaining that he had purchased supplies for the North West Army that Harrison had not requested even though, Harrison contended, Orr knew about "the immense supplies we had on our hands."[72] Orr had received the commissary contract from Secretary Armstrong, and Harrison's circumventing his authority in the supply of rations and their transport to the frontier displeased him. The Orr & Greeley dispute with Harrison eventually became a sore point with Armstrong and the source of rumors concerning the general's supposed peculation in commissary supplies. Orr was a Washington, DC, grocer and a former city alderman who had numerous connections within the administration and with congressmen who believed his anti-Harrison charges.

Attacks on Fort Meigs and Fort Stephenson

On 24 June Harrison left Franklinton with elements of the 24th, 26th, 17th, and 19th U.S. Infantry Regiments, amounting to approximately 1,270 officers and men. Behind him were the 27th U.S. Infantry and Lt. Col. James V. Ball's dragoons. In addition he expected the arrival of the 28th Infantry, which Col. Thomas D. Owings recruited from Kentucky. Because Colonel Johnson's mounted regiment was already at Fort Meigs, Harrison considered General Clay in a strong position to resist any force the British and their allies could bring against him. Instead of going all the way to Lower Sandusky, Harrison stopped his corps at what became known as Camp Seneca (Old Fort, Ohio), where they encamped. Taking approximately three hundred men from the 24th U.S. Infantry, he marched to the Maumee Rapids to personally assess the situation. While there he sent Colonel Johnson on a scouting mission to the River Raisin, where he gathered considerable intelligence information from the francophone population. Having learned that a British-Indian attack was delayed, not knowing its probable target, and having determined that the augmentation of the Fort Meigs garrison with Johnson's mounted Kentuckians and

Colonel Anderson's men made the post well defended, Harrison hurried on to Fort Stephenson and then to Cleveland, where he reinforced the garrison protecting the bateaux and the supplies stored there.[73]

For the British, the situation on Lakes Erie and Ontario grew increasingly bleak during the spring and summer of 1813. The list of defeats and tactical failures grew steadily longer. An American army-navy raid at York in late April was followed by a successful seizure of Fort George at the mouth of the Niagara River a month later. The British evacuated Fort Erie at the headwaters of the Niagara a few days after this. Now the principal logistical route over the Niagara escarpment between the lower two Great Lakes was in American hands. A British attack in late May against the American naval base at Sackets Harbor, New York, failed. Added to this was the failure to take Fort Meigs in early May, the growing American naval strength at Erie, and the obvious preparations for an American offensive into Michigan. Yet the Royal Navy and American fleets on Lakes Ontario and Erie had not met in decisive engagement, and the British Army with its Canadian and native allies remained intact.

The British right division—its regular army strength was about half a regiment—existed as a forlorn hope, with its rear threatened if the Americans gained control of Burlington Heights (modern Hamilton, Ontario) at the northwest end of Lake Ontario or if Kingston fell to them at the northeast end of the lake. From the perspective of those at Fort Malden, Fort Meigs looked like a dagger pointed at the Detroit River Valley. The loss of Forts George and Erie meant that Procter's tenuous supply line rested on a primitive road network from Burlington Bay to Long Point, opposite Erie, Pennsylvania. From there they could use water transport. If Perry's squadron ever sailed out of Presque Isle Bay, that logistical lifeline would be severed unless the new British ship being slowly constructed at Amherstburg could join with Commander Robert H. Barclay's other vessels in a decisive victory over Perry. Even before Perry entered the lake, the logistical situation became desperate at Fort Malden. The soldiers and natives and their families consumed fourteen thousand rations a day. This created an unsustainable supply situation. Already the beef supply was exhausted, and soon the supply of grain and forage would be gone. Procter looked enviously at the mountains of supplies and hundreds of cattle that Harrison was accumulating on Erie's south shore. That bane of many unsuccessful commanders throughout history—insufficient logistical support—caused the British commander to lament, "The want of meat does operate much against

us. As does the want of Indian arms and goods. In short, our wants are so serious that the enemy must derive great advantage from them alone."[74]

Then things became more complicated. Down the Detroit River came dozens upon dozens of brightly decorated birch bark canoes filled with at least
twelve hundred warriors from the upper lakes and the Mississippi Valley. One
observer described it as "one of the wildest and most grand and beautifull
Indian sights" he ever beheld. British flags flew from the canoes, and warriors
chanted war songs as they approached Procter's headquarters in Sandwich.
At a signal "they commenced fiering their guns and turned the bows of their
canoes towards . . . [the] Canada shore, landing in beautiful order one after the
other." Led by Robert Dickson of the British Indian Agency, these Menominee, Winnebago, Ojibwa, Sioux, Ottawa, Sac, and Fox tribesmen represented
both an opportunity and a problem for General Procter. According to Captain McAfee, they "were a horde of as wild and cruel savages as ever disgraced
human nature."[75] However great the hyperbole in the Kentuckian's rhetoric,
these additions forced Procter to engage in another offensive against a target
he wanted to avoid.

On the positive side, these arriving natives nearly doubled Procter's Native American combat strength. On the negative side, this latest addition
to native strength and their Detroit River colleagues focused on Fort Meigs
and demanded that the Maumee River outpost be their first objective. They
undoubtedly had heard many tales concerning the victory, scalps, and booty
secured in the first siege. The new arrivals also increased British commissary
requirements. In vain Procter sought to convince them that the supply depots
at Lower and Upper Sandusky were more vulnerable and more valuable targets. Procter found to his "Mortification . . . that instead of being a disposable
one, or under my Direction, our Movements would be subject to the Caprices
and Prejudices of the Indian Body, to the Degree in which my regular Force
was disproportionate to their Numbers." So it was that with gunboats, bateaux,
and canoes, they sailed out of the Detroit River and headed for Maumee Bay.[76]
Procter's self-justifying epistle omits the fact that Fort Stephenson at Lower
Sandusky had few supplies and that Harrison's entrenched encampment at
Camp Seneca interposed between the British-Indian armada and the Upper
Sandusky depot. Because it would be difficult for the British to transport any
supplies they might capture at either Fort Winchester or Fort Wayne, Indiana,
Harrison expected Procter to advance on his depots on either the Sandusky

River or the Cuyahoga River at Cleveland. Once the supplies were captured, Procter could easily move them via Lake Erie to the Detroit Valley. So Harrison sent additional troops to Cleveland while he turned his attention to Fort Meigs.[77]

Meanwhile, American naval dominance of Lake Erie remained in abeyance and recruitment for the regular army regiments lagged. While Secretary Armstrong found the "want of *Seamen* [for Perry's squadron] astonishing," he finally recognized that volunteers were a necessary source of manpower for the North West Army. Samuel Huntington, Duncan McArthur, Lewis Cass, and Richard Johnson declared that the regular "recruiting service is very dull" and volunteer units of limited duration should be authorized. After considerable delay, Armstrong reluctantly authorized Harrison "to take what in your judgement will be necessary" to complete the army's requirements from militia units—giving preference to Kentucky units already in service and to the Pennsylvania regiment stationed at Erie. Harrison's aide-de-camp, Maj. David Trimble, carried a letter to Governor Shelby requesting between four hundred and two thousand men to come north as soon as possible. He also suggested that the governor command the troops from Kentucky. Respecting the governor's age and experience, Harrison suggested that Shelby would "be the guiding Head and I the Hand" in such an arrangement. Using one of his typical Roman historical allusions, Harrison noted that such an understanding was not without precedent: "Scipio the Conqueror of Carthage did not disdain to act as the Lieutenant of his younger and less experienced Brother Lucius" in 190 BC at the battle of Magnesia, near Smyrna, in modern Turkey. So it would be that Shelby, senior in age and experience, subordinated himself to Harrison. To assist Shelby in his task, Harrison ordered the quartermasters at Newport, Kentucky, to furnish the governor with "any quantity of the arms and other munitions of war which he may demand or you are able to supply." Shelby agreed to the proposal and directed volunteers to rendezvous at Newport (opposite Cincinnati) at the end of August. President Madison also wrote Shelby encouraging the Kentuckians to answer Harrison's call. The solicitation of Kentuckians with no similar request to Ohio's young men aroused Governor Meigs's resentment. Harrison sought to mollify the Ohio leader by suggesting he consolidate the currently active Ohio units into two full militia regiments (approximately a thousand officers and men) to be stationed at Upper Sandusky until it was determined "whether their Services will be wanted." In addition he hoped Meigs would encourage more Ohioans to enlist in the 26th U.S. Infantry as twelve-month recruits.[78] One can understand why the nonuse of Ohio militia units eventually caused resentment among many who saw the general as favoring Kentuckians.

Also in mid-July Armstrong slightly enlarged the Eighth Military District by placing the Pennsylvania militiamen guarding Perry's squadron in Erie under Harrison's command. Harrison ordered Col. Rees Hill's regiment stationed there to embark on Perry's ships once they left Erie.[79]

When news of the British advance toward Fort Meigs reached Harrison, three critical decisions resulted. First, he trusted General Clay and left the defense of his outpost to the troops now encamped at the Maumee Rapids. Second, he thought Fort Stephenson too vulnerable to British assault for its small garrison to resist, so he directed Major Croghan to evacuate the post. Third, he decided not to reinforce either fortification, thereby avoiding opening his corps to attack from the numerous Indians that he knew eagerly awaited a possible ambush.

Perhaps the third of these decisions best represents the typical William Henry Harrison military style—he was a cautious commander. He had fewer than a thousand troops at Camp Seneca, and he knew there were at least three thousand native warriors wandering the woods and swamps of northwest Ohio. Indians had an aversion to attacking fortifications, and Harrison's position was as secure as an encampment could be made in a few days. It was also nine miles beyond the point to which the British could bring their gunboats and cannon by water. Hence he was safe from artillery bombardment. Tecumseh's allies waited in vain for Harrison's march to assist in the Fort Meigs defense. The Eighth Military District commander anticipated Perry's squadron would start to leave Erie in a few days and would dominate the lake until the British ship being built at Amherstburg was completed. The men at Camp Seneca represented the vanguard of the troops he expected to use in an amphibious attack on the Canadian shore. Their preservation for the cross-lake invasion was a primary consideration in not risking them in the Black Swamp. Prudent commanders do not endanger critical forces for secondary objectives.

Harrison placed considerable confidence in and responsibility on Green Clay. Fifteen years older than the Eighth Military District's commander, Clay was a Virginia-born Kentucky entrepreneur who reputedly was the commonwealth's wealthiest citizen. General Clay was a veteran of the Continental Army and of early Kentucky politics. A few weeks earlier he had witnessed the destruction of two-thirds of his relieving force in Dudley's massacre, a memory that made him much more cautious than many volunteer soldiers. The next few days would test his courage and resolve as Procter and his host moved toward the Maumee Rapids.

Clay's scouts discovered their presence on 21 July, and the Kentuckian reported that his troops were "in high spirits—and most woefully will the enemy be deceived in their anticipation of conquest." Harrison, noting that his garrison was of insufficient size to do anything but remain in a defensive posture, wrote General Duncan McArthur urging him to ask Governor Meigs to call up the Ohio militia for reinforcements.[80]

This would not be a repeat of the first siege, with heavy artillery confronting the wooden ramparts and earthen traverses of the fort. These pieces could not be forwarded on the small craft available to the British. Instead, Procter, Tecumseh, and their men staged a mock battle east of the fort, involving a few British regulars and various natives, with the intention to deceive the Americans into coming to the rescue of American reinforcements. A British observer waiting in the ambush said it was so effective that even he was in "half doubt" as to "whether the battle was a sham one or a real." Many of Clay's officers urged him to make a sortie to rescue their countrymen, but he forbade it because he knew Harrison was not sending reinforcements. Clay remained resolute in his decision, and the British found themselves "utterly foiled in the grand design of the expedition."[81]

Their ruse failing, both the British commander and the native chiefs faced a new operational decision. Procter wanted to press forward toward his original objective of the supply base at Upper Sandusky. Many natives, especially those whose families had moved from Ohio, Indiana, and Illinois to the Detroit Valley, did not want to leave Fort Meigs behind them because this would make their families vulnerable to a counterattack while they were in Ohio. They knew only too well that a raid by Colonel Johnson's cavalrymen could devastate their villages. For that reason many withdrew to Michigan to protect their homes and loved ones. Procter and many allies left the Maumee by water on 28 July, on the gunboats *Eliza* and *Myers*, commercial schooners *Nancy* and *Ellen*, several bateaux, and scores of Indian canoes. In addition several hundred mounted Indians marched overland toward Lower Sandusky. By 1 August the armada was off the mouth of Sandusky Bay. Its objective was obvious to Harrison.[82]

He ordered Major Croghan to withdraw his two companies from Fort Stephenson. That directive became one of the most controversial of Harrison's career. Croghan had 160 men and seven officers from the 17th Infantry at the small post and only two hundred barrels of flour. From Harrison's standpoint, it was too much risk for too little materiel. He, of course, did not know of the massive withdrawal of Procter's Indian allies to Michigan, nor did he know of the modest size of Procter's artillery onboard the gunboats that accompanied the British. General Clay's reports estimated the British strength at five thousand. Procter, on the other hand, believed there were only about fifty Americans at the post and that it contained a large amount of commissary goods. He did not know that the American general had replaced the "mutinous militia" with over three times that many men and a small artillery piece. Harrison ordered Croghan to abandon Fort Stephenson and proceed to Camp Seneca, after destroying the fort and its contents. He issued the order on 29 July, but because the men carrying it became disoriented, it did not arrive until midmorning of the 30th. Croghan replied that because the order was received so late, he could no longer safely evacuate the fort, and his troops were "determined to maintain this place, and by heavens we can."[83]

Such insubordination did not sit well with Harrison. Even though Croghan had been the commanding general's aide-de-camp, and even though Harrison's accolades for his gallant conduct during the first siege of Fort Meigs had gotten him promoted to major, Croghan's disobedience to a specific order brought down the general's wrath. He ordered Col. Samuel Wells to Lower Sandusky and directed him to relieve Croghan of command, and the dragoons sent with Wells were to bring Croghan under arrest to Camp Seneca. "The General, of course, was nettled," recalled Sergeant Alfred Brunson. "The Major was a pet of his; had been in service with him through the war, from Tippecanoe to this time; and to get such a letter from his pet, was rather too much for friendship to bear; and, besides subordination must be preserved or the army would be ruined." In Harrison's mind Major Croghan waited too long to abandon the post, but "it was the error of a Brave Man," he wrote Governor Shelby.[84]

En route to Fort Stephenson, the dragoons engaged in a brief skirmish with Indian warriors. They repulsed the ambush but informed Harrison about it when they brought Croghan to Camp Seneca. That episode plus the bravado of the twenty-one-year-old major convinced Harrison that perhaps the post could be successfully defended. He allowed Croghan to return to his command. Central to the successful defense of the post was the management of an aged sixpounder (called "Old Bess") by a gentleman private of the Petersburg, Virginia, volunteers. Croghan's victory over a force of British regulars at least three times

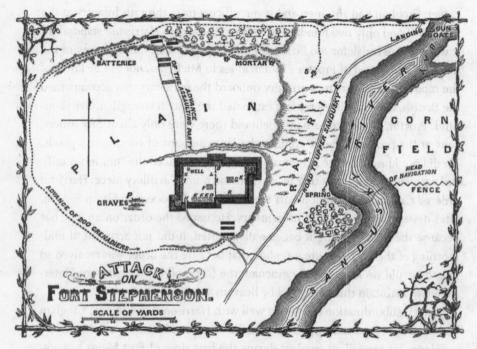

Battle of Fort Stephenson. Reprinted from Benson J. Lossing, *Pictorial Field-Book of the War of 1812* (New York: Harper Brothers, 1869)

his number became legendary. With Croghan promoted to lieutenant colonel for his exploit, the incident provided ammunition to those who derided Harrison's military leadership capabilities. Too few of Harrison's critics understood the adage of Capt. Daniel Cushing of the 2nd U.S. Artillery. A veteran of both sieges of Fort Meigs, Cushing opined, "Caution is one of the greatest traits of military glory that a General can be possessed of. The commanding officer cannot be too cautious of his enemy; they will come like a thief in the night when they are least expected."[85] Harrison's wariness was too often seen as weakness when in fact it was the most prudent course of action.

Harrison sought to rectify the impression of lacking confidence in Croghan by lauding his performance: "It will not be amongst the least of Genl. Proctors [Procter's] mortification[s] to find that he has been baffled by a youth who has just passed his 21st year." Croghan, he wrote Secretary Armstrong, was a "Hero worthy of his gallant Uncle (Genl. [George Rogers] Clark) and I bless my good fortune in having first introduced this promising Shoot of a Distinguished family to the notice of the Government."[86]

For the British, the dire consequences of their failures on the Maumee and Sandusky Rivers emerged. Their casualty list was very long—at least a hundred regulars killed, wounded, and missing. The episode shattered the *esprit de corps* of the right division. The Indian alliance splintered. Many of Dickson's warriors headed north, and others began negotiations with Harrison. A disillusioned Tecumseh threatened to leave the British. The defenses of Forts Meigs and Stephenson vindicated Harrison's strategic caution and his construction of defensible fortresses that threatened the British and Indians in the Detroit Valley. Two days after Croghan's victory, Perry's fleet crossed over the bar at Presque Isle Bay. and the Americans achieved naval dominance on the lake. Now, Harrison prophesied, "we shall transfer the *labouring Oar* to the enemy and oblige him to encounter Some of the labours and difficulties which we have undergone in waging a defensive warfare and protecting our extensiv[e] frontier against a Superior force."[87] The only hope the British had was that HMS *Detroit* would soon be finished and that it, with the remainder of the Royal Navy squadron on the lake, might reverse the strategic situation.

The transfer of the "labouring oar" would take longer than Harrison anticipated. He grew increasingly skeptical about the military capabilities of the officers and men of the Ohio militia. His call to Governor Shelby indicates a reliance on Kentuckians over those men that Governor Meigs could enlist. But Shelby could not muster his expected troops until 31 August, and it would take nearly three weeks for his mounted infantry to arrive at Lake Erie's southern shore. Perry might be over the bar, but he lacked sufficient officers and men to maneuver on the lake. It would not be until 9 August that a few additional tars arrived; even so, his squadron was still undermanned. Three days later Perry's little squadron raised anchor and sailed off to immortality. Navy Secretary William Jones believed Perry's complaints regarding an insufficiency of officers and men were exaggerated and that it might be a case of "laying an anchor to the windward"—that is, establishing an excuse to be used in case of defeat or allowing for excessive merit on his part should he achieve victory.[88]

Each day of delay postponed the objectives the Washington command authorities expected of the general and the master commandant: secure naval dominance on the upper lakes, capture Fort Malden and Detroit, eliminate the right division of the British Army, destroy the Indian alliance, retake Fort Michilimackinac, and advance against the British-Canadian forces on the Niagara frontier.[89] This was a tall order, one that Harrison and Perry set out to achieve. But Perry needed more crew members; Governor Shelby's men only slowly mobilized south of the Ohio River; the British expected to launch their new ship, which had heavier armament than any vessel in the American squadron; and the summer's end and fall storms might adversely affect naval operations. Every delay increased the possibility that not all of the items on Washington's wish list would be accomplished.

Chapter Six

Invading Canada

O n 10 September 1813, the sound of guns echoed across Lake Erie; the rumble was heard from Detroit to Cleveland. But the outcome of the long-expected naval engagement was unknown to those on shore; even those at Put-in-Bay and the mouth of the Detroit River could not discern from the smoke-obscured lake which side had won. The next day General Harrison ordered his troops garrisoned at Camp Seneca to march to Lower Sandusky, even though no one knew the result. But before the arriving troops had time to pitch their tents, a boat came up the river "with all the speed oars could give her." Shortly after Lt. Dulaney Forrest, the officer commanding the vessel, reached Harrison's headquarters at Fort Stephenson, the troops "heard a tremendous shout and hurrahing, and then the booming of cannon. All eyes were turned in that direction, knowing that something glorious had occurred, what, we could not guess." Harrison had just read one of the best-known dispatches in American military history: "We have met the enemy, and they are ours—two ships, two brigs, one schooner and one Sloop." Soon, recalled Supply Sergeant Alfred Brunson, a man came "running down the hill at a break-neck speed" and announced to the anxious soldiers the news of the American victory on the lake. There then ensued universal shouting and rejoicing. Everyone knew the consequences of the destruction of the British squadron on the lake—the invasion of Canada was about to begin.[1]

By far the most immediate consequence of the naval victory on Lake Erie was the American invasion that followed. In less than four weeks, Harrison's troops altered the military situation on the upper Great Lakes and defeated the hopes of many Canadians and Native Americans for changing the 1783 northwestern boundary of the United States.

Harrison and Perry Cooperate

Interservice cooperation received a blow when Secretary of War John Armstrong and Secretary of the Navy William Jones issued joint regulations on 8

April specifically delineating command relationships between army and navy commanders in the field. Army officers found themselves prohibited from commanding any naval vessel, and navy officers were forbidden to command any army troops.[2] This regulation prohibited Perry from placing in a command position Capt. Henry Brevoort of the army, who had previously commanded the army supply brig *Adams* on Lakes Erie and Huron and was a far more experienced ship master and commander than many of Mstr. Comdt. Oliver Hazard Perry's very junior subordinates. Harrison and Perry soon violated the order concerning ground troops on naval vessels so as to fill empty billets on Perry's ships. They found that some "volunteers" would not become sailors unless their junior officers commanded them.[3]

In early July Harrison and Perry began exchanging letters from which blossomed a spirit of cooperation. The army commander suggested Put-in-Bay as an ideal port for Perry's use and one that also would provide security for Harrison's forces in northern Ohio. Harrison also noted it would take some time to assemble enough troops for a cross-lake invasion. Inherent in these observations was a belief that the embarkation point would be somewhere west of Cleveland, since Harrison required Kentucky volunteers to bolster his forces. Perry forwarded ordnance stores from Pittsburgh to Fort Meigs via Erie. Army quartermasters transferred necessary supplies to Perry's squadron. One of Harrison's staff officers wrote of the general's "perfect conviction, that no exertion will be omitted on [Perry's] part to give the Crisis an issue of Profit and Glory to the arms of our Country."[4]

The first opportunity for "profit and glory" had already passed. Harrison wanted Perry to sail to western Lake Erie while Procter was attacking either Fort Meigs or Fort Stephenson, thereby entrapping Procter in Ohio. The lack of officers and seamen to man Perry's squadron frustrated this option. Had the Lake Erie squadron been able to sail ten days before it did, the pursuit of the British right wing to the Thames battlefield would have been unnecessary. Defeat of the British forces in early August would have allowed the transfer of Harrison's army to the subsequent missions with which it was charged: the recapture of Fort Michilimackinac and the redeployment of regular troops to the Niagara frontier. As Perry wrote Harrison, "My anxiety to joining you is very great, and, had seamen been sent to me in time, I should now [5 August], in all probability, have been at the head of the lake acting in conjunction with you."[5]

A second opportunity for "profit and glory" required the two service commanders to coordinate their activities. It was in Sandusky Bay, on 19 August, that Harrison first met Perry. They, their senior commanders, and their staffs consulted for three days. They shaped the operational planning for the next several weeks with a series of decisions. First, Perry would try to entice Barclay and his squadron out of the Detroit River and the protection of Fort Malden's guns and onto the lake, where Perry expected to defeat the Royal Navy force. Second, Harrison would begin moving most of his forces to the mouth of the Portage River (modern Port Clinton, Ohio), where they would be joined by Maj. Thomas Jesup's boats. Third, Harrison would solicit Gov. Isaac Shelby of Kentucky to quickly bring the volunteers from his state to reinforce Harrison's regular regiments, which were still woefully undermanned and depleted by sickness. Fourth, Harrison would provide enough volunteer militia and regular army troops to fill the still-vacant billets in Perry's vessels. Finally, once Perry captured, depleted, blockaded, or reduced to insignificance the British naval squadron, his vessels would escort and tow the Schenectady landing craft to the Canadian shore.[6] Theirs would be the most complex, sophisticated, and integrated joint operation in the brief history of American warfare.

The delays in naval operations and the lack of success on Lakes Ontario and Erie began to irritate some in Washington. President Madison expressed an appreciation of the need for caution by both Cmdr. Isaac Chauncey on the lower lake and Perry on the upper lake that indicated a desire not to be "hurried, by an impatience to fix the public opinion" in their favor. In particular, he concluded that for Perry, delay probably would have little effect on the outcome of battle. Secretary Jones noted to the president that Perry "had gone to Cooperate with Gen. Harrison."[7]

On 10 September Cmdr. Robert H. Barclay brought his Royal Navy flotilla out of the Detroit River and onto Lake Erie. Perry, with approximately 130 of Harrison's soldiers onboard his vessels, won a dramatic victory that resulted in the capture of the entire Royal Navy squadron. One Kentuckian recalled Perry saying "that had it not been for the [army] volunteers the battle would have been lost." Both the militiamen and the regulars that fought with Perry constituted an important segment of his manpower during the battle, in which he achieved extraordinary fame for the navy.[8] Now Perry could return the favor by supporting army endeavors.

This required what modern military terminology calls a "joint operation." The official Pentagon dictionary describes joint operations as "military actions conducted by joint forces," that is, by forces of two or more military services.[9] In the early twentieth century, to achieve optimum results in combined army-navy operations, the United States military devised a set of "Principles of War," one of which was "Unity of Command." This term argues that the "decisive application of full combat power" is obtained "by the coordinated action of all forces toward a common goal. While coordination may be attained by cooperation, it is best achieved by vesting a single commander with requisite authority."[10]

In the early nineteenth century, however, the U.S. military lacked the benefit of decades of Command and General Staff College and War College indoctrination of its officers in the implementation of joint commands that we know today. There was no way the Department of the Navy was going to allow a Department of War general to have operational command over its officers, ships, or their crews. Instead, interservice synchronization required a "unity of effort" between cooperating generals and commodores to achieve the desired "coordination and cooperation toward common objectives, even if the participants are not necessarily part of the same command or organization."[11]

Such a unity of effort was difficult to achieve; one only needs to witness the on-again, off-again cooperation between Commodore Isaac Chauncey on Lake Ontario and a variety of army commanders from the Niagara frontier to the St. Lawrence Valley.[12] Early in the war, a spirit of interservice cooperation was the intention of Washington authorities. Secretary of the Navy Paul Hamilton had notified his various part commanders (including O. H. Perry at Newport, Rhode Island) that "to provide against a deficiency in the munitions of war," ordnance officers of the army and navy should cover the deficiencies of the other service as far as possible. A few months later, Acting Secretary of War James Monroe concluded that "it is obvious that the Command of Lake Erie would dissipate many difficulties which now weigh heavy on us"—that is, on the ground forces.[13] Still, none of this required the close interservice cooperation necessary for Harrison and Perry to achieve the desired results on the Lake Erie littoral. Their unity of effort would not be the consequence of advanced military educational training, joint service doctrinal manuals, or departmental orders. Instead it was the result of personal coordination and interaction that exceeded the wildest expectations of those in Washington.

Harrison wrote Secretary William Eustis on 12 December that an "Army advancing to Detroit along a line of Operation passing so near" Fort Malden risked being logistically cut off, as General Hull had been, by interruptions of the supply lines from Ohio. Consequently, he argued, "the attack ought not to be directed against Detroit, but against Malden." But Harrison sought to accomplish this task not through naval operations but rather by attacking across Lake Erie or the Detroit River when they were frozen.[14]

The type of coordination expected in the first instance was logistical, not command; in the second, it involved the navy gaining dominance on the lake, not any direct army effort or interservice coordination. Therefore the degree of cooperation, coordination, and interdependence that existed between Maj. Gen. William Henry Harrison and Mstr. Comdt. Oliver Hazard Perry merits special attention for its level of mutual effort and operational success without much Washington direction.

On 3 April 1813, Secretary Armstrong issued a long directive to Harrison in which he listed several objectives, including (1) gaining command of the lakes, which could be achieved by early June, and curtailing land operations until then; and (2) approaching Fort Malden by an amphibious operation using the boats built by Major Jesup in Cleveland, rather than engaging in a "difficult, dangerous and enormously expensive" overland campaign out of Fort Meigs.[15]

Following the naval triumph on Lake Erie, Harrison wrote the secretary of war what he considered his operational objectives to be: (1) driving the enemy from Detroit and Fort Malden, (2) capturing Forts Michilimackinac and St. Joseph at the northern tip of Lake Huron, (3) securing the Western District of Upper Canada for the United States, and (4) moving troops down to Lake Erie to assist operations on the Niagara frontier. Harrison expected contrary orders from the secretary should he have other ideas for directing the North West Army. This letter was directed to departmental offices in Washington, where it was sent to the president with a copy to the secretary, who was at Sackets Harbor.[16] The delay in communication between Harrison and Armstrong meant that directives from the secretary were often received by the general after he had already acted.

Delay along the Detroit River

Along the Detroit River, the British waited anxiously to learn the results of the naval engagement. Looking through the smoke, they could not determine the outcome. But on the morning of 11 September, the ships sailed away toward South Bass Island and no small vessel returned carrying Barclay's expected victory message. Soon it dawned on them: not only had the Royal Navy been beaten, but the entire squadron was lost. Such an unexpected outcome completely changed the situation for the right wing of His Majesty's forces in Can-

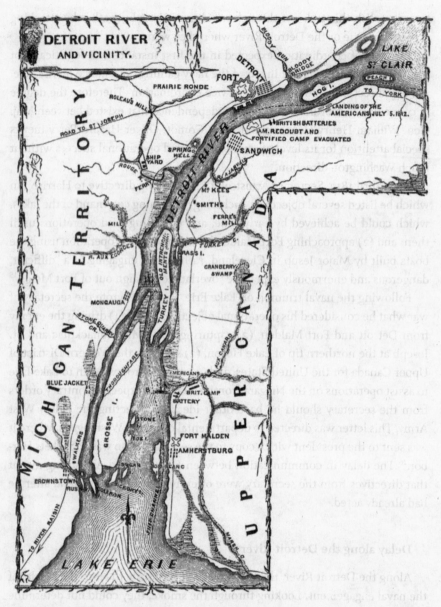

Detroit Valley. Reprinted from Benson J. Lossing, *Pictorial Field-Book of the War of 1812* (New York: Harper Brothers, 1869).

ada and for their native allies. As a new reality confronted the residents of the Detroit River Valley, they reacted in differing ways.

Native Americans split. Some sent word to Harrison that they were willing to negotiate; in fact, they might even support American forces. Others quietly left and returned to their homes to the north. Led by Tecumseh, a few hundred warriors and their families accompanied the retreating British, the last remnants of the coalition Tecumseh and Tenskwatawa had formed just a few years before.

Amongst the Canadians there were obvious misgivings. Few rallied to the British flag; most went home. For the most part, militia units of the Western District of Upper Canada went unmustered. Their livelihoods, property, and families were in jeopardy. The Americans living inside British-occupied Michigan worried that they might be attacked by the retreating natives before their countrymen arrived,. They awaited the advancing North West Army with the expectation that their yearlong nightmare was about to end.

General Procter faced a dilemma. He had long promised the native allies that he would never yield a foot of Canadian soil. Militarily it was obvious that his staying at Fort Malden and Detroit was no longer tenable. The British had stripped the fort's artillery to equip the Royal Navy's *Detroit*, which had been lost in the battle of Lake Erie. The British feared retreat would bring the wrath of the Indians upon them. Consequently, Procter delayed making a decision and acting decisively. The results would be catastrophic for the 41st Regiment of Foot and the British Indian Department.

Few had more to lose than Matthew Elliott, the British Indian Agent operating out of Amherstburg. For years he and his agents had funneled food, weapons, and ammunition to natives living inside the United States. Now his whole system of alliances was on the verge of collapse. In fact, he feared the natives might turn on him, his property, and his family. On the other hand, he knew the Americans wanted his scalp; there would be no mercy for the man many thought was to blame for Indian depredations on the frontier. Many Americans designated him personally responsible for the massacre at the River Raisin.[17]

The Kentuckians also blamed General Procter for the loss of their friends and relatives at the River Raisin and Fort Miamis; revenge was on their minds, and the British commander knew it. Still Procter dallied, letting precious days go by while he contemplated his options. He was dispensing to the Indians fifteen thousand rations per day, and no more would arrive to replace them.

Describing Barclay's defeat as "a most calamitous Circumstance," the British commander recognized that there was no advantage in occupying his "present extensive Position, which can be so easily turned by means of the entire Command of the Waters here which the Enemy now has."[18]

On 13 September General Procter called a council of war at Sandwich to which his senior subordinate, Lt. Col. Alexander Warburton, was not summoned. This illustrates the growing animosity between the army's second-in-command and its commanding general. Procter ordered the schooners and gunboats, the few remaining artillery pieces, and the hundreds of muskets and rifles captured at Detroit to be moved to the mouth of the Thames River. He proclaimed martial law so that he might confiscate supplies and counter actions by "all traitorous or disaffected persons." Still he waited until 17 September, a week after Perry's victory, to collect all livestock and provisions below Malden, both for his own use and to keep them from the invading Americans. He moved his headquarters northward to Sandwich, but it was not until 20 September that he ordered Col. Warburton to burn and destroy Fort Malden and the navy yard at Amherstburg. Then he rescinded the order for six more days. Dozens of wagons loaded with family possessions and valuables lined the roadways—Elliott's family brought nine wagons and thirty horses. Still Procter did not issue the order to withdraw up the Thames River Valley and move his army toward the central wing of the British Army on the Niagara Peninsula. At the same time, his commander in Upper Canada, Maj. Gen. Francis, Baron de Rottenburg, did "not clearly see the necessity or expedience, of your immediately retiring" from the Detroit frontier.[19]

This lingering along the Detroit River was also a consequence of, for Procter, a personally embarrassing speech made by Tecumseh on 18 September. The Shawnee warrior reminded Procter that the British had twice before given "the hatchet to his [Majesty's] red children," and twice before they had betrayed them at a peace conference from which the natives were excluded. Now, for a third time, "our British father" gave the natives "the tomahawk and told us that he was then ready to strike the American; that he wanted our assistance; and that he would certainly get us our lands back." Tecumseh wanted to remain at Amherstburg and fight to the end. If "they defeat us, we will then retreat." In the most dramatic moment of this speech, Tecumseh turned toward Procter and condemned his plans to withdraw, comparing the general's conduct to that of "a fat dog, that carries its tail upon its back, but when affrighted, it drops it between its legs and runs off."[20]

Implicit, but not explicit, in Tecumseh's address was the threat that if a stand were not made, the natives might turn on their outnumbered British allies. The Indians were not red pawns to be sacrificed at the whims of the British commander. They made their own moves across the chessboard of self-interest, even to the point of threatening their former allies. It took Matthew Elliott's most persuasive diplomacy to convince Tecumseh to bring his men, their wives, and their children up the Thames River to a point where they might make a stand. Still, many natives withdrew from the retreating column, especially the Miami, Potawatomi, Chippewa, and Ottawa. Tecumseh's once proud confederation dwindled to approximately a thousand warriors. The British and their native allies began moving out of Sandwich on 27 September, more than two weeks after the Americans had gained control of Lake Erie. The delay gave General Harrison time to assemble the water craft and troops necessary to land on Canadian soil. Burdened as the British and their allies were with women, children, supply boats, and wagons, the question was whether they could move fast enough to elude the advancing Americans. On the same day that Procter left Sandwich, Harrison's army landed on the Lake Erie shore south of Amherstburg, and by evening they raised the American flag over the smoldering ruins of Fort Malden.

Cross-Lake Amphibious Operation

Procter's delays allowed Harrison and Perry to assemble their supplies, troops, and vessels along Ohio's north shore in preparation for an attack on southwestern Upper Canada. Harrison amassed his forces in the vicinity of modern Port Clinton, Ohio. This involved awaiting the mounted infantry coming from Kentucky, training the regular and volunteer forces under his immediate command, and pushing forward all supplies not only from the Ohio Valley but also from Erie and Cleveland. Restrained by too many defeats and disappointments, President Madison cautioned that the sickness among Perry's crews and of Perry himself, along with the launching of HMS *Detroit* at Amherstburg, created circumstances that were "not favorable; I trust they will be over balanced by those that are so."[21]

Trying to make the circumstances more favorable to victory, Harrison encouraged the training of his recruits, both regular and volunteer. A General Order of 8 August directed every officer to pay "the most unremitted attention to the Drill" of his troops because "the perfection of their Corps in decipline and the success of our operations so much depends upon it." He was particularly concerned with his young officers, who might omit or neglect this duty. Such officers "are too Apt to imagine that bravery is the only qualification which it is necessary for them to Possess," when in reality they will "discover that intrepidity without skill" will lead to defeat.[22]

Once the news of Perry's victory reached Harrison, the Eighth Military District commander began issuing orders to subordinates to concentrate their forces at the mouth of the Portage River. After Perry's squadron drove its Royal Navy counterparts into the Detroit River in August, Major Jesup concentrated the Schenectady bateaux at Sandusky Bay. Following the American naval victory, the boats were pulled across the narrow Marblehead Peninsula dividing that body of water from the Portage mouth. Secretary Armstrong described these vessels as not being decked but as "strong & high sided & very competent to the navigation of the Lake, particularly between the chains of Islands & the West Shore" of Lake Erie. Gen. Duncan McArthur reduced the fortifications at Fort Meigs to a small blockhouse and then moved his men toward the rendezvous point. Most of Gen. Greene Clay's Kentuckians joined them, even though their enlistments were about to expire. Meanwhile, Perry sent several of his vessels to the Maumee Rapids to pick up supplies that McArthur had left behind. At Fort Meigs, only Col. Richard M. Johnson's cavalrymen remained, with orders to wait until launching of the invasion fleet before marching toward Detroit.[23]

Harrison directed that supplies accumulating at Upper Sandusky and Camp Seneca be forwarded downstream and brought across the narrow isthmus, thereby avoiding over forty miles of navigation that might expose the goods to the hazards of Lake Erie storms. Pennsylvania, Ohio, and Kentucky volunteers arrived, although many of the Pennsylvanians had "constitutional scruples" about invading a foreign country and refused to cross the lake. By far the most important component of the assemblage was the mounted Kentuckians commanded by their governor, Isaac Shelby.[24]

A key ingredient in Harrison's strategy was to use friendly natives in the American cause and to disengage as many hostile Indians as possible from supporting the British. The general urged friendly Wyandot, Shawnee, and Seneca in the vicinity to join him in the enterprise, and approximately 260 did. At this conference, Harrison told the natives they "must conform to our mode of warfare. You are not to kill defenceless prisoners, old men, women, or children." Harrison's conduct in this matter drew lavish praise from Captain McAfee. And his Indian allies obeyed the general's injunction. The Kentuckian then casti-gated the British:

> Had the Indians been employed by the British on the condition that they
> must conform to the rules of civilized warfare, no instance of savage cruelty
> in this war would now be recorded against them . . . but they employed the
> savages on a different principle . . . If the British officers in Upper Canada
> did not directly instigate, they at least very willingly permitted the savages
> to massacre the prisoners, who had surrendered, not to the savages, but to
> themselves after receiving a solemn promise of protection.[25]

The general subsequently sent some of these Wyandot allies to meet with disgruntled fellow tribesmen north of the River Raisin to see whether they would remain neutral during an American advance in the Detroit Valley. Instead of just the Wyandot, however, Indian Agent Elliott saw to it that repre-sentatives of the most hostile tribes were also present at this meeting. Reput-edly, Wyandot war chief Walk-in-the-Water secretly passed a message for Har-rison that he would try to keep his people out of the pending fight. Harrison remained skeptical of this possibility; he was going to be pleasantly surprised.[26]

The mounted units built a strong fence of brush and fallen timber across the two-mile-wide peninsula extending between the Portage and Sandusky Rivers, and turned their horses loose to graze there and await their owners' return. This meant that Shelby's mounted Kentuckians now became infantrymen.[27] The only mounted troops remaining were the approximately one thousand riflemen commanded by Col. Richard M. Johnson at Fort Meigs.

Meanwhile, Harrison's troops moved from the embarkation point at the Portage River mouth to South Bass Island. Sergeant Alfred Brunson of the 27th U.S. Infantry recalled how he and twenty-six others boarded a vessel and sailed to the island in the midst of gale winds. It took them eleven hours to go twelve miles, but they finally came under the lee of the island and found sailing much easier. They arrived at Put-in-Bay and received their first glimpse of the dam-aged American and British fleets. HMS *Detroit* "had not a spar left standing. The masts, bowsprit, and the davits were all shot away. Her side next to our guns in the battle was so full of balls, shot, and holes made by heavy shot that it seemed to me that an man's hand, laid on her at any place, would touch more or less of them." The U.S. brig *Lawrence* "was bored through and through" by the fire of the enemy's long guns. Years later, Capt. Stanton Sholes of the 2nd U.S. Artillery vividly remembered the *Lawrence*'s deck "covered from stem to stern, with blood and gore, and all parts of the human body, but the sight and smell, was too sickening for me to stay but a few moments."[28]

Following the naval victory, which had been assisted by army troops, it was Perry's turn to assist Harrison. For the cross-lake operation, Perry directed his efforts in three different areas. First, the navy transported most of Harrison's army from the mouth of the Portage River for an attack on Fort Malden. Second, Perry planned for supporting naval gunfire during the Canadian landing (it was unneeded, however, because there was no British opposition), and third, his gunboats provided logistical support to the ground forces in their advance up the Thames River. Once this was accomplished, he maintained naval superiority on the Detroit River and Lake St. Clair—a relatively minor task, given the capture of most of the Royal Naval vessels on Lake Erie a few days before.[29] These efforts constituted a degree of naval support for army operations unequalled in the War of 1812.

On 26 September General Harrison and newly promoted Captain Perry, with members of their staff and senior officers, sailed on the *Ariel* to reconnoiter the Canadian shore. They found the blockhouse at Bar Point at the mouth of the Detroit River destroyed and the coastline north of it uncommonly tranquil. Harrison suspected that this was a ruse to induce his landing without proper precautions and that he might fall into an ambush. Accordingly, he prepared for the worst possible encounter on the enemy's shore, a spot about three miles south of Amherstburg opposite the lower end of Bois Blanc (Bob-Lo) Island.

That night he issued his landing instructions. Nowhere is the level of army-navy cooperation more apparent than in the operational order General Harrison issued that evening. The minutely detailed directive attempted to cover all expected exigencies. The original draft of this order was written by Major Wood, who apparently served in the capacity of what modern military personnel would call an operations officer—G-3. Harrison divided his army into two wings: the right wing commanded by Governor Shelby acting as a major general and the left wing containing the regular brigades under Brigadier Generals Duncan McArthur and Lewis Cass plus the light infantry of Lt. Col. James Ball of the 2nd U.S. Light Dragoons. The landing site they selected was three miles north of Bar Point at the river's mouth. It contained both open ground, which was most conducive to fighting by regulars, and wooded areas (where he suspected Canadian militia and Indians would be placed), most conducive to combat by the Kentucky volunteers experienced in irregular warfare.

Harrison's initial landing parties were to be led by some of his most experienced officers. Colonel Ball and his dismounted dragoons led the left wing, along with the battalion of riflemen commanded by Lt. Col. James Simrall. On landing, these two units were to proceed "with the utmost celerity consistent with the preservation of good order" and to "seize the most favorable position for annoying the enemy, and covering the debarkation of the troops of the line." Once they had secured the landing area, the remaining troops of the two regular army generals would follow. Harrison would accompany General Cass's brigade on the regular army's right flank, thus positioning himself near the center of the landing area. On the American right, General Shelby, assisted by Major Generals Joseph Desha and William Henry, commanded two divisions of Kentuckians comprising five brigades under the command of Brigadier Generals Markes Calmes, John King, Samuel Caldwell, James Allen, and David Chiles. Governor Shelby's troops constituted the second wave and would begin disembarking as soon as the regulars' boats returned to the fleet.

The general's directions for the navy were much less specific. The order merely required that the "arrangements for landing the troops will be made entirely under the direction of an officer of the navy whom Commodore Perry has been so obliging as to offer for that purpose. The debarkation of the troops will be covered by the cannon of the vessels." Given this latitude, Perry assigned each warship to tow several of the bateaux during the approach toward the shore. Perry superintended the squadron's fire support; Elliott managed "the debarkation of the troops."[30] Since both officers had participated in the landings at Fort George a few months earlier, they brought a considerable understanding of joint operations to the fore.

A few of Perry's directives provide additional evidence of these cooperative efforts. He directed the commanders of two of his smaller vessels to "proceed to the Portage river . . . & take on board as many of Col. [Thomas] Smith's Reg. of Riflemen, as [your vessels] will carry & land them at Malden. If you are not able to bring them all, you will return to the river for the remainder." To Lt. Thomas Holdup he wrote, "You will keep as near the Army with the *Caledonia* as possible, that you may be enabled to deliver them provisions as called for." Lt. George Senat of the *Porcupine* received a directive to "proceed to the Lake St. Clair, and join me at the mouth of the river Thames, where the baggage you have on board for the army will be landed." With the *Scorpion*, *Tigress*, and *Porcupine*, Master Commandant Elliott sailed up the Thames, providing artillery and logistical support and river-crossing transportation for Harrison's rapidly advancing ground troops, while Perry served the general as an aide-de-camp. As Perry informed Secretary Jones, "Every possible exertion will be made by the officers & men under my command to assist the advance of the Army, and it affords me great pleasure . . . to say, that the utmost harmony prevails between the Army and Navy." General Harrison confirmed this when he noted that "Commodore Perry gives me every assistance in his power."[31]

Finally, General Harrison consulted Perry on joint operational matters and heeded the naval officer's technical advice. The pursuit of Procter could have gone either along the Thames or by water to a point on the north shore of Lake Erie, where a short march would have placed the Americans in a blocking position capable of capturing the whole of Procter's force. Taking Perry's advice to use the land option rather than risk the fall storms on the lake, Harrison marched his combined columns east from Sandwich (now Windsor, Ontario) with Perry's gunboats supporting him.[32]

Stationed at the much-reduced Fort Meigs and apprehensive about their being used in the campaign, Col. Richard M. Johnson's Kentucky cavalry finally received orders to advance to Detroit. Harrison, and to some degree Colonel Johnson, feared the natives living in the Brownstown area would engage them in an unequal battle. This notion was confirmed when one of Johnson's patrols captured a Shawnee named Misselmetaw, who informed them they could expect a battle at the crossing of the Huron River north of Frenchtown. And yet when word came that the Kentuckians were to march northward, they eagerly accepted the assignment. Harrison sequenced the cavalry movement at a slower pace than the amphibious one so that the Indians would learn of the capture of Fort Malden before Johnson's men came into their vicinity. Consequently, the mounted Kentuckians found little opposition as they moved toward Detroit, which they entered on 30 September, a day after McArthur's troops had occupied the town via Canada.[33]

As they neared the River Raisin, Johnson's troops discovered the bones of their comrades killed during the battle there the previous January. Feral hogs and wild animals had eaten the flesh from the scattered skeletons. According to Captain McAfee, the sight of these human remains "had a powerful effect on the feelings of the men. The wounds inflicted by that barbarous transaction were again torn open. The bleaching bones still appealed to heaven, and called on Kentucky to avenge this outrage on humanity." General Harrison knew the urge for vengeance that surged through his Kentuckians. At about the same time Colonel Johnson's men observed these bones, Harrison spoke to those Kentucky soldiers engaged in the amphibious portion of his advance:

"Remember the river Raisin; but remember it only, whilst victory is suspended. The revenge of a soldier cannot be gratified on a fallen enemy."[34] The question remained, could Harrison restrain his Kentuckians from vengeance or would there be a bloodbath if the Americans could bring the British and Indians to stand and engage them?

Planning the Pursuit along the Thames

While a variety of craft ferried Johnson's men and horses across the river on 1 October, Harrison held a conference with Governor Shelby. As Captain McAfee recalled, the two concluded that if they followed the British along the southern shore of Lake St. Clair and then eastward along the Thames River, they might catch Procter's force in less than four days. They also considered the option of having Perry's squadron tow the Schenectady boats loaded with his soldiers and their baggage to Long Point on the Canadian shore, where a short march northward would interpose these forces between Procter's and the Niagara Peninsula.

After concluding his conference with Shelby, Harrison called a meeting of all the generals and Perry. Should they pursue the enemy by land or by water? The water option was particularly inviting. They could land forces around Long Point on northeastern Lake Erie (opposite modern Erie, Pennsylvania) and make a short march northward to cut off the retreating British and Native American forces before they reached the Niagara–Burlington Heights area and joined up with other British forces. This option had a number of positive ingredients: it maximized American naval dominance of the lake; it used the American fleet and the dozens of Schenectady boats that had brought most of Harrison's army across Lake Erie to a landing near the mouth of the Detroit River; and it promised to annihilate the retreating enemy, which would be moving at a slower pace than the waterborne operation. Moreover, the regular army forces in Harrison's command would then be located in an area of critical operations in the Lake Ontario littoral. It was there that Secretary of War John Armstrong wanted most of his regulars stationed, in what was considered the most critical sector of the American war effort. In addition, American logistical support to the army via Lake Erie could be more easily accomplished through supply depots at Erie and Cleveland than via the Detroit River–Lake St. Clair–Thames River line.

But the water option had several liabilities. First, because most of Harrison's troops were Kentucky volunteers, taking them that far eastward inconvenienced them individually during the harvest season and imposed a large logistical burden on the government just to return them to their homes as enlistment terms expired. Second, Captain Perry feared the fall storms on the lake might endanger troops on the bateaux during their transit. In fact, even as they debated their operational future, these flag officers witnessed a heavy storm that brought rain and high winds on their troops. What might happen to these landsmen in open, shallow-draft vessels on Lake Erie's treacherous waters?

The land option had similar positive and negative aspects. The British had only two days' head start, and their families and baggage hampered their retreat. It might be possible for the Americans to advance at a greater speed and engage them. Since Col. Richard M. Johnson's mounted infantry constituted a major portion of Harrison's force, their speed might allow them to overtake the British-Indian force. On the other hand, the British had a better chance of escaping the Americans if the land option were taken. Harrison planned to use his mounted and dismounted Kentuckians as the major portion of his force. The Americans did not suffer the civilian logistical burden that encumbered the British, but they could find themselves in a relatively uninhabited Canadian wilderness without adequate supplies as they advanced up the Thames River. Most importantly, however, the delay in the departure of the British rearguard from Sandwich until 1 October meant the American advance would be only two days behind their foes if they departed the same town on 2 October. There were also apprehensions that Procter might pick up Canadian militia reinforcements as he withdrew.[35]

According to McAfee, Harrison announced to the assembled senior officers that "the governor thinks, and so do I, that the best way will be to pursue the enemy . . . by land." The assembled officers agreed, and they issued orders for departure the following morning. It is about the decision making at this conference that a bitter controversy arose. A strong Harrison partisan, Captain McAfee apologized to his readers for the excessive detail in his account of what transpired in Sandwich. Some later argued that "General Harrison never would have pursued farther than Sandwich, and had it not been for Governor Shelby, and that he differed with the governor, respecting the route to be taken." Instead, McAfee said, "there never was a difference of opinion between them [Shelby and Harrison], neither on the propriety of the pursuit nor the manner of performing it . . . The chief object of the councils was to obtain the approbation of the governor and general officers for the route he [Harrison] preferred."[36] This final sentence creates something of a conundrum: why did Harrison need to get the governor's approbation if he already had it?

Years later, political rivals wishing to discredit Harrison's military competence would argue that the land pursuit option was Governor Shelby's idea and that it was the Kentuckian who convinced Harrison to prefer it. Those who made this point entirely avoided discussing Perry's role in the decision-making discussion. Whatever the case, a good commander considers the options his subordinates provide and makes his decision after deliberating over their recommendations. Harrison certainly acted in an appropriate manner in this instance.[37]

The anxiety in Washington rose, even though the acquisition of Fort Malden had created optimism. President Madison wrote Secretary Armstrong, who was in upstate New York, that he trusted that Harrison "in his pursuit will not forget the traps & tricks of an artful enemy."[38]

Battle of the Thames

To set the project in motion, Colonel Johnson's mounted infantry, which had come to Detroit via Fort Meigs, had to be ferried across the river to Sandwich. Stormy weather complicated the task. Still, they were on the Canadian shore by late in the evening of 1 October. While attaching himself to Harrison's staff as an aide-de-camp, Captain Perry issued directives to his subordinates to assist in the advance. As he wrote Secretary of the Navy William Jones, "Every possible exertion will be made by the officers & men under my command to assist the advance of the Army, and it affords me great pleasure . . . to say, that the utmost harmony prevails between the Army and Navy." He placed Mstr. Cmdt. Jesse D. Elliott in command of the brigs and sloops that carried army supplies. Typical of Perry's orders was one to Lt. George Senat of the *Porcupine* to "proceed to the Lake St. Clair, and join me at the mouth of the river Thames, where the baggage you have on board for the army will be unloaded." On 3 October they were at the mouth of the Thames River. Perry left the brig *Caledonia* there and placed Elliott in charge of the schooners *Scorpion* and *Tigress* and the sloop *Porcupine*, which carried supplies and provided artillery cover and cross-river transport for Harrison's rapidly advancing force. Behind them came a flotilla of smaller craft loaded with provisions and baggage.[39]

Harrison's allocation of forces under his command seems almost deliberately done to incite the dismay and opposition of Secretary of War Armstrong. The regular army infantry brigades of Generals McArthur and Cass remained on both sides of the Detroit River where they protected the residents from the natives and the Indians from the Kentuckians.[40] It was feared that the Miami and Potawatomi who remained in Michigan might attack Detroit during Harrison's pursuit. An equal rationale for leaving the regulars behind involved the depletion of their numbers over the past several months due to illness. Except for the small number of regulars commanded by Colonel Paull, General Cass's brigade remained in Sandwich awaiting equipment and supplies that had been left behind.

For the secretary of war, this force distribution was an affront to his emphasis on employing regulars over volunteers when possible. As it was highly probable that the pursuit might result in an encounter with British regulars, Armstrong feared the volunteers lacked the discipline and training necessary for formal combat. General Harrison thought his Kentuckians had more combat experience and military zeal than the recently recruited regulars. Moreover, the troops in General Cass's brigade had left their knapsacks and blankets on Middle Sister Island and had to await their arrival before moving forward. Harrison took with him only 150 regulars from the 27th U.S. Infantry (which had been raised in Ohio) and about 200 Native Americans, in a force numbering nearly 3,000.

Years later Harrison would be accused of favoring Kentuckians over Ohioans during this pursuit. There is some justification for this charge. It is doubtful that the commanding general could have restrained the Kentuckians had he wanted to do so. But his employment of all the Kentucky volunteers and so few regulars and Ohioans, many of whom were in the brigades of McArthur and Cass, was going to excite the envy and animosity of those left behind and those who felt their service or state had been discriminated against. On the other hand, to deny the Kentuckians an opportunity to vindicate their military prowess following the River Raisin and Dudley massacres would have been an affront to the Bluegrass State that Governor Shelby could not accept.

At sunrise on 2 October, the Americans began their march. With Colonel Johnson's cavalrymen in the lead, the army troops set a rugged pace and covered twenty-five miles the first day, and they encamped only nine miles from the mouth of the Thames. The primitive roads were lined with trees in their full fall colors, and the barns were filled with the plenty from the recent harvest. It took great restraint on the officers' part to keep the amount of looting as low as they could. Apparently, General Procter did not expect a land pursuit. He left bridges intact and during the first couple of days seems not to have had a rear guard of scouts to ascertain Harrison's actions. Elliott left the *Ariel* and *Caledonia* at the river's mouth and proceeded with the gunboats *Scorpion*, *Tigress*, and *Porcupine*, following the army's advance along the Thames. It was not until 3 October that the cavalry encountered a small patrol that was trying to destroy a bridge over Jeannettes Creek, the first crossing of a Thames tributary. That bridge and one shortly thereafter were captured before the British had completely destroyed them and were soon repaired. In the first two days, the Americans covered over forty miles. Procter now knew that Harrison was no more than a day behind him, and he knew the Americans lacked the burdensome logistical train and families that accompanied the British and the natives. As now became obvious, Procter was going to be compelled to stand and fight an opponent that deeply detested him personally.

On 3 October the trail grew increasingly fresh and the expedition reached Matthew Dolsen's farm near Chatham, the location where Procter had told Tecumseh he would make his stand—which he did not do. One of Procter's junior officers recalled that the "only resemblance this place could boast to that from which it takes its name was its being also situated on the river Thames, for instead of a populous town and cultivated county, a solitary hut and a little plantation alone met the view." Lieutenant Colonel Warburton, commander of the rear guard, became outraged when he found that General Procter had not fortified the place as promised. Harrison, meanwhile, allowed a band of about sixty Wyandot headed by Walk-in-the-Water, "naturally preferring their own welfare to the interest of Britain (to which in justice it must be owed they had hitherto been most faithful warriors)," to peacefully go to their homes in Michigan without engaging in further hostilities.[41] At this point the Americans abandoned their gunboats because the high banks of the river made the vessels' guns inoperable and the trees along the embankment allowed the enemy to pick off sailors. Harrison left behind a detachment of troops to guard the vessels and some prisoners they had taken. There were several other times he left security forces behind during the advance up the Thames.

At McGregor's Creek the Indians decided to make a preliminary stand. There were two bridges a mile apart, and the surrounding woods made ideal cover for Tecumseh's marksmen. When Johnson's men discovered their foes ahead, they stopped and sent for the commanding general because he had warned them about a possible ambush. Harrison instructed the cavalrymen to advance cautiously by columns, but when scattered fire arose (which may have been a deliberate enticement to induce the usually impulsive Kentuckians to charge), the general brought forward two six-pounder artillery pieces and their grape shot dispersed the foes. The infantry doused the flames on the bridge and repaired it, while Johnson's mounted troopers went up the creek to a second bridge, which they seized after a brief skirmish.[42]

Both armies were hampered by an incessant rain that slowed their progress. The rains had made the roads so impassable that along the primitive wilderness trail, the British were abandoning military and personal baggage and wagons. Procter began with approximately eight hundred regulars and militiamen plus about twelve hundred natives. While Tecumseh's warriors harassed the American advance parties, they caused no significant delay. Meanwhile, tensions rose between General Procter and his chief subordinate, Lieutenant Colonel Warburton, who found himself wondering just what his commander's intentions were.[43]

As the Americans neared the hamlet of Moraviantown, or Fairfield (where Moravian missionaries had established a settlement for the Christian Delaware), evidence of the hasty and obviously over-encumbered British-Indian retreat appeared. The British had left a schooner containing military stores burning in the river, and they had torched a house in an effort to destroy hundreds of shoulder weapons stored inside. The Americans rescued many of the weapons from the flames. After a march of a few more miles, the Americans found another vessel in flames, and nearby a distillery containing ordnance and naval stores was also afire. The British abandoned the last of their supply bateaux, with approximately 174 wounded and sick men, who surrendered. The speed of the American advance also forced the British to abandon several canoes and other small vessels, and Harrison's men used the abandoned vessels to cross the Thames to its northern shore, along which the British Army was retreating. The Americans also captured two twenty-four-pounder artillery pieces with shells and balls. The loss of the bateaux meant no British rations were available on 4 October. That evening the Americans encamped. Unlike at Tippecanoe, Harrison's soldiers built a breastwork around their bivouac, and Harrison closely inspected the defensive positions until well after dark. Governor Shelby supervised his lines and finally, exhausted, went to sleep under a blanket he shared with one of his soldiers. Procter and Tecumseh reconnoitered the American position and decided against a night attack.[44]

Both armies bivouacked short of the Moravian mission. The hamlet consisted of a single mud street lined by log huts and a small church. Around the habitation were a few hundred acres of fenced, cleared ground with ripened grain crops. It is doubtful the British could have fought in the town as it was filled with wagons, horses, and women and children, both white and Indian, fleeing the American advance.[45]

General Procter decided to engage the Americans just west of the village. Given the troop limitations, he chose terrain where he might best employ his soldiers and the native warriors. Later, one of his often-critical subordinates facetiously remarked that "the intended disposition of his small force certainly [provided] evidence [of] some judgement and knowledge of his profession."[46] Actually, the position was probably as good as Procter could find, given the available terrain. No attempt was made to entrench or to impede the American advance; this may have been the consequence of the loss of shovels and axes in the supply vessels. Everyone knew that Harrison's men were hard on their heels, but the British had no obstacles constructed to provide cover and concealment or to hamper a cavalry charge.

By this time, Procter claimed, he had fewer than 400 redcoats and 500 Indians at his disposal. If so, he was outnumbered almost three to one by his opponents; such odds were not all that unfavorable, however, given that he was on the defensive. But his actual strength was probably greater than this. Harrison estimated there were 1,000 natives allied with the British and present on the field. While this may be an overestimate, it is highly probable that Procter had several hundred more than the 500 figure he gave. His assertion that there were 400 British/Canadian effectives was a self-serving underestimation. Even though the Amherstburg-based redcoats were severely hurt by the losses at the sieges of Forts Meigs and Stephenson, by the losses in Barclay's squadron in the battle of Lake Erie, and by desertions during the withdrawal from Sandwich, there seem to have been more British soldiers than this. Based on deserters' and Michiganders' reports, Harrison estimated that before leaving Sandwich, there were 580 British regulars and between 600 and 1,000 Indians. No Canadian militiamen were included. Yet Harrison records the capture of 601 British/Canadian troops and 12 dead on the battlefield (perhaps the only figures from either side one can assume to be accurate). The prisoner total undoubtedly includes some captured before and after the battle itself, but the vast majority must have been taken on the Thames battlefield. In addition, Procter recorded that 247 of his soldiers gathered at Ancaster after the fighting. This means Procter had 870 to 900 or more troops when he left Sandwich.

Even given that a number of these men were sick, wounded, or injured and others had to be on escort duty, his total of combat effectives had to be greater than 500.

How many soldiers did Harrison have on the battlefield? Originally he estimated 3,000, but after consultation with Governor Shelby he reduced that figure to less than 2,500. The largest portion of these was Col. Richard M. Johnson's Kentucky mounted infantry, numbering approximately 1,000. These men bore the brunt of the battle and, with few exceptions, were the only Americans who actually fought the British and Indians.[47] On the British side, even if one accepts the 900 total effective personnel given by Procter, these soldiers and warriors were of nearly equal strength to the total of actively engaged Americans.

On Procter's left flank was the River Thames and the road to Detroit, and it was there he kept his grenadiers from the 41st Foot and his remaining six-pounder, which apparently lacked either ammunition or a gun crew determined to fire it. The remaining infantry he deployed in extended order on either side of Backmetack Marsh. One junior officer recalled that the men were really in no order but rather huddled, with sometimes four or five men behind various trees. In other words, there were numerous open spaces between the infantrymen. Procter kept himself and his thirty-eight cavalry men in the rear. Tecumseh's Indians were in the woods on the right flank. The position was ideal for their style of warfare, allowing them to use the woods for cover and concealment while the swamp behind them provided an avenue for escape through which their foe would find pursuit difficult and hazardous. By anchoring his line on the Thames and the marsh, Procter exploited the terrain as well as possible. Except for the area in the vicinity of the road, the battlefield was lightly to heavily wooded, making it difficult to determine the actions of one's friends or foes. The woods also made it difficult for advancing American infantry to maintain their formations.

Thus the redcoats "silently awaited" the attack, "each determined to do his duty, but very few with any doubt as to the result."[48] But this recollection of British bravado does not accord with the 41st Foot's demoralization after the failures to take Forts Meigs and Stephenson and the losses of soldiers serving in Barclay's squadron at the battle of Lake Erie. There was also considerable British apprehension about just how the Kentuckians would react to strenuous resistance, given their anger over the massacre at the River Raisin and the one inflicted on Dudley's men.

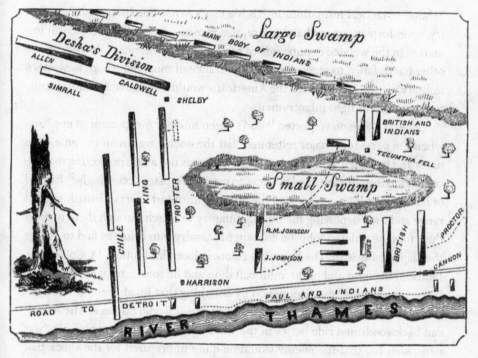

Battle of the Thames. Reprinted from Benson J. Lossing, *Pictorial Field-Book of the War of 1812* (New York: Harper Brothers, 1869).

As was his wont, General Harrison conducted his pre-battle arrangements with caution. He aroused his troops at 0500 hours on 5 October, and they began a slow march toward their now deployed foe. He estimated Procter's strength as approximately twenty-one hundred, though it was about half that. While Colonel Johnson wanted to lead his men on a charge at the enemy position, Harrison must have recalled another Kentucky cavalryman named Joseph Daviess whose impetuosity cost him his life at Tippecanoe, a death for which some critics blamed Harrison. Prudently, he dispatched the recently promoted Maj. Eleazer Wood to survey the situation. Wood was a staff officer with many talents who served as Harrison's chief engineer, artillery commander, and all-around military consultant (his staff tasks conformed to those of a modern operations officer). Major Wood returned and reported that the British were in an open order. Harrison could not believe his ears; this was not the anticipated formation for British troops. He expected the redcoats to be in close order and seemed not to have understood the importance of the "American

School" of tactical formations in His Majesty's Army. Emphasizing light infantry, open formations, and aimed fire, this proved a most effective tactical formation in the wooded countryside of eastern North America.[49] Procter, on the other hand, failed to recognize the importance of mounted troops to western military tactics. He expected the Americans would use regular infantry formations against his light infantrymen.

General Harrison respected Wood's "keen military & experienced eye," and when the persistent major reiterated that the enemy was in an extreme open order and that there were neither entrenchments nor abatis protecting the redcoats, Harrison "determined at once" to modify his plans accordingly.[50] Instead of having Johnson's cavalry lead the advance until just short of British musket range and then deploying the trailing infantry to march through them to meet their foes, he ordered Johnson to form his cavalry into columns and to charge the dispersed British. The Kentucky colonel placed his brother, Lt. Col. Joseph Johnson, in command of the right battalion and he took command of the left. It was a maneuver "not Sanctioned by any thing that I had Seen or heard of," wrote Harrison, "but I was fully Convinced that it would Succeed. The American backwoodsmen ride better in the woods than any other people." He "was persuaded too that the enemy would be quite unprepared for the shock that they could not resist it."[51] He was correct.

But rather than following Harrison's order to the letter, Colonel Johnson decided to do something completely unauthorized. Leaving his brother to attack the British on the right, he turned his column toward the left flank and marched through the small swamp to attack the British and natives on the American left. The denseness of the vegetation forced many of the troopers to dismount and continue their advance afoot. The maneuver reminds one of what Kentucky Col. William Dudley did a few months earlier at the first siege of Fort Meigs, with disastrous consequences. Colonel Johnson later excused his disobedience on the grounds that there was not enough maneuver room for the horsemen of the two battalions on the same side of the smaller swamp. Regardless of his rationale, the maneuver ensured the Kentuckian immortality in the annals of American warfare and eventual elevation to the vice presidency of the United States.

Behind the horsemen, Harrison arranged his infantry. There were five "brigades" of foot troops averaging about three hundred men each—in other words, they were battalion sized and should have been commanded by lieutenant colonels and majors. Instead, colonels and brigadier generals were in command. No wonder Secretary of War Armstrong deplored the high rank given to too many volunteer officers. Facing the main British line were three brigades commanded by Col. George Trotter, Brig. Gen. John E. King, and Brig. Gen. David Chiles—the latter deployed to the rear as a reserve corps. These three units constituted a division commanded by Gen. William Henry. On the American left flank facing the large swamp, the Native Americans were poised to strike a division commanded by Gen. Joseph Desha, consisting of the brigades of Col. John Allen and Gen. Samuel Caldwell and the battalion of dragoons commanded by Lt. Col. James Simrall. This formation denied the Indians the opportunity to outflank the Americans' left and strike at their rear.

At the obtuse angle between Colonel Simrall's troopers and Colonel Trotter's infantry, Governor Shelby directed operations in this critical junction should the occasion require it. Harrison posted himself on the road near the infantry front lines and behind Colonel Johnson's cavalry. This gave him a clear view of the key avenue of approach toward the enemy lines. In effect, Governor Shelby—perhaps the most experienced soldier in the American army—and General Harrison were at the two ends of the main line. Harrison's two aides-de-camp, Capt. Charles S. Todd (Shelby's son-in-law) and Lt. John O'Fallon, and his volunteer aides, General Cass and Captain Perry, coordinated the positioning of the infantry units.

Close by the commander were Col. George Paull and his 150 regulars from the 27th U.S. Infantry with about 200 allied Indians. This constituted Harrison's reserve force, which had an additional assignment of attacking through the trees between the road and the river in case the mounted infantry needed them. Harrison told them before the battle began that he did not know how his volunteers would act and that "if they give way, my whole dependence is on you, and if you fail me, I'll bury my head in sorrow and disgrace to-day."[52] Fortunately the volunteers fought well and the regulars never fired a shot.

Finally, at 1430 hours Harrison signaled for the cavalry to attack, with a cry of "Charge them, my brave Kentuckians!" A bugle sounded on the right, and its call was soon echoed by others along the American line. Lieutenant Colonel Johnson's battalion dashed forward shouting "Remember the River Raisin" and soon drove through the left wing of the British infantry, causing them to flee to a second line. The Kentuckians soon surrounded these, and they quickly surrendered. It was all over in less than ten minutes, maybe less than five. The demoralized redcoats feared that continued resistance would incite the "savage" Kentuckians to inflict their vengeance upon the British enlisted men and officers. General Procter lamented that his troops did "not seem to have had that Confidence in themselves that they have shewn, on every former Occasion." He continued, "Having in vain endeavoured to call the Men to a Sense of Duty and having no Chance, by remaining, but of being captured, I reluctantly quitted the Ground."[53] Few commanding officers in history have "reluctantly quitted" a battlefield more expeditiously than Henry Procter.

His reluctance to retire from the battlefield rings hollow because, as soon as he noted the American penetration of his line, General Procter, Indian Agent Elliott, and their cavalry escort fled to the rear, dashing past the column of wagons, women, and children along the road and disappearing into the woods. Both Procter and Elliott knew full well that no prisoner-of-war legalisms could spare them from the wrath of the Kentuckians, who wanted revenge on the men they felt were the architects of the River Raisin and Maumee River slaughters. There was no doubt, wrote one contemporary observer, that while the Kentuckians would spare the British soldiers who surrendered, there was the exception of Procter and Elliott—"these, neither the authority of Harrison nor of Shelby could have saved."[54] Seeing his foe fleeing, Harrison assigned Major Wood to command a cavalry squadron to chase after Procter and Elliott. They failed to catch them, in part because of the delay caused by the crowded road and because the fleeing British leaders eventually left the road and hid in a swamp. The detachment did capture numerous rearguard elements and sick evacuees during their pursuit. After a several-mile chase, Major Wood gave up and returned to the army encampment in Moraviantown.[55]

But the rout of the British left did not end the battle. From the trees on the American left, the Indians opened fire all along the line commanded by General Desha. At the center of this melee struggled Col. Richard Johnson's horsemen, most of whom had been dismounted by the dense underbrush and native gunfire. As this scattered and somewhat disorganized force emerged from the marsh, it hit the flank of the British-Indian line. At the same time, some of Lt. Col. Joseph Johnson's men moved to the British rear. Tecumseh's voice could be heard giving orders to his warriors as they resisted the ragged line of Kentuckians on their flank and the horsemen advancing at their rear. The American line was cut up; Colonel Johnson was wounded five times, and several of his men were killed. Still the colonel and his dismounted troopers advanced, and Johnson claimed that he killed a prominent Indian before remounting his wounded horse and returning to have his wounds dressed. Whether or not the Kentucky colonel killed Tecumseh will remain a controversy, but there is little doubt that the native chieftain died from a bullet fired by someone in Johnson's regiment.[56]

As they saw or learned of Tecumseh's death, the natives' resistance began to wither. When they realized their charismatic leader was gone, a low moan arose from the Indian warriors, a cry unknown to their opponents and one that haunted them for the rest of their lives. The remnants of Tecumseh's defiant confederacy withdrew into the large swamp, unpursued by the Americans. For most of these natives, the era of armed resistance to American advance into the Ohio Valley and the Great Lakes had now ended.[57] The battle of the Thames—or of Moraviantown, as the Canadians call it—was the most important American land victory so far in this war.

The combatant and casualty figures for this campaign are elusive. British sources want to reduce their numbers of combatants and those of their native allies and to overestimate the size of their opponent's army. American sources reduce the number in Harrison's army and inflate the numbers in Procter's and Tecumseh's. Harrison reported the capture of 601 British soldiers, including 25 officers, with 12 others killed in action. Thirty-three Indian bodies remained on the ground, and additional bodies were carried away by native allies, including, say some, that of Tecumseh. In addition the Americans captured five thousand small arms, six brass cannons, two iron twenty-four-pounder artillery pieces, and small naval craft, military equipment, and supplies. As noted above, Harrison estimated there were 1,000 native foes, twice the number claimed by Procter. American losses were 7 killed and 22 wounded. Procter retreated to Ancaster (part of modern Hamilton, Ontario), where he gathered the retreating natives and British soldiers.[58]

The Battle's Aftermath

William Henry Harrison made no effort to pursue the remnants of Procter's forces. Instead he encamped at Moraviantown for two days and then withdrew to the Detroit River Valley, after putting the community to flames so that it would not become a staging area for subsequent British operations. His Kentuckians were content with their few scalps and loot. Besides, their sixty-day volunteer enlistments expired in a few days, and they eagerly awaited a victorious return to the Bluegrass State. Throughout the Thames campaign, the navy provided logistical support to the army, especially in bringing supplies from Erie and Cleveland to the rapidly moving North West Army as it advanced deep into the Western District of Upper Canada. Now Perry's naval logistical support had reached its limits. Even if Harrison had all his regulars with him, advancement over the inadequate road system into the homeland of the Iroquois in the Grand River Valley and into the heart of the central wing of His Majesty's army would risk all that had been won.

Besides, directives from the secretary of war and the secretary of the navy gave Harrison and Perry other missions. First, if possible, they were to advance into Lake Huron and seize Fort Michilimackinac. Second, Harrison was to assign any surplus of regulars in his command to the Niagara frontier and Perry was to transport them there.

As the Kentuckians went home, Harrison and General McArthur prepared for the Mackinac Island expedition. They awaited the arrival of two supply vessels—the *Chippawa* and *Ohio*—before departing, only to find some baggage and provisions the vessels were carrying washed up on the shore of western Lake Erie. They presumed the ships had foundered, but they later learned that the crews had thrown their cargoes overboard in an effort to save the vessels. In this they were successful; the winds drove the two ships the length of the lake, and they ran aground near Buffalo and survived. A conference involving Generals Harrison, McArthur, and Cass and including Captain Perry and Master Commandant Elliott determined that the winds of October were too precarious for an expedition on a dangerous lake where none of the naval officers had sailed. Also, a rumor (incorrect) reported that the British had abandoned the post. The council cancelled the Mackinac expedition and turned to the second mission.[59]

They decided to use Perry's squadron to transport elements of the North West Army from Detroit to the Niagara frontier. There were so few regulars that they sailed on Perry's ships, not the Schenectady bateaux.

Harrison's and Perry's joint conduct merits one last commendation. In victory, Harrison and Perry sought redemption, not revenge. They cooperated with one another and integrated their respective services toward a common goal—victory. At the same time, their conduct with hundreds of prisoners of war differed considerably from that imposed on American soldiers captured on the banks of the River Raisin and Maumee River in the previous ten months. On the waters of Lake Erie and on the banks of the Thames River, both their victories and their post-battle conduct redeemed the sacrifices made on the banks of the Raisin and Maumee, without atrocities like those inflicted on some American prisoners.

The Harrison-Perry cooperation constitutes one of the few successful joint efforts in early American military history. Seldom have commanders from different services worked together more closely and efficiently than these young officers—Harrison was just forty and Perry only twenty-nine years old. The two achieved that unity of effort that was critical to the national objective. They overcame interservice ambitions and operational biases to focus on a common goal. Undoubtedly some of this was because of Perry's deference to Harrison's rank, experience, and professionalism. And Harrison exhibited a degree of respect toward his junior colleague in his laudatory reports on the naval commander's actions. Perhaps the best example of this mutual admiration came when Harrison allowed Perry to cosign a proclamation establishing government in the recently conquered area of Upper Canada. Such an honor was indeed singular, especially since none of the general officers under Harrison's command signed the document.[60] Their collaboration was an excellent example of how unity of effort may be achieved by cooperation without vesting command authority in a single individual. Yet, as distinguished military historian Mark Grimsley writes, "while these successes secured the western U.S. frontier, they contributed little toward ending the war."[61]

In a strict military sense, Harrison and Perry were not the "saviors of the Old Northwest" they are sometimes acclaimed to be (the British Army, fur traders, and their native allies would control Michigan's Upper Peninsula and the future Wisconsin through the end of the war). But there can be little doubt that the American victories on Lake Erie and at the Thames River influenced His Majesty's negotiators at Ghent to reaffirm the 1783 boundary rather than readjust it in accordance with the military situation at the war's end. Without these two victories, the chances of such a *status quo ante bellum* conclusion to the War of 1812 remain in doubt.[62]

Whatever may be said against General Procter and his redcoats, they accomplished a great deal by delaying American efforts in the Detroit River region. Their sacrifice represented an extraordinary economy-of-force effort that postponed the American triumph until such a seasonally late date that U.S. objectives at Fort Michilimackinac and the Niagara frontier remained unfulfilled. The result was the American failure on Mackinac Island and the stalemate along the shores of the Niagara River in 1814. The Great Lakes offensive waged by Gen. Isaac Brock in 1812 had required Native American assistance to secure and sustain. General Brock's designs to create an Indian barrier state between the Mississippi River and Lake Huron failed both on the shores of the Thames

River and in decisions at Whitehall. Consequently, His Majesty's government, for a third time, sacrificed Native Americans' desires on the altar of diplomacy.

From the Washington viewpoint, one usually ignored consequence of Harrison's victory was its effect on the Creek and other southern Indians fighting in modern Alabama. The president, Secretary of State James Monroe, and Secretary Armstrong all agreed that news of the Thames battle would soon be known among the southern Indians and would discourage them.[63] Far more significant, however, was the victory of Andrew Jackson's forces at the battle of Horseshoe Bend the following March.

The life of Tecumseh has provoked an extraordinarily positive response among Americans and Canadians. Generally he receives laudatory treatment, as he is portrayed as a humane warrior for a lost cause. But among those who engaged in warfare against him, the commentary was often highly critical. Contemporary writer Henry Brackenridge of Pennsylvania called him "one of the most celebrated warriors that ever raised the tomahawk against us." But this "untutored man was the determined foe of civilization, and had for years been laboring to unite all the Indian tribes in resisting the progress of our settlements to the westward." Tecumseh, he continued, "had received the stamp of greatness from the hand of nature; and had his lot been cast in a different state of society, he would have shone as one of the most distinguished of men." In the final analysis, however, "he was the champion of barbarism at a period when he could only draw down destruction on his own head." Isaac Shelby, after learning of Jackson's victory at Horseshoe Bend, observed that "those Miserable writches will have occasion long to Mourn the day that they listened to Tecumseh's talks."[64]

In recounting Dudley's defeat and the subsequent massacre of his surrendered troops, Captain McAfee attributed to Tecumseh "more humanity, magnanimity, and civilization, than Proctor [Procter] with all his British associates in command, displayed through the whole war on the northwestern frontiers." But the Kentuckian made no final summary of Tecumseh's career and contributions in his conclusions regarding the battle of the Thames.[65] It is this theme of the native chieftain's humanity when compared with other Indians and with British leaders that dominates much of the early commentary on Tecumseh.

Lewis Cass, who also served at the Thames, described the Indian chieftain as "a man of more enlarged views than are often found among the Indian chiefs, a brave warrior and a skillful leader, politic in his measures and firm in his purposes. But he was jealous and ambitious and prepared to sacrifice the happiness of his people to his own impracticable objects."[66]

In his analysis, historian Gregory Evans Dowd ends with a telling conclusion: the War of 1812 "was not pan-Indianism's greatest triumph, as it is often portrayed in studies of Tecumseh. Instead, the War of 1812 stands as pan-Indianism's most thorough failure, its crushing defeat, its disappointing anticlimax."[67] From a contemporary perspective, Lewis Cass may have been correct: Tecumseh sacrificed the happiness of his people on the altar of impracticability.

We will never know whether the path of accommodation advocated by Tarhe and Black Hoof would have resulted in a different solution to the Native American problem that confronted the leaders of the young republic. But we do know that the wave of violence that many Indians unleashed in the first dozen years of the nineteenth century transformed the political culture of the United States after the War of 1812 from the self-serving paternalism of the Jeffersonian age into a racist policy of removal of Native Americans from the Eastern Woodlands onto the North American grasslands.

Thus it was that Harrison's triumph at the battle of the Thames marked the end of the very policy he had attempted to implement as the governor of Indiana Territory. More important than the death of Tecumseh, perhaps, was the attempted assassination of Black Hoof. This event acknowledged that the pathway of integration of Native Americans into Euroamerican culture was no longer viable in the Indian-hating mood of the frontiersmen. If Tecumseh's hope for a military solution to his American problem had failed, so had Harrison's and Jefferson's policy that naively envisioned the Indians would peacefully transform their culture and tolerate white settlement in their ancient hunting and farming grounds.[68]

Chapter Seven

The Politics of Victory

T he nation received William Henry Harrison's triumph on the Thames with great enthusiasm. Some hailed the Eighth Military District commander as the "Washington of the West." A nation whose army had been humiliated, defeated, and disgraced throughout the previous year now had a general with a winning record. The victory at the Thames redeemed the surrender of Detroit, the River Raisin massacre, and Dudley's defeat. Harrison's troops repelled British sieges of Fort Meigs twice, did the same at Fort Stephenson, engaged in an amphibious assault on Canadian soil, destroyed the right wing of His Majesty's forces in Canada, and eliminated native foes as a military threat. Some thought the government should revive the military rank of lieutenant general and that Harrison should be awarded three stars. Gov. Isaac Shelby wrote Secretary of War John Armstrong that he trusted the president would reward Harrison for his inspired leadership during the campaign.[1] Given these credits, it is hard to believe that just a few months later Harrison would resign his commission, with his honor besmirched, his military reputation tarnished, and his financial integrity questioned.

Aftermath of Victory

Immediately after his retirement to Detroit in early October 1813, Harrison wrote two letters to Secretary of War Armstrong. The first described the Thames River campaign; the second, written on 10 October, outlined his disposition of the Indians and the armistice he had made with the formerly hostile tribes. He concluded that further Indian war in the region was unlikely so long as the United States delicately managed and monitored the situation or "unless we suffer the British again to get footing in our territory." While this agreement curtailed native depredations in Ohio, Indiana, Illinois, and the lower peninsula of Michigan, he recognized that it would not affect the more northern tribes, from Mackinac Island to modern Wisconsin and along the shores of Lake Superior. Until the United States was "in Possession of Montreal," he concluded, "the northern Indians will be entirely independent of us." His selection of Montreal as a national objective is somewhat mystifying—was he unexpectedly becoming more of a national strategist and less of a regional one or was he angling for command of an expedition in the St. Lawrence Valley, or both? As the Eighth Military District commander, he should have been more interested in Mackinac Island than Montreal. It is clear that Harrison now had bigger ambitions than commanding the North West Army.

While Governor Shelby's troops marched to their home state and mustered out, Harrison began working on several items that remained on his agenda: planning an expedition against Fort Michilimackinac, concluding an armistice with the Indians, establishing civil government in Michigan and the occupied Western District of Upper Canada, and moving many of his regulars to the Niagara Peninsula on Perry's vessels. He also found himself responsible for providing food for both natives and whites living on the Detroit frontier and conveying British prisoners to Ohio and Kentucky. This was a full plate, and he had no instructions from the War Department on how to proceed.

The provisioning of the natives and the American and Canadian residents of the Detroit frontier posed a problem. A combination of poor harvests and British and Indian confiscation of foodstuffs and livestock, along with Perry's dominance of Lake Erie in August and September, destroyed the region's ability to feed its inhabitants. As a Michigan resident recalled, "The miserable inhabitants now once more free, were at a loss how to live or what to do for many had lost their all and few but what had sufered exceedingly." He pleaded for the national government to relieve the residents in their hour of need. The necessity for federal intervention was best illustrated by General Cass, who described a region where the "whole resources . . . are exhausted, & there being no means of transportation upon the Lake, but by public vessels." Harrison heard these pleas and directed Ohio Brig. Gen. John S. Gano to forward to Detroit "with as much expedition as possible" all beef cattle in his logistical lifeline. Indian Agent John Johnston in Piqua, Ohio, received directives to send flour under his control to the Indians living near Detroit. This use of government supplies to aid private suffering was somewhat unusual in the early national period.[2] Eventually this policy became part of a dispute between Harrison and the provisions contractor Orr & Greeley over accusations of financial irregularities.

Harrison and Captain Perry sought to restrict commercial and military cooperation between the Indians and the British in the upper region by retaking Fort Michilimackinac and seizing Fort St. Joseph in the St. Marys River between the United States and Canada. With his Kentuckians heading south, Harrison coordinated with Gen. Duncan McArthur to make use of his regular army troops in such an enterprise.[3] They cancelled the expedition to Fort Michilimackinac, however, because weather intruded into their plans. On 15 October Col. Thomas A. Smith of the U.S. Rifle Regiment reported from Amherstburg that trunks, saddle bags, and other luggage had been washed up on the Canadian shore, apparently a consequence of the loss of two of Perry's supply vessels (the *Chippawa* and *Ohio*) carrying necessary equipment and provisions for the Lake Huron voyage. That information, combined with Perry's fears that the seasonal storms would endanger the ships and troops on a lake where none of the U.S. Navy officers had sailed, was enough for Harrison to cancel the expedition.[4] The American attempt to retake Mackinac Island the following year would be unsuccessful.

Simultaneously, Harrison was conducting negotiations with the Indians. Again, he had no War Department instructions on what to do, and he operated on his own initiative. He certainly brought to the table a wide experience in such efforts, given his activities as governor of Indiana Territory, 1800–1812.[5] The 14 October meeting with representatives of the Miami, Potawatomi, Wyandot, Ottawa, and Chippewa tribes resulted in an armistice with three major points: (1) the suspension of hostilities, with the tribes retiring to their traditional hunting grounds; (2) a promise to punish those committing murder or other depredations on American citizens; and (3) a requirement that the tribes provide hostages into U.S. custody until a council between the tribes determined the final disposition of relations between the natives and the American government. Harrison promised that if they remained faithful to this agreement, the tribes would receive their previously agreed-to annuities.[6]

Six weeks later Cass observed that "the professions of many of the Indian tribes are hollow & deceitful." He blamed this situation on "the art with which the enemy have impressed the Indians that our success is their destruction." He found "that the Indians are suspicious & jealous, doubtful of our sincerity, & apprehensive for the future." By mid-December Cass reported the Indians to be "restless and uneasy." He feared the Canadian authorities would "use every exertion to regain their former influence with the Indian tribes." To counter this he advised a sound policy to extend "the hand of friendship, to be liberal in our supplies of clothing, and provisions; and to invite them, as soon as circumstances will permit, to hold a general treaty." The president agreed with this, and Daniel Parker, the War Department's chief clerk, informed General Cass that the issuing of rations to both the Indians and the suffering white inhabitants of Michigan was authorized.[7] It is clear that Cass and Harrison were of the same mind regarding the necessity of supplying provisions to both the Native Americans and the white residents of the Detroit region; federal authorities heeded their pleas.

The following July, Harrison told a delegation of Indian chiefs to disregard the assertions of some British informants that the end of the Napoleonic wars would bring France and the anti-Napoleon allies into the war on the side of the United Kingdom. Informants designed this fabrication "to answer their usual purposes of deception." He then brought out statements from his former opponents—Pecan of the Miami and Walk-in-the-Water of the Wyandot—that reaffirmed their support of an agreement with the United States.[8]

Establishing a government in Michigan and the Western District of Upper Canada became one of Harrison's more complex problems. Since General Procter had placed the Western District under martial law prior to his departure, Harrison continued that form of government and awaited directions from Washington on what should be done. He appointed General Cass as the civil and military commander of the Western District of Upper Canada and, in a joint proclamation with Captain Perry, directed civil magistrates there to continue in their functions after taking an oath "to be faithful to the Government of the U. States as long as they Shall be in the possession" of that country. The proclamation abolished the Canadian militia in the areas under American control. One of the most interesting documents of this period was a protection order for John Askin of Sandwich, a leading merchant and Canadian militia officer whose sons were also in British service. Harrison's order directed "all Officers and privates of my Army . . . to abstain from any acts of violence or outrage towards" Askin and his household.[9]

From the beginning, the American general recognized that the upper level of administration in Michigan had been eliminated by the British occupation and the subsequent emigration of its civil government officers to areas controlled by the national government. Civil government in the territory ceased to exist. Harrison pleaded for the president to appoint civil officials as soon as possible. He decided to reorganize and rearm the territorial militia on his own initiative. He placed this force and a few regulars under the command of

General Cass. Before the month of October was out, President James Madison appointed Cass as territorial governor. This appointment began Cass's long and distinguished political career in Michigan and national politics.[10]

One might assume that this singular triumph in the Northwest provided enough opportunities for individual and unit commendations that would leave little room for controversy. The decisions made at Sandwich resulted in an American victory of large significance. These decisions allowed American occupation of the Western District of Upper Canada; they ended serious Native American resistance in Indiana, Ohio, and southern Michigan; and they permitted the Kentuckians to return home with scalps, souvenirs, accolades, and stories of valor that produced electoral victories for a generation. Despite this success, from the beginning, the decisions at Sandwich were controversial.

First, they aggravated the tensions between General Harrison and Secretary of War Armstrong. Harrison's decision to use a force almost entirely made up of volunteer Kentuckians with only a small battalion of regulars constituted a slap in the face for the secretary of war, who believed that regulars should make up the main component of his army. Armstrong never understood the military competence of the Ohio Valley's wartime volunteers or the relative inexperience of the recently formed regular army units. Through a series of maneuvers, Armstrong violated Harrison's sense of honor and prestige and eventually, in 1814, caused him to resign. Second, Armstrong wanted Harrison's regulars to be sent to the Niagara frontier as soon as Detroit had been redeemed. This meant that Harrison either should have chosen the water route to entrap General Procter or should have used regulars for the major portion of the troops sent on the land route. Harrison had done neither. His Sandwich decisions increased Armstrong's animus toward Harrison.

Some of their animosity can be attributed to the different military experiences of the two men. Armstrong's Revolutionary War career was with the Continental Army and carried with it a contempt for militia units as undisciplined and unreliable. Having spent most of his career in eastern Pennsylvania and New York, he had little understanding of westerners and their military experiences over the previous two decades. He made no distinction between the common militia and volunteer units. Harrison's regular army career was brief and involved a combination of regular and volunteer units. Although Anthony Wayne's Fallen Timbers campaign is heralded as laying the foundations of the regular army, it also involved mounted volunteer soldiers who contributed significantly to the American victory.[11] Harrison's Tippecanoe campaign was another combination of regulars and volunteers in which both types of units contributed to the tactical victory. Although a few of the volunteer units were less than valorous, others fought with distinction and sustained many casualties without breaking.[12]

Armstrong also failed to understand that most of the regular units attached to Harrison's command were very new and contained many inexperienced officers and enlisted men. Many in the volunteer units were men with substantially more military experience than their regular counterparts. For instance, Ohio's Alfred Brunson of the 27th U.S. Infantry enlisted for a year in early 1813, was named a noncommissioned officer without any previous military service, and experienced his first combat in the battle at Moraviantown that October. In contrast, Daniel Sibert served as a fourth sergeant in a volunteer company that participated in the fall and winter campaign of 1812-13, before being discharged at Fort Meigs in March. After returning to Kentucky, he heeded Governor Shelby's call to arms the following August and reenlisted with the rank of orderly sergeant in a mounted infantry company that headed north. He left his horse at the Marblehead Peninsula of Ohio and, like Brunson, sailed across Lake Erie and fought at the battle of the Thames.[13] Neither man fired a shot in the battle. No one could argue that Brunson, a regular army soldier, had more service than Sibert and that he was better trained, armed, and experienced than the Kentucky volunteer. Nor could one make the case that these two were necessarily typical of soldiers in either type of unit. However, Kentuckians had been fighting Indians for the previous two decades, and their military experience at the midlevel officer and senior enlisted ranks was extensive. One of the Kentucky mounted riflemen remembered that his "officers were men, almost without exception, who had been brought up to war, and they instilled into the raw recruits an enthusiasm that made them irresistible."[14]

Col. Richard M. Johnson was well known for the training of his mounted rifle units. For instance, while Perry's fleet fought on Lake Erie, Johnson's troopers spent the day "in training, and in fighting sham battles, the exact miniature of that which they were soon to fight in reality. A line of infantry was formed, and the horses were practiced to charge through it at full speed; and such was the tractability and the force of custom in this noble animal, that in a little time there was scarcely a horse in the regiment that would flinch at a line of infantry enveloped in a blaze of fire and smoke."[15] This exemplified the best training to be found in professional military units. Johnson's troopers probably were the best-trained mounted soldiers in either the regular army or the volunteers.

The quality of Johnson's leadership is best illustrated by the fact that his unit was the only one in the 1814 campaign to have a full complement of authorized troops.

And one cannot forget Isaac Shelby. One of the most experienced military leaders in the United States, his reputation rested on his leadership in the victory over the British at the battle of Kings Mountain, South Carolina, in 1780. At Moraviantown he again led backcountry volunteers against a disciplined foe. His reputation as a commander brought more volunteers to Harrison's army than any other leader could bring. What was unique about Shelby was his willingness to subordinate himself to a man more than twenty years his junior who had much less combat experience. The supportive relationship between Shelby and Harrison is best exemplified by the governor's consultation with the Eighth Military District commander before the senior officers' meeting at Sandwich. Even though he never served with either the Continental Army or the U.S. Army, Shelby's status as a military leader was such that newly elected president James Monroe offered him the post of secretary of war in 1817.[16] And as we shall see, Shelby refused to accept congressional accolades of victory if Harrison did not receive at least equal recognition. Shelby's relationship with Harrison contrasts sharply with that of James Winchester and John Armstrong.

The Armstrong-Harrison Rivalry Continues

The battle smoke had scarcely cleared from the Thames Valley when the recriminations began. Secretary Armstrong bemoaned the absence of a substantial number of regulars at the battle. Apparently he never congratulated Harrison on the triumph. Even before he officially knew of Perry's victory, the secretary specifically directed Harrison not "to pursue the Indians into their woody & distant recesses" and instead to move his regulars down the lake to the Niagara Peninsula. In other words, he preferred pursuit by water rather than by land. The delay in communication between the frontier and the secretary meant that Armstrong and his staff did not know what Harrison and Shelby were doing until a week to ten days after they had acted. Thus a directive authorizing the use of Shelby's volunteers in the campaign was written the day Harrison's Kentucky forces landed on the Canadian shore. Another order for Harrison to move the regular troops to the Niagara Peninsula was sent after he had arrived there.[17]

Harrison felt compelled to act on his own assessment of the situation. He wrote the secretary, "Not having received your directions and being entirely ignorant of the State of our military operations" on the Niagara frontier, "I was much at a loss to Know how to proceed." Thus he left General Cass in charge of operations in the Detroit River region and concluded "that I could not do better than to move down the Lake [Erie] with the remaining part of the Troops." There he awaited Armstrong's directions on what to do next. He sent this missive with Colonel Gaines, who was leaving to join his regiment at Sackets Harbor.[18]

It became increasingly apparent that the secretary of war would not give Harrison an opportunity for another victory, nor would he allow him to assume command outside the Eighth Military District. Harrison was outside the Eighth District at Niagara, and Armstrong maneuvered to deny him an opportunity for military success there.[19]

The accolades given Perry and Harrison in Erie portended political problems for Armstrong. As the victors on Lake Erie and at the Thames docked at the Pennsylvania port, they were met by cheering residents and treated to a lavish celebration that included banners proclaiming "WE HAVE MET THE ENEMY," "TENTH OF SEPTEMBER," "HARRISON—VICTORY," "FIFTH OF OCTOBER." Armstrong deplored such outbursts, especially aimed at someone who won with volunteers.[20]

While in Erie, the general wrote the secretary indicating that he had brought Gen. Duncan McArthur's brigade and a battalion of U.S. riflemen (totaling no more than eleven hundred men) to Niagara but had no idea how the War Department wanted him to use them. When he arrived at Buffalo on 24 October, he still was without directions from the secretary.[21] Unbeknownst to Harrison, Armstrong had expected the general to use his regulars in the Thames campaign and then to march from there to the Niagara frontier. Armstrong intended Harrison to confront Maj. Gen. Francis, Baron de Rottenburg's British troops from the rear, while New York Maj. Gen. George McClure moved against their front by advancing from Fort Erie, Upper Canada (opposite Buffalo). This directive was sent after Harrison had already withdrawn to Detroit, and the messenger carrying it was lost in the storm that beached the *Chippawa* near Buffalo. The secretary sent another message to Harrison on 30 October in which he understood that the general was at Fort Erie. Knowing that de Rottenburg had withdrawn to Burlington Heights (modern Hamilton, Ontario), the secretary now urged Harrison and McClure to force the British off the western end of Lake Ontario past York (modern Toronto). "The capture or destruction of this [de Rottenburg's] Corps would be a glorious *finale* to your Campaign," concluded Armstrong.[22] This last order is contained only in the copy of the letter in War Department files, not the version in Harrison's papers. The first two paragraphs of the letters are the same until, in the War Department version, Armstrong directs the attack toward Burlington Heights and on to York. Had the general been able to accomplish the secretary's objective on the Niagara Peninsula, the bloodletting there in 1814 might have been avoided. Why this discrepancy exists between the Library of Congress copy of Harrison's papers and the War Department version in the National Archives is unexplained. Given the defeat of Gen. Wade Hampton's corps at Chateaugay on 25 October, the secretary may well have reconsidered how to make use of Harrison's regulars and decided not to employ them on the Niagara Peninsula. Therefore the order was never sent. Armstrong may have changed his mind regarding Harrison's troops on the Niagara frontier and revised the directive to the version the general received.

Even though he did not receive the secretary's directive to move on Burlington Heights and York, it is clear that Harrison agreed with those objectives. On 1 November he wrote New York Governor Daniel D. Tompkins that the "enemy must not be suffered to occupy the head of Lake Ontario thro' the winter or from thence they may attempt the recovery of the Upper District." But all of General McArthur's troops and their baggage had not yet arrived at Niagara. Therefore Harrison directed General McClure to call for volunteers or militia units from western New York for a thirty-day tour, in his effort to dislodge the British from the Niagara-to-Toronto frontier. He used McClure because he did not want to waste the time needed for a message to be sent to the governor in Albany and for a gubernatorial order calling up troops to be sent to Buffalo. Moreover, intelligence reports concluded that the British were sending troops from York to Kingston, thereby increasing his chances of taking the former objective.[23]

Concurrently, he planned to bring General Cass's brigade from Detroit to the Niagara peninsula to assist in the assault on Burlington Heights. But his order to Cass went undelivered when the vessel carrying it was driven ashore. He subsequently learned that Mstr. Comdt. Jesse Duncan Elliott, USN, now commanding the Lake Erie naval squadron, refused to devote sufficient shipping to transport the Detroit brigade in a timely manner. He therefore canceled the order to Cass. He also noted that the previous transfer of Col. Winfield Scott's regiment from the Niagara frontier to Sackets Harbor deprived him of the use of this regiment in operations at the head of Lake Ontario.[24]

Secretary Armstrong, meanwhile, changed his mind about the disposition of McArthur's brigade. On 3 November he ordered McArthur's troops to be sent to Sackets Harbor, New York, and directed Cmdr. Isaac Chauncey to pick up the brigade at the mouth of the Niagara River. Their purpose was to join less than a thousand regulars commanded by Colonel Scott in the defense of the U.S. Navy's base near the eastern end of Lake Ontario from a possible over-the-ice British attack from Kingston, Upper Canada. The two units together constituted what the secretary thought would be enough to defend the critical naval base and its shipyard.[25]

One can attribute motives both positive and sinister to this move. Certainly the defense of the only U.S. naval base and shipyard on Lake Ontario was a high priority for the army. Gen. James Wilkinson's expedition toward Montreal was underway, so the necessity of having enough troops at Sackets Harbor to protect it against a *coup de main* could be justified as prudent. On the other hand, one can attribute devious motives to Armstrong's decision. He deprived Harrison of an opportunity to exploit British weaknesses on the Niagara frontier. Given the decision of the British leadership regarding the necessary employment of most of their forces against Wilkinson, an attack on Sackets Harbor was unlikely. And the chance of Harrison's success against de Rottenburg was reasonable.[26] At the very least, Armstrong did not exhibit the kind of risk taking that characterized Maj. Gen. Isaac Brock and resulted in his capture of Detroit in 1812.

Armstrong's directive deprived Harrison of an opportunity for attacking the British at Burlington Bay on the northwest side of Lake Ontario. It also discouraged the New York militia commanded by General McClure from remaining on duty, thereby leaving Forts George (Niagara-on-the-Lake, Ontario) and Niagara (Youngstown, New York) without sufficient troops for their defense. General McClure was outraged at the failure to exploit the opportunity Harrison and his regulars and the militia presented to the Niagara frontier. Harrison could only plead that Armstrong's orders left him no alternative. One of the unintended consequences of the victory at the Thames may have been that survivors reinforced the British forces on the Niagara Peninsula and assisted His Majesty's troops in that vicinity at a critical juncture. The two forts would subsequently fall to the British and remain in their hands for the rest of the war.[27] General Wilkinson's disastrous defeat at Crysler's Farm (11 November) had not occurred when Armstrong issued his order. Certainly that loss provided an opportunity for a British attack on the critical naval base at Sackets Harbor. Thus, in hindsight, the move may be seen as cautious foresight on the secretary's part.

But why did Armstrong change the force disposition when he did? We will never know what Col. Edmund Pendleton Gaines told Secretary Armstrong when the two met in early November. Gaines had been seconded from his command of the 25th U.S. Infantry to serve as Harrison's adjutant general. He was now en route to command his regiment in Wilkinson's campaign. Did he make derogatory comments about Harrison's military capabilities? Gaines was ill during the Thames campaign so he did not witness Harrison's performance and his use of the volunteers there. Or did Gaines merely mention to Armstrong the enthusiasm for the general in the West and how it might be parlayed into his military and political careers? Did this prompt the secretary to seek Harrison's demise as a potential rival to his own presidential ambitions? The secretary's dislike and distrust of Harrison was in sharp contrast to the growing sentiment that the Eighth District Commander might become the army's commanding general.[28]

An "order," not a suggestive letter, of 3 November directing the movement of McArthur's troops to Sackets Harbor contained another item of interest. It authorized Harrison and McArthur to visit their families.[29] If McArthur did not accompany his troops to Sackets Harbor, Col. Winfield Scott would be the commanding officer there. Secretary Armstrong was already favorably inclined toward Scott (and would see to his promotion to brigadier general the following May). Both generals understood this order as a directive to return to their own district.[30]

All this speculation regarding Harrison's military future provoked regional and personal animosities. In Albany, Governor Daniel Tompkins had Maj. Gen. Wade Hampton, army chief engineer Col. Joseph Swift, Secretary Armstrong, and Harrison over for breakfast. Relations between Armstrong and Harrison remained testy. Afterward they journeyed by steamboat to New York City (Harrison's first steamboat ride), where the secretary and the George Clinton faction in New York politics tried to ignore the general and where Tompkins and his allies had him feted. From there Harrison rode to Philadelphia, where he attended a special dinner in his honor. At a time when the secretary, frustrated at the lack of enlistments in the regular army, sought to have Congress pass a conscription law, Harrison used the opportunity to defy him. In a voluntary toast at the dinner, Harrison lauded the militia. "I will give you," said the Thames commander, "The Militia of the United States. They possess the Roman spirit and when our Government shall think it proper to give them that organization and discipline of which they are susceptible they will perform deeds that will emulate those of legions led by Marcellus and Scipio."[31] This toast was a direct affront to the secretary of war, and undoubtedly news of this insult reached him quickly.

Besides the militia issue, there was another side of Armstrong's opposition to Harrison. A disgusted young ensign wrote his father that the "people at Washington have got scared at Harrison's victories. They are afraid a few more might make him President!" He warned that Harrison would not be given an active command and observed in a sarcastic conclusion that the war "from the start has been about three parts politics to one part war."[32] Policy prejudice or political opportunism, the young man's observation appears a very close approximation of the attitudes of some at the War Department.

There were those who expected Congress to create a lieutenant general rank, and the expectation was that Harrison might be the one so honored. After all, with the disgrace of Generals Dearborn, Wilkinson, and Hampton, who else might ascend to that post? A letter to the *Freeman's Journal* of Philadelphia foresaw Harrison's becoming "commander-in-chief of our armies in Canada." Or as Perry put it in a letter to the general, "I expect to hail you as the chief who is to redeem the honor of our arms in the North."[33]

But this was not to be the case. Armstrong and his confidant William Duane of the important Philadelphia newspaper *Aurora* were determined to push Harrison aside. Theirs was a continuation of the attacks on Harrison that appeared in the *Aurora* earlier in the year. After spending a week in Washington, to which Armstrong had not yet returned, the general wrote the secretary regarding both the defense of the Michigan frontier and Indian relations.[34] He then returned to Cincinnati and to the arms of his beloved Anna, who had given birth to their ninth child in his absence. While all this was going on, Armstrong and Duane began an attack on Harrison's generalship. The core of the anti-Harrison argument was that the Eighth District Commander sacrificed Brig. Gen. James Winchester at Frenchtown and thereby contributed to the River Raisin massacre of January 1813, blundered in his treatment of Maj. George Croghan during the defense of Fort Stephenson in August, and failed to capture British General Procter at the Thames in October. The capture of Procter could have happened if only Harrison had used the Lake Erie route to quickly maneuver between Procter and the British forces on the Niagara Peninsula. In other words, Harrison was incompetent and not deserving of further combat leadership.[35]

Despite the increasing criticism of Armstrong's leadership at the War Department, President Madison remained unwilling to dismiss him. His "going to the front" to direct the Wade Hampton and James Wilkinson operations in the St. Lawrence Valley instead of remaining in Washington typified Armstrong's self-image of being a commanding general as well as a secretary of war. This effort ended with his making no positive contribution to the campaign. For all of Armstrong's reputation for promoting able commanders—Jacob Brown and Winfield Scott, for example—the reverse applies to his relationship with Harrison. Armstrong's placement of Wilkinson and Hampton, whose mutual dislike of one another was well known, in what were supposedly mutually supportive campaigns constituted an administrative error of the first magnitude.[36]

While Armstrong dallied in Philadelphia, Harrison had waited in Washington. He held conferences on Indian affairs with President Madison, western congressional leaders, and Daniel Parker, the War Department's chief clerk. Before leaving the capital, he wrote Armstrong regretting that they had not had another meeting and noting that he would await "your further instructions" in Cincinnati. He also detailed a list of options for his district. Because General Cass had been named territorial governor, the government withdrew his military authority in the Detroit Valley. Unaware of the illness that would lead to Gen. Benjamin Howard's death in a few months (in September 1814), Harrison recommended the St. Louis commander be sent to Detroit. Finally, Harrison urged attention be paid to Indian affairs, particularly to undercutting potential British efforts to bring the hostile tribes in alliance with His Majesty's government. He looked forward to receiving specific instructions on the treatment of various tribes.[37]

While Armstrong's criticisms of Harrison's military abilities emerged in the *Aurora*, another critique appeared within the Eighth Military District.

The Mississippi Valley Theater

Harrison's command included not only Kentucky, Ohio, and Michigan, where he concentrated his efforts in 1813, but also the territories of Indiana, Illinois, and Missouri, a vast region that extended up both sides of the Mississippi from St. Louis to its headwaters. For the most part, Harrison neglected the region and left its defense to Governor Howard of Missouri Territory. Like so many commanders throughout history, Howard envisioned the war through the narrow lens of his theater of operations. In January 1813 he wrote the War Department outlining his strategic and operational suggestions. He understood clearly that British control of Mackinac Island allowed them to influence the region west of Lake Michigan through their Indian agents and the large number of voyageurs that worked for various fur trading companies. The question he posed was whether it was more expedient for the United States "to act on the defensive on our frontiers until our differences are settled with Great Britain, or carry on a Campaign to reduce" the hostile tribes and their allies. He recognized westerners' vulnerability to native depredations as a consequence of the Indians' mobility by canoes that plied the numerous waterways in the region. Howard understood that limited efforts to push Indian villages deeper into the wilderness constituted a "fashionable but fallacious" strategy because it only drove them away from American forces while allowing native warriors more opportunity to attack frontier settlements with little fear that their own villages would be assailed. If, he argued, Americans depended on a defensive policy, the Indians would defy "every vigilance" and be enabled "to distress our frontier from its vast extent." Moreover, he contended, it would require more men and money to defend the region than to engage in offensive operations deep inside the native habitations.

The Missouri governor proposed a multipronged offensive with four thousand mounted troops engaged for at least six months, unless sooner discharged. Campaigns were to be sent up the Wabash, Illinois, and Rock Rivers, then would join and move along the western Lake Michigan shore from Chicago to Green Bay. Forts were to be erected on the Illinois River (near modern Peoria), on the upper Rock River, and at the mouth of the Wisconsin River (Prairie du Chien). Howard's central argument revolved around his perception of the relative military unimportance of the Wabash and southern Michigan tribes when compared with those in what is now northern Illinois and Wisconsin. In other words, Tecumseh's confederation was less threatening than the alliances under the direction of Robert Dickson. And from his St. Louis vantage point this was correct; from that perspective, the seizure of Fort Malden was relatively unimportant. In effect, Howard endorsed an operational scheme contrary to that adopted by Harrison in 1813. Secretary Armstrong saw this grandiose plan as impractical from a strategic, manpower, and financial viewpoint and refused to endorse it. Nonetheless, Howard received a brigadier general's commission in March 1813. General William Clark (of Lewis and Clark fame) received the Missouri Territory governorship.[38]

Technically, Howard was subordinate to Harrison in the Eighth Military District, but in a practical sense he operated independently of the theater commander because Harrison devoted his 1813 efforts to the campaign to retake Detroit. From the beginning, Secretary Armstrong corresponded directly with General Howard and neglected to send copies of his messages to Harrison. Some of this can be justified on the grounds of the secretary's inability to communicate quickly with Harrison because of the latter's constant movement throughout Ohio during most of 1813. On the other hand, the secretary made few attempts to keep the general informed of his communications with Howard and thereby undercut Harrison's authority in the Mississippi Valley. He learned while perusing War Department files that Armstrong had made Howard an independent commander in the Mississippi Valley. When Harrison returned to Cincinnati in early 1814, his status relative to Howard remained unclear. Similar problems occurred within the Department of the Navy, with Mstr. Cmdt. Oliver Hazard Perry being subordinate to Great Lakes Commodore Isaac Chauncey on Lake Ontario, and the secretary of the navy communicating directly with Perry, and vice versa, without Chauncey's being informed.[39]

Hoping to keep Harrison in the comparatively inactive Midwestern theater, Secretary Armstrong ordered General Howard to report to the district commander in Cincinnati, since Harrison "has returned to resume his Command within the 8th Military District, & has been instructed to adopt measures for the next Campaign." It is clear that this directive superseded Armstrong's previous orders regarding Howard's operational independence. Thus Armstrong gave Harrison more district authority than he had previously had while at the same time keeping him in a theater of secondary importance for the 1814 campaigns.[40]

Howard's major military accomplishment of 1813 involved organizing offensive operations for 1814. Of particular note was the construction of four gunboats with high, thick, small arms–resistant sides for use on the Mississippi and its tributaries. As Governor Clark reported in mid-December, "Those savage bands [of Indians] between Lake Michigan & the Mississippi, we must Consider as our Enemies—They have not shewn that Anxiety to become our friends as was expected." From the St. Louis perspective, American victories on Lake Erie and at the Thames had not calmed the war tendencies of the Mississippi Valley tribes. Until Michilimackinac and Prairie du Chien were taken and the Native Americans' connection "with the British and their Traders [was] entirely" cut off, no peace could be expected in the upper Mississippi Valley.[41]

Despite Harrison's victories in the Detroit region, Robert Dickson kept "alive that ascendency which the British had" with the tribes between Lake Michigan and the Mississippi River. To counter this, Governor Clark recommended establishing a fortification at Prairie de Chien.[42] The governor wrote directly to Secretary Armstrong rather than to Harrison, but this may have been because he did not know whether Harrison still commanded the Eighth Military District and he did know that General Howard was becoming increasingly incapacitated by his illness. That May, the general proposed sending Clark and a gunboat to Prairie du Chien and establishing a fort there. But, he warned, "rest assured that the Garrison will be assailed as soon as they [the British] receive notice and can embody the Indians." This effort constituted a major operational proposal for Harrison's district of which Howard did not notify the district commander.[43]

On Indian affairs, Harrison continued to be a figure of importance to those in Washington. He suggested the government make "no attempt at Obtaining an Extinguishment of title to lands" until the war was over. Even if the natives consented to this, "the jealousy of the Warriors" might force the chiefs "once more to throw themselves in the arms of the enemy." Land cessions, he warned, were "the rock upon which the popularity of Tecumseh was founded and that upon which the influence of the *Little Turtle* was wrecked." With Madison's approval, Armstrong replied positively to the suggestion "of not mingling with the question of peace any proposals for either buying or exchanging Lands." Harrison continued to make suggestions on Indian affairs throughout the next two years.[44]

As evidence mounted that the British were reinforcing and resupplying Fort Michilimackinac, Harrison urged that Mstr. Cmdt. Jesse D. Elliott, commander of the Lake Erie squadron now that Perry had gone east, should send vessels to Detroit in anticipation of a cruise to intercept boats on Lake Huron that were "destined to take Supplies to Michilimacinac or Indian Goods to Lake Superior." And he warned Armstrong that the British were constructing vessels on Georgian Bay to supply the critical outpost at the junction of Lakes Huron and Michigan.[45]

Still, the threat in the west was not as strategically serious as that in the St. Lawrence Valley and the Lake Ontario littoral. As 1813 came to an end, Secretary Armstrong clearly wanted to retain General Harrison in the Eighth Military District where military action would be nationally insignificant, while Harrison expected a more active theater command in the northeast.

Resignation

As winter turned to spring in 1814, it became increasingly apparent to Harrison's staff that Armstrong was not going to place their commander in an active theater of war. Capt. Charles S. Todd of Harrison's Inspector General Office bemoaned, "Certainly the War dept. cannot mean to put [Maj. Gen. Jacob J.] Brown and [Maj. Gen. George] Izard in Competition with General H[arrison].—the truth is, Sir, the mass of the U.S. have such confidence in the latter and so little in any other, that the Govt. must appoint him Com. In Chief."[46] Although both Brown and Izard were junior to Harrison, Armstrong had no intention of using Harrison in preference to one of them. Izard had little combat leadership experience at that time, and Brown, who was most famous for his defense of Sackets Harbor in May 1813, received a major general commission in January 1814.

Congressman James Pleasants Jr. of Virginia warned Harrison about the animosity of Secretary Armstrong that contributed to Harrison's not being "employed in a situation in which you may be of use to your country."[47] "I believe the Secy of War is not my friend," Harrison wrote Shelby, "and believing him to be a most dangerous man to act under I would immediately retire from the Service—If I did not believe that Such a Step would Meet the disapprobation of the greater part of my fellow Citizens."[48] Besides the secretary's hostility toward Harrison, also contributing to the general's non-assignment were his inexperience with fighting British regulars and his favoritism toward volunteer soldiers in a military district containing most of the regular army. Armstrong therefore named Brown instead of Harrison to command the combat-intensive Ninth Military District.[49] That decision became the final straw as far as the Eighth Military District commander was concerned.

Soon other grievances emerged. One critical complaint between the general and the secretary began in mid-April when Col. Anthony Butler took leave from his post in Detroit and Harrison placed recently promoted Lt. Col. George Croghan in command there. Armstrong later provoked Croghan when he wrote an order to Maj. Andrew H. Holmes directing him to command the Fort Michilimackinac expedition without informing either the Detroit commander or Harrison. Such disregard for the chain of command was normal for Armstrong but irritated subordinate commanders.[50]

While Armstrong succeeded in disparaging Harrison in some military quarters, the general continued to have a solid reputation. Brig. Gen. Andrew Jackson reputedly spoke of Harrison's military abilities "in respectful terms." Newly promoted Brig. Gen. Edmund P. Gaines wrote Harrison an informative letter from Sackets Harbor to continue their acquaintanceship and update him on affairs in that quarter. A friendly letter from Harrison's Fallen Timbers campaign superior, Maj. Gen. James Wilkinson, described Secretary Armstrong as "a blundering, vain glorious minister, who is a mere military Emperic"—that is, a charlatan.[51] But then Wilkinson had his own troubles with Armstrong.

Secretary of the Navy William Jones paid Harrison the respect due a district commander when he wrote Armstrong and the general concerning the proposed expedition to Lake Huron to be undertaken by Capt. Arthur Sinclair, USN, who had replaced Elliott as naval commander on Lake Erie. He requested U.S. control of the St. Clair River shores so that the British or Indians might not intercept vessels going from one lake to the other. Croghan implemented Jones's request by sending his engineer officer, Capt. Charles Gratiot Jr., to erect a fort at what is now Port Huron, Michigan.[52]

On 11 May Harrison wrote Secretary Armstrong a letter in which he forwarded, through him, a request for "the President to accept my resignation of the appointment of Major General in the army." The way this was written implied that the president should make the decision to accept, and the general may have expected Madison to decline to do so. On the other hand, his letter to Madison written the same day implies that Armstrong would accept the resignation. Whatever Harrison's intent, in Madison's absence from Washington, Armstrong accepted the resignation and immediately nominated Andrew Jackson for the vacancy thus created. Harrison suggested a court martial concerning his conduct with Orr & Greeley, but Armstrong avoided this possible embarrassment by not creating a military tribunal. Consequently, Harrison turned to the House of Representatives for vindication.[53]

Of Medals and Money

Meanwhile, a coterie of Kentuckians wanted the accolades for the Thames victory to go to Governor Shelby, not General Harrison. The leader of this group was Gen. Joseph Desha, who coordinated with Jonathan Jennings, Indiana's territorial delegate to the House of Representatives and a longtime Harrison foe. Part of Desha's rationale was commonwealth xenophobia. Why, when it was Kentuckians who won the battle on the banks of the Thames and Shelby who brought them to Canada, should the accolades of victory go to Harrison? Central to Desha's argument was that in the senior officers' conference at Sandwich, it was Shelby who insisted on the land route while Harrison vacillated between the two options.[54]

Desha led the attack on Harrison from his position as a member of the U.S. House of Representatives. After the war's end, Congress began awarding gold medals to senior victorious commanders. Often it awarded the commander and the second-in-command separate medals. For example, Oliver Hazard Perry and his second-in-command Jesse Duncan Elliott received medals for the Lake Erie victory. The top three naval commanders at the battle of Lake Champlain also received such decorations.[55] So it was not unusual for Congress to recognize more than one officer for combat gallantry in the same battle. In fact, one can make the case that Colonel Johnson should also have received such honors for his conduct on the River Thames. Certainly one would think that Harrison and Shelby would be so rewarded.

Desha and Jennings had other ideas. Harrison's post-victory career was cloudy: he resigned his commission in 1814 during a dispute with Secretary of War Armstrong, and there were allegations of corruption in the awarding of supply contracts in his Eighth Military District. Both of these charges contributed to the controversy over awarding Harrison a medal.

Jennings, Harrison's arch-foe in Indiana, served as that territory's delegate to Congress until late 1816, when he became the new State of Indiana's first governor. In Congress he was a principal advocate of the corruption charges against Harrison. The case arose out of the manner of purchasing and delivering supplies to the North West Army. Jennings claimed to have papers that would "produce the political damnation of Genl. Harrison." As early as March 1814, influential Washington contractor Benjamin G. Orr of the firm of Orr & Greeley argued that Harrison violated a commissary contract, given to Orr's firm by Secretary Armstrong, to provide salted beef, bacon, and hams to the North West Army. Instead, Harrison employed a leading Cincinnati merchant to provide the meat that Orr & Greeley was supposed to supply. Harrison countered by arguing that the Orr & Greeley meat was not salted and that on the eve of the invasion of September 1813, he had to use John H. Piatt's firm for provisions. Both sides in this dispute had vested interests at stake: Orr's firm was closely allied to Secretary Armstrong, and Piatt was a personal friend and subsequent business partner of Harrison.[56]

The charges brought by Jennings went to a House committee chaired by Congressman Jonathan Fisk of New York, who reputedly said that information received from Jennings and the firm of Orr & Greeley impeached Harrison's integrity. Although the committee published an adverse report, Fisk denied making the censorious statement attributed to him by Jennings and said that the investigation into Harrison's conduct was not completed. The general described the committee's account as containing "Vilanous Misrepresentations of my Conduct" as commander of the North West Army. Fisk allowed Harrison to make a detailed reply against the "artful falsehoods" of his detractors and to describe how Orr & Greeley was responsible for the deficiency in provisions that occurred in late 1813 and how if he "had relied entirely upon them the army would have starved."[57]

In December 1815 Harrison dictated a long statement and enclosed a variety of affidavits from other interested parties attesting to his fiscal propriety and to the necessity to use other contractors when Orr & Greeley could not or would not provide necessary provisions to Detroit and Fort Malden. He accused Benjamin G. Orr of an "artful combination of truth and falsehood" in recounting the situation on Lake Erie in the fall and winter of 1813–14. While their relationship might have been satisfactory in the spring and summer, by fall it had become strained when Harrison would not allow Orr to draw what he considered an excessive advance for supplies. This episode "gave the first shock to the good understanding which had subsisted between us, and my taking him severely to task, when the army was crossing the lake, for not providing vessels to transport his provisions, entirely destroyed it." While he would "not have blamed the contractors for not performing impossibilities," he felt Orr made no effort to procure a means of transporting provisions across the lake as his contract required. This failure continued while Harrison was in New York and Washington during the winter, when Orr & Greeley botched requisitions by the Detroit and Put-in-Bay commanders. Should I, Harrison asked, have countermanded such requests, which were necessary to keep the troops and local populace provisioned "for fear that I should deprive Mr. Orr of the opportunity of making three hundred thousand dollars instead of one hundred thousand?" To which Fisk replied that if the materials now received from Harrison had been available at the time of the original inquiry, "they would have made an impression upon the minds of the committee different from that produced by the imperfect information which was received."[58]

Meanwhile, Desha charged that Harrison was no better as a general than William Hull (who had surrendered Detroit in 1812) and that Harrison joined in the pursuit up the Thames only because Shelby said he would lead the Kentuckians by himself if Harrison would not. No positive credit was given to Harrison's careful consideration of the options and his command decision to pursue Procter by land. Nor did Harrison's detractors mention Perry's opposition to the water route. Harrison found both his honor and his reputation under attack when in 1815 the Senate voted 13 to 11 to expunge Harrison's name from a bill honoring both him and Shelby.[59]

Kentucky's governor immediately condemned this slight. It appalled Governor Shelby that Harrison would not be honored with himself. The governor wrote Henry Clay saying he would decline the honor if Harrison were not equally rewarded. In the aftermath of the Thames campaign, Shelby had informed Armstrong of Harrison's "indefatigable zeal and industry during the Campaign." On receiving notice of the resolution against of Harrison's gold medal, Shelby wrote the former North West Army commander, "How mortified I should feel to be noticed if you were not—who had rendered ten times more service to the nation than I had." He then proposed a counterattack: "You must spare no pains to get into Congress." A similar proposal came from Harrison's former aide Charles S. Todd, who presciently prophesied, "This cold blooded persecution will I trust eventually benefit your fame—it will lead to a full investigation and your merits will consequently be the more conspicuous."[60]

A campaign biography of 1840 repeated this evaluation of Harrison's critics: much to the surprise of General Harrison and his partisans, the "Washington of the West" found himself consigned to "a service far inferior to that which he had a right to expect." According to this biographer, "the notorious John Armstrong, saw fit to assign to him the command of a district where he would be compelled to remain inactive, while others were appointed to those more arduous duties which he had heretofore fulfilled with so much honour to himself, and to the nation."[61] This became the excuse for Harrison's resignation: he was slighted by an envious and devious secretary of war.

Was there a way he might redeem his honor? Writing from Washington, a friend deplored "some members of Congress, who, instead of performing the sacred duty of their station, by bestowing that reward (to which the North Western Army, and its officers are so eminently entitled) . . . have been plotting to deprive you and your brave and patriotic army of the . . . praise to which is so eminently due." He too urged Harrison to seek the congressional seat from the Cincinnati area.[62]

Both the financial improprieties charge and the Senate's slight concerning a gold medal influenced Harrison to run for the House seat being vacated by John McLean. He won easily and thus was enabled to confront his accusers in the nation's capital. By then Armstrong had resigned his position as a consequence of the debacle that resulted in the capture and burning of Washington, so Harrison's case underwent a more neutral investigation by the War Department than he might have expected. Avoiding any direct confrontation with Harrison, Desha slackened his criticism, and Jennings was back in Indiana. A House committee headed by Congressman Richard M. Johnson (whose mounted riflemen had been major actors in Harrison's success at the Thames) was "unanimously of opinion that General Harrison stands above suspicion" for any pecuniary improprieties, nor did he "wantonly or improperly interfere with the rights of the contractors." Subsequently Congress resolved on gold medals for both Harrison and Shelby. Harrison's medal lauded his services at both Fort Meigs and the Thames.[63]

William Henry Harrison medal. Reprinted from Benson J. Lossing, *Pictorial Field-Book of the War of 1812* (New York: Harper Brothers, 1869).

Even though exonerated by Congress, Harrison would be dogged by repetitions of these charges. And they would not be forgotten by those who wished, for political gain, to disparage his military leadership.[64]

Harrison and the American Military Tradition

One must understand Harrison's career in the context of the broader development of the American military tradition. Educated in military imperatives in the regular army by an astute military organizer, the young Virginian learned the importance of logistics, leadership, and drill in the development of army units, whether of the regular army or of volunteers. His years as a territorial governor confirmed his impression about the importance of mounted units, of volunteer and regular infantry, and of well-built and effectively defended frontier outposts. In War of 1812 histories, too much is made of the regulars' performance at Chippawa and Lundy's Lane in 1814 and not enough of the volunteers' performances at Fort Meigs, the Thames, Baltimore, and New Orleans. The difference was not whether the troops were regulars or not but whether there was effective leadership and pre-battle training.

Unit cohesion is the key to effective combat performance. It is the product of effective and concerned leadership, from the small unit to higher headquarters. In the War of 1812, it affected regulars and volunteers. The defeats of regular units and the ineffectiveness of regular army commanders were a common phenomenon of the war. Certainly the collapse of the 17th U.S. Infantry at the battle of Frenchtown compares quite unfavorably with the conduct of the Kentucky volunteers in the same engagement. Volunteer leaders like Richard M. Johnson, Green Clay, and Isaac Shelby raised, trained, and effectively led their units in several campaigns. For every William Dudley there was a James Winchester. Harrison's troubles with Secretary Armstrong over the use of volunteers demonstrated his belief in the efficacy of the Jeffersonian tradition of the citizen soldier.

Harrison was certainly not an anti–regular army crusader, as his opposition to the proposed cuts in 1800 demonstrates. On the other hand, his reading of Roman history led him to the conclusion that republican values were best inculcated when a society required universal male military obligation. But he understood more than most that the citizen soldier needed effective officers, efficient and frequent training, government-funded equipment, and adequate financial compensation. Thus his proposals to Governor Scott in 1810 advocating militia reforms constituted a mature assessment of the possibilities, but they went far beyond the achievable in that day. In his Philadelphia toast that outraged Secretary Armstrong, the general made no distinction between the regular militia and the volunteer units he commanded in the Thames campaign. He toasted a myth that had little relevance to the militia reality of 1813.

And Harrison had a recurring tendency to make political enemies. Some of this may have come from his habit of constantly reminding his correspondents of his knowledge of sometimes obscure ancient history when using examples to bolster his rationale for his military decisions.[65] He possessed a Virginia-gentry hauteur that irritated self-made men like Jonathan Jennings and Joseph Desha. To such men Harrison represented an old-style elitism that their more populist-oriented attitudes sought to replace. Both of these men were born in the middle colonies and struggled to establish their political base against traditional gentry-level leaders like Harrison and Henry Clay.[66]

To John Armstrong, Harrison represented a western variant of the Virginia political dynasty. Harrison appeared as a rube, a country bumpkin who wore hunting shirts rather than an elegant uniform, preferred militiamen over regulars, and failed to understand the grand strategies evolving in the mind of the secretary of war. Armstrong emphasized Harrison's mistakes and shifted the mistakes of his subordinates to his discredit. He never fully recognized the difficulties Harrison faced; he never understood the nature of frontier warfare and the complexities of raising, training, and supplying armies in the wilderness. We will not ever fully know the essence of Armstrong's hostility toward Harrison. Certainly Harrison demonstrated in the 1813 campaign an ability to find capable officers, inspire westerners to join his army despite its earlier record, require effective training of his inexperienced enlisted men, and solicit and consider conflicting opinions on operational matters.[67]

This was the key to Harrison's success as a frontier warrior. He knew his men and he knew how to use them effectively. Anthony Wayne taught him the importance of fortifications at critical transportation nodes, such as at the portage between the Maumee and Wabash Valleys that became Fort Wayne. So he constructed an outpost at the Maumee Rapids, which both resisted British-Indian attacks and pointed toward an advance on the Detroit River Valley. From Wayne he also learned the usefulness of military training before engaging in combat and of combining the best ingredients of regular and volunteer forces. The victorious commander at Fallen Timbers also trained his young aide to be prudent and cautious as he marched toward a foe. To this list Harrison added the importance of using native allies, of maintaining a secure logistical lifeline, of selecting, using, and promoting proven subordinates, of merging the combat arms of infantry, cavalry, and artillery in effective proportions, of cooperating with naval forces and making use of their expertise to add flexibility to his operational capabilities, and of applying mass, firepower and shock action to achieve victory. It may have been that his theater allowed mounted soldiers more opportunity than did others, but Harrison's effective employment of R. M. Johnson's troopers was conspicuously absent in other districts, with the exception of Brig. Gen. John Coffee under Andrew Jackson.

But he was not the perfect commander. His calling forth unwarranted numbers of volunteers in the fall of 1812 contributed significantly to excessive logistical requirements and the demise of his campaign against Detroit that fall. He could not control the impulsive and hazardous actions of his subordinates James Winchester and William Dudley that led to defeat and significant losses. He also seems to have been excessively ambitious and to have had an inflated opinion of his leadership capabilities.

The consequences of the animosity of Secretary of War John Armstrong leave the student of Harrison's career without evidence of his capabilities as a Ninth District commander. Would his reputation have brought more volunteers into the field that might have changed the outcome of the 1814 Niagara campaign? Could he have done better than Jacob Brown at Chippawa or Lundy's Lane? Would he have directed the sortie from Fort Erie in the manner that resulted in the death of his beloved subordinate Eleazer Wood, then a lieutenant colonel? Would he have been able to cooperate with Commodore Isaac Chauncey and the U.S. Navy on Lake Ontario as he had with Oliver Hazard Perry? Nor do we know what might have happened in the Eighth Military District if he had not allowed his ego and sense of honor to compel his resignation. Would the 1814 failures on Mackinac Island and at Prairie du Chien have occurred had Harrison been commanding the district?

No other individual exemplified the triumph of American arms in that vast region between the Ohio Valley and the Great Lakes more than William Henry Harrison. He alone witnessed the demise of the greatest Native American coalition in U.S. history during the Fallen Timbers campaign; he alone watched the tedious but successful negotiations that brought about the Treaty of Greenville; he alone used the examples learned in Ohio to conduct consultations with native leaders that expanded the areas for Euroamerican settlement in what became Indiana and Illinois; he alone frustrated the ambitions of Tenskwatawa and Tecumseh to stop pioneer settlement of the Midwest; and he alone organized and commanded the fateful campaign of 1813 that terminated British assistance to Native Americans living in the central United States and ended significant native resistance in the Old Northwest.

To this day, many Americans recall the 1840 campaign slogan of "Tippecanoe and Tyler too," which Whig partisans—faithfully avoiding serious issues—meant to evoke the controversial engagement on a tributary of the Wabash River. Undoubtedly it is the poetic rhythm of the Indian name for the stream that makes it memorable; who would campaign under a slogan of "Thames and Tyler too"? Generally, Harrison and his western theater are given short shrift in American military annals. War of 1812 studies focus mostly on the combat on the Niagara frontier and eastward, where the regular army earned laurels and fostered a new generation of leaders. In reality, Harrison was a far better soldier than he is generally credited with being, and he campaigned in an environment that challenged his leadership skills to the utmost. It was the War of 1812 that allowed him to develop and exhibit his military talents. Far more than the battle for which he is best remembered, his struggles in defending Ohio and Indiana from British-Indian invasion, in cooperating with the U.S. naval forces on Lake Erie, in coordinating volunteer and regular army units in a campaign to retake Detroit and invade southwestern Upper Canada against combined British and native opposition, and in concluding an armistice with hostile tribes that terminated a long war between natives and Americans in the Old Northwest—all these accomplishments collectively constitute achievements worthy of greater remembrance than those in the Wabash Valley.

In at least two ways, Harrison's career represents both the future and the past in the American military tradition. He correctly understood that the republic depended on its citizens for manpower needs in serious military encounters. From the War of 1812 through the Vietnam War, the nation required the services of volunteers and conscripts to augment a relatively small regular military. Yet his vision of universal military training in the manner of the Roman Republic exceeded the political will and military requirements of the new nation. There are hints that he saw promise in the emerging volunteer military units (precursors to the National Guard of the late nineteenth century) and understood that they needed federal support in doctrine, organization, training, weaponry, equipment, and salary. Thus he epitomized the Jeffersonian idealization of the citizen soldier while comprehending the need for maintaining reserve forces capable of mobilization and employment on short notice.

If Harrison's ideas constituted a step toward the future in preparing the nation for wartime mobilization, his career represents a past in which leadership at the highest levels of army command came from the ranks of citizen soldiers. The War of 1812 is the last American war in which the senior generals would be prominent citizens rather than professional soldiers. Harrison, Andrew Jackson, James Winchester, Jacob Brown, Lewis Cass, and many other commanders in this conflict had limited military experience prior to the declaration of war and received high rank because of their political status, not their military careers. Nothing so typifies the U.S. Army after this war than the dominance of professional soldiers at senior command levels. Some, like Winfield Scott, Alexander Macomb, and Edmund P. Gaines, emerged from midlevel regular army careers to senior rank; others, like Jacob J. Brown and John E. Wool, rose from civilian obscurity to high rank through meritorious conduct on the battlefield. These officers dominated army leadership for the next thirty years. At the same time, the U.S. Military Academy produced additions to the officer corps trained in military engineering, history, and tactics that proved highly useful in the postwar army. Collectively such men created a professional military subculture that exalted the regular soldier and officer and disdained the amateur for his lack of training, discipline, and leadership. No longer would the United States see men like George Washington, Nathanael Greene, Andrew Jackson, and William Henry Harrison elevated from civilian status to senior command.[68] Harrison was one of the last of a breed that died with the War of 1812.

But Harrison was not one who disdained the professional soldier. As his critique of the Republicans' efforts to reduce the regular army while he was the Northwest Territory's delegate to Congress demonstrated, he understood the necessity of a professional and immediately ready ground force. His comments to Governor Charles Scott on the eve of the War of 1812 acknowledged the necessity of a trained corps of professional soldiers in excess of that currently on the government's roles. The performance of Eleazer Wood as his engineer officer certainly confirmed and reinforced his opinions about the requirement for well-trained regular army leadership in critical positions. The fear that a standing army might become the source of an American Caesar or Napoleon Bonaparte did not dominate his ideology as it did that of so many of his political associates.

***

In many ways, William Henry Harrison reconciled himself to the consequences of resignation. As he told Oliver Hazard Perry, the "domestic happiness" with which he found himself surrounded had in "great Measure tranquillised the feelings produced by public ingratitude & private Malice."[69] Yet there arose a sense of remorse over the termination of his military career. After the British burned Washington, he wrote Governor Shelby inquiring about "the propriety of an auxiliary force marching from the Western Country to the assistance" of such threatened cities as Baltimore, Philadelphia, and New York. He told Andrew Jackson, "How gladly would I have joined you & Served under your Command even at the Head of a Regiment." A military melancholy overcame him. By resigning, he had burned his army bridges and irrevocably condemned himself to what he called "a life of ease & retirement when my whole Soul was devoted to the profession which I had been Compelled to abandon."[70] The ghosts of things done and undone continued to haunt him.

As "Old Tip" ended his military career, a political one loomed before him. But he, like so many soldiers before and after him, rested his political reputation on his military success, and in the end it elevated him to the chief magistracy of the young American republic. More than any one man, William Henry Harrison embodied the United States' efforts to wrest control of the territory between the Ohio River and the Great Lakes from both the Indians and the British. From the time Ensign Harrison reported for duty in Cincinnati to the day he resigned his major general commission, no one was more closely involved in the conquest of the Midwest than he.

This page intentionally left blank

Notes

CHAPTER ONE: **Apprenticeship in Frontier Warfare**

1. WHH to Eustis, 28 Oct., 18 Nov. 1811, in Douglas E. Clanin et al., eds., *The Papers of William Henry Harrison, 1800–1815*, 10 microfilm reels (Indianapolis: Indiana Historical Society, 1993–99), 5:19–20, 47–51 (hereafter, *WHH Papers*); Nellie Armstrong Robertson and Dorothy Riker, eds., *The John Tipton Papers*, 3 vols. (Indianapolis: Indiana Historical Society, 1942), 2:829.

2. "Biographical Memoirs of Major Gen. William Henry Harrison," *Port Folio*, 3rd ser., 5 (Apr. 1815): 305–25, quotations on 305.

3. The standard biographies are Dorothy Burne Goebel, *William Henry Harrison: A Political Biography*, Indiana Historical Collections, vol. 14 (Indianapolis: Indiana Library and Historical Department, 1926); Freeman Cleaves, *Old Tippecanoe: William Henry Harrison and His Times* (New York: Charles Scribner's Sons, 1939); and James A. Green, *William Henry Harrison: His Life and Times* (Richmond: Garret and Massie, 1941). None of these pay much attention to Harrison's early life. Far better in this regard are Hendrik Booraem V, "William Henry Harrison Comes to Cincinnati," *Queen City Heritage* 45 (fall 1987): 3–22; and Booraem, *A Child of the Revolution: William Henry Harrison and His World, 1773–1798* (Kent, OH: Kent State University Press, 2012); Reginald Horsman, "William Henry Harrison: Virginia Gentleman in the Old Northwest," *Indiana Magazine of History* 96 (June 2000): 125–49; Robert G. Gunderson, "A Search for Old Tip Himself," *Register of the Kentucky Historical Society* 86 (autumn 1968): 330–51; Gunderson, "William Henry Harrison: Apprentice in Arms," *Northwest Ohio Quarterly* 65 (winter 1993): 3–29; and Adam Jortner, *The Gods of Prophetstown: The Battle of Tippecanoe and the Holy War for the American Frontier* (New York: Oxford University Press, 2012), 38–49, 62–67.

4. William Gribbin, "Rollin's Histories and American Republicanism," *William and Mary Quarterly* 29 (1972): 611–22; Henry Steele Commager, "The American Enlightenment and the Ancient World: A Study in Paradox," *Proceedings of the Massachusetts Historical Society* 83 (1972): 3–7. For a review of the importance of Julius Caesar in Harrison's life, see Allan R. Millett, "Caesar and the Conquest of the Northwest Territory: The Wayne Campaign, 1792–95," *Timeline* 14 (May–June 1997): 2–21; and Millett, "Caesar and the Conquest of the Northwest Territory: The Harrison Campaign, 1811," *Timeline* 14 (July–Aug. 1997): 2–19.

5. The role of "honor" in early American society is explored in Bertram Wyatt-Brown, *Southern Honor: Ethics and Behavior in the Old South* (New York: Oxford University Press, 1982); Joanne B. Freeman, *Affairs of Honor: National Politics in the New Republic* (New

Haven, CT: Yale University Press, 2001); and Rodney P. Carlisle, "The American Maritime Code Duello," *Northern Mariner* 21 (Apr. 2011): 159–69.

6. For WHH's version of his background, see "Biographical Memoirs of Harrison"; WHH to Erastus Brooks, 20 July 1839, Harrison MSS, New York Historical Society, New York, NY. See also Booraem's "William Henry Harrison Comes to Cincinnati" and *Child of the Revolution.* On WHH's father, see Howard W. Smith, *Benjamin Harrison and the American Revolution* (Williamsburg: Virginia Independence Bicentennial Commission 1978). For an introduction to the largest planters of Virginia, see Jackson T. Main, "The One Hundred," *William and Mary Quarterly* 11 (1964): 354–84; and Emory G. Evans, *A "Topping People": The Rise and Decline of Virginia's Old Political Elite, 1680–1790* (Charlottesville: University Press of Virginia, 2009).

7. Leroy V. Eid, "'The Slaughter Was Reciprocal': Josiah Harmar's Two Defeats, 1790," *Northwest Ohio Quarterly* 65 (spring 1993): 51–67; Michael S. Warner, "General Josiah Harmar's Campaign Reconsidered: How the Americans Lost the Battle of Kekionga," *Indiana Magazine of History* 83 (Mar. 1987): 43–64; Wilkinson quoted in Edward M. Coffman, *The Old Army: A Portrait of the American Army in Peacetime, 1784–1898* (New York: Oxford University Press, 1986), 7.

8. This concept comes from Frank J. Sulloway's controversial *Born to Rebel: Birth Order, Family Dynamics, and Creative Lives* (New York: Pantheon Books, 1996), 430–39. Kevin Leman, in *Birth Order Book: The Why You Are the Way You Are,* 2nd ed. (Grand Rapids, MI: Revell, 2009), claims that last-borns are charming and manipulative persons, a description that certainly fits Harrison's personality.

9. Joyce Oldham Appleby, *Inheriting the Revolution: The First Generation of Americans* (Cambridge, MA: Belknap Press of Harvard University Press, 2000).

10. Lawrence H. Keeley, *War before Civilization* (New York: Oxford University Press, 1996), 39.

11. Wayne E. Lee, "Peace Chiefs and Blood Revenge: Patterns of Restraint in Native American Warfare, 1500–1800," *Journal of Military History* 71 (July 2007): 713–15. See also Anthony F. C. Wallace, *The Death and Rebirth of the Seneca* (New York: Vintage Books, 1972), 44–48; and Daniel K. Richter, *The Ordeal of the Longhouse: The Peoples of the Iroquois League in the Era of European Colonization* (Chapel Hill: University of North Carolina Press, 1992), 33–37.

12. Lee, "Peace Chiefs," 703.

13. Richter, *Ordeal of the Longhouse,* 35; Keeley, *War before Civilization,* 64, 109; Lee, "Peace Chiefs," 707; Leroy V. Eid, "'National War' among Indians of Northeastern North America," *Canadian Review of American Studies* 16 (1985): 125–54.

14. Pierre Pouchot, *Memoirs on the Late War in North America between France and England* (Youngstown, NY: Old Fort Niagara Association, 1994), 461.

15. Keeley, *War before Civilization,* 12–13. 64.

16. Pouchot, *Memoirs,* 459–60.

17. Dean L. Anderson, "The Flow of European Trade Goods into the Western Great Lakes Region, 1715–1760," in Jennifer S. H. Brown, W. J. Eccles, and Donald P. Heldman, eds., *The Fur Trade Revisited: Selected Papers of the Sixth North American Fur Trade Conference, Mackinac Island, Michigan, 1991* (East Lansing: Michigan State University Press, 1994), 109; Pouchot, *Memoirs,* 460.

18. Gregory Evans Dowd, *A Spirited Resistance: The North American Indian Struggle for Unity, 1745–1815* (Baltimore: Johns Hopkins University Press, 1992), 181; John Sugden, *Tecumseh: A Life* (New York: Henry Holt, 1997), 99–100, 129–31.

19. John Mack Faragher, *Daniel Boone: The Life and Legend of an American Pioneer* (New York: Henry Holt, 1992), 218.

20. Paul David Nelson, "General Charles Scott, the Kentucky Mounted Volunteers, and the Northwest Indian Wars, 1784–94," *Journal of the Early Republic* 6 (1986): 219–51.

21. Guy Chet, *Conquering the American Wilderness: The Triumph of European Warfare in the Colonial Northeast* (Amherst: University of Massachusetts Press, 2003), 143–45.

22. Brian Leigh Dunnigan, "Fortress Detroit, 1701–1826," in David Curtis Skaggs and Larry L. Nelson, eds., *The Sixty Years' War for the Great Lakes, 1754–1824* (East Lansing: Michigan State University Press, 2001), 167–85.

23. Matthew C. Ward, *Breaking the Backcountry: The Seven Years' War in Virginia and Pennsylvania, 1754–1765* (Pittsburg, PA: University of Pittsburg Press, 2004), 45–57, 60–70; Gregory Evans Dowd, *War under Heaven: Pontiac, the Indian Nations, and the British Empire* (Baltimore: Johns Hopkins University Press, 2002), 114–47.

24. Susan Sleeper-Smith, *Indian Women and French Men: Rethinking Cultural Encounter in the Western Great Lakes* (Amherst: University of Massachusetts Press, 2001); Francis Jennings, *Empire of Fortune: Crowns, Colonies, and Tribes in the Sever Years War in America* (New York: W. W. Norton, 1988), 261n21.

25. John Grenier, *The First Way of War: American War Making on the Frontier* (New York: Cambridge University Press, 2005), esp. 170–203.

26. Keeley, *War before Civilization*, 74. See also Grenier, *First Way of War*.

27. Ward, *Breaking the Backcountry*, 95–100.

28. John Shy, *Toward Lexington: The Role of the British Army in the Coming of the American Revolution* (Princeton, NJ: Princeton University Press, 1965), 192–204, 223–31, 260–66, 271–74, 402–4, and maps on 238, 328, 419.

29. Ward, *Breaking the Backcountry*, 77–90, 236–40.

30. Fred Anderson, *Crucible of War: The Seven Years' War and the Fate of Empire in British North America, 1754–1766* (New York: Alfred Knopf, 2000), 267–79; Jane T. Merritt, *At the Crossroads: Indians and Empires on a Mid-Atlantic Frontier, 1700–1763* (Chapel Hill: University of North Carolina Press, 2003), 231.

31. Jennings, *Empire of Fortune*, 467.

32. David Hackett Fischer, *Albion's Seed: Four British Folkways in America* (New York: Oxford University Press, 1989), 765–66.

33. Merritt, *At the Crossroads*, 282–88; Ward, *Breaking the Backcountry*, 236–40, 260; Eric Hinderaker, *Elusive Empires: Constructing Colonialism in the Ohio Valley, 1673–1800* (New York: Cambridge University Press, 1997), 175.

34. Jennings, *Empire of Fortune*, 417. For the Shawnee response, see Colin G. Calloway, *The Shawnees and the War for America* (New York: Viking, 2007).

35. For an introduction to the American Revolution in the West, see Jack M. Sosin, *The Revolutionary Frontier, 1763–1783* (New York: Holt, Rinehart and Winston, 1967), 82–92, 104–23, 133–41.

36. Dowd, *Spirited Resistance*, 68–89; Leonard Sadosky, "Rethinking the Gnadenhutten Massacre: The Contest for Power in the Public World of the Revolutionary Frontier,"

in Skaggs and Nelson, *Sixty Years' War*, 187–213, quotation on 201; Rob Harper, "Looking the Other Way: The Gnadenhutten Massacre and the Contextual Interpretation of Violence," *William and Mary Quarterly* 64 (July 2007): 621–44, quotation on 643.

37. "General Scott to Secretary of War Knox: Destruction of Ouiatanon," 28 June 1791, in *American State Papers, Military Affairs*, 3 vols. (Washington: Gales and Seaton, 1832), 1:131–32.

38. Stephen Aron, *How the West Was Lost: The Transformation of Kentucky from Daniel Boone to Henry Clay* (Baltimore: Johns Hopkins University Press, 1996), 127; Lee Soltow, "Horse Owners in Kentucky in 1800," *Register of the Kentucky Historical Society* 79 (summer 1981): 203–10.

39. Procter to Prevost, 4 July 1813, in *Michigan Pioneer and Historical Society Collections*, 40 vols. (Lansing, MI: Wynkoop Hallenbeck Crawford, 1877–1929), 15:331.

40. Nelson Vance Russell, "Transportation and Naval Defense, in the Old Northwest during the British Régime, 1760–96," *University of Michigan Historical Essays* 9 (1937): 113–39; Brereton Greenhous, "A Note on Western Logistics in the War of 1812," *Military Affairs* 34 (Apr. 1970): 41–44; Barry Gough, *Fighting Sail on Lake Huron and Georgian Bay: The War of 1812 and Its Aftermath* (Annapolis, MD: Naval Institute Press, 2002), 6–19, 69–71; C. P. Stacey, "Naval Power on the Lakes, 1812–1814," in Philip P. Mason, ed., *After Tippecanoe: Some Aspects of the War of 1812* (East Lansing: Michigan State University Press, 1963), 49–59.

41. Philip Lord Jr., "The Mohawk/Oneida Corridor: The Geography of Inland Navigation across New York," in Skaggs and Nelson, *Sixty Years' War*, 275–90.

42. See, for instance, Aron, *How the West Was Lost*; Elizabeth A. Perkins, *Border Life: Experience and Memory in the Revolutionary Ohio Valley* (Chapel Hill: University of North Carolina Press, 1998); J. Winston Coleman, *The British Invasion of Kentucky* (Lexington: University Press of Kentucky, 1951); Faragher, *Daniel Boone*; John Sugden, *Blue Jacket: Warrior of the Shawnees* (Lincoln: University of Nebraska Press, 2000); and Sugden, *Tecumseh*.

43. Robert B. McAfee, *History of the Late War in the Western Country* (Bowling Green, OH: Historical Publications Co., 1919 [1816]), 11–12.

44. Dave R. Palmer, *1794: America, Its Army, and the Birth of the Nation* (Novato, CA: Presidio, 1994), 201; William O. Odom, "Destined for Defeat: An Analysis of the St. Clair Expedition of 1791," *Northwest Ohio Quarterly* 65 (spring 1993): 68–93; James T. Currie, "The First Congressional Investigation: St. Clair's Military Disaster of 1791," *Parameters* 20 (Dec. 1990): 95–102. Somewhat sympathetic to St. Clair are Patrick J. Furlong, "The Investigation of General Arthur St. Clair, 1792–93," *Capitol Studies* 5 (fall 1977): 65–86; and Alan D. Gaff, *Bayonets in the Wilderness: Anthony Wayne's Legion in the Old Northwest* (Norman: University of Oklahoma Press, 2004), 3–8. Debate continues over whether Miami chief Little Turtle or Shawnee chief Blue Jacket was the architect of this victory. For the other side, see Sugden, *Blue Jacket*, 113–27.

45. WHH to E. Brooks, 20 July 1839, Harrison MSS; Booraem, *Child of the Revolution*, 195n8.

46. "Winthrop Sargent's Diary While with General St. Clair's Expedition against the Indians," *Ohio Archeological and Historical Quarterly* 33 (July 1924): 272; Gaff, *Bayonets*, 11–12. On Wilkinson's career, see Thomas R. Hay and M. R. Werner, *The Admirable Trum-*

peter: *A Biography of General James Wilkinson* (Garden City, NY: Doubleday, 1941); James R. Jacobs, *Tarnished Warrior: Major-General James Wilkinson* (New York: Macmillan, 1938); and Andro Linklater, *An Artist in Treason: The Extraordinary Double Life of General James Wilkinson* (New York: Walker and Co., 2010).

47. Cleaves, *Old Tippecanoe*, 11–12.

48. Alan Borer, "William Henry Harrison and the Rhetoric of History," *Northwest Ohio Quarterly* 68 (summer/autumn 1996): 116–32; Robert Silverberg, *Mound Builders of Ancient America: The Archaeology of a Myth* (Greenwich, CT: New York Graphic Society, 1968), 76.

49. B. H. Pershing, "Winthrop Sargent," *Ohio Archeological and Historical Quarterly* 35 (Oct. 1926): 589–98; "Biographical Memoirs of Harrison."

50. Richard H. Kohn, *Eagle and Sword: The Beginnings of the Military Establishment in America* (New York: Free Press, 1975), 116–24.

51. For an introduction to the problems of recovery, see George J. Andreopoulos and Harold E. Selesky, *The Aftermath of Defeat: Societies, Armed Forces, and the Challenge of Recovery* (New Haven, CT: Yale University Press, 1994), 2–9.

52. Garrison Orders, 11 May 1792, Sargent Papers, Massachusetts Historical Society, Boston, MA; Gaff, *Bayonets*, 14–15; Booraem, *Child of the Revolution*, 94–96.

53. Wayne to WHH, 3 July 1792, Wayne Papers, Pennsylvania Historical Society, Philadelphia, PA.

54. Wayne to Knox, 9 May 1793, Wayne Papers. European organizational developments of the late eighteenth century increased the emphasis on light infantry and marksmanship. See, for instance, Peter Paret, "Colonial Experience and European Military Reform at the End of the Eighteenth Century," *Bulletin of the Institute of Historical Research* 37 (1964): 47–59; and J. F. C. Fuller, "The Revival and Training of Light Infantry in the British Army, 1757–1806," *Journal of the Royal United Service Institute* 57 (1913): 1187–214.

55. WHH to Howell, 7 Apr. 1838, in *Cincinnati Daily Gazette*, 19 May 1838; Cleaves, *Old Tippecanoe*, 15; Coffman, *Old Army*, 23, 32.

56. WHH to Tipton, 6 Dec. 1833, in Logan Esarey, ed., *Messages and Letters of William Henry Harrison*, 2 vols. (Indianapolis: Indiana Historical Society, 1922), 2:745–46.

57. For a review of the American-Indian negotiations of the era, see Lisa Brooks, "Two Paths to Peace: Competing Visions of Native Space in the Old Northwest," and Frazer Dorian McGlinchey, "'A Superior Civilization': Appropriation, Negotiation, and Interaction in the Northwest Territory, 1787–1795," both in Daniel P. Barr, ed., *The Boundaries between Us: Natives and Newcomers along the Frontiers of the Old Northwest Territory, 1750–1850* (Kent, OH: Kent State University Press, 2006), 87–117, 118–42.

58. Wayne to Wilkinson, 7 Feb. 1794, Wayne Papers; Kohn, *Eagle and Sword*, 198; Richard H. Kohn, "General Wilkinson's Vendetta with General Wayne: Politics and Command in the American Army, 1791–1796," *Filson Club History Quarterly* 45 (Oct. 1971): 361–72. For more on the Wayne-Wilkinson rivalry, see Gaff, *Bayonets*, 180–81, 256, 272.

59. Kohn, *Eagle and Sword*, 153–55.

60. Paul David Nelson, *Anthony Wayne: Soldier of the Early Republic* (Bloomington: Indiana University Press, 1985), 245–47.

61. William Henry Harrison, *A Discourse on the Aborigines of the Ohio Valley* (Chicago: Fergus, 1883), 38.

62. C. M. Burton, ed., "General Wayne's Orderly Book," in *Michigan Pioneer*, 34:544; Paul A Hutton, "William Wells: Frontier Scout and Indian Agent," *Indiana Magazine of History* 74 (1978): 183–222; William Heath, "William Wells: From Miami Warrior to American Spy," *Northwest Ohio History* 78 (spring 2011): 102–13; Donald H. Gaff, "Three Men from Three Rivers," in Barr, *Boundaries between Us*, 143–60.

63. Wayne to J. Edwards, 22 Oct. 1793, to Knox, 23 Oct. 1793, to Elliott and Williams, 16 Oct., 23 Oct., 12 Nov., 3 Dec. 1793, and 1 Jan., 17 Apr., 22 Apr., 23 Apr., 1 May, 6 May 1794, Wayne Papers. See also Nelson, *Anthony Wayne*, 246–47. For a brief introduction to logistical issues in the early military, see James A. Huston, *The Sinews of War: Army Logistics 1775–1953*, Army Historical Series (Washington, DC: Office of the Chief of Military History, 1966), 86–96.

64. See, for instance, Carl A. Brettschneider, "Some of the Personalities and Problems of Supply Affecting the Indian Campaign of 1792–1794," *Bulletin of the Historical and Philosophical Society of Ohio* 9 (Oct. 1951): 299–318.

65. WHH to M. C. Perry, 16 Apr. 1821, Rodgers Papers, Library of Congress, Washington, DC.

66. Burton, "Wayne's Orderly Book," 529, 535.

67. Nelson, *Anthony Wayne*, 245.

68. Dwight L. Smith, "A North American Neutral Indian Zone: Persistence of a British Idea," *Northwest Ohio Quarterly* 61 (spring–autumn 1989): 46–63; Reginald Horsman, "The British Indian Department and the Resistance to General Anthony Wayne, 1793–1795," *Mississippi Valley Historical Review* 49 (Sept. 1962): 269–90; Paul R. Reynolds, *Guy Carleton: A Biography* (Toronto: Gage Publishing, 1980); Sugden, *Blue Jacket*, 159.

69. Gaff, *Bayonets*, 239–53; Richard White, *The Middle Ground: Indians, Empires, and Republics in the Great Lakes Region, 1650–1815* (New York; Cambridge University Press, 1991), 467; Larry L. Nelson, "'Never Have They Done So Little': The Battle of Fort Recovery and the Collapse of the Miami Confederacy," *Northwest Ohio Quarterly* 64 (Spring 1992): 43–55.

70. Helen Hornbeck Tanner, "The Glaize in 1792: A Composite Indian Community," *Ethnohistory* 25 (winter 1978): 15–39; Randall L. Buchman, *The Confluence: "The Site of Fort Defiance"* (Defiance, OH: Defiance College Press, 1994); Gaff, *Bayonets*, 265–89; C. M. Burton, "Anthony Wayne and the Battle of Fallen Timbers," in *Michigan Pioneer*, 31:472–89.

71. Accounts of the battle of Fallen Timbers are numerous. Among the more recent secondary accounts are Palmer, *1794*, 253–62; Gaff, *Bayonets*, 265–313, Schaumburgh quoted on 307; and Jortner, *Gods*, 67–71. The danger of an aide's conspicuous presence when galloping across the battlefield relaying information may be seen in the death of General Wilkinson's aide, Lt. Campbell Smith, during the battle. Jortner, *Gods*, 311. Harrison's own version of the battle is in WHH to C. Scott, 17 Apr. 1801, *WHH Papers*, 3:816–18. For the archaeology of the battlefield, see G. Michael Pratt, "The Archaeology of the Fallen Timbers Battlefield: A Report of the 1995 Field Survey" (1995), www2.heidelbergs .edu/FallenTimbrs/FTFinalMaster.html.

72. WHH to Tipton, 6 Dec. 1813, in Esarey, *Messages*, 2:746–47.

73. The treaty is reprinted in Clarence Edwin Carter, ed., *The Territorial Papers of the*

United States, 28 vols. (Washington, DC: Government Printing Office, 1934–75), 2:525–35. See also Dwight L. Smith, "Wayne and the Treaty of Greene Ville," *Ohio State Archaeological and Historical Quarterly* 16 (Jan. 1954): 1–7; and Andrew R. L Cayton, "'Noble Actors' upon 'the Theatre of Honor': Power and Civility in the Treaty of Greenville," in Andrew R. L. Cayton and Fredrika J. Teute, eds., *Contact Points: American Frontiers from the Mohawk Valley to the Mississippi, 1750–1830* (Chapel Hill: University of North Carolina Press, 1998), 235–69. Robert M. Owens, *Mr. Jefferson's Hammer: William Henry Harrison and the Origins of American Indian Policy* (Norman: University of Oklahoma Press, 2007), 28–36, outlines the Greenville treaty negotiations and consequences; the rest of Owens's book provides an excellent account of Harrison's subsequent negotiations with the Native Americans.

74. See, for instance, Harrison's Speech at an Indian Council Held at Vincennes, 12 Sept., Negotiations at an Indian Council, 12–17 Sept., Notes of Speeches at an Indian Council, 15 Sept. 1802, *WHH Papers*, 1:373–96. See also Owens, *Jefferson's Hammer*, 35.

CHAPTER TWO: **To Tippecanoe**

1. The law is reprinted in Peter S. Onuf, *Statehood and Union: A History of the Northwest Ordinance* (Bloomington: Indiana University Press, 1987), 60–64, quotation on 60.

2. On Harrison's marriage, see Andrew R. L. Cayton, *Frontier Indiana* (Bloomington: Indiana University Press, 1996), 172–78, 181–82.

3. Sargent to T. Pickering, 21 May 1798, in Dunbar Rowland, ed., *Mississippi Territorial Archives, 1798–1804*, 2 vols. (Nashville, TN: Brandon Printing, 1905), 1:16; WHH to Harper, 26 May 1798, in Dorothy Burne Goebel, *William Henry Harrison: A Political Biography*, Indiana Historical Collections, vol. 14 (Indianapolis: Indiana Library and Historical Department, 1926), 38–40. On the duties of the secretary, see St. Clair to Sargent, 1 Dec. 1796, in William H. Smith, ed., *The St. Clair Papers*, 2 vols. (Cincinnati, OH: R. Clarke, 1882), 2:413–17. For an introduction to territorial politics, see R. Douglas Hurt, *The Ohio Frontier: Crucible of the Old Northwest, 1720–1839* (Bloomington: Indiana University Press, 1996); Andrew R. L. Cayton, *The Frontier Republic: Ideology and Politics in the Ohio Country, 1780–1825* (Kent, OH: Kent State University Press, 1986); and Donald J. Ratcliffe, *Party Spirit in a Frontier Republic: Democratic Politics in Ohio, 1793–1821* (Columbus: Ohio State University Press, 1998). On the Northwest Ordinance and its importance, see Onuf, *Statehood and Union*.

4. WHH to Brooks, 20 July 1839, Harrison Papers, New York Public Library, New York, NY.

5. *American State Papers, Military Affairs*, 3 vols. (Washington, DC: Gales and Seaton, 1832), 6th Cong., 1st Sess., cols. 376, 426, 509–10, 523, 529ff., 660ff. For introductions on land policy, see Malcolm J. Rohrbough, *The Land Office Business: The Settlement and Administration of American Public Lands, 1789–1837* (New York: Oxford University Press, 968); and Paul W. Gates, *History of Public Land Law Development* (Washington, DC: U.S. Government Printing Office, 1968). On the impact of these laws on Ohio, see Hurt, *Ohio Frontier*; Cayton, *Frontier Republic*; and Ratcliffe, *Party Spirit*. WHH's enthusiasm for what he had accomplished in land policy is best reflected in his Circular Letter, 14 May 1800, in Douglas E. Clanin et al., eds., *The Papers of William Henry Harrison, 1800–1815*, 10 micro-

254 Notes to Pages 46–49

film reels (Indianapolis: Indiana Historical Society, 1993–1999), 1:74–83(hereafter, *WHH Papers*). On the ongoing Vincennes land titles issue, see Dearborn to WHH, 23 Jan., 17 June, WHH to Dearborn, 26 Feb. 1802, *WHH Papers*, 1:247, 270–73, 320–22.

6. *Annals of Congress [The Debates and Proceedings in the Congress of the United States]*, 42 vols. (Washington, DC: Gales and Seaton, 1834–56), 6th Cong., 1st Sess., cols. 286, 316.

7. [Oliver Wolcott] to WHH, 1 Feb., WHH Circular Letter, 14 May 1800, *WHH Papers*, 1:19, 76; *Annals of Congress*, 6th Cong., 1st Sess., col. 513.

8. *Annals of Congress*, 6th Cong., 1st Sess., col. 705, and 8th Cong., 2nd Sess., cols. 69, 1002. The case of Robert Elliott bothered Harrison for years, and he subsequently would not directly attack Elliott's son, Capt. Jesse Duncan Elliott, USN, in Captain Elliott's disputes with Oliver Hazard Perry in the aftermath of the battle of Lake Erie. WHH to M. C. Perry, 16 Apr. 1821, Rodgers Papers, Library of Congress, Washington, DC.

9. Nomination of WHH to Be Governor of Indiana Territory, 13 May 1800, *WHH Papers*, 1:70, 71; *Public Statutes at Large of the United States*, 8 vols. (Boston: Little, Brown, 1845–46), 1: chap. 41, pp. 58–59.

10. Susan Symmes to Maria (Symmes) Short, 21 June 1802, Harrison Papers, 1:53, Library of Congress, Washington, DC; WHH to J. Dayton, 30 Nov. 1781, *WHH Papers*, 1:215. See also Freeman Cleaves, *Old Tippecanoe: William Henry Harrison and His Time* (New York: Charles Scribner's Sons, 1939), 31–32.

11. WHH to Jefferson, [Oct. 1801], *WHH Papers*, 1:193.

12. John Badollet's often–embittered critique of the Harrison administration is published in Gayle Thornbrough, ed., *The Correspondence of John Badollet and Albert Gallatin, 1804–1836*, Indiana Historical Society Publications, vol. 22 (Indianapolis: Indiana Historical Society, 1963). Badollet was a federal official operating under the jurisdiction of Secretary of the Treasury Gallatin, and his criticism of Harrison reached the highest levels of the administrations of Jefferson and Madison.

13. Andrew R. L. Cayton, *Frontier Indiana* (Bloomington: Indiana University Press, 1996), 226–60. See also John Craig Hammond, *Slavery, Freedom, and Expansion in the Early American West* (Charlottesville: University of Virginia Press, 2007), 98–123.

14. Robert M. Owens, *Mr. Jefferson's Hammer: William Henry Harrison and the Origins of American Indian Policy* (Norman: University of Oklahoma Press, 2007), 145. See also Goebel, *William Henry Harrison*, 76–87; Cleaves, *Old Tippecanoe*, 45–48; and George W. Geib, "Jefferson, Harrison, and the West: An Essay on Territorial Slavery," in Darrel E. Bingham, ed., *The Indiana Territory, 1800–2000: A Bicentennial Perspective* (Indianapolis: Indiana Historical Society, 2001), 99–124.

15. Appointment of John Small et al., 6 Feb. 1801, *WHH Papers*, 1:123. See also appointment documents 12 Sept. 1801, 20 July, 19 Aug., 24 Sept. 1802, *WHH Papers*, 1:179, 180, 337, 363, 364, 408.

16. General Orders, 10 May, Militia Appointments, 28 July 1803, *WHH Papers*, 1:556, 614.

17. WHH address to General Assembly, 1805, in Gayle Thornbrough and Dorothy Riker, eds., *Readings in Indiana History*, Indiana Historical Collections, vol. 36 (Indianapolis: Indiana Historical Bureau, 1956), 105.

18. Francis S. Philbrick, ed., *Laws of Indiana Territory, 1801–1809*, Collections of the Illinois State Historical Library, vol. 21 (Springfield: Illinois State Historical Library, 1930),

chap. 42, pp. 399–425, quotations on 399. Philbrick's long introduction (ix–ccxxv) provides an excellent overview to the government of the territory but has virtually nothing dealing with military affairs.

19. On the background of the early militia, see such secondary works as John K. Mahon, *The American Militia: Decade of Decision, 1789–1800* (Gainesville: University of Florida Press, 1960); Richard H. Kohn, *Eagle and Sword: The Beginnings of the Military Establishment in America* (New York: Free Press, 1975); Lawrence D. Cress, *Citizens in Arms: The Army and Militia in American Society to the War of 1812* (Chapel Hill: University of North Carolina Press, 1981); and C. Edward Skeen, *Citizen Soldiers in the War of 1812* (Lexington: University of Kentucky Press, 1999).

20. Gibson (for WHH) to Hargrove, 4 Oct., 4 Nov. 1807, *WHH Papers*, 3:1, 41–43.

21. Kennedy to WHH, 24 Feb. 1808, *WHH Papers*, 3:115–17.

22. *Vincennes Western Sun*, 9 July 1808; General Orders, 8 Sept. 1808, *WHH Papers*, 3:237–39.

23. WHH to Eustis, 14–19 June 1810, *WHH Papers*, 4:38. Harrison's disparagement of the militia may be a consequence of his desire for more regulars in Indiana. When push came to shove, in 1811 he used both regulars and militiamen in the Tippecanoe campaign and became an outspoken advocate of militiamen in that battle's aftermath.

24. WHH to Eustis, 26 June, 11 July 1810, *WHH Papers*, 4:71, 95.

25. WHH to Scott, 10 Mar., 17 Apr. 1810, *WHH Papers*, 3:758–69, 807–24. The following discussion of Harrison's thesis and all quotations are from these two letters. For the evolving volunteer tradition, see Marcus Cunliffe, *Soldiers and Civilians: The Martial Spirit in America, 1775–1865* (New York, Free Press, 1973).

26. Message to Territorial Assembly, 17 Oct. 1809, *WHH Papers*, 3:584–85.

27. Message to Territorial Assembly, 27 Sept. 1808, *WHH Papers*, 3:249.

28. Richard White, *The Middle Ground: Indians, Empires, and Republics in the Great Lakes Region, 1650–1815* (New York: Cambridge University Press, 1991), 93.

29. Ibid., 420; Elizabeth A. Perkins, "War as Cultural Encounter in the Ohio Valley," in David Curtis Skaggs and Larry L. Nelson, eds., *The Sixty Years' War for the Great Lakes, 1754–1814* (East Lansing: Michigan State University Press, 2001), 217.

30. Bernard W. Sheehan, *Seeds of Extinction: Jeffersonian Philanthropy and the American Indian* (Chapel Hill: University of North Carolina Press, 1973), 10–11. See also such studies as Reginald Horsman, *Expansion and American Indian Policy, 1783–1812* (East Lansing: Michigan State University Press, 1964); and Francis Paul Prucha, *American Indian Policy in the Formative Years: The Indian Trade and Intercourse Acts, 1790–1834* (Cambridge, MA: Harvard University Press, 1962).

31. Reginald Horsman, "The Indian Policy of the 'Empire for Liberty,'" in Frederick E. Hoxie, Ronald Hoffman, and Peter J. Albert, eds., *Native Americans in the Early Republic* (Charlottesville: University Press of Virginia, 1999), 52.

32. Harvey Lewis Carter, *The Life and Times of Little Turtle: First Sagamore of the Wabash* (Urbana: University of Illinois Press, 1987); Amy C. Schutt, *People of the River Valleys: The Odyssey of the Delaware Indians* (Philadelphia: University of Pennsylvania Press, 2007).

33. WHH to Jefferson, 12 May 1804, *WHH Papers*, 1:798.

34. WHH to Jefferson, [Oct. 1801], *WHH Papers*, 1:193–95. For more on this problem, see Francis Paul Prucha, *American Indian Policy in the Formative Years: The Indian Trade and

Intercourse Acts, 1790–1834 (Cambridge, MA: Harvard University Press, 1962), 188–212; Robert F. Berkhofer Jr., *The White Man's Indian: Images of the American Indian from Columbus to the Present* (New York: Vintage Books, 1979), 134–49; and Bruce C. Smith, "Negotiating Law on the Frontier: Responses to Cross-Cultural Homicide in Illinois, 1810–1825," in Daniel P. Barr, ed., *The Boundaries between Us: Natives and Newcomers along the Frontiers of the Old Northwest Territory, 1750–1850* (Kent, OH: Kent State University Press, 2006), 161–77.

35. WHH to Dearborn, 15 July 1801, Dearborn to WHH, 23 Feb. 1802, *WHH Papers*, 1:151–54, 265–66. See also WHH to Dearborn, [26 Feb. 1802], Eustis to WHH, 14 July 1810, *WHH Papers*, 1:270–75, 4:100. For a broader perspective on this issue, see Prucha, *American Indian Policy*, 139–87.

36. WHH to Dearborn, 15 July 1801, *WHH Papers*, 1:152–53.

37. WHH to Dearborn, 15 July, Proclamation, 20 July 1801, *WHH Papers*, 1:152, 161.

38. WHH to Jefferson, 29 Oct. 1803, WHH to Indiana Assembly, 30 July 1805, *WHH Papers*, 1:682, 2:263. The letter from Dearborn to WHH, 6 Jan. 1804, provides the governor with the authority to regulate trade. *WHH Papers*, 1:747. See also WHH Proclamation, 7 Aug. 1805, *WHH Papers*, 2:277. For a detailed account of the federal, state, and territorial efforts to regulate whiskey sales to Indians, see Prucha, *American Indian Policy*, 102–38.

39. Owens, *Jefferson's Hammer*, 31. See also, M. Teresa Baer, "William Henry Harrison and the Indian Treaty Land Cessions," in Bingham, *Indiana Territory*, 167–86.

40. Notes of Speeches at an Indian Council, 15 Sept., Memorandum of Agreement, 17 Sept. 1802, *WHH Papers*, 1:387–404, quotations on 388, 394. One interesting aside is the signature of Carter B. Harrison on the treaty. The former congressman, the governor's older brother, must have been visiting Vincennes at the time. See also Owens, *Jefferson's Hammer*, 63–66. The interactions of Little Turtle, Richardville, and William Wells are imaginatively explored in Donald H. Gaff, "Three Men from Three Rivers: Navigating between Native and American Identity in the Old Northwest Territory," in Barr, *Boundaries between Us*, 143–60.

41. Jefferson to WHH, 27 Feb. 1803, *WHH Papers*, 1:519–24. For a further elaboration of these policies, see S/War Henry Dearborn to WHH, 21 Feb. 1803, *WHH Papers*, 1:512–13.

42. Treaty of Kaskaskia, 13 Aug. 1803, *WHH Papers*, 1:632–36. On another large cession along the Mississippi northward to the Wisconsin, see Treaty with Sac & Fox, 3 Nov. 1804, *WHH Papers*, 2:3–10. For more details on the Kaskaskia treaty, see Robert M. Owens, "Jean Baptiste Ducoigne, the Kaskaskias, and the Limits of Thomas Jefferson's Friendship," *Journal of Illinois History* 5 (summer 2002): 109–36.

43. WHH to Dearborn, 3 Mar. 1805, *WHH Papers*, 2:113.

44. WHH to Jefferson, 12 May 1805, Dearborn to WHH, 21 June 1805, Treaty with Delawares, 18 Aug. 1804 through 3 Mar. 1805, Treaty with Piankashaw, 27 Aug. 1804 through 3 Mar. 1805, *WHH Papers*, 1:797–99, 819–20, 856–60, 881–83; Dearborn to WHH, 17 Jan. 1805, *WHH Papers*, 2:79–80. See also Owens, *Jefferson's Hammer*, 84–85, and the map of these treaties on xxiv.

45. WHH to Dearborn, 3 Mar., 26 Apr., 20 July 1805, *WHH Papers*, 2:104–15, 157, 245–49; Gaff, "Three Men," 145–46, 152–57. For subsequent developments on this issue, see

WHH to Jefferson, 18 June, Report of John Gibson and Francis Vigo, 6 July 1805, *WHH Papers*, 2:222, 235–42.

46. Dearborn to WHH, 24 May, Grouseland Treaty, 21 Aug., WHH to Dearborn, 26 Aug. 1805, *WHH Papers*, 2:188–89, 287–92, 324–27.

47. WHH to Dearborn, 18 Feb. 1808, *WHH Papers*, 3:113.

48. WHH to Jefferson, 29 Aug. 1805, *WHH Papers*, 2:328.

49. Yelabahcan speech at an 1816 Council, Lewis Cass Papers, William L. Clements Library, University of Michigan, Ann Arbor, MI.

50. Colin G. Calloway, *The Shawnees and the War for America* (New York: Viking, 2007), 133.

51. Tecumseh Speech, 20 Aug., WHH to Eustis, 4 July, 22 Aug., 28 Aug. 1810, *WHH Papers*, 4:79, 159, 169, 179–80.

52. Standard references include R. David Edmunds, *The Shawnee Prophet* (Lincoln: University of Nebraska Press, 1983); Edmunds, *Tecumseh and the Quest for Indian Leadership* (Boston: Little, Brown, 1984); John Sugden, *Tecumseh: A Life* (New York: Henry Holt, 1997); Calloway, *Shawnees*, 126–54; Owens, *Jefferson's Hammer*, 121–27; and Adam Jortner, *The Gods of Prophetstown: The Battle of Tippecanoe and the Holy War for the American Frontier* (New York: Oxford University Press, 2012); Alfred Cave, *Prophets of the Great Spirit: Native American Revitalization Movements in Eastern North America* (Lincoln: University of Nebraska Press, 2006), esp. 66–79; Patrick Bottiger, "Prophetstown for Their Own Purposes: The French, Miamis, and Cultural Identities in the Wabash-Miami Valley," *Journal of the Early Republic* 33 (spring 1913): 29–60.

53. WHH to Eustis, 11 July 1810, *WHH Papers*, 4:92.

54. WHH to Eustis, 18 July, Message to the Shawnee Prophet, 19 July 1810, *WHH Papers*, 4:103–4, 106–7.

55. WHH to Eustis, 25 July 1810, *WHH Papers*, 4:113.

56. Ibid., 116.

57. Sugden, *Tecumseh*, ix. See also Andrew R. L. Cayton, *Frontier Indiana* (Bloomington: Indiana University Press, 1996), 196–220.

58. WHH to Eustis, 28 Aug. 1810, *WHH Papers*, 4:180.

59. Gregory Evans Dowd, *A Spirited Resistance: The North American Indian Struggle for Unity, 1745–1815* (Baltimore: Johns Hopkins University Press, 1992), 181.

60. Richard White, *The Middle Ground: Indians, Empires, and Republics in the Great Lakes Region, 1650–1815* (New York: Cambridge University Press, 1991); R. David Edmunds, "Forgotten Allies: The Loyal Shawnees and the War of 1812," in Skaggs and Nelson, *Sixty Years' War*, 337 –51; Edmunds, "'A Watchful Safeguard to Our Habitations': Black Hoof and the Loyal Shawnees," in Hoxie, Hoffman, and Albert, *Native Americans*, 162–99; Calloway, *Shawnees*, 109–25.

61. T. Forsyth to N. Edwards, 13 July 1812, in Clarence Edwin Carter, ed., *The Territorial Papers of the United States*, 28 vols. (Washington, DC: Government Printing Office, 1934–75), 16:252.

62. Dowd, *Spirited Resistance*, 184.

63. Douglas A. Birk, "When Rivers Were Roads: Deciphering the Role of Canoe Portages in the Western Lake Superior Fur Trade," in Jennifer S. H. Brown, W. J. Eccles, and

Donald P. Heldman, eds., *The Fur Trade Revisited: Selected Papers of the Sixth North American Fur Trade Conference, Mackinac Island, Michigan, 1991* (East Lansing: Michigan State University Press, 1994), 359–60.

64. Robert S. Allen, *His Majesty's Indian Allies: British Indian Policy in the Defence of Canada, 1774–1815* (Toronto: Dundurn Press, 1992), 110–17; Timothy D. Willig, *Restoring the Chain of Friendship: British Policy and the Indians of the Great Lakes, 1783–1815* (Lincoln: University of Nebraska Press, 2008), 199–242; Cecil K. Boyd, "The Northwest Indians and the British Preceding the War of 1812," *Indiana Magazine of History* 38 (1942): 31–50.

65. Journal of the Treaty Negotiations, [1 Sept.–1 Oct. 1809], *WHH Papers*, 3:487–530; for the treaty, see *WHH Papers*, 3:531–38.

66. WHH to Armstrong, 20 Mar. 1814, in Carter, *Territorial Papers*, 10:1–4, quotation on 2.

67. WHH to J. Mansfield, 15 July 1811, in Carter, *Territorial Papers*, 8:127.

68. Eustis to WHH, 10 May, WHH to Eustis, 14 June, Johnston to WHH, 24 June, Brouillette to WHH, 30 June, WHH to Eustis, 4 July, 11 July, 18 July, 6 Aug. 1810, in *WHH Papers*, 4:9, 38–47, 58–61, 78–84, 93–95; Edmunds, *Shawnee Prophet*, 86–90, 103–5, 126–30.

69. WHH to J. Mansfield, 15 July, D. Sullivan to Mansfield, 15 July 1811, in Carter, *Territorial Papers*, 8:127.

70. WHH to Eustis, 6 Aug., 7 Aug. 1811, *WHH Papers*, 4:126–30, 684–88. See also Sugden, *Tecumseh*, 220–25; and Owens, *Jefferson's Hammer*, 211–16.

71. WHH to Eustis, 7 Aug. 1811, *WHH Papers*, 4:684–85.

72. WHH to Eustis, 6 Aug., 7 Aug. 1811, *WHH Papers*, 4:126–30, 684–88; Eustis to WHH, 22 Aug., 3 Oct. 1811, in Carter, *Territorial Papers*, 8:130–31, 135–36; M. Irwin to Eustis, 13 May, Edwards to Eustis, 27 June, 6 July, 11 Aug. 1811, in Carter, *Territorial Papers*, 16:159–60, 162–66, 169–71; Eustis to Madison, 21 Aug., Madison to Eustis, 24 Aug. 1811, in Robert A. Rutland et al., eds., *The Papers of James Madison, Presidential Series*, 7 vols. to date (Charlottesville: University Press of Virginia, 1984–), 3:426–27, 429.

73. Eustis to WHH, 17 Sept. 1811, in Carter, *Territorial Papers*, 8:133–34.

74. Cleaves, *Old Tippecanoe*, 87–89.

75. Nellie Armstrong Robertson and Dorothy Riker, eds., *The John Tipton Papers*, 3 vols. (Indianapolis: Indiana Historical Society, 1942), 1:75–76.

76. Accounts of the Tippecanoe campaign are provided in Owens, *Jefferson's Hammer*, 215–19; and Alfred A. Cave, "The Shawnee Prophet, Tecumseh, and Tippecanoe: A Case of Historical Myth-Making," *Journal of the Early Republic* 22 (winter 2002): 636–73.

77. Robertson and Riker, *Tipton Papers*, 1:75n.

78. WHH General Orders, 28 Oct., WHH to Eustis, 28 Oct. 1811, *WHH Papers*, 5:18–20.

79. WHH to Eustis, 2 Nov., WHH General Orders, 2 Nov. 1811, *WHH Papers*, 5:23–25, 28.

80. Tippecanoe Journal, in Robertson and Riker, *Tipton Papers*, 1:62–83, quotation on 68.

81. WHH to Lexington, Kentucky, *Reporter*, *WHH Papers*, 5:312.

82. Ibid., 310–14.

83. Important primary sources on the battle of Tippecanoe include WHH to Eustis, 18 Nov. 1811, and an exchange of letters between WHH and Prescott over the controversy

with Colonel Boyd, 9 Feb., 10 Feb. 1812, *WHH Papers*, 5:47–63, 347–51, 354–55; Boyd to Sec. of War, 11 Dec. 1811, in *Washington, DC, National Intelligencer*, 8 Feb. 1812; S. G. Hopkins to WHH, 15 Jan. 1812, in Carter, ed., *Territorial Papers*, 8:161–62; Isaac Naylor's reminiscences in Thornbrough and Riker, *Readings in Indiana History*, 36:131–37; John Tipton's comments in Robertson and Riker, *Tipton Papers*, 1:62–88, 2:825–33; Richard G. Carlson, ed., "George P. Peters' Version of the Battle of Tippecanoe (November 7, 1811)," *Vermont History* 45 (1977): 38–43; and Statement by Officers, 19 Nov., Resolutions & Toasts, 27 Dec. 1811, Adam Walker, "A Journal of the Campaigns of the Fourth Regiment of U.S. Infantry," T. Scott to Dawson, 25 July 1823, Larrabee to Dawson, 12 Oct. 1823, and W. Polk to *National Intelligencer*, 10 Feb. 1840, all in Logan Esarey, ed., *Messages and Letters of William Henry Harrison*, 2 vols. (Indianapolis: Indiana Historical Commission, 1922), 1:634, 680–82, 693–723. A fine brief secondary account is Allan R. Millett, "Caesar and the Conquest of the Northwest Territory: The Harrison Campaign, 1811," *Timeline* 14 (July–Aug. 1997): 2–19. See also Cleaves, *Old Tippecanoe*, 83–111; Goebel, *William Henry Harrison*, 118–127; Edmunds, *Shawnee Prophet*, 94–116; Sugden, *Tecumseh*, 220–36; Jortner, *Gods*, 187–200; Cave, "Shawnee Prophet"; Alfred Pirtle, *The Battle of Tippecanoe*, Filson Club Publication, vol. 15 (Louisville, KY: Filson Club, 1900); Harry D. Tunnell IV, *To Compel with Armed Force: A Staff Ride Handbook for the Battle of Tippecanoe* (Fort Leavenworth, KS: Combat Studies Institute, 2000); and Robert J. Holden, "The Pen *Replaces* the Sword: Governor William Henry Harrison and the Battle of Tippecanoe Controversy," *Indiana Academy of the Social Sciences Proceedings* 22 (1987): 57–68. Cave, with Jortner concurring, argues that the battle was an accident in which non–hostile native scouts were shot by American sentinels, which provoked the subsequent Indian attack. This seems doubtful because the sustained Indian assault began immediately after the sentinels fired.

84. Snelling to WHH, 20 Nov. 1811, *WHH Papers*, 5:70–73.

85. Geoffrey Perret, *A Country Made by War: From the Revolution to Vietnam—The Story of America's Rise to Power* (New York: Random House, 1989), 105; Edmunds, *Shawnee Prophet*, 115.

CHAPTER THREE: **The Politics of Command**

1. WHH to Eustis, 5 July 1809, in Douglas E. Clanin et al., eds., *The Papers of William Henry Harrison, 1800–1815*, 10 microfilm reels (Indianapolis: Indiana Historical Society, 1993–1999), 3:446–55, quotations on 449, 450 (hereafter, *WHH Papers*).

2. Army Act of 11 Jan. 1812, 2 Stat. 671; WHH to Eustis, 14 Jan. 1812, in Clarence Edwin Carter, ed., *The Territorial Papers of the United States*, 28 vols. (Washington, DC: Government Printing Office, 1934–75), 8:159–60. For a brief account of the Tippecanoe campaign, see Allan R. Millett, "Caesar and the Conquest of the Northwest Territory: The Harrison Campaign, 1811," *Timeline* 14 (July–Aug. 1997): 2–19.

3. The letter of Col. John P. Boyd and Capt. George W. Prescott to Eustis, 11 Dec. 1811, was printed in the *Washington, DC, National Intelligencer*, 11 Jan. 1812, and in the *Vincennes Western Sun*, 8 Feb. 1812. The letter is reprinted in Richard C. Knopf, ed., *Document Transcriptions of the War of 1812 in the Northwest*, 10 vols. (Columbus, OH: Anthony Wayne Parkway Board and Ohio State Historical Society, 1957–62), 5, pt. 1: 39–40; Harrison's 18 Nov. 1811 report on the battle is on 22–28. See also Samuel G. Hopkins to WHH, 15 Jan.

1812, in Carter, *Territorial Papers*, 8:161–62; Dorothy Burne Goebel, *William Henry Harrison: A Political Biography*, Indiana Historical Collections, vol. 19 (Indianapolis: Indiana Library and Historical Department, 1926), 124–27.

4. *Washington, DC, National Intelligencer*, 8 Feb. 1812. An exchange of letters between WHH and Prescott over this controversy, 9 Feb., 10 Feb. 1812, is in *WHH Papers*, 5:347–51, 354–55. See also Robert J. Holden, "The Pen Replaces the Sword: Governor William Henry Harrison and the Battle of Tippecanoe Controversy," *Indiana Academy of the Social Sciences Proceedings* 22 (1987): 57–68.

5. Cass to Worthington, 19 May, McArthur to Worthington, 26 June 1812, in Knopf, *Document Transcriptions*, 3:89, 101.

6. Worthington to Harrison, 28 Nov. 1812, in Carter, *Territorial Papers*, 8:218; Robert B. McAfee, *History of the Late War in the Western Country* (Bowling Green, OH: Historical Publications Co., 1919 [1816]), 148.

7. Badollet to Gallatin, 29 Apr. 1812, in Gayle Thornbrough, ed., *The Correspondence of John Badollet and Albert Gallatin, 1804–1836*, Indiana Historical Society Publications, vol. 22 (Indianapolis: Indiana Historical Society, 1963), 226–27.

8. *Washington, DC, National Intelligencer*, 29 Feb. 1812. See also Reginald Horsman, *Matthew Elliott: British Indian Agent* (Detroit: Wayne State University Press, 1964).

9. John Sugden, *Tecumseh: A Life* (New York: Henry Holt, 1997), 275.

10. Eustis to WHH, 28 Feb., 2 May, 14 May 1812, in Carter, *Territorial Papers*, 8:168, 179, 181; B. F. Stickney to Eustis, 7 June 1812, in Gayle Thornbrough, ed., *Letterbook of the Indian Agency at Fort Wayne, 1809–1815*, Indiana Historical Society Publications, vol. 21 (Indianapolis: Indiana Historical Society, 1961), 136.

11. Eustis to Hull, 19 Apr. 1812, in Knopf, *Document Transcriptions*, 8:21.

12. John Taylor to Madison, 7 July 1812, in Robert Rutland et al., eds., *The Papers of James Madison, Presidential Series*, 7 vols. to date (Charlottesville: University Press of Virginia, 1984–), 4:572

13. The letter no longer exists but is summarized in Clay to Eustis, 22 Aug. 1812, in James F. Hopkins, et al., eds., *The Papers of Henry Clay*, 10 vols. (Lexington: University of Kentucky Press, 1959–91), 1:717. See also Barry Gough, "Michilimackinac and Prairie du Chien: Northern Anchors of British Authority in the War of 1812," *Michigan Historical Review* 38 (spring 2012): 83–105.

14. Primary sources on the Detroit campaign are located in E. A Cruikshank, ed., *Documents Relating to the Invasion of Canada and the Surrender of Detroit, 1812*, Publications of Canadian Archives, no. 7 (Ottawa: Government Printing Bureau, 1912); and John C. Parish, ed., *The Robert Lucas Journal of the War of 1812 during the Campaign under General Hull* (Iowa City: State Historical Society of Iowa, 1906). Among the better secondary accounts are Robert S. Quimby, *The U.S. Army in the War of 1812: An Operational and Command Study*, 2 vols. (East Lansing: Michigan State University Press, 1997); Alec R. Gilpin, *The War of 1812 in the Old Northwest* (East Lansing: Michigan State University Press, 1958); George F. G. Stanley, *The War of 1812: Land Operations* (Toronto: National Museums of Canada and Macmillan, 1983); Sandy Antal, *A Wampum Denied: Procter's War of 1812*, Carleton Library Series, vol. 191 (Ottawa: Carleton University Press, 1997); Antal, "Michigan Ceded: Why and Wherefore?" *Michigan Historical Review* 38 (spring 2012): 1–26; and Anthony J. Yanik,

The Fall and Recapture of Detroit in the War of 1812: In Defense of William Hull (Detroit: Wayne State University Press, 2011).

15. McAfee, *History*, 121; *Scioto Gazette* quoted in *Washington, DC, National Intelligencer*, 8 Sept. 1812; *Washington, DC, National Intelligencer*, 15 Sept. 1812.

16. Dayton to Madison, [ca. 17 Sept. 1812], in Rutland et al., *James Madison*, 5:325.

17. Johnson to Madison, 3 Sept. 1812, in Rutland et al., *James Madison* 5:261; *Biographical Directory of the United States Congress, 1774–1989*, Senate Document no. 100–34, 100th Cong., 2nd Sess.(Washington, DC: Government Printing Office, 1989), 1267–68, 1270.

18. Badollet to Gallatin, 19 May 1812, in Thornbrough, *Correspondence of John Badollet*, 232.

19. WHH to Eustis, 12 Aug. 1812, in Carter, *Territorial Papers*, 8:190. For an introduction to raiding versus persisting strategies, see Archer Jones, *Civil War Command and Strategy: The Process of Victory and Defeat* (New York: Free Press, 1992), 138–41, 183–86.

20. On the Michilimackinac surrender, see Matthew Irwin to John Mason, 16 Oct. 1812, in Carter, *Territorial Papers*, 10:411–15.

21. WHH to Eustis, 12 Aug. 1812, in Carter, *Territorial Papers*, 8:191.

22. McAfee, *History*, 121–24. Harrison's appointment raised hackles in the family of Samuel Hopkins, who thought WHH should not receive a Kentucky major generalship because the post was already allotted to Hopkins. Hopkins's son, Samuel G. Hopkins, wrote Harrison an angry letter declaring that he was "severely stung" by Harrison's brevet major general's commission and that the episode dissolved "all ties of friendship" between the Hopkins family and Governor Scott and others who had advised that Harrison be appointed. S. G. Hopkins to WHH, 24 Feb. 1813, *WHH Papers*, 7:607.

23. Clay to Monroe, 25 Aug., to Eustis, 26 Aug. 1812, in Hopkins et al., *Henry Clay*, 1:719–22; Allen to Madison, 25 July 1812, in Knopf, *Document Transcriptions*, 6, pt. 2: 136.

24. Eustis to WHH, 18 July, WHH to Eustis, 12 Aug. 1812, in Carter, *Territorial Papers*, 8:188; Eustis to WHH, 22 Aug., 28 Aug., 30 Aug. 1812, in Knopf, *Document Transcriptions*, 8:69, 71, 73.

25. Findlay to WHH, 29 Aug. 1812, *WHH Papers*, 6:28.

26. For Governor Scott's orders, see *Washington, DC, National Intelligencer*, 10 Sept. 1812.

27. Eustis to Wadsworth, 5 Sept. 1812, in Knopf, *Document Transcriptions*, 10:151.

28. Tupper and Perkins to Meigs, 16 Feb. 1813, in Knopf, *Document Transcriptions*, 7, pt. 1: 114.

29. Madison to Monroe, 5 Sept., to Eustis, 6 Sept., 10 Sept. 1812, in Rutland et al., *James Madison*, 5:270–71, 277, 295; Monroe to Clay, 17 Sept. 1812, in Hopkins et al., *Henry Clay*, 1:727.

30. Madison to Monroe, 6 Sept. 1812, in Rutland et al., *James Madison*, 5:278.

31. Monroe to Madison, 7 Sept., Madison to Eustis, 8 Sept., Madison to Monroe, 8 Sept. 1812, in Rutland et al., *James Madison*, 5:284–87. On the Monroe gambit, see J. C. A. Stagg, *Mr. Madison's War: Politics, Diplomacy, and Warfare in the Early American Republic, 1783–1830* (Princeton, NJ: Princeton University Press, 1983), 213–26.

32. WHH to Eustis, 29 Aug. 1812, *WHH Papers*, 6:35–36.

33. Eustis to Winchester, 31 Aug. 1812, in Knopf, *Document Transcriptions*, 8:74.

34. Eustis to WHH, 1 Sept. 1812, *WHH Papers*, 6:56; Eustis to Meigs, 1 Sept. 1812, in Knopf, *Document Transcriptions*, 8:75.

35. WHH to Eustis, 3 Sept. 1812, *WHH Papers*, 6:76–80.

36. The letter from Winchester to Eustis, 2 Sept. 1812, was docketed by the War Department on 11 September but no longer survives. See Monroe to Madison, 12 Sept. 1812, in Rutland et al., *James Madison*, 5:312, 312n1; R. M. Johnson to Madison, 18 Sept. 1812, in Rutland et al., *James Madison*, 5:332, 332n1. Harrison's orders from Speech to Field Officers, 21 Sept. 1812, *WHH Papers*, 6:210. For Winchester's version of these and subsequent controversies, see James Winchester, *Historical Details Having Relation to the Campaign of the North-Western Army, under Generals Harrison and Winchester during the Winter of 1812–13* (Lexington, KY: Worsley and Smith, 1818), 9–11, 23–39.

37. S. G. Hopkins to Winchester, 11 May 1817, in Winchester, *Historical Details*, 76–77. These conspiratorial sentiments were echoed in Capt. T. Eastland to Winchester, July 1817, in Winchester, *Historical Details*, 83–88.

38. WHH to Eustis, 21 Sept. 1812, *WHH Papers*, 6:204; Rbt. Johnson to Monroe, 3 Sept., R. M. Johnson to Madison, 18 Sept., Meigs to Madison, 24 Nov. 1812, in Rutland et al., *James Madison*, 5:262, 332, 470. See also Monroe to Madison, 10 Sept., D. Jones to Madison, 30 Nov. 1812, in Rutland et al., *James Madison*, 5:297, 474.

39. WHH to Winchester, 21 Sept. 1812, *WHH Papers*, 6:208.

40. Monroe to Madison, 2 Sept. 1812, in Rutland et al., *James Madison*, 5:252.

41. Monroe to Clay, 17 Sept. 1812, in Hopkins et al., *Henry Clay*, 1:727.

42. Eustis to WHH, 17 Sept., WHH to Eustis, 13 Oct. 1812, *WHH Papers*, 6:173–74, 381.

43. Worthington to WHH, 28 Nov. 1812, in Carter, *Territorial Papers*, 8:217–18. Worthington was mistaken; Hull had refused to resign his governorship to accept the regular army post, and the Madison administration eventually allowed him to hold both positions. Yanik, *Fall and Recapture*, 23.

44. Worthington to WHH, 28 Nov. 1812, in Carter, *Territorial Papers*, 8:218.

45. Order to Jesse Hunt, 17 Jan. 1813, *WHH Papers*, 7:230.

46. Address and Resolutions in Columbia Township, Hamilton Co., 16 Jan. 1813, *WHH Papers*, 7:207–10; Franklin Co. resolution, 20 Jan. 1813, in Rutland et al., *James Madison*, 5:600.

47. Johnson to Madison, 21 Jan. 1813, in Carter, *Territorial Papers*, 8:231–32.

48. WHH to Armstrong, 16 Feb. 1813, in Carter, *Territorial Papers*, 8:237–38. WHH's manuscript letter of resignation as Indiana Territory governor has not been located, but copies of it were published in various Ohio newspapers in early 1813. The published letter is in WHH to S/State, 28 Dec. 1812, in Carter, *Territorial Papers*, 8:227–28.

49. Goebel, *William Henry Harrison*, 163–65. On creation of the various military districts, see *American State Papers: Military Affairs*, 7 vols. (Washington, DC: Gales and Seaton, 1832–61), 4:147.

50. Armstrong to Wm. Duane, 16 Mar. 1813, in "Selections from the Duane Papers," *Historical Magazine*, 2nd ser., 4 (1868): 61.

51. W. S. Hunt to wife, 22 Sept. 1812, *WHH Papers*, 6:216.

CHAPTER FOUR: **The Failed Counteroffensive**

1. Among the best summaries of the British-Indian situation are those in Robert S. Allen, *His Majesty's Indian Allies: British Indian Policy in the Defence of Canada, 1774–1815* (Toronto: Dundurn Press, 1992); Timothy D. Willig, *Restoring the Chain of Friendship: British Policy and the Indians of the Great Lakes, 1783–1815* (Lincoln: University of Nebraska Press, 2008); Colin G. Calloway, *Crown and Calumet: British-Indian Relations, 1783–1815* (Norman: University of Oklahoma Press, 1987); Reginald Horsman, "British Indian Policy in the Northwest, 1797–1812," *Mississippi Valley Historical Review* 45 (1958–59): 51–66; Horsman, *Matthew Elliott: British Indian Agent* (Detroit: Wayne State University Press, 1964), 60–208; Louis A. Tohill, "Robert Dickson, British Fur Trader on the Upper Mississippi," *North Dakota Historical Quarterly* 2 (Oct. 1928): 51–66, 3 (Jan. 1929): 83–128, and 3 (Apr. 1929): 182–203; and E. A. Cruikshank, "Robert Dickson, The Indian Trader," *Collections of the State Historical Society of Wisconsin*, 31 vols. (Madison: State Historical Society of Wisconsin, 1888–1931), 12:133–53. On Brock, see Wesley B. Turner, *British Generals in the War of 1812: High Command in the Canadas* (Montreal: McGill-Queen's University Press, 1999), 58–83; Turner, *The Astonishing General: The Life and Legacy of Sir Isaac Brock* (Toronto: Dundurn, 2011); and Jonathon Riley, *A Matter of Honour: The Life, Campaigns, and Generalship of Isaac Brock* (Montreal: Robin Brass Studio, 2011).

2. Brock to Prevost, 2 Dec. 1811, in William C. H. Wood, ed., *Select British Documents of the Canadian War of 1812*, Publications of the Champlain Society, 4 vols. (Toronto: Champlain Society, 1920–28), 1:271–78.

3. W. A. B. Douglas, "The Anatomy of Naval Incompetence: The Provincial Marine in Defence of Upper Canada before 1813," *Ontario History* 1 (Sept. 1979): 3–26; Turner, *Astonishing General*, 72–105; Riley, *Matter of Honour*, 147–67.

4. On Dickson's career and influence, see Allen, *His Majesty's Indian Allies*, 125–30, 140–42, 151–56, 163–64, 223–24; and Tohill, "Robert Dickson," 2 (Oct. 1928): 5–49, and 3 (Jan. 1929): 83–128, 182–203. On the Canadian fur traders and their opposition to U.S. expansion into the upper Great Lakes, see Julius W. Pratt, "Fur Trade Strategy and the American Left Flank in the War of 1812," *American Historical Review* 40 (Jan. 1935): 246–73.

5. Clegg to Dickson, 27 Feb., Dickson to Clegg, 18 June 1812, in E. A. Cruikshank, ed., *Documents Relating to the Invasion of Canada and the Surrender of Detroit, 1812*, Publications of the Canadian Archives, no. 7 (Ottawa: Government Printing Bureau, 1913), 17–18, 31–32. For an introduction to the real and fictive kinship groups arising from the marriage of Native American women with Euroamerican men, see Susan Sleeper-Smith, *Indian Women and French Men: Rethinking Cultural Encounter in the Western Great Lakes* (Amherst: University of Massachusetts Press, 2001); Sylvia Van Kirk, *Many Tender Ties: Women in Fur Trade Society, 1679–1870* (Norman: University of Oklahoma Press, 1990); and Jennifer S. H. Brown, *Strangers in Blood: Fur Trade Company Families in Indian Country* (Vancouver: University of British Columbia Press, 1980).

6. Quoted in Allen, *His Majesty's Indian Allies*, 223–24.

7. John Sugden, *Tecumseh: A Life* (New York: Henry Holt, 1997), 163–64, 216–17, 285; R. David Edmunds, "Main Poc: Potawatomi Wabeno," *American Indian Quarterly* 9 (1985): 259–72.

8. See http://usregularo.tripod.com/1usstations.

9. Act of 2 Jan. 1812, 2 Stat. 670, and Act of 20 Feb. 1812, 2 Stat. 678; Eustis to WHH, 28 Feb., 7 Mar., 2 May, 14 May 1812, in Clarence Edwin Carter, ed., *The Territorial Papers of the United States*, 28 vols. (Washington, DC: Government Printing Office, 1934–75), 8:168, 170, 179, 181.

10. Russell to Eustis, 1 July, 24 Aug., 31 Oct. 1812, in Carter, *Territorial Papers*, 16:238–40, 257–58, 268–69.

11. WHH to Eustis, 13 May 1812, *WHH Papers*, 5:564–65.

12. Edwards to Eustis, 12 May 1812, in Richard C. Knopf, ed., *Document Transcriptions of the War of 1812 in the Northwest*, 10 vols. (Columbus, OH: Anthony Wayne Parkway Board and Ohio State Historical Society, 1957–62), 6, pt. 1: 197; W. Perry to T. Worthington, 17 June 1812, in Knopf, *Document Transcriptions*, 3:97; Stickney to Hull, 20 June 1812, in Gayle Thornbrough, ed., *Letter Book of the Indian Agency at Fort Wayne, 1809–1815*, Indiana Historical Society Publications, vol. 21 (Indianapolis: Indiana Historical Society, 1961), 141.

13. Stickney to J. Johnston, 20 July 1812, in Thornbrough, *Letter Book*, 165.

14. Gray Memo, 13 Jan., Pothier Memo, 13 Jan. 1812, in Wood, *Select British Documents*, 1:286–87.

15. After the fall of Fort Dearborn, Matthew Irwin, United States factor at Chicago, received notice that his services were no longer needed, but the government would continue his salary until the Chicago store could be reopened. John Mason to Irwin, 27 Oct. 1812, in Carter, *Territorial Papers*, 16:267. For a more detailed account of the federal factory system, see Edgar B. Wesley, "The Government and the Factory System among the Indians, 1795–1832," *Journal of Economic and Business History* 4 (1931–32): 487–511. On the Chicago area in this period, see Ann Durkin Keating, *Rising Up from Indian Country: The Battle of Fort Dearborn and the Birth of Chicago* (Chicago: University of Chicago Press, 2012).

16. Brian Leigh Dunnigan, *A Picturesque Situation: Mackinac before Photography, 1615–1860* (Detroit: Wayne State University Press, 2008), 101–2; Dunnigan, *The British Army at Mackinac, 1812–1815*, Reports in Mackinac History and Archaeology, no. 7 (Lansing, MI: Mackinac Island State Park Commission, 1980).

17. Quote in John Askin Jr. to John Askin, 19 July 1812, in *Michigan Pioneer and Historical Society Collections*, 40 vols. (Lansing, MI: Wynkoop Hallenbeck Crawford, 1877–1929), 32:482–83. Essential documents on the Mackinac situation are in Wood, *Select British Documents*, 1:419–42. Some secondary accounts describe the North West Co. brig *Caledonia* participating in the Mackinac Island attack, but none of the primary sources I located confirm this. On the other hand, the *Caledonia* was at St. Joseph Island shortly before the British set off for Mackinac and arrived there shortly after the surrender. Detailed treatments of the Michilimackinac affair are in Barry Gough, *Fighting Sail on Lake Huron and Georgian Bay: The War of 1812 and Its Aftermath* (Annapolis, MD: Naval Institute Press, 2002), 14–26; and Dunnigan, *British Army at Mackinac*.

18. Roberts to Baynes, 17 July 1812, in Wood, *Select British Documents*, 1:433.

19. Hull's letter no longer exists but is summarized in Clay to Eustis, 22 Aug. 1812, in James F. Hopkins, ed., *The Papers of Henry Clay*, 10 vols. (Lexington: University of Kentucky Press, 1959–91), 1:717.

20. Primary sources on the Detroit campaign are located in Cruikshank, *Documents*; Milo M. Quaife, ed., *The John Askin Papers*, 2 vols. (Detroit: Detroit Library Commission, 1931), 2:708–23; and Daniel Dobbin's Account of 11 Sept. 1812, Lewis Cass Papers, William L. Clements Library, University of Michigan, Ann Arbor, MI. Among the better secondary accounts are Robert S. Quimby, *The U.S. Army in the War of 1812: An Operational and Command Study*, 2 vols. (East Lansing: Michigan State University Press, 1997); Alec R. Gilpin, *The War of 1812 in the Old Northwest* (East Lansing: Michigan State University Press, 1958); George F. G. Stanley, *The War of 1812: Land Operations* (Toronto: National Museums of Canada and Macmillan, 1983); and C. Edward Skeen, *Citizen Soldiers in the War of 1812* (Lexington: University Press of Kentucky, 1999).

21. LeClair Report, 14 July 1812, in Carter, *Territorial Papers*, 16:254.

22. Forsyth to Howard, 7 Sept. 1812, in Carter, *Territorial Papers*, 16:261–63; Mentor L. Williams, ed., "John Kinzie's Narrative of the Fort Dearborn Massacre," *Journal of the Illinois State Historical Society* 46 (1953): 343–62; Heald to Eustis, 23 Oct. 1812, in Cruikshank, *Documents*, 225–27. The standard secondary account is in Milo M. Quaife, *Chicago and the Old Northwest, 1673–1835: A Study of the Evolution of the Northwestern Frontier, Together with a History of Fort Dearborn* (Chicago: University of Chicago Press, 1913), 211–26.

23. Howard to Eustis, 13 Jan. 1812, in Carter, *Territorial Papers*, 14:505; Boilvin to Howard, 5 Jan. 1812, Blandeau to Howard, [?] Jan. 1812, in Carter, *Territorial Papers*, 16:186–88; WHH to Eustis, 18 Nov. 1811, *WHH Papers*, 5:61.

24. M. Irwin to Eustis, 16 Apr. 1812, in Carter, *Territorial Papers*, 16:212.

25. St. Clair Co. Militia Officers, 7 Feb. 1812, in Carter, *Territorial Papers*, 16:188–89.

26. T. Forsyth to N. Edwards, 7 Sept. 1812, in Carter, *Territorial Papers*, 16:263–64.

27. Hull's Proclamation, 13 July 1812, in Cruikshank, *Documents*, 59.

28. Allen, *His Majesty's Indian Allies*, 131.

29. Howard to Eustis, 15 Sept. 1812, in Knopf, *Document Transcriptions*, 6, pt. 1: 210.

30. WHH to Eustis, 12 Aug. 1812, in Carter, *Territorial Papers*, 8:191; Eustis to WHH, 2 Sept. 1812, *WHH Papers*, 6:56.

31. For an introduction to the annihilation versus attrition strategy in U.S. military history, see Russell F. Weigley, *The American Way of War: A History of United States Military Strategy and Policy* (New York: Macmillan, 1973). In this strategy, Harrison followed the colonial tradition of anti-Indian warfare explored in Guy Chet, *Conquering the American Wilderness: The Triumph of European Warfare in the Colonial Northeast* (Amherst: University of Massachusetts Press, 2003); and John Grenier, *The First Way of War: American War Making on the Frontier* (New York: Cambridge University Press, 2005).

32. For Winchester's version of these and subsequent controversies, see James Winchester, *Historical Details Having Relation to the Campaign of the North-Western Army, under Generals Harrison and Winchester during the Winter of 1812–13* (Lexington, KY: Worsley and Smith, 1818).

33. William H. Merritt, "Journal of Events Principally on the Detroit and Niagara Frontiers," in Wood, *Select British Documents*, 3, pt. 2: 563; Robert B. McAfee, *History of the Late War in the Western Country* (Bowling Green, OH: Historical Publications Co., 1919 [1816]), 108.

34. Hamilton to Chauncey, 31 Aug., 4 Sept. 1812, in William S. Dudley and Michael J.

Crawford, eds., *The Naval War of 1812: A Documentary History*, 3 vols. to date (Washington, DC: Naval Historical Center, 1985–), 1:297–302. A month later Hamilton ordered Lt. Thomas Macdonough, USN, to command the naval forces on Lake Champlain. Hamilton to Macdonough, 28 Sept. 1812, in Dudley and Crawford, *Naval War*, 1:319–20.

35. Hamilton to Dobbins, 11 Sept., 15, Sept., Hamilton to Chauncey 11 Sept., Hamilton to Tingey, 15 Sept., and Dobbins to Chauncey, 28 Sept. 1812, in Dudley and Crawford, *Naval War*, 1:306–11.

36. Elliott to Chauncey, 14 Sept. 1812, in Dudley and Crawford, *Naval War*, 1:312–14. On Chauncey's efforts on Lake Ontario, see letters from him to Hamilton, 8 Oct. through 26 Nov. 1812, in Dudley and Crawford, *Naval War*, 1:336–53. The best secondary account is Robert Malcomson, *Lords of the Lake: The Naval War on Lake Ontario, 1812–1814* (Toronto: Robin Brass Studio, 1998), 3–56.

37. Elliott to Hamilton, 9 Oct., Brock to Prevost, 11 Oct. 1812, in Dudley and Crawford, *Naval War*, 1:328–33.

38. Leonard D. White, *The Jeffersonians: A Study in Administrative History, 1801–1829* (New York: Macmillan, 1951), 213.

39. James A. Huston, *The Sinews of War: Army Logistics, 1775–1953* (Washington, DC: Office of the Chief of Military History, 1966), 102.

40. Crawford to Monroe, 16 Aug. 1812, quoted in Huston, *Sinews of War*, 104.

41. White, *Jeffersonians*, 216–19.

42. WHH to Eustis, 13 Dec., WHH General Orders, 19 Dec. 1812, *WHH Papers*, 6:802–4, 839.

43. Eustis to WHH, 17 Sept., 18 Sept., to Stoddard, 17 Sept., 19 Sept., to Morrison, 18 Sept., to Hart, 28 Nov. 1812, in Knopf, *Document Transcriptions*, 8:86, 118; WHH to Eustis, 15 Oct. 1812, *WHH Papers*, 6:393–95; enclosure in WHH to Eustis, 13 Dec. 1812, *WHH Papers*, 6:804.

44. McAfee, *History*, 125, 307–12.

45. Eustis to WHH, 23 Sept. 1812, *WHH Papers*, 6:222.

46. Eustis to W. Piatt, 30 Sept. 1812, in Knopf, *Document Transcriptions*, 8:98.

47. Eustis to McArthur, 6 Oct. 1812, in Knopf, *Document Transcriptions*, 8:101.

48. WHH to Monroe, 20 Jan. 1813, *WHH Papers*, 7:259–60; J. C. A. Stagg, *Mr. Madison's War: Politics, Diplomacy, and Warfare in the Early American Republic, 1783–1830* (Princeton, NJ: Princeton University Press, 1983), 218.

49. WHH to Eustis, 13 Oct. 1812, *WHH Papers*, 6:380.

50. J. Wheaton to Madison, 29 Dec., 31 Dec. 1812, in Robert A. Rutland et al., eds., *The Papers of James Madison: Presidential Series*, 7 vols. to date (Charlottesville: University of Virginia Press, 1984–), 5:532–33, 538.

51. Eustis to Edwards, 22 Aug., 22 Oct. 1812, in Carter, *Territorial Papers*, 16:256–57, 266; Eustis to Howard, 22 Aug., 22 Oct. 1812, in Carter, *Territorial Papers*, 14:592, 602. A recent study of the war in the Mississippi Valley is Gillum Ferguson, *Illinois in the War of 1812* (Champaign: University of Illinois Press, 2012).

52. WHH to Shelby, 28 June 1812, *WHH Papers*, 6:18. Barbour was U.S. Army Major Zachary Taylor's brother-in-law.

53. Sandy Antal, *A Wampum Denied: Procter's War of 1812*, Carleton Library Series, vol. 191 (Ottawa: Carleton University Press, 1997), 103–6.

54. Clark to Eustis, 13 Feb. 1812, in Carter, *Territorial Papers*, 14:519–20.

55. Stark to Bissell, 7 Feb., Howard to Bissell, 13 Feb., Edwards to Bissell, 14 Feb., Bissell to Eustis, 19 Feb. 1812, in Carter, *Territorial Papers*, 14:520–23. See also Howard to Eustis, 19 Mar. 1812, in Carter, *Territorial Papers*, 14:531–34.

56. Howard to Eustis, 14 June 1812, in Carter, *Territorial Papers*, 14:563–69.

57. Howard to Eustis, 20 Sept. 1812, in Carter, *Territorial Papers*, 14:593–94.

58. S. Bond and E. Hempstead to S/War, 18 Jan. 1813, in Carter, *Territorial Papers*, 16:291–93.

59. Eustis to Edwards, 22 Aug., 7 Oct. 1812, in Carter, *Territorial Papers*, 16:256–57, 266.

60. Russell to Eustis, 31 Oct. 1812, in Carter, *Territorial Papers*, 16:268–69.

61. See, for instance, Edwards to Madison, 16 Jan., Bond and Hempstead to Monroe, 18 Jan. 1813, in Carter, *Territorial Papers*, 16:285–93.

62. WHH to Edwards, 29 Apr., to Eustis, 29 Apr., 2 May 1812, in *WHH Papers*, 5:535–40, 540, 543.

63. Noble to WHH, 6 May, WHH to Eustis, 13 May 1812, *WHH Papers*, 5:549–50, 565.

64. WHH to Eustis, 29 Apr., 3 June 1812, *WHH Papers*, 5:541–42, 616.

65. WHH to Eustis, 13 May 1812, *WHH Papers*, 5:564.

66. WHH to Eustis, 13 May, Eustis to WHH, 14 May, WHH to Scott, 26 May 1812, *WHH Papers*, 5:566, 569–70, 588.

67. WHH to Eustis, 27 May, to Greenup, 29–30 May, to Eustis, 3 June 1812, *WHH Papers*, 5:595–96, 600, 616. See also Sugden, *Tecumseh*, 264–71.

68. Stickney to WHH, 16 June 1812, *WHH Papers*, 5:638; Stickney to M. Elliott, 30 May 1812, in Thornbrough, *Letter Book*, 133–34.

69. WHH to Eustis, 12 Aug. 1812, *WHH Papers*, 5:755–61.

70. WHH to Shelby, 28 Aug., WHH to Worthington, 28 Aug., Shelby to WHH, 28 Aug. 1812, *WHH Papers*, 6:18–19, 23, 25. See also Quimby, *U.S. Army*, 110–11.

71. WHH to Eustis, 3 June, to Scott, 6 June 1812, *WHH Papers*, 5:621, 626.

72. Quimby, *U.S. Army*, 94–95; Procter to Brock, 30 Sept., 3 Oct., Charles Askin Journal, in Wood, *Select British Documents*, 1:524, 527, 544–45.

73. *WHH Papers*, 6:3–55.

74. WHH to Clay, 29 Aug. 1812, *WHH Papers*, 6:32.

75. Taylor to WHH, 10 Sept. 1812, *WHH Papers*, 6:141–46; Quimby, *U.S. Army*, 100–101.

76. Quimby, *U.S. Army*, 101.

77. WHH to Shelby 28 Aug., WHH to Worthington, 28 Aug., Shelby to WHH, 28 Aug. 1812, *WHH Papers*, 6:18–19, 23, 25. See also Quimby, *U.S. Army*, 110–11.

78. WHH to Eustis, 13 Oct. 1812, *WHH Papers*, 6:376–77.

79. WHH to Eustis, 21 Sept. 1812, *WHH Papers*, 6:202–6.

80. S. W. Culbertson to *Zanesville (Ohio) Messenger*, in *Washington, DC, National Intelligencer*, 19 Sept. 1812.

81. W. S. Hunt to wife, 22 Sept. 1812, *WHH Papers*, 6:216; Eustis to WHH, 1 Sept., WHH to Hopkins, 22 Sept. 1812, *WHH Papers*, 6:56, 218.

82. Ibid., Shelby to WHH, 26 Sept. 1812, *WHH Papers*, 6:259–60.

83. T. Forsyth to Howard, 7 Sept., Edwards to Eustis, 21 Sept., Russell to Eustis, 31 Oct., Petition to Congress by the [Illinois] Territorial Legislature, 30 Nov., Memorial to the

President, 6 Dec. 1812, in Carter, *Territorial Papers*, 16:261–66, 268–69, 271–75; Shelby to WHH, 1 Nov., 7 Nov. 1812, *WHH Papers*, 6:504–5. On General Hopkins's failed campaign, see Skeen, *Citizen Soldiers*, 57–58.

84. Edwards to Madison, 16 Jan., Bond and Hempstead to Monroe, 18 Jan. 1813, in Carter, *Territorial Papers*, 16:285–93, Howard to Monroe, 10 Jan. 1813, in Carter, *Territorial Papers*, 14:614–22.

85. Armstrong to Howard, 10 Apr. 1813, in Knopf, *Document Transcriptions*, 8:142–43.

86. WHH to Eustis, 22 Sept. 1812, *WHH Papers*, 6:219–20.

87. WHH to Winchester, 24 Sept. 1812, *WHH Papers*, 6:230. The regulars were commanded by Col. Samuel Wells; Capt. William Garrard commanded a troop of twelve-month dragoons. The three Kentucky regiments that constituted the bulk of Winchester's forces were commanded by Colonels John M. Scott, John Allen, and William Lewis. See WHH to Shelby, 22 Sept. 1812, *WHH Papers*, 6:219–20.

88. Eustis to WHH, 23 Sept., WHH to Denny, 24 Sept., WHH to Jennings, 24 Sept., Jennings to WHH, 26 Sept. 1812, *WHH Papers*, 6:223, 226, 228, 257.

89. WHH to Eustis, 24 Sept. 1812, *WHH Papers*, 6:230–33.

90. Winchester to WHH, 24 Sept. 1812, *WHH Papers*, 6:236.

91. "To the People of Kentucky," 25 Sept., WHH to T. Buford and to Shelby, 25 Sept. 1812, *WHH Papers*, 6:241–42, 244, 246–47.

92. Eustis to WHH, 17 Sept. 1812, *WHH Papers*, 6:173–74.

93. This analysis is based on numerous WHH letters from August to November 1812, *WHH Papers*, 6. In particular, see WHH to Eustis, 26 Oct., 15 Nov. 1812, *WHH Papers*, 6:465–68, 597–605. Harrison summarizes the situation in a letter to Monroe, 4 Jan. 1813, *WHH Papers*, 7:126–34.

94. WHH to S. Perkins, 1 Nov., to A. Porter, 1 Nov. 1812, *WHH Papers*, 6:496, 498–99.

95. Tupper to Perkins, 9 Nov., WHH to Piatt, 11 Oct., 30 Nov. 1812, *WHH Papers*, 6:355, 555–56, 715.

96. WHH to Eustis, 12 Dec. 1812, *WHH Papers*, 6:792.

97. Winchester to WHH, 27 Nov., WHH to Eustis, 14 Dec. 1812, *WHH Papers* 6:700, 809–10; Samuel R. Brown, *Views of the Campaigns of the North-Western Army* (Troy, NY: Francis Adancourt, 1814), 31–32. Black Hoof, in particular, has been frequently analyzed; such studies include R. David Edmunds, "Forgotten Allies: The Loyal Shawnees and the War of 1812," in David Curtis Skaggs and Larry L. Nelson, eds., *The Sixty Years' War for the Great Lakes, 1754–1824* (East Lansing: Michigan State University Press, 2001), 337–51; Edmunds, "Evil Men Who Add to Our Difficulties: Shawnees, Quakers & William Wells, 1807–1808," *American Indian Culture and Research Journal* 14 (1990): 1–14; Edmunds, "'A Watchful Safeguard to Our Habitations': Black Hoof and the Loyal Shawnees," in Frederick E. Hoxie, Ronald Hoffman, and Peter J. Albert, eds., *Native Americans and the Early Republic* (Charlottesville: University Press of Virginia, 1999), 162–99; Collin G. Calloway, *The Shawnees and the War for America* (New York: Viking, 2007), 109–25; Horsman, *Matthew Elliott*, 202; and McAfee, *History*, 172.

98. WHH to B. F. Stickney, 1 Dec., Perkins to WHH, 19 Dec. 1812, *WHH Papers*, 6:723, 845. On Tarhe and the Wyandot, see John P. Bowes, "Transformation and Transition: American Indians and the War of 1812 in the Lower Great Lakes," *Journal of Military History* 76 (Oct. 2012): 1129–46. On the Delaware, see Daniel P. Barr, "Odyssey's End: The

Battle of Lake Erie and the Failure of the Delaware Indian Struggle for Autonomy," in David Curtis Skaggs, *The Battle of Lake Erie and Its Aftermath* (Kent, OH: Kent State University Press, 2013), 101–25.

99. WHH to Eustis, 24 Sept. 1812, *WHH Papers*, 6:230–31.

100. John Payne letter in *Washington, DC, National Intelligencer*, 14 Jan. 1813; WHH orders to Campbell, 25 Nov. 1812, *WHH Papers*, 6:685–89; Campbell to WHH, 25 Dec. 1812, 1 Jan. 1813, WHH General Orders, 2 Jan. 1813, Ball to WHH, 3 Jan. 1813, with enclosure from Ball to Campbell, 25 Dec. 1812, *WHH Papers*, 7:25–39, 93–94, 96–101, 104–13; J. Simrall to T. Speed, 17 Feb. 1813, in James Simrall Letters, Filson Historical Society, Louisville, KY; Brown, *Views of the Campaigns*, 33.

101. WHH to Monroe, 3 Jan. 1813, *WHH Papers*, 7:121–22.

102. WHH to Tupper, 4 Oct., to Winchester, 4 Oct. 1812, *WHH Papers*, 6:320–24.

103. Winchester to WHH, 26 Oct., 30 Oct., E. W. Tupper to WHH, 10 Nov. 1812, *WHH Papers*, 6:470–72, 490–91, 571–72.

104. Winchester to WHH, 30 Oct., WHH to Eustis, 26 Oct., Trimble to WHH, 21 Oct., WHH to Perkins, 12 Nov., with enclosure of orders to Perkins from Meigs, 14 Nov., WHH to Trimble, 18 Nov. 1812, *WHH Papers*, 6:416–19, 467, 470–72, 491, 581–83, 637. The Tupper court of inquiry report is in General Orders, 17 Feb. 1813, *WHH Papers*, 7:538–40. Clay to Monroe, 23 Dec. 1812, in Hopkins et al., *Henry Clay*, 1:748–49. For more on Tupper's dispute with Winchester, see articles by Maj. Horace Nye in the *Marietta (OH) Register* in 1847, reprinted in 1878, posted in the Draper MSS (123 microfilm reels), 62, Wisconsin Historical Society, Madison, WI. General Beall was eventually acquitted of the charges of refusing to obey a direct order and subsequently resigned his commission.

105. Johnson to WHH, 3 Nov., WHH to Johnson, 14 Nov., WHH to *Liberty Hall* eds., 14 Nov., WHH to Eustis, 17 Nov. 1812, *WHH Papers*, 6:517–18, 593, 595–96, 626–27.

106. Winchester to WHH, 13 Nov. 1812, *WHH Papers*, 6:589–91.

107. Tupper to WHH, 16 Nov., General Order, 19 Nov. 1812, *WHH Papers*, 6:615–21, 639.

108. WHH to Symmes, 30 Nov. 1812, *WHH Papers*, 6:719–21.

109. Winchester to WHH, 10 Dec., Bordley to WHH, 11 Dec., Perkins to WHH, 11 Dec., Morrison to WHH, [before 12 Dec.], WHH to Eustis, 12 Dec., Perkins to WHH, 12 Dec. 1812, *WHH Papers*, 6:771–72, 774–77, 784–85, 788–94, 798.

110. Dorothy Burne Goebel, *William Henry Harrison: A Political Biography* (Indianapolis: Indiana Library and Historical Department, 1926), 146.

111. Orders to Winchester, 18 Dec. 1812, *WHH Papers*, 6:835.

112. Perkins to WHH, 19 Dec. 1812, *WHH Papers*, 6:845.

113. Winchester to WHH, 12 Jan., Perkins to WHH, 16 Jan., Winchester to Perkins, 15 Jan. 1813, *WHH Papers*, 7:190, 222–23.

114. WHH to Perkins, 16 Jan. 1813, *WHH Papers*, 7:214. See also Moses Dawson, *A Historical Narrative of the Civil and Military Services of Major-General William H. Harrison and a Vindication of His Character and Conduct* (Cincinnati: M. Dawson, 1824), 341–43.

115. WHH to Eustis, 12 Dec. 1812, *WHH Papers*, 6:788–94, quotation on 791–92.

116. WHH to Monroe, 4 Jan. 1813, *WHH Papers*, 7:126–35, quotations on 130. See also WHH to Monroe, 6 Jan. 1813, *WHH Papers*, 7:142–54.

117. WHH to Symmes, 30 Nov. 1812, *WHH Papers*, 6:719.

118. Winchester, *Historical Details*; Laurent Durocher letter, 13 Jan. 1858, Lewis Bond, "Journal of the Battle and Massacre of the River Raisin, January 22 & 23, 1813, and of the War of 1812," in Knopf, *Document Transcriptions*, 10, pt. 1: 39–41, 188–97; Isaac Day to WHH, [12 Jan. 1813], *WHH Papers*, 7:180–81; Perkins to Meigs, 28 Jan. 1813, in Knopf, *Document Transcriptions*, 2:225; Elias Darnell, *Journal Containing an Accurate and Interesting Account of the Hardships, Sufferings, Battles, Defeat, and Captivity of Those Heroic Kentucky Volunteers and Regulars, Commanded by General Winchester* (Philadelphia: Lippincott, Grambo, 1854). Winchester read Day's letter concerning the situation on the River Raisin before deciding to go to Frenchtown. Winchester to WHH, 17 Jan. 1813, *WHH Papers*, 7:236. For secondary accounts, see Gilpin, *War of 1812*, 163–70.

119. Winchester, *Historical Details*, 25–28.

120. Winchester to WHH, 17 Jan., 19 Jan., Lewis's Report, 20 Jan. 1813, *WHH Papers*, 7:236, 252, 279–83.

121. Orders to Tupper, 19 Jan., Orders to Leftwich, 22 Jan., WHH to Shelby, 22 Jan. 1813, *WHH Papers*, 7:242, 298, 300.

122. WHH to Shelby, 19 Jan., Whittlesey letter, 19 Jan. 1813, *WHH Papers*, 7:248–49, 251.

123. WHH to Monroe, 20 Jan., Winchester to WHH, 21 Jan. 1813 (two letters), *WHH Papers*, 7:259, 277, 293. Procter's name was also often spelled "Proctor."

124. Bond, "Journal," in Knopf, *Document Transcriptions*, 10, pt. 1:194–95; Procter to Sheaffe, 13 Jan., J. Baby to G. Jacob, 19 Jan., Procter to Sheaffe, 25 Jan. 1813, in Wood, *Select British Documents*, 2:3–9.

125. Perkins to Meigs, 28 Jan. 1813, in Knopf, *Document Transcriptions*, 2:225; Darnell, *Journal*, 50–51.

126. Hart to WHH, [ca. 21] Jan. 1813, *WHH Papers*, 7:295.

127. WHH to Tupper, 21 Jan. 1813, *WHH Papers*, 7:269; Tupper to Meigs, 16 Feb. 1813, in Knopf, *Document Transcriptions*, 2:117.

128. Interesting details on aspects of the British attack on the Kentuckians inside the fencing are given in *Proceedings of a Court Martial, Holden at Quebec, For the Trial of Lieutenant Benoit Bender of the 41st Regiment of Foot, in July 1815* (Montreal: J. Lane, 1817).

129. The discussion of the battle at Frenchtown is based on Winchester, *Historical Details*, 26–45; Durocher letter, 13 Jan. 1858, Bond, "Journal," in Knopf, *Document Transcriptions*, 10, pt. 1:39–41, 188–97; Day to WHH, [12 Jan. 1813], WHH to Meigs, 24 Jan., WHH to Monroe, 24 Jan. 1813, *WHH Papers*, 7:180–81, 309–20; Perkins to Meigs, 28 Jan. 1813, in Knopf, *Document Transcriptions*, 2:225; Darnell, *Journal*; Brown, *Views of the Campaigns*; Procter to Sheaffe, 25 Jan. 1813, in Wood, *Select British Documents*, 2:7–12; James Cochrane, "The War in Canada, 1812–1814" (unpublished MS, ca. 1840), Welsh Regimental Museum, Cardiff Castle, South Wales, UK. Secondary sources include Quimby, *U.S. Army*, 132–38; Antal, *Wampum Denied*, 161–83; Anthony J. Yanik, *The Fall and Recapture of Detroit in the War of 1812: In Defense of William Hull* (Detroit: Wayne State University Press, 2011), 171–75; James W. Hammack, *Kentucky in the Second American Revolution: The War of 1812* (Lexington: University of Kentucky Press, 1976); Dennis Au, *War on the Raisin* (Monroe, MI: Monroe County Historical Commission, 1981); G. Glenn Clift, *Remember the Raisin!* (Frankfort: Kentucky Historical Society, 1961); and Ralph Naveaux, *Invaded on All Sides: The Story of Michigan's Greatest Battlefield Scene of the Engagements at French-*

town and the River Raisin in the War of 1812 (Marceline, MO: Walsworth, 2008). Distinguished Canadian historical editor William Wood admitted that "the infuriated Indians . . . got out of hand. The fight was not closed on civilized principles. But there was now, as before and afterwards, war to the knife between the Indians and the dispossessing and exterminating Americans—a war which was inevitable between two races who were natural enemies under existing conditions. There were the usual accusations and recriminations; also the usual exaggerations." Wood, *Select British Documents*, 1:51–52. Canadian Capt. William Merritt summarized the situation on the River Raisin in a typical excuse for the British failure to secure prisoners by blaming the Kentuckians: "I regret to say that some unavoidable cruelty occurred after this action [at the River Raisin]. Our army fearing the approach of Gen. Harrison, retreated immediately to Amherstburgh. Some of the wounded were left in the house near the action. The Indians getting drunk, most inhumanly and brutally massacred them in cold blood; although the officers of the department exerted themselves in an extraordinary manner to prevent it . . . This is the first instance, I am shocked to relate it of deliberate murder by our Indians. The only thing that will in the least extenuate it is the conduct of some of the Kentucky riflemen, who were nearly as savage as the natives." Capt. W. H. Merritt, "Journal of Events Principally on the Detroit and Niagara Frontiers," in Wood, *Select British Documents*, 3, pt. 2: 567.

130. WHH to Winchester, 20 Jan., to Meigs, 20 Jan., to Monroe, 20 Jan. 1813, *WHH Papers*, 7:256–60.

131. Woodward to Monroe, 22 Mar. 1813, in Carter, *Territorial Papers*, 10:434.

CHAPTER FIVE: **Defending Ohio**

1. Carey to Madison, 21 Jan. 1793, in Robert A. Rutland et al., eds., *The Papers of James Madison: Presidential Series*, 7 vols. to date (Charlottesville: University Press of Virginia, 1984–), 5:603. The best biography of Armstrong is Carl E. Skeen, *John Armstrong, Jr., 1758–1843: A Biography* (Syracuse, NY: Syracuse University Press, 1982). See also J. C. A. Stagg, *Mr. Madison's War: Politics, Diplomacy, and Warfare in the Early Republic, 1783–1830* (Princeton, NJ: Princeton University Press, 1983), 277–88.

2. Morrison to WHH, 25 Apr. 1813, in Douglas E. Clanin et al., eds., *The Papers of William Henry Harrison, 1800–1815*, 10 microfilm reels (Indianapolis: Indiana Historical Society, 1993–1999), 8:119 (hereafter, *WHH Papers*); *Philadelphia Aurora*, 20 Mar. 1813.

3. This discussion of the River Raisin Massacre is based on Lewis Bond, "Journal of the Battle and Massacre of the River Raisin, January 22 & 23, 1813, and of the War of 1812," and Laurent Durocher letter, 13 Jan. 1858, in Richard C. Knopf, ed., *Document Transcriptions of the War of 1812 in the Northwest*, 10 vols. (Columbus: Ohio Historical Society, 1957–62), 10, pt. 1: 39–41, 188–97; Perkins to Meigs, 28 Jan. 1813, in Knopf, *Document Transcriptions*, 2:225; Elias Darnell, *Journal Containing an Accurate and Interesting Account of the Hardships, Sufferings, Battles, Defeat, and Captivity of Those Heroic Kentucky Volunteers and Regulars Commanded by General Winchester, in the Years 1812–13* (Philadelphia: Lippincott, Grambo, 1854), 58–63; Affidavit of Medard Descomps dit Labadie, 11 Feb. 1813, *WHH Papers*, 7:475–77; Robert B. McAfee, *History of the Late War in the Western Country* (Bowling Green, OH: Historical Publications, 1919 [1816]), 231–48; Samuel R. Brown, *Views of the Campaigns of the North-Western Army* (Troy, NY: Francis Adancourt, 1814), 34–39;

Procter to Sheaffe, 25 Jan. 1813, in William C. H. Wood, ed., *Select British Documents of the Canadian War of 1812*, Publications of the Champlain Society, 4 vols. (Toronto: Champlain Society, 1920–28), 2:7–12; and James Cochrane, "The War in Canada, 1812–1814" (unpublished MS, ca. 1840), Welsh Regimental Museum, Cardiff Castle, South Wales, UK. Secondary sources include Robert S. Quimby, *The U.S. Army in the War of 1812: An Operational and Command Study*, 2 vols. (East Lansing: Michigan State University Press, 1997), 132–38; Sandy Antal, *A Wampum Denied: Procter's War of 1812*, Carleton Library Series, vol. 191 (Ottawa: Carleton University Press, 1997), 161–83; Dennis Au, *War on the Raisin* (Monroe, MI: Monroe County Historical Commission, 1981); G. Glenn Clift, *Remember the Raisin!* (Frankfort: Kentucky Historical Society, 1961); and Ralph Naveaux, *Invaded on All Sides: The Story of Michigan's Greatest Battlefield Scene of the Engagements at Frenchtown and the River Raisin in the War of 1812* (Marceline, MO: Walsworth, 2008), 202–54.

4. Richardson to John Askin, 7 Feb. 1813, in Milo M. Quaife, ed., *The John Askin Papers*, 2 vols. (Detroit: Detroit Library Commission, 1928–31), 2:750.

5. Indiana Assembly Resolution, 18 Feb., Tupper, Perkins, et al., 20 Feb., H. Hurst to WHH, 23 Feb. 1813, *WHH Papers*, 7:560–61, 571–73, 595.

6. WHH to Meigs, 28 Jan., to J. Morrison, 29 Jan., 28 Feb., to Armstrong, 11 Feb. 1813, *WHH Papers*, 7:357–58, 362–63, 467–73, 636–37.

7. Johnston to WHH, 4 Feb. 1813, *WHH Papers*, 7:417.

8. Crooks to Leftwich, 26 Jan. 1813, Leftwich Papers, Alderman Library, University of Virginia, Charlottesville, VA.

9. WHH to Meigs, 4 Feb. 1813, *WHH Papers*, 7:414.

10. Eleazer D. Wood, "Journal of the Northwestern Campaign of 1812–1813," in George W. Cullum, ed., *Campaigns of the War of 1812 against Great Britain* (New York: James Miller, 1879), 369–72. See also Joseph Wheaton to Madison, 10 Feb., 4 Mar., 12 Mar. 1813, in Rutland et al., *James Madison*, 6:9–11, 83–85, 110–14. Wheaton was a Continental Army veteran who served as the first sergeant at arms of the U.S. House of Representatives, 1789–1807; he lost the post probably because of associations with Aaron Burr. Beginning in 1812 he wrote obsequious letters to Madison requesting new government employment, eventually receiving the minor post of assistant deputy quartermaster general in the Eighth Military District. He continued to write the president about matters in the district, to which Madison seems not to have replied. See Rutland et al., *James Madison*, 3:502–3, 503n; Wheaton to Madison, 5 Feb., 29 May, 27 June 1812, in Rutland et al., *James Madison*, 4:167–68, 423–24, 513–15; Wheaton to Madison, 10 Feb., 26 Feb., 4 Mar., 12 Mar., 26 Apr., 1 May 1813, in Rutland et al., *James Madison*, 6:9–10, 72–73, 83–84, 110–12, 241–43, 273–74.

11. Wheaton to Madison, 12 Mar. 1813, in Rutland et al., *James Madison*, 6:111.

12. Ibid., 112.

13. E. Wood, *Journal*, 374–75. The standard history of the post is Larry L. Nelson, *Men of Patriotism, Courage, & Enterprise! Fort Meigs in the War of 1812* (Canton, OH: Darling Books, 1985). See also Nelson, "The Maumee River Campaign, 1812–1813," in David Curtis Skaggs, ed., *The Battle of Lake Erie and Its Aftermath* (Kent, OH: Kent State University Press, 2013), 11–31; Rex L. Spencer, "The Gibraltar of the Maumee: Fort Meigs in the War of

1812" (PhD diss., Ball State University, 1988); and Lee A. Wallace Jr., "The Petersburg Volunteers, 1812–1813," *Virginia Magazine of History and Biography* 82 (1974): 458–85. Today, a reconstructed Fort Meigs in Perrysburg, Ohio, is a historical site of considerable interest for those wishing to understand why this outpost was so important to the War of 1812.

14. Daniel Cushing, *Fort Meigs in the War of 1812*, Harlow Lindley, ed. (Columbus: Ohio Historical Society, 1975), 102; General Orders, 24 Apr. 1813, *WHH Papers*, 8:96; Wheaton to Madison, 12 Mar. 1813, in Rutland et al., *James Madison*, 6:112. Harrison, on the other hand, suspected Wheaton of having "at least $10,000 of public Money in his possession." WHH to Armstrong, 21 Apr. 1813, *WHH Papers*, 8:82, 82n7. For more on this subject, see Armstrong to WHH, 8 May, WHH to Armstrong, 19 May 1813, *WHH Papers*, 8:283–86. On the evolution of U.S. Army artillery doctrine, see Donald E. Graves, "'For Want of This Precaution . . . Many Men Lose Their Arms': Official, Semiofficial, and Unofficial American Artillery Texts, 1775–1815," *Military Collector and Historian* 64 (summer 2012): 79–99, and 64 (fall 2013): 190–207.

15. Cushing, *Fort Meigs*, 105; E. Wood, *Journal*, 376.

16. Orders to Leftwich, 3 Mar. 1813, *WHH Papers*, 7:653–55.

17. E. Wood, *Journal*, 377–78. The Virginia Brigade's quartermaster, C. W. Gooch, noted that rumors were circulating disparaging Leftwich's character but were "not worthy of your notice." Gooch to Leftwich, 29 Apr. 1813, Leftwich Papers. Leftwich would subsequently be accused by Virginia authorities of failure to account for all the arms and supplies paid for by the Commonwealth. He denied the charges. Gooch to Leftwich, 19 Apr., Leftwich to [?], 12 June, Gooch to VA Gov., 14 Aug. 1813, Leftwich Papers.

18. WHH to Meigs, 8 Apr., to Shelby, 9 Apr., to Armstrong, 21 Apr. 1813, *WHH Papers*, 8:11, 14–15, 82.

19. WHH to Armstrong, 17 Mar. 1813, *WHH Papers*, 7:11.

20. Wheaton to Monroe, 26 Apr. 1813, in Rutland et al., *James Madison*, 6:242; WHH to Armstrong, 21 Apr. 1813, *WHH Papers*, 8:83.

21. Forsyth to Howard, 7 May 1813, in Clarence Edwin Carter, ed., *The Territorial Papers of the United States*, 28 vols. (Washington, DC: Government Printing Office, 1934–75), 16:326.

22. Orders to J. H. Piatt, 18 Feb., Morrison to WHH, 9 Apr., 11 Apr. 1813, *WHH Papers*, 7:549, 8:18–20, 22–23. For a look at the trivial problems a general officer encountered, see W. Sprague to WHH, 17 Apr. 1813, *WHH Papers*, 8:58.

23. WHH to Armstrong, 21 Apr. 1813, *WHH Papers*, 8:82. For another critique of Ohio militia officers, see Alexander Bourne, "The Siege of Fort Meigs Year 1813," *Northwest Ohio Quarterly* 17 (Oct. 1945): 139–154, and 18 (Jan. 1946): 39–48.

24. General Orders, 12 Apr., 22 Apr. 1813, *WHH Papers*, 8:26–27, 90–91.

25. Shelby to Armstrong, 21 Feb. 1813, in Knopf, *Document Transcriptions*, 7, pt. 1: 122–23. Shelby amplified these views in a letter to WHH, 27 Mar. 1813, *WHH Papers*, 7:784–86.

26. Monroe to WHH, 17 Jan., Armstrong to WHH, 5 Mar., 7 Mar. 1813, *WHH Papers*, 7:232–34, 663–65, 668–69; Armstrong to Jesup, 9 Mar., to S. Huntington, 1 Apr. 1813, in Knopf, *Document Transcriptions*, 8:132; Hawkins to Sec/War, 14 Feb., Jesup to Armstrong, 27 Mar. 1813, in Knopf, *Document Transcriptions*, 7, pt. 1: 105–8, 198.

27. Armstrong to WHH, 3 Apr. 1813, *WHH Papers*, 7:832–34. The seven infantry regi-

ments in the Eighth Military District were the 1st, 17th, 19th, 24th, 26th, 27th, and the Regiment of Riflemen.

28. WHH to Armstrong, 17 Mar. 1813, *WHH Papers*, 7:706–13, quotation on 712.

29. Armstrong Orders, 17 Mar. 1813, *WHH Papers*, 7:704.

30. M. D. Hardin to Clay, 7 July 1813, in Rutland et al., *James Madison*, 1:809; Jackson to W. B. Lewis, 9 Apr., to Armstrong, 24 Apr. 1813, in Sam B. Smith et al., *The Papers of Andrew Jackson*, 8 vols. to date (Knoxville: University of Tennessee Press, 1980–), 2:401–3; WHH to Armstrong, 17 Mar. 1813, *WHH Papers*, 7:706–13.

31. WHH to Armstrong, 27 Mar. 1813, *WHH Papers*, 7:766–71, quotation on 767.

32. WHH to Armstrong, 30 Mar. 1813, *WHH Papers*, 7:802–3.

33. WHH to Wingate, to Stoddard, to Armstrong, to Leftwich, 30 Mar. 1813, *WHH Papers*, 7:800–803, 805, 807.

34. Crooks to WHH, 31 Mar. 1813, *WHH Papers*, 7:811–12.

35. WHH to Armstrong, 21 Apr. 1813, *WHH Papers*, 8:83.

36. Armstrong to WHH, 11 Apr., 18 Apr., WHH to Cushing, 24 Apr. 1813, *WHH Papers*, 8:22–23, 60, 107.

37. Shelby to WHH, 27 Mar., 4 Apr. 1813, *WHH Papers*, 7:784–87, 839–40. The reports on Dudley's defeat turned Henry Clay against Harrison for a brief time, until details of the incident became more definitive. Clay to M. D. Hardin, 26 May 1813, in Hopkins et al., *Henry Clay*, 1:799. The Dudley defeat and massacre are described later in the chapter.

38. Johnston to WHH, 31 Mar. 1813, *WHH Papers*, 7:814–16.

39. WHH to Armstrong, 17 Apr., 21 Apr., Wingate to WHH, 19 Apr., WHH to Wingate, 24 Apr., WHH to Johnston, 4 Mar., 24 Apr., Wingate to WHH, 28 May 1813, *WHH Papers*, 7:659, 8:51–52, 73–74, 84, 101, 104, 327–28. On Indians as auxiliaries, see also Shelby to WHH, 27 Mar. 1813, *WHH Papers*, 7:786.

40. Tupper to Meigs, 26 Jan. 1813, in Knopf, *Document Transcriptions*, 2:116; Jeff L. Patrick, ed., "'We Lay There Doing Nothing': John Jackson's Recollection of the War of 1812," *Indiana Magazine of History* 38 (June 1992): 125.

41. J. Johnston to WHH, 4 Feb., Speech at Indian Council, 21 June 1813, *WHH Papers*, 7:417, 8:429–30. On Tarhe, see John P. Bowes, "Transformation and Transition: American Indians and the War of 1812 in the Lower Great Lakes," *Journal of Military History* 76 (Oct. 2012): 1129–46.

42. Speech of Shawnee chiefs, 17 July, Stickney to WHH, 18 July 1813, *WHH Papers*, 8:547–49, 557–60.

43. General Orders, 12 Apr. 1813, *WHH Papers*, 8:26–27. For more detail on this vessel, see Robert Malcomson and Thomas Malcomson, *HMS Detroit: The Battle of Lake Erie* (Annapolis, MD: Naval Institute Press, 1990).

44. WHH to Green Clay, 26 Mar., 1 Apr., 8 Apr., 13 Apr., WHH to J. Wingate, 8 Apr., WHH to Gov. Meigs, 8 Apr., WHH to Gov. Shelby, 9 Apr., WHH to Armstrong, 14 Apr., Shelby to WHH, 18 Apr. 1813, *WHH Papers*, 7:765, 823, 8:3–4, 7–8, 11, 14–15, 33–34, 71–72. For R. M. Johnson's proposal for mounted riflemen, see Johnson to Madison, [ca. 10] Dec. 1812, in Rutland et al., *James Madison*, 5:491–94.

45. On R. M. Johnson's receiving authorization to raise such a regiment, see Johnson to WHH, 28 Feb., 25 Mar. 1813, *WHH Papers*, 7:640–41, 759–62.

46. Morrison to WHH, 31 Mar., WHH to Shelby, 1 Apr. 1813, *WHH Papers*, 7:819, 825.

47. Armstrong to Cass, 28 Apr., WHH to Armstrong, 28 Apr., General Orders, 29 Apr. 1813, *WHH Papers*, 8:133–35, 137, 143.

48. McAfee, *History*, 277–83; Shelby to WHH, 20 Mar. 1813, *WHH Papers*, 7:733–37; Cochrane, "War in Canada," 32–33; P. L. Rainwater, ed., "The Siege of Fort Meigs," *Mississippi Valley Historical Review* 19 (1932): 261–64; Bourne, "Siege of Fort Meigs"; Antal, *Wampum Denied*, 221–23; Nelson, *Men of Patriotism*, 67–70; E. Wood, "Journal," 388–89.

49. McAfee, *History*, 392–93.

50. E. Wood, "Journal," 285–86; WHH to Armstrong, 5 May 1813, *WHH Papers*, 8:177–79; Johnson to Armstrong, 28 Mar. 1813, in Knopf, *Document Transcriptions*, 7, pt. 1: 201.

51. For a brief account of Colonel. Miller's sortie, see Private Nathaniel Vernon's memoir in John C. Fredriksen, ed., *The War of 1812 in Person: Fifteen Accounts by the United States Army Regulars, Volunteers, and Militiamen* (Jefferson, NC: McFarland, 2010), 302–4.

52. WHH to Tipton, 6 Dec. 1833, in Logan Esarey, ed., *Messages and Letters of William Henry Harrison*, 2 vols. (Indianapolis: Indiana Historical Society, 1922), 2:747.

53. Cochrane, "War in Canada," 33–36; John Richardson, *Richardson's War of 1812* (Toronto: Historical Publishing, 1902), 148–56. The commanders' after-action reports are in Procter to Prevost, 14 May 1813, in W. Wood, *Select British Documents*, 2:33–37; and Clay to WHH, 9 May, General Orders, 9 May, WHH to Armstrong, 9 May 1813, *WHH Papers*, 8:205–7, 218–22, 226–29. The best secondary accounts are Larry L. Nelson, "Dudley's Defeat and the Relief of Fort Meigs during the War of 1812," *Register of the Kentucky Historical Society* 104 (2006): 5–42; Nelson, *Men of Patriotism*, 67–86, Alec R. Gilpin, *The War of 1812 in the Old Northwest* (East Lansing: Michigan State University Press, 1958), 179–91; Antal, *Wampum Denied*, 218–36; and John Sugden, *Tecumseh: A Life* (New York: Henry Holt, 1997), 325–39.

54. Wingate to WHH, 15 June 1813, *WHH Papers*, 8:399–403.

55. *Cincinnati Liberty Hall*, 25 May 1813; WHH to Meigs, 6 May 1813, *WHH Papers*, 8:189.

56. WHH to Procter, 7 May, Articles of Agreement, 7 May 1813, *WHH Papers*, 8:198–99.

57. Procter to Prevost, 14 May 1813, General Order, 21 May 1813, in W. Wood, *Select British Documents*, 2:33–40.

58. General Orders, 9 May 1813, *WHH Papers*, 8:218; Sugden, *Tecumseh*, 339.

59. Shelby to H. Clay, 16 May 1813, in Rutland et al., *James Madison*, 6:316–18. Former U.S. senator Jonathan Dayton of New Jersey also wrote Madison, 26 May 1813, suggesting revisions in Harrison's operations; in Rutland et al., *James Madison*, 6:345–46.

60. Morrison to WHH, 22 Feb. 1813, *WHH Papers*, 7:587–88.

61. See David Curtis Skaggs, *Oliver Hazard Perry: Honor, Courage, and Patriotism in the Early U.S. Navy* (Annapolis, MD: Naval Institute Press, 2006), 80–84.

62. WHH to Armstrong, 19 May, General Orders, 20 May, 5 June, 11 June, Armstrong to WHH, 31 May 1813, *WHH Papers*, 8:283–84, 289, 333, 344, 358–62.

63. Orders to Piatt, 18 June, WHH to Orr, 20 June 1813, *WHH Papers*, 8:413, 424. On logistical problems, see also R. M. Johnson to Madison, 9 Aug. 1813, in Rutland et al., *James Madison*, 6:504–6.

64. WHH to Armstrong, 23 May, 8 June, Johnson to WHH, 23 May, 25 May, General Order, 11 June, Disposition of General Court-Martial, 12 June 1813, *WHH Papers*, 8:296–97, 300–301, 311–12, 351, 358–65, 376.

65. Armstrong to WHH, 9 June, Johnson to WHH, 4 July, 9 July, WHH to Armstrong, 9 July, Armstrong to WHH, 14 July 1813, *WHH Papers*, 8:355, 500–501, 515, 523–27, 539, 541; Johnson to Madison, 14 July 1813, in Rutland et al., *James Madison*, 6:438.

66. WHH to Johnson, 11 June, to Armstrong, 11 June 1813, *WHH Papers*, 8:366–69, 372–74.

67. Stickney to WHH, 18 July 1813, *WHH Papers*, 8:560.

68. WHH to Armstrong, 23 May, 8 June, WHH to Howard, 24 May, WHH to Buntin, 25 May, WHH to Purdy, 25 May, Anderson to WHH, 26 May, WHH to Armstrong, 26 May, Jesup to WHH, 26 May, WHH to Dearborn, 13 June 1813, *WHH Papers*, 8:296–97, 302–4, 308–9, 313–14, 316–17, 321–22, 352, 385.

69. WHH to Armstrong, 15 June, 18 June, 23 June 1813, *WHH Papers*, 8:397, 416, 443.

70. WHH to Howard, 24 May 1813, *WHH Papers*, 8:304.

71. Clay to WHH, 20 June, Orders to Perry, 23 June, WHH to Jesup, 27 June, WHH to Armstrong, 24 June 1813, *WHH Papers*, 8:418–20, 449, 454, 463.

72. Orr to WHH, 22 June, WHH to Orr, 22 June, WHH to Armstrong, 24 June 1813, *WHH Papers*, 8:433–36, 454.

73. WHH to Clay, 26 June 1813, *WHH Papers*, 8:461.

74. Procter to McDouall, 16 June 1813, quoted in George F. G. Stanley, *The War of 1812: Land Operations* (Toronto: Macmillan of Canada, 1983), 156.

75. Richard J. Wright, ed., *The John Hunt Memoirs* (Maumee, OH: Maumee Valley Historical Association, 1977), 25; McAfee, *History*, 322.

76. Procter to Prevost, 9 Aug. 1813, in W. Wood, *Select British Documents*, 2:44–47.

77. WHH to Armstrong, 2 July, to Bartlet, 2 July 1813, *WHH Papers*, 8:484–86, 493.

78. Huntington to Monroe, 14 Jan., Johnson to Armstrong, 31 Mar., McArthur and Cass to Armstrong, 31 Mar. 1813, in Knopf, *Document Transcriptions*, 7, pt. 1: 30, 208–9; Armstrong to WHH, 14 July, WHH to Shelby, 20 July, WHH to Bryson, 21 July, WHH to Meigs, 6 Aug., Shelby to WHH, 2 Aug. 1813, *WHH Papers*, 8:541, 573–74, 589, 674–75; Madison to Shelby, 12 Aug., Madison's notes, 23 Aug. 1813, in Rutland et al., *James Madison*, 6:513, 552.

79. Armstrong to WHH, 14 July, Order to Hill, 23 July 1813, *WHH Papers*, 8:541, 592, 729–30.

80. Clay to WHH, 22 July, WHH to McArthur, 22 July, WHH to Meigs, 22 July 1813, *WHH Papers*, 8:583, 587, 590.

81. Richardson, *War of 1812*, 178; Procter to Prevost, 9 Aug. 1813, in W. Wood, *Select British Documents*, 2:44; Clay to WHH, 26 July, 28 July, 1 Aug., WHH to Armstrong, 28 July 1813, *WHH Papers*, 8:611, 618, 620–21, 644, 676–80; Cushing, *Fort Meigs*, 134–39; "Daniel Sibert's Reminiscences of the War of 1812—Letters to His Brother Jeremiah Sibert," *Register of the Kentucky State Historical Society* 36 (1938): 66–71. Secondary accounts include Larry L. Nelson, "'A Mysterious and Ambiguous Display of Tactics': The Second Siege of Fort Meigs, July 21–28, 1813," *Ohio History* 120 (2013): 5–28; Nelson, *Men of Patriotism*, 101–11; Gilpin, *War of 1812*, 201–5; Sugden, *Tecumseh*, 346–49; Quimby, *U.S. Army*, 1:204–6; Stanley, *War of 1812*, 156–58; and Antal, *Wampum Denied*, 252–55.

82. Clay to WHH, 1 Aug. 1813, *WHH Papers*, 8:644.

83. Orders to Croghan, 29 July, Croghan to WHH, 30 July, 3 Aug. 1813, *WHH Papers*, 8:633, 636, 683.

84. Orders to Croghan, 30 July, WHH to Shelby, 2 Aug. 1813, *WHH Papers*, 8:639, 672; Alfred Brunson, *A Western Pioneer*, 2 vols. (Cincinnati: Hitchcock and Walden, 1872), 116–19.

85. Cushing, *Fort Meigs*, 139.

86. Procter to Prevost, 9 Aug., 3 Sept. 1813, in W. Wood, *Select British Documents*, 2:44–47, 50–51; Croghan to WHH, 3 Aug., 5 Aug., WHH to Armstrong, 4 Aug. 1813, *WHH Papers*, 8:683, 695–701, quotations on 697, 714–17. Secondary accounts of the Fort Stephenson battle are in Bruce Bowlus, "A 'Signal Victory': The Battle for Fort Stephenson, August 1–2, 1813," *Northwest Ohio Quarterly* 63 (summer/autumn 1991): 43–57; Gilpin, *War of 1812*, 205–8; Antal, *Wampum Denied*, 254–63; Quimby, *U.S. Army*, 1:208–11; and Stanley, *War of 1812*, 158–61.

87. WHH to Armstrong, 4 Aug. 1813, *WHH Papers*, 8:700.

88. Jones to Madison, 11 Aug. 1813, in Rutland et al., *James Madison*, 6:511.

89. On the operational expectations of the Navy and War Departments, see Armstrong to WHH, 4 Aug. 1813, *WHH Papers*, 8:700; Jones to Perry, 3 July 1813, in William S. Dudley and Michael J. Crawford, eds., *The Naval War of 1812: A Documentary History*, 3 vols. to date (Washington, DC: Naval Historical Center, 1985–), 2:487–88.

CHAPTER SIX: **Invading Canada**

1. Alfred Brunson, *A Western Pioneer*, 2 vols. (Cincinnati: Hitchcock and Walden, 1872), 1:121. Similar sentiments are found in Eleazer D. Wood, "Journal of the Northwestern Campaign of 1812–13," in George W. Cullum, ed., *Campaigns of the War of 1812–15* (New York: James Miller, 1879), 404–7; and Robert B. McAfee, *History of the Late War in the Western Country* (Bowling Green, OH: Historical Publications Co., 1919 [1816]), 304–5, 390.

2. Regulations, 8 Apr. 1813, in Richard C. Knopf, ed., *Document Transcriptions of the War of 1812 in the Northwest*, 10 vols.(Columbus, OH: Anthony Wayne Parkway Board and Ohio State Historical Society, 1957–62), 8:141.

3. John Norris to A. S. Goodman, 27 Mar. 1869, in Knopf, *Document Transcriptions*, 10:157. In one case, Lt. James Coburn of Capt. John Paine's troop of Kentucky cavalry led fifteen of his men on the *Caledonia*. These "horse marines" later brought the British ship *General Hunter* to Put-in-Bay.

4. WHH to Perry, 23 July 1813, in Douglas E. Clanin et al., eds., *The Papers of William Henry Harrison, 1800–1815*, 10 microfilm reels (Indianapolis: Indiana Historical Society, 1993–1999), 8:597 (hereafter, *WHH Papers*).

5. WHH to Perry, 23 July, Perry to WHH, 5 Aug. 1813, *WHH Papers*, 8:597, 727.

6. WHH to Armstrong, 22 Aug. 1813, *WHH Papers*, 9:17–18; Samuel Hambleton Diary, 17 Aug., 22 Aug. 1813, MS 983, Maryland Historical Society, Baltimore, MD; John C. Fredriksen, ed., *Surgeon of the Lakes: The Diary of Dr. Usher Parsons, 1812–1814* (Erie, PA: Erie County Historical Society, 2000), 46–47.

7. Madison to Armstrong, 8 Sept., Jones to Madison, 23 Aug. 1813, in Robert A. Rutland et al., eds., *The Papers of James Madison: Presidential Series*, 7 vols. to date (Charlottesville: University Press of Virginia, 1984–), 6:556, 601–2.

8. Perry to WHH, 10 Sept., to Jones, 10 Sept. 1813. in William S. Dudley and Michael

J. Crawford, eds., *The Naval War of 1812: A Documentary History*, 3 vols. to date (Washington, DC: Department of the Navy, 1985–), 2:553–54; John Norris to A. T. Goodman, 7 Apr. 1869, in Knopf, *Document Transcriptions*, 10:158. On the battle of Lake Erie, see David Curtis Skaggs and Gerard T. Altoff, *A Signal Victory: The Lake Erie Campaign, 1812–1813* (Annapolis, MD: Naval Institute Press, 1997), 118–48; Ernest A. Cruikshank, "The Contest for the Command of Lake Erie in 1812–13," in Morris Zaslow, ed., *The Defended Border: Upper Canada in the War of 1812* (Toronto: Macmillan, 1964), 84–104; Jeff Seiken, "'To Obtain Command of the Lakes': The United States and the Contest for Lakes Erie and Ontario, 1812–1815," in David Curtis Skaggs and Larry L. Nelson, eds., *The Sixty Years' War for the Great Lakes, 1754–1814* (East Lansing: Michigan State University Press, 2001), 353–72; Walter R. Rybka, "Observations on the Sailing Characteristics of the U.S. Brig *Niagara*," in David Curtis Skaggs, *The Battle of Lake Erie and Its Aftermath* (Kent, OH: Kent State University Press, 2013), 236–49. More than a week after Perry's victory, news of it had not yet reached Washington. Madison to Armstrong, 18 Sept. 1813, in Rutland et al., *James Madison*, 6:636.

9. Department of Defense, *Dictionary of Military and Associated Terms*, Joint Pub. 1–02 (Washington, DC: Department of Defense, 2001), 295.

10. Armed Forces Staff College, *The Joint Staff Officer's Guide*, AFSC Pub. 1 (Norfolk, VA: Armed Forces Staff College, 1991), 1–3; Maurice Matloff, ed., *American Military History* (Washington, DC: Office of the Chief of Military History, 1969), 9.

11. Defense, *Dictionary*, 585. See also Department of the Army, *Operations*, FM 100–5 (Washington, DC: Department of the Army, 1976), 2–6 to 2–8. In effect, Harrison and Perry developed a joint task force that "performs missions having specific, limited objectives or missions of short duration. It dissolves when it has achieved its purpose." Army, *Operations*, 15–3. For early nineteenth-century doctrine on service command distinctions, see War Department Regulation, 8 Apr. 1813, in Knopf, *Document Transcriptions*, 8:141.

12. William S. Dudley, "Commodore Isaac Chauncey and U.S. Joint Operations on Lake Ontario, 1813–14," in William B. Cogan, ed., *New Interpretations in Naval History: Selected Papers from the Eighth Naval History Symposium* (Annapolis, MD: Naval Institute Press, 1989), 139–55.

13. Circular, Hamilton to Selected Officers, 20 June 1812, in Dudley and Crawford, *Naval War*, 1:140; Monroe to WHH, 26 Dec. 1812, *WHH Papers*, 7:63–69.

14. WHH to Eustis, 12 Dec. 1812, *WHH Papers*, 6:791.

15. Armstrong to WHH, 5 Mar. 1813, *WHH Papers*, 7:663–65. Secondary sources include Frederick C. Drake, "Loss of Mastery: The British Squadron on Lake Erie, May–September 1813," *Journal of Erie Studies* 17 (fall 1989): 54–57; and Howard S. Miller and Jack Alden Clarke, "Ships in the Wilderness: A Note on the Invasion of Canada," *Ohio History* 71 (July 1962): 124–28.

16. WHH to Armstrong, 15 Sept. 1813, in Rutland et al., *James Madison*, 6:631. The editorial notes on this letter indicate it was received in Washington on 22 September, when copies were sent to Madison and Armstrong. By the time Armstrong received it, Harrison was in Upper Canada. The secretary was giving directions for WHH's movements on Lake Erie after the general had arrived at Buffalo. Armstrong to Madison, 20 Oct. 1813, in Rutland et al., *James Madison*, 6:705–6.

17. Reginald Horsman, *Matthew Elliott, British Indian Agent* (Detroit: Wayne State University Press, 1964), 211–14; Timothy D. Willig, *Restoring the Chair of Friendship: British Policy and the Indians of the Great Lakes, 1783–1815* (Lincoln: University of Nebraska Press, 2008), 253–54.

18. Procter to de Rottenburg, 12 Sept. 1813, in William C. H. Wood, ed., *Select British Documents of the Canadian War of 1812*, 3 vols. (Toronto: Champlain Society, 1920–28), 2:272–73.

19. J. Harvey to Procter, 17 Sept., Prevost to Procter, 23 Sept. 1813, in W. Wood, *Select British Documents*, 2:282, 284–85; James Cochrane, "The War in Canada, 1812–1814" (unpublished MS, ca. 1840), 55–59, Welsh Regimental Museum, Cardiff Castle, South Wales, UK; Horsman, *Matthew Elliott*, 212.

20. McAfee, *History*, 400–404.

21. Madison to Armstrong, 18 Sept. 1813, in Rutland et al., *James Madison*, 6:636.

22. General Order, 8 Aug. 1813, *WHH Papers*, 8:746.

23. McAfee, *History*, 379–81, 391–400; Armstrong to WHH, 8 May 1813, *WHH Papers*, 8:202.

24. D. Parker (for Armstrong) to Shelby, 27 Sept. 1813, in Knopf, *Document Transcriptions*, 8:159–60; Madison to Shelby, 12 Aug. 1813, in Rutland et al., *James Madison*, 6:513.

25. McAfee, *History*, 328–29.

26. Ibid., 375.

27. Brunson, *Western Pioneer*, 1:129; McAfee, *History*, 391–95.

28. Brunson, *Western Pioneer*, 1:129; Stanton Sholes, "A Narrative of the Northwestern Campaign of 1813," M. M. Quaife, ed., *Mississippi Valley Historical Review* 15 (1929): 522.

29. General Orders, 27 Sept. 1813, directing the joint landings on the shore south of Ft. Malden, *WHH Papers*, 9:273–78. For secondary accounts on army-navy cooperation, see David Curtis Skaggs, "Joint Operations during the Detroit–Lake Erie Campaign, 1813," in William Cogar, ed., *New Interpretations in Naval History: Selected Papers from the Eighth Naval History Symposium of the U.S. Naval Academy* (Annapolis, MD: Naval Institute Press, 1989), 121–38; and Skaggs, "River Raisin Redeemed: William Henry Harrison, Oliver Hazard Perry and the Midwestern Campaign, 1813," *Northwest Ohio History* 77 (spring 2010): 67–84.

30. Harrison's General Orders, 27 Sept. 1813, *WHH Papers*, 9:273–79; Perry to Officers in Charge of Prime Vessels, 22 Sept. 1813, Order Book, Lake Erie, 1813, Perry Papers, William L. Clements Library, University of Michigan, Ann Arbor, MI; Eleazer D. Wood, *Journal of the Northwestern Campaign of 1812–1813*, Robert B. Boehm and Randall L. Buchman, eds. (Defiance, OH: Defiance College, 1975), 31; McAfee, *History*, 391–400; Sholes, "Narrative," 522–23.

31. Perry to J. E. McDonald, to Thomas Holdup, to Senat, 2 Oct., in Order Book, Lake Erie, 1813, Perry to Jones, 20 Oct. 1813, Perry Papers; WHH to Armstrong, 9 Oct. 1813, *WHH Papers*, 9:323–34.

32. McAfee, *History*, 411–12; Harrison's After-Action Report to Armstrong, 9 Oct. 1813, *WHH Papers*, 9:323–34.

33. McAfee, *History*, 406–10; Johnson to Madison, 27 Sept. 1813, in Rutland et al., *James Madison*, 6:660.

34. McAfee, *History*, 400, 408.

35. For Procter's slow departure from the Detroit River area after Perry's 10 September 1813 defeat of the British naval squadron on Lake Erie, see Sandy Antal, *A Wampum Denied: Procter's War of 1812*, Carleton Library Series, vol. 191 (Ottawa: Carleton University Press, 1997), 297–309; George F. G. Stanley, *The War of 1812: Land Operations*, Canadian War Museum Historical Publication no. 18 (Toronto: Macmillan of Canada, 1983), 204–9.

36. McAfee, *History*, 411–12.

37. Freeman Cleaves, *Old Tippecanoe: William Henry Harrison and His Times* (New York: Charles Scribner's Sons, 1939), 234–37.

38. Madison to Armstrong, 11 Oct. 1813, in Rutland et al., *James Madison*, 6:688.

39. Perry to Senat, 2 Oct. 1812, in Order Book, Lake Erie, 1813, Perry to Jones, 20 Oct. 1813, Perry Papers; Lewis Bond, "Journal of Battle and Massacre of the River Raisin, January 22 & 23, 1813, and of the War of 1812," in Knopf, *Document Transcriptions*, 10:210–11.

40. McArthur to Armstrong, 6 Oct. 1813, in Knopf, *Document Transcriptions*, 5, pt. 2: 237. A fine secondary account of the movement of both armies up the Thames River Valley is in Fred Coyne Hamil, *The Valley of the Lower Thames, 1640–1850* (Toronto: University of Toronto Press 1951), 82–95.

41. Cochrane, "War in Canada," 59, 61; McAfee, *History*, 417.

42. McAfee, *History*, 416–17.

43. Ibid., 413–18; Cochrane, "War in Canada," 59–61. McAfee's journal for October provides a solid primary account of the pursuit. Book and Journal of Robert B. McAfee's Mounted Company, Kentucky Historical Society, Frankfort, KY.

44. Procter to de Rottenburg, 23 Oct., 16 Nov. 1813, in W. Wood, *Select British Documents*, 2:323–27, 338–41; McAfee, *History*, 417–18.

45. On the background to the Moravian mission, see John P. Bowes, "The Gnadenhutten Effect: Moravian Converts and the Search for Safety in the Canadian Borderlands," *Michigan Historical Review* 34 (spring 2008): 101–17.

46. Cochrane, "War in Canada," 60–62.

47. WHH to Armstrong, 30 Sept., 9 Oct., 11 Oct. 1813, *WHH Papers*, 9:294, 330–33, 355; WHH to Meigs, 11 Oct. 1813, *WHH Papers*, 9:356–57.

48. Cochrane, "War in Canada," 63. Throughout his discussion of the engagement, Lieutenant Cochrane has nothing but derisive comments on Procter's command competence. For an opposite opinion, see Victor Lauriston, "The Case for General Procter," in Zaslow, *Defended Border*, 121–29; and Antal, *Wampum Denied*, 315–28.

49. John Grenier, *The First Way of War: American War Making on the Frontier* (New York: Cambridge University Press, 2005), 102–14; Jonathon Riley, *A Matter of Honour: The Life, Campaigns, and Generalship of Isaac Brock* (Montreal: Robin Brass, 2011), 16–20.

50. WHH to Armstrong, 9 Oct. 1813, *WHH Papers*, 9:323–34; WHH to Benjamin Drake, "Defence of His Conduct, & Mode of Conducting the Thames Campaign of 1813," ca. 1840, Draper MSS (123 microfilm reels), 62:48, Wisconsin Historical Society, Madison, WI; Procter to de Rottenburg, 23 Oct. 1813, in W. Wood, *Select British Documents*, 2:323–27.

51. WHH to Armstrong, 9 Oct. 1813, *WHH Papers*, 9:328–29.

52. While most accounts give this force a mission of moving between the river and the road to seize the enemy cannon located on the road, Sergeant Brunson of the 27th Infantry makes clear that Harrison intended this force as a reserve. Brunson, *Western Pioneer*, 1:139.

53. Procter to de Rottenburg, 23 Oct. 1813, in W. Wood, *Select British Documents*, 2:326. According to the 9 Oct. 1813 letter of Maj. Thomas Toland of the 27th U.S. Infantry, "The British Officers are cursing Proctor for a coward and a rascal." *Washington, DC, National Intelligencer*, 17 Nov. 1813.

54. Samuel R. Brown, *Views of the Campaigns of the North-Western Army* (Troy, NY: Francis Adancourt, 1814), 74.

55. WHH to Armstrong, 9 Oct. 1813, *WHH Papers*, 9:323–34.

56. Johnson's claim to have personally killed the Indian chieftain would lead to the most inane campaign slogan in American history: "Rumpsey dumpsey, rumpsey dumpsey, Colonel Johnson killed Tecumseh." Regardless of who killed Tecumseh, there is no doubt that he died at the hand of one of Johnson's men. John O'Fallon, WHH's aide at the time of the battle, later claimed that Colonel Johnson was wounded near where Tecumseh was killed. But there was no direct witness to Johnson's having personally killed Tecumseh. O'Fallon said that, in 1818, a friend of Johnson had asked him, "Admitting that Col. Johnson killed an Indian (which I never doubted) was there not a greater probability that he had killed Tecumseh than any other person, to which I [O'Fallon] replied in the affirmative because I had never doubted that Col. Johnson was engaged and received his wound near about the spot where I saw Tecumsehs body." O'Fallon to WHH, 21 Apr. 1834, John O'Fallon Papers, Filson Historical Society, Louisville, KY. However, no positive identification of Tecumseh's body was made on the field, as WHH was the only American present who had met the Shawnee warrior, and he could not identify Tecumseh from among the thirty-three dead on the battlefield. WHH to Tipton, 2 May 1834, in Logan Eseray, ed., *Messages and Letters of William Henry Harrison*, 2 vols. (Indianapolis: Indiana Historical Commission, 1911), 2:749–55. See also Lowell H. Harrison, "Nat Crain and the Battle of the Thames," *Filson Club History Quarterly* 64 (July 1990): 377–83; Crain asserted that Tecumseh's killer was Pvt. Joshua Brown (381–82).

57. For secondary sources on the Thames campaign, see Antal, *Wampum Denied*, 297–353; Stanley, *War of 1812*, 201–14; John Sugden, *Tecumseh: A Life* (New York: Henry Holt, 1997), 368–80; Robert S. Quimby, *The U.S. Army in the War of 1812: An Operational and Command Study*, 2 vols. (East Lansing: Michigan State University Press, 1997), 1:270–92; Cleaves, *Old Tippecanoe*, 188–205; James Hanny, *History of the War of 1812 between Great Britain and the United States of America* (Toronto: Morang, 1905), 195–201; Katherine B. Coutts, "Thamesville and the Battle of the Thames," in Zaslow, *Defended Border*, 114–20; Dennis Carter-Edwards, "The War of 1812 along the Detroit Frontier: A Canadian Perspective," *Michigan Historical Review* 13 (fall 1987): 25–50; and Marshall Smelser, "Tecumseh, Harrison, and the War of 1812," *Indiana Magazine of History* 65 (1969): 25–44. An undocumented and sometimes erroneous survey of the 1812–14 campaigns in the region is in Fred C. Hamil, "Michigan in the War of 1812," *Michigan History* 44 (Sept. 1960): 257–91.

58. WHH to Armstrong, 9 Oct. 1813, *WHH Papers*, 9:323–34; Procter to de Rottenburg, 23 Oct., 16 Nov. 1813, in W. Wood, *Select British Documents*, 2:323–27, 338–41.

59. McAfee, *History*, 435–36.

60. A Proclamation, 17 Oct. 1813, *WHH Papers*, 9:435–36.

61. Mark Grimsley in Robert A. Doughty et al., *American Military History and the Evolution of Warfare in the Western World* (Lexington, MA: D. C. Heath, 1996), 76.

62. George F. G. Stanley, "The Indians in the War of 1812," *Canadian Historical Review*

31 (June 1950): 145–65, esp. 164–65; Robert S. Allen, *His Majesty's Indian Allies: British Indian Policy in the Defence of Canada, 1774–1815* (Toronto: Dundurn, 1992), 144–46; Colin G. Calloway, *Crown and Calumet: British-Indian Relations 1783–1815* (Norman: University of Oklahoma Press, 1987), 248–50; Gregory Evans Dowd, *A Spirited Resistance: The North American Indian Struggle for Unity, 1745–1815* (Baltimore: Johns Hopkins University Press, 1992), 184–85; Richard White, *The Middle Ground: Indians, Empires, and Republics in the Great Lakes Region, 1650–1815* (New York: Cambridge University Press, 1991), 516–17; Timothy D. Willig, *Restoring the Chain of Friendship: British Policy and the Indians of the Great Lakes, 1783–1815* (Lincoln: University of Nebraska Press, 2008), 243–71; John P. Bowes, "The Late War: Black Hawk and the Legacies of Violence in the Great Lakes Region," in Skaggs, *Battle of Lake Erie*, 143–56.

63. Madison to Armstrong, 11 Oct., Monroe to Madison, 17 Oct. 1813, in Rutland et al., *James Madison*, 6:688–89, 702.

64. H. M. Brackenridge, *History of the Late War between the United States and Great Britain* (Philadelphia: James Kay, 1844 [1816]), 163; Shelby to WHH, 23 Apr. 1814, *WHH Papers*, 10:105.

65. McAfee, *History*, 294.

66. Lewis Cass, "Indians of North America," *North American Review* 22 (1826): 98.

67. Dowd, *Spirited Resistance*, 183.

68. On the experience of the Wyandot during and after the war, see John P. Bowes, "Transformation and Transition: American Indians and the War of 1812 in the Lower Great Lakes," *Journal of Military History* 76 (Oct. 2012): 1143–46. On the Sauk, see Bowes, "The Late War," in Skaggs, *Battle of Lake Erie*, 143–56. On the Delaware, see Daniel P. Barr, "Odyssey's End: The Battle of Lake Erie and the Failure of the Delaware Indian Struggle for Autonomy," in Skaggs, *Battle of Lake Erie*, 101–25.

CHAPTER SEVEN: **The Politics of Victory**

1. Shelby to Armstrong, 19 Nov. 1813, in Richard C. Knopf, ed., *Document Transcriptions of the War of 1812 in the Northwest*, 10 vols. (Columbus: Ohio Historical Society, 1957–62), 7, pt. 3: 105–6.

2. Lewis Bond, "Journal of Battle and Massacre of the River Raisin, January 22 & 23, 1813, and of the War of 1812," in Knopf, *Document Transcriptions*, 10, pt. 1: 207–10; Cass to Armstrong, 28 Oct. 1813, in Knopf, *Document Transcriptions*, 7, pt. 3: 99; WHH to Johnston, 15 Oct., WHH to Gano, 16 Oct., Gano to WHH, 15 Oct. 1813, in Douglas E. Clanin et al., eds., *The Papers of William Henry Harrison, 1800–1815*, 10 microfilm reels (Indianapolis: Indiana Historical Society, 1993–99), 9:394, 402, 408 (hereafter, *WHH Papers*). The problems of supply are also illustrated in Cass to Armstrong, 4 Dec., 11 Dec. 1813, in Knopf, *Document Transcriptions*, 10, pt. 1: 115–16, 118–19.

3. WHH to Armstrong, 10 Oct., to Meigs, 11 Oct., General Orders, 12 Oct. 1813, *WHH Papers*, 9:342–45, 356–57, 366–68. For Harrison's orders concerning Shelby's troops, see WHH to Gano, 12 Oct., General Orders, 13 Oct. 1813, *WHH Papers*, 9:376–77.

4. Smith to WHH, [12 Oct.], WHH to Armstrong, 16 Oct., Notice to the Kentucky Militia, 23 Oct. 1813, *WHH Papers*, 9:374, 410–11, 451–52. As described in chapter 6, rather than the ships being destroyed, the crews had thrown the cargo overboard to lighten the

ships in a storm, and the vessels were driven ashore near Buffalo, New York. The same storm on Lake Huron nearly destroyed the Royal Navy schooner *Nancy* on the Canadian lee shore, near Manitoulin Island. Even though its officers and crew were familiar with the lake, the vessel nearly foundered in the high seas. Barry Gough, *Fighting Sail on Lake Huron and Georgian Bay: The War of 1812 and Its Aftermath* (Annapolis, MD: Naval Institute Press, 2002), 62–64. Perry and Harrison's decision to forgo the Mackinac expedition was clearly well advised.

5. On Harrison's negotiations with Native Americans while governor, see Robert M. Owens, *Mr. Jefferson's Hammer: William Henry Harrison and the Origins of American Indian Policy* (Norman: University of Oklahoma Press, 2007).

6. Armistice Agreement, [14 Oct.], WHH to Armstrong, 16 Oct. 1813, *WHH Papers*, 9:384–86, 410–11.

7. Cass to Armstrong, 4 Dec., 17 Dec., Parker to Cass, 2 Dec. 1813, in Knopf, *Document Transcriptions*, 7, pt. 3: 115–16, 123, and 8:166.

8. Journal of Treaty Negotiations, 21 July 1814, *WHH Papers*, 10:341–44.

9. Protection order, 15 Oct., General Orders, 17 Oct., WHH-Perry Proclamation, [18 Oct.], General Orders [extract], 18 Oct. 1813, *WHH Papers*, 9:401, 418–19, 435, 439.

10. Woodward to Procter, 2 Feb., 10 Feb. 1813, in Knopf, *Document Transcriptions*, 5:202–3; General Orders, 17 Oct., WHH-Perry Proclamation, [18 Oct.] 1813, *WHH Papers*, 9:418–19, 435–36. On Cass's career, see Willard C. Klunder, *Lewis Cass and the Politics of Moderation* (Kent, OH: Kent State University Press, 1996).

11. Dave R. Palmer, *1794: America, Its Army, and the Birth of the Nation* (Novato, CA: Presidio Press, 1994).

12. Primary sources on the Tippecanoe campaign include the anti-Harrison letter of Col. John P. Boyd and Capt. George W. Prescott to Secretary of War Eustis, 11 Dec. 1811, printed in the *Washington (DC) National Intelligencer*, 11 Jan. 1812, and the *Vincennes Western Sun*, 8 Feb. 1812, and reprinted in Knopf, *Document Transcriptions*, 5, pt. 1: 39–40. Harrison's 18 Nov. 1811 report on the battle is in Knopf, *Document Transcriptions*, 5, pt. 1: 22–28. See also Samuel G. Hopkins to WHH, 15 Jan. 1812, in Clarence Edwin Carter, ed., *Territorial Papers of the United States*, 28 vols. (Washington, DC: Government Printing Office, 1934–75), 8:161–62.

13. Alfred Brunson, *A Western Pioneer*, 2 vols. (Cincinnati: Hitchcock and Walden, 1872), 1:108–42; "Daniel Sibert's Reminiscences of the War of 1812," *Register of the Kentucky State Historical Society* 36 (1938): 66–71.

14. Lowell H. Harrison, ed., "Nat Crain and the Battle of the Thames," *Filson Club History Quarterly* 64 (July 1990): 380.

15. Robert B. McAfee, *History of the Late War in the Western Country* (Bowling Green, OH: Historical Publications Co., 1919 [1816]), 378–79.

16. The standard biography is Sylvia Wrobel and George Grider, *Isaac Shelby: Kentucky's First Governor and Hero of Three Wars* (Danville, KY: Cumberland Press, 1974).

17. Armstrong to WHH, 20 Oct., 30 Oct., 3 Nov. 1813, *WHH Papers*, 9:445, 460–61, 473–77; Parker to Shelby, 27 Sept. 1813, in Knopf, *Document Transcriptions*, 8:158–60, 161–63.

18. WHH to Armstrong, 24 Oct. 1813, *WHH Papers*, 9:453–54.

19. Jonathan Hooks examines this issue in detail in "A Study of the Rivalry between James Madison and John Armstrong" (MA thesis, East Carolina University, 2002).

20. Freeman Cleaves, *Old Tippecanoe: William Henry Harrison and His Time* (New York: Charles Scribner's Sons, 1939), 206–13. On Armstrong's anti-southern biases, see C. Edward Skeen, *John Armstrong, Jr., 1758–1843: A Biography* (Syracuse, NY: Syracuse University Press, 1991), 123.

21. WHH to Armstrong, 22 Oct., 24 Oct. 1813, *WHH Papers*, 9:449, 453–54.

22. There are two versions of this letter in Harrison's papers; Armstrong to WHH, 30 Oct. 1813, *WHH Papers*, 9:460–62 (esp. Clanin's n. 1 on 9:462). Harrison acknowledges receipt of the letter on 30 October, the same day it was supposedly written—an impossibility. Since the secretary was at Wilma, New York (near Watertown), it is entirely possible that the letter was delivered by a fast packet boat and that Harrison did not write the correct date of receipt.

23. WHH to Tompkins, 1 Nov., to Armstrong, 11 Nov. 1813, *WHH Papers*, 9:468–69, 511–13.

24. WHH to Armstrong, 8 Nov. 1813, *WHH Papers*, 9:499–500. Harrison obviously wrote this letter before receiving Armstrong's of 3 November.

25. Armstrong to WHH, 3 Nov. 1813, *WHH Papers*, 9:473–75; Armstrong to Madison, Nov. 1813, in Robert A. Rutland et al., eds., *The Papers of James Madison: Presidential Series*, 7 vols. to date (Charlottesville: University Press of Virginia, 1984–), 7:9.

26. Vincent to de Rottenburg, 15 Nov. 1813, in William C. H. Wood, ed., *Select British Documents of the Canadian War of 1812*, 3 vols. (Toronto: Champlain Society, 1920–28), 2:332–38; P. B. Porter to WHH, 3 Nov. 1813, *WHH Papers*, 9:487–88.

27. McClure to WHH, 15 Nov., WHH to McClure (two letters), 15 Nov. 1813, *WHH Papers*, 9:522–23, 526–27, 530–31; Wilkinson to Armstrong, 7 Jan. 1814, in Rutland et al., *James Madison*, 7:184–85, 186n1.

28. On Gaines, see James W. Silver, *Edmund P. Gaines, 1777–1849* (Baton Rouge: Louisiana State University Press, 1949).

29. Armstrong Order to WHH, 3 Nov. 1813, *WHH Papers*, 9:474.

30. McAfee, *History*, 437–38.

31. *Kentucky Reporter* (Lexington), 21 Dec. 1813.

32. David Buell to his father, 25 Nov. 1813, quoted in Cleaves, *Old Tippecanoe*, 214.

33. *Franklinton (OH) Freeman's Journal*, 16 Dec. 1813; Perry to WHH, [Dec. 1813], *WHH Papers*, 9:602. Henry Dearborn disgraced himself in an abortive campaign toward Montreal in late 1812; James Wilkinson and Wade Hampton failed in their leadership of the St. Lawrence campaign of 1813.

34. WHH to Armstrong, 21 Dec. 1813, *WHH Papers*, 9:573–75.

35. *Philadelphia Aurora*, 20 Mar. 1813, 4 Jan., 11 Jan., 14 Jan. 1814; *Franklinton (OH) Freeman's Chronicle*, 4–7 June 1813. See also WHH to [James Barnes?], 18 Apr. 1813, *WHH Papers* 8:66–670, esp. n. 1.

36. Skeen, *John Armstrong*, 168. Skeen pays little attention to the Armstrong-Harrison relationship.

37. WHH to Armstrong, 21 Dec. 1813, *WHH Papers*, 9:573–75.

38. Howard to War Department, 10 Jan., Armstrong to Howard, 11 Feb. 1813, in Carter, *Territorial Papers*, 14:614–22, 631. Similar sentiments are in Illinois Governor Ninian Edwards to Madison, 16 Jan. 1813, in Carter, *Territorial Papers*, 16:286–88.

39. On the Chauncey-Perry controversy, see David Curtis Skaggs, *Oliver Hazard Perry: Honor, Courage, and Patriotism in the Early U.S. Navy* (Annapolis, MD: Naval Institute Press, 2006), 63–64, 66–67, 71–73, 79–81, 131.

40. Armstrong to Howard, 31 Dec. 1813, in Carter, *Territorial Papers*, 14:724.

41. Clark to Armstrong, 31 July, 18 Dec. 1813, in Carter, *Territorial Papers*, 14:691–92, 723–24.

42. Clark to Armstrong, 6 Jan. 1814, in Carter, *Territorial Papers*, 14:726.

43. Howard to Armstrong, 15 May 1814, in Carter, *Territorial Papers*, 16:423. Howard's letter was written four days after Harrison submitted his resignation, but Howard had no way of knowing of the district commander's decision. A fine secondary account of the Mississippi Valley campaign of 1814 is given in Robert M. Quimby, *The U.S. Army in the War of 1812: An Operational and Command Study*, 2 vols. (East Lansing: Michigan State University Press, 1997), 2:734–37.

44. WHH to Armstrong, 20 Mar., Armstrong to WHH, 21 Apr. 1814, *WHH Papers*, 10:1–2, 88. On the continued discussions of tribal affairs, see, for example, WHH to Armstrong, 22 Mar. 1814, *WHH Papers*, 10:11–18.

45. WHH to Armstrong, 3 Apr., 10 Apr., WHH to Elliott, 3 Apr. 1814, *WHH Papers*, 10:52, 54, 66. Preparations for the 1814 campaign on Lake Huron are recorded in Elliott to Chauncey, 16 Jan., Prevost to Drummond, 8 Jan., Drumond to Prevost, 28 Jan., R. McDouall to Drummond, 26 May, Chauncey to Jones, 27 May 1814, in William S. Dudley and Michael J. Crawford, eds., *The Naval War of 1812: A Documentary History*, 3 vols. to date (Washington, DC: Naval Historical Center, 1985–), 374, 379–83, 501–4. For a general discussion of the British efforts in this regard, see Gough, *Fighting Sail*, 67–81.

46. Todd to John O'Fallon, 12 Apr. 1814, John O'Fallon Papers, MSS A 031, Filson Historical Society, Louisville, KY.

47. Pleasants to WHH, 18 Apr. 1812, *WHH Papers*, 10:80.

48. WHH to Shelby, 20 Mar. 1814, *WHH Papers*, 10:9.

49. For Brown's and Izard's careers, see John P. Morris, *Sword of the Border: Major General Jacob Jennings Brown, 1775–1828* (Kent, OH: Kent State University Press, 2000); and John C. Fredriksen, "A Tempered Sword Untested: The Military Career of General George Izard," *Journal of America's Military Past* 25 (fall 1998): 5–18, and 25 (winter 1999): 5–17.

50. WHH to Armstrong, 17 Apr., Croghan to WHH, 15 May, 27 May 1814, *WHH Papers*, 10:74, 160, 201–2.

51. Wm. Bradford to WHH, 5 Apr., Gaines to WHH, 20 Apr., Wilkinson to WHH, 28 Apr. 1814, *WHH Papers*, 10:58, 83, 110. Modern dictionaries spell Wilkinson's word *empiric*.

52. Jones to Armstrong and WHH, 23 Apr., Croghan to WHH, 15 May 1814, *WHH Papers*, 10:101–2, 160.

53. WHH to Armstrong, 11 May, WHH to Madison, 11 May, Armstrong to WHH, 24 May 1814, *WHH Papers*, 10:150, 153, 188; Armstrong to Madison, 20 May 1814, in Rutland et al., *James Madison*, 7:505. Secondary accounts of this incident are in Cleaves, *Old Tippecanoe*, 221–24; Dorothy Burne Goebel, *William Henry Harrison: A Political Biography*, Indiana Historical Collections, vol. 14 (Indianapolis: Indiana Library and Historical Department, 1926), 194–98; J. C. A. Stagg, *Mr. Madison's War: Politics, Diplomacy, and Warfare in*

the Early American Republic, 1783–1830 (Princeton, NJ: Princeton University Press, 1983), 398–99; and Skeen, *John Armstrong*, 136–37.

54. The standard Harrison biographies provide a limited discussion of this dispute; see Goebel, *William Henry Harrison*, 198–203; and Cleaves, *Old Tippecanoe*, 232–38.

55. For illustrations of the Perry and Elliott medals and the Harrison and Shelby medals, see Benson J. Lossing, *The Pictorial Field-Book of the War of 1812* (New York: Harper and Brothers, 1868), 535, 558–59; illustrations of the medals of the three senior naval officers of the battle of Lake Champlain are on 868, 878.

56. Cleaves, *Old Tippecanoe*, 220–22, 232–36; Goebel, *William Henry Harrison*, 195–200.

57. WHH to Fisk, 17 Sept., 20 Oct. 1814, WHH to J. H. Hawkins, 17 Sept. 1814, Fisk to WHH, 3 Oct. 1814, WHH Statement, 20 Dec. 1815, and affidavits, *WHH Papers*, 10:389–90, 392–401, 415–16, 422–33, 723–38.

58. Fisk to WHH, 30 Jan. 1815, *WHH Papers*, 10: 479–80.

59. *Annals of Congress [The Debates and Proceedings in the Congress of the United States]*, 42 vols. (Washington, DC: Gales and Seaton, 1834–56), 14th Cong., 1st sess., cols. 253, 316, 334, 1196–99, 1456; 15th Cong., 1st sess., cols. 283–84. This dispute eventually resulted in letters that were published in the leading Washington newspaper of the day. See Harrison to the Soldiers Who Fought at the Thames, 10 July 1816, and other documents in *Washington (DC) National Intelligencer*, 12 Aug. 1816. Some of this controversy may have arisen from the publication in 1816 of McAfee's *History*, which lauded Harrison's generalship and said little about that of Desha, but Desha began the controversy in late 1813. On Desha's 1813 charge against Harrison, see Taylor to Tompkins, 14 Jan. 1814, in *Washington (DC) Globe*, 29 Aug. 1840. The *Globe* was an anti-Harrison paper that, in this 29 August issue, published several documents supporting Desha's stance. An anti-Harrison propaganda booklet of 1840 echoed charges made after the 1811–13 campaigns: ". . . the loss of her [Kentucky's] gallant sons at Tippecanoe, Raisin and Dudley's defeat; all which disasters, I have long since satisfied myself, were brought about by the bungling imbecility of the modern 'hero,' whose fame has suddenly been brought into existence by the magic wand of a whig nomination for the presidency!" Daniel Garrard, *An Address to the Young Men of Kentucky, Comprising a Brief Review of the Military Services of General William Henry Harrison, during the Late War between Great Britain and the United States* (Frankfort, KY: Robinson and Adams, 1840), 5.

60. Shelby to Armstrong, 19 Nov. 1813, in Knopf, *Document Transcriptions*, 7, pt. 1: 5–6; Shelby to WHH, 21 Apr. 1813, *WHH Papers*, 8:87; O. H. Perry's substantiation of Shelby's comments in Perry to WHH, 18 Aug. 1817, in Logan Esarey, ed., *Messages and Letters of William Henry Harrison*, 2 vols. (Indianapolis: Indiana Historical Commission, 1922), 2:568–70; Todd to WHH, 25 Apr. 1816, Draper MSS (123 microfilm reels), 62:69, Wisconsin Historical Society, Madison, WI. In letters to Shelby in late 1813, Desha did not indicate any anti-Harrison feelings; he apparently recognized that such attitudes would not be well received by the governor. Desha to Shelby, 12 Oct., 11 Dec. 1813, Draper MSS, 62:49, 55.

61. *The Civil Services of William Henry Harrison* (Philadelphia: C. Sherman, [1840]), 20.

62. A. Beatty to WHH, 24 June 1816, Draper MSS, 62:73.

63. *American State Papers, Military Affairs*, 3 vols. (Washington, DC: Gales and Seaton, 1832), 1:644–61; *Annals of Congress*, 14th Cong., 2nd sess. col. 394. Similar problems

between field commanders and the firm of Orr & Greeley are reported in S. Tupper to Armstrong, 17 Sept. 1813, in Knopf, *Document Transcriptions*, 7, pt. 2: 79–80. For elaboration on these issues, see Cleaves, *Old Tippecanoe*, 240–42; and Goebel, *William Henry Harrison*, 199–202.

64. Goebel, *William Henry Harrison*, 203.

65. See Allan R. Millett's "Caesar and the Conquest of the Northwest Territory: The Wayne Campaign, 1792–95," *Timeline* 14 (May–June 1997): 2–21; "Caesar and the Conquest of the Northwest Territory: The Harrison Campaign, 1811," *Timeline* 14 (July–Aug. 1997): 2–19; and "Caesar and the Conquest of the Northwest Territory: The Second Harrison Campaign, 1813," *Timeline* 14 (Sept.–Oct. 1997): 2–21.

66. The issue is best confronted in Stephen Aron, *How the West Was Lost: The Transformation of Kentucky from Daniel Boone to Henry Clay* (Baltimore: Johns Hopkins University Press, 1996); Randy K. Mills, *Jonathan Jennings: Indiana's First Governor* (Indianapolis: Indiana Historical Society, 2005); Andrew R. L. Cayton, *Frontier Indiana* (Bloomington: Indiana University Press, 1996); and Owens, *Mr. Jefferson's Hammer*.

67. For similar conclusions, see Russell F. Weigley, *History of the United States Army* (New York: Macmillan, 1967), 131–32; and Richard A. Herrera, "Toward an American Army: U.S. Soldiers, the War of 1812, and National Identity," *Army History*, summer 2013, 42–57.

68. On the changing nature of high command in the U.S. Army, see William B. Skelton, *An American Profession of Arms: The Army Officer Corps, 1784–1861* (Lawrence: University Press of Kansas, 1992) and Samuel J. Watson, *Jackson's Sword: The Army Officer Corps on the American Frontier, 1810–1821* (Lawrence: University Press of Kansas, 2012).

69. WHH to Perry, 31 July 1815, *WHH Papers*, 10:579.

70. WHH to Shelby, 6 Sept. 1814, to Jackson, 20 Apr. 1815, *WHH Papers*, 10:386, 502.

This page intentionally left blank

Essay on Sources

Any study of William Henry Harrison must begin with the two biographic studies of the early twentieth century: Dorothy Burne Goebel, *William Henry Harrison: A Political Biography*, Indiana Historical Collections, vol. 14 (Indianapolis: Indiana Library and Historical Department, 1926), and Freeman Cleaves, *Old Tippecanoe: William Henry Harrison and His Time* (New York: Charles Scribner's Sons, 1939). Neither of these explores Harrison's military career in detail. Unfortunately, Indiana University's Robert G. Gunderson never completed his biography of which we have preliminary glimpses in his "A Search for Old Tip Himself," *Register of the Kentucky Historical Society* 86 (autumn 1968): 330–51, and "William Henry Harrison: Apprentice in Arms," *Northwest Ohio Quarterly* 65 (winter 1993): 3–29. A brief inquiry of importance is Reginald Horsman, "William Henry Harrison: Virginia Gentleman in the Old Northwest," *Indiana Magazine of History* 96 (June 2000): 125–49.

Hendrik Booraem V continues his psychological studies of presidents with "William Henry Harrison Comes to Cincinnati," *Queen City Heritage* 45 (fall 1987), 3–22, and *A Child of the Revolution: William Henry Harrison and His World, 1773–1798* (Kent, OH: Kent State University Press, 2012); I was privileged to read the latter before its publication. Useful analyses of Harrison's relations with Native Americans are found in Robert M. Owens, *Mr. Jefferson's Hammer: William Henry Harrison and the Origins of American Indian Policy* (Norman: University of Oklahoma Press, 2007), and Adam Jortner, *The Gods of Prophetstown: The Battle of Tippecanoe and the Holy War for the American Frontier* (New York: Oxford University Press, 2012).

Allan R. Millett explores the classical Roman influence on Harrison's outlook in three articles: "Caesar and the Conquest of the Northwest Territory: The Wayne Campaign, 1792–95," *Timeline* 14 (May–June 1997): 2–21; "Caesar and the Conquest of the Northwest Territory: The Harrison Campaign, 1811," *Timeline* 14 (July–Aug. 1997): 2–19; and "Caesar and the Conquest of the Northwest Territory: The Second Harrison Campaign, 1813," *Timeline* 14 (Sept.–Oct. 1997): 2–21. William Gribbin examines the importance of Charles Rollin's writings to the eighteenth-century understanding of the classical world in "Rollin's Histories and American Republicanism," *William and Mary Quarterly* 29 (1972): 611–22. The breadth of classical references in Harrison's correspondence demonstrates his preference for Rollin over Caesar.

David Curtis Skaggs published several articles concerning Harrison's career: "Joint Operations during the Detroit–Lake Erie Campaign, 1813," in William Cogar, ed., *New Interpretations in Naval History: Selected Papers from the Eighth Naval History Symposium of the U.S. Naval Academy* (Annapolis, MD: Naval Institute Press, 1989), 121–38; "River Raisin Redeemed: William Henry Harrison, Oliver Hazard Perry and the Midwestern Campaign, 1813," *Northwest Ohio History* 77 (spring 2010): 67–84; "The Making of a Major General: William Henry Harrison and the Politics of Command, 1812–13," *Ohio Valley History* 10 (spring 1910): 32–52; and "Decisions at Sandwich: William Henry Harrison and the Pursuit to the Thames," *Michigan Historical Review* 38 (spring 2012): 107–28.

Harrison's Indiana career is explored in Andrew R. L. Cayton, *Frontier Indiana* (Bloomington: Indiana University Press, 1996): 226–60, John Craig Hammond, *Slavery, Freedom, and Expansion in the Early American West* (Charlottesville: University of Virginia Press, 2007), and Darrel. E. Bingham, ed., *The Indiana Territory, 1800–2000: A Bicentennial Perspective* (Indianapolis: Indiana Historical Society, 2001). For early Ohio politics, see R. Douglas Hurt, *The Ohio Frontier: Crucible of the Old Northwest, 1720–1839* (Bloomington: Indiana University Press, 1996), Andrew R. L. Cayton, *The Frontier Republic: Ideology and Politics in the Ohio Country, 1780–1825* (Kent, OH: Kent State University Press, 1986), and Donald J. Ratcliffe, *Party Spirit in a Frontier Republic: Democratic Politics in Ohio, 1793–1821* (Columbus: Ohio State University Press, 1998).

On the War of 1812, important surveys are J. C. A. Stagg, *Mr. Madison's War: Politics, Diplomacy, and Warfare in the Early American Republic, 1783–1830* (Princeton, NJ: Princeton University Press, 1983), Stagg, *The War of 1812: Conflict for a Continent* (New York: Cambridge University Press, 2012), and Donald R. Hickey, *The War of 1812: A Forgotten Conflict* (Urbana: University of Illinois Press, 1989). For the international context of the war, see Jeremy Black, *The War of 1812 in the Age of Napoleon* (Norman: University of Oklahoma Press, 2009), and Troy Bickham, *The Weight of Vengeance: The United States, the British Empire, and the War of 1812* (New York: Oxford University Press, 2012). Critical military analyses include Richard H. Kohn, *Eagle and Sword: The Beginnings of the Military Establishment in America* (New York: Free Press, 1975), Guy Chet, *Conquering the American Wilderness: The Triumph of European Warfare in the Colonial Northeast* (Amherst: University of Massachusetts Press, 2003), John Grenier, *The First Way of War: American War Making on the Frontier* (New York: Cambridge University Press, 2005), and Robert M. Quimby, *The U.S. Army in the War of 1812: An Operational and Command Study*, 2 vols. (East Lansing: Michigan State University Press, 1997). Of continuing importance, if only for its illustrations, is Benson J. Lossing, *The Pictorial Field-Book of the War of 1812* (New York: Harper and Brothers, 1868). References to particular campaigns and battles are found in the chapter notes.

Exploring British-Indian relations begins with Robert S. Allen, *His Majesty's Indian Allies: British Indian Policy in the Defence of Canada, 1774–1815* (Toronto: Dundurn Press, 1992), Timothy D. Willig, *Restoring the Chain of Friendship: British Policy and the Indians of the Great Lakes, 1783–1815* (Lincoln: University of Nebraska Press, 2008), Colin G. Calloway, *Crown and Calumet: British-Indian Relations, 1783–1815* (Norman: University of Oklahoma Press, 1987), Daniel P. Barr, ed., *The Boundaries between Us: Natives and Newcomers along the Frontiers of the Old Northwest Territory, 1750–1850* (Kent, OH: Kent State University Press, 2006), Gregory Evans Dowd, *A Spirited Resistance: The North American Indian Struggle for Unity, 1745–1815* (Baltimore: Johns Hopkins University Press, 1992), Helen Hornbeck Tanner, *Atlas of Great Lakes Indian History* (Norman: University of Oklahoma Press, 1987), and Reginald Horsman, "British Indian Policy in the Northwest, 1797–1812,"

Mississippi Valley Historical Review 45 (1958–59): 51–66. Biographical studies of importance include Reginald Horsman, *Matthew Elliott: British Indian Agent* (Detroit: Wayne State University Press, 1964), R. David Edmunds, *The Shawnee Prophet* (Lincoln: University of Nebraska Press, 1983), Edmunds, "Main Poc: A Potawatomi Wabeno," *American Indian Quarterly* 9 (1985): 259–72, John Sugden, *Tecumseh: A Life* (New York: Henry Holt, 1997), Sugden, *Blue Jacket: Warrior of the Shawnees* (Lincoln: University of Nebraska Press, 2000), and Louise A. Tohill, "Robert Dickson, British Fur Trader on the Upper Mississippi," *North Dakota Historical Quarterly* 2 (Oct. 1928): 51–66, 3 (Jan. 1929): 83–128, and 3 (Apr. 1929): 182–203.

Biographical studies of Harrison's contemporaries include Carl E. Skeen, *John Armstrong, Jr., 1758–1843: A Biography* (Syracuse, NY: Syracuse University Press, 1982), John Mack Faragher, *Daniel Boone: The Life and Legend of an American Pioneer* (New York: Henry Holt, 1992); Jonathon Riley, *A Matter of Honour: The Life, Campaigns, and Generalship of Isaac Brock* (Montreal: Robin Brass Studio, 2011), Willard C. Klunder, *Lewis Cass and the Politics of Moderation* (Kent, OH: Kent State University Press, 1996), Randy K. Mills, *Jonathan Jennings: Indiana's First Governor* (Indianapolis: Indiana Historical Society, 2005), David Curtis Skaggs, *Oliver Hazard Perry: Honor, Courage, and Patriotism in the Early U.S. Navy* (Annapolis, MD: Naval Institute Press, 2006), Sandy Antal, *A Wampum Denied: Procter's War of 1812*, Carleton Library Series, vol. 191 (Ottawa, ON: Carleton University Press, 1997), Sylvia Wrobel and George Grider, *Isaac Shelby: Kentucky's First Governor and Hero of Three Wars* (Danville, KY: Cumberland Press, 1974), Paul David Nelson, "General Charles Scott, the Kentucky Mounted Volunteers, and the Northwest Indian Wars, 1784–94," *Journal of the Early Republic* 6 (1986): 219–251, Nelson, *Anthony Wayne: Soldier of the Early Republic* (Bloomington: Indiana University Press, 1985), James R. Jacobs, *Tarnished Warrior: Major-General James Wilkinson* (New York: Macmillan, 1938), and Andro Linklater, *An Artist in Treason: The Extraordinary Double Life of General James Wilkinson* (New York: Walker and Co., 2010).

No study of Harrison's early career can accomplished without Douglas E. Clanin et al., eds., *The Papers of William Henry Harrison, 1800–1815*, 10 microfilm reels (Indianapolis: Indiana Historical Society, 1993–99), which should be supplemented with Logan Esarey, ed., *Messages and Letters of William Henry Harrison*, 2 vols. (Indianapolis: Indiana Historical Commission, 1922). Other critical published writings of Harrison's contemporaries are found in Robert A. Rutland et al., eds., *The Papers of James Madison, Presidential Series*, 7 vols. to date (Charlottesville: University Press of Virginia, 1984–), William C. H. Wood, ed., *Select British Documents of the Canadian War of 1812*, Publications of the Champlain Society, 4 vols. (Toronto: Champlain Society, 1920–28), William H. Smith, ed., *The St. Clair Papers*, 2 vols. (Cincinnati: R. Clarke, 1882), Nellie Armstrong Robertson and Dorothy Riker, eds., *The John Tipton Papers*, 3 vols. (Indianapolis: Indiana Historical Society, 1942), Gayle Thornbrough, ed., *The Correspondence of John Badollet and Albert Gallatin, 1804–1836*, Indiana Historical Society Publications, vol. 22 (Indianapolis: Indiana Historical Society, 1963), *Michigan Pioneer and Historical Society Collections* 40 vols. (Lansing: Wynkoop Hallenbeck Crawford, 1877–1929), and Richard C. Knopf, ed., *Document Transcriptions of the War of 1812 in the Northwest*, 10 vols. (Columbus, OH: Anthony Wayne Parkway Board and Ohio State Historical Society, 1957–62)

Government records of importance are found in *Annals of Congress* [*The Debates and*

Proceedings in the Congress of the United States], 42 vols. (Washington, DC: Gales and Seaton, 1834–56), *American State Papers, Military Affairs*, 3 vols. (Washington, DC: Gales and Seaton, 1832), Clarence Edwin Carter, ed., *Territorial Papers of the United States*, 28 vols. (Washington, DC: Government Printing Office, 1934–75), Francis S. Philbrick, ed., *Laws of Indiana Territory, 1801–1809*, Collections of the Illinois State Historical Library, vol. 21 (Springfield: Illinois State Historical Library, 1930), E. A. Cruikshank, ed., *Documents Relating to the Invasion of Canada and the Surrender of Detroit, 1812*, Publications of the Canadian Archives, no. 7 (Ottawa, ON: Government Printing Bureau, 1912); and William S. Dudley and Michael J. Crawford, eds., *The Naval War of 1812: A Documentary History*, 3 vols. to date (Washington, DC: Naval Historical Center, 1985–).

Index

Abbreviations